HANDBOOK OF MENTAL HEALTH AND MENTAL DISORDER AMONG BLACK AMERICANS

Handbook of Mental Health and Mental Disorder Among Black Americans

Edited by

Dorothy S. Ruiz

Foreword by

James P. Comer

Greenwood Press
New York • Westport, Connecticut • London

To my sons, Jason and Alexander
and
To my parents, Willie and Mary Smith

Library of Congress Cataloging-in-Publication Data

Handbook of mental health and mental disorder among Black Americans /
    edited by Dorothy S. Ruiz ; foreword by James P. Comer.
    p. cm.
    Includes bibliographical references (p.).
    ISBN 0–313–26330–2 (lib. bdg. : alk. paper)
    1. Afro-Americans—Mental health. 2. Cultural psychiatry—United
States. I. Ruiz, Dorothy S.
RC451.5.N4H36 1990
362.2'089'96073—dc20   89–71401

British Library Cataloguing in Publication Data is available.

Library of Congress Catalog Card Number: 89–71401
ISBN: 0–313–26330–2

First published in 1990

Greenwood Press, 88 Post Road West, Westport, CT 06881
An imprint of Greenwood Publishing Group, Inc.

Printed in the United States of America

The paper used in this book complies with the
Permanent Paper Standard issued by the National
Information Standards Organization (Z39.48–1984).

10 9 8 7 6 5 4 3 2 1

CONTENTS

FOREWORD

James P. Comer

Historically, Western social and behavioral scientists have focused largely on the individual as the major source of psychological and social dysfunction or impaired mental health. Such a focus facilitated a political and economic system that valued individuality highly. But it caused social and behavioral scientists and social policy-makers alike to ignore the power of social structures and practices and their impact on individual behavior. Several efforts have been made to move the discipline to a broader and more interactive perspective, but these have had limited success.

The positive mental health movement attempted to move us away from an almost exclusive focus on psychopathology. Social and community psychiatry directly called our attention to the impact of social structures and practices, but a discipline driven by research and treatment income—and continued political imperatives—has not been eager to pay significant attention. For this reason, social and community psychiatry never amounted to much more than local and more flexible approaches to the treatment of individuals or small groups. In the last decade there has been a powerful movement away from social and community approaches and toward an intense interest in the biological roots and causes of impaired mental health.

Because of the unique status of minorities in this country—probably more than any other factor—the question of the role of social structures and practices in individual behavior will not go away. Minority mental health theorists, researchers, and practitioners share experiences and interest with minority clients in a way that is both insightful and challenging. The level and kind of pathology, identification issues, and social problems reflective of a low level of mental health found among minority populations will not permit minority mental health people—and should not permit any—to ignore the power of social structures and practices.

It is not easy to observe early elementary school black children who function well, go on to function less well in middle school, and eventually express a myriad of behavioral and social problems in high school and later life, and then simply give them labels indicative of internal pathology. Do we really believe that the disproportionate number of black males in correctional facilities—many of whom would be in mental health facilities without their minority status—are simply products of family or community pathology unrelated to our political, economic, and social policies and practices over the years? Do we believe that the heightened levels of depression, hypertension, and other psychosomatic problems among blacks are unrelated to minority status?

The black experience suggests that social structures and practices play a prominent role in individual behavior. Afro-Americans had much of the structure inherent in the culture of Africa torn away—like trees pulled from the ground, with a few roots and some soil intact and transplanted in new soil. And the new soil was less nurturing; in fact, it was highly damaging. Our modern knowledge of mental health tells us that slavery created three of the most troublesome conditions possible for people who were expected to function well in a society that valued independence highly.

First, slavery was a system of forced dependency; second, it fostered a sense of inferiority for individuals and the group; and third, it provided no hope that a slave could work for better conditions in a lifetime or in the lifetime of his or her offspring. This prevented adequate social cohesion among a large number of the slaves. This made the acquisition of political, economic, and social power after slavery more difficult. Even where there was group cohesion, outright violence and repression made it impossible for many to acquire power, protect their rights, and promote the opportunities that would permit them to be independent, to experience adequacy, and to develop a better future orientation.

Despite these devastating sociocultural experiences, the black population utilized some remnants of African culture and fused them with the elements of the new culture to which they had access (e.g., the religion), and they created guiding and psychologically and socially protective institutions.

Families enmeshed in what amounted to an amalgam of African, religious, and rural Southern culture were able to function adequately—many even thrived from a mental health standpoint—despite economic and racial abuse. This is why so many blacks are angered by the pathology label that is often placed on the black family. Such a perception ignores the destructive role of societal structures and practices and dismisses the protective role of Afro-American culture.

The way in which sociocultural forces affected the behavior of individuals is obvious even in the above brief encapsulation of the black experience. The attitudes, feelings, and concerns that Afro-Americans hold—in sickness and in health—about themselves, their group, and others in the society, and related behaviors, are greatly affected by these past sociocultural structures and practices. And yet, many American mental health workers—theorists, researchers, and practitioners—have never even studied the black experience.

A number of social and behavioral scientists never accepted the traditional research and treatment paradigms that focus primarily on individuals. A question about the usefulness of established mental health approaches, particularly as they relate to blacks, led to a number of important developments in the late 1960s and the early 1970s.

Black and other minority caucuses were founded in most of the established mental health organizations. Minority mental health associations, journals, and treatment facilities were established. Action taken by the Black Psychiatrists of America led to the establishment of the Center for Minority Mental Health Studies at the National Institute of Mental Health in the 1970s. Programs established by the center promoted a focus on minority psychological health in most of the mental health–related disciplines. These programs have produced a small nucleus of minority mental health students and workers seeking to develop more useful research and treatment paradigms for minorities. And while the effort to do so has not gone away, neither has the resistance to looking at and addressing minority mental health issues differently. This is unfortunate in that our society will not be able to address minority mental health problems effectively until we take a more interactive perspective—individual and sociocultural—and consider the minority experience within this context.

A circular problem is created by our limited knowledge. Without adequate knowledge of the black experience, and acknowledgment of the negative psychosocial consequences of denial and abuse, we continue to develop social policies and programs that contribute to existing problems rather than address needs. For example, in many foreign countries subsidies are given to well-functioning families so that they will remain in housing projects with less well-functioning families. In our country, we denied a negative impact on family functioning among the descendents of slaves, former sharecroppers, and tenant farmers, and forced the best-functioning families out of housing projects and helped to create large concentrations of poorly functioning, eventually alienated and angry, families. This, in turn, adversely affected child development and individual functioning.

Education, public welfare, and every other social program have been adversely affected by our unwillingness to pay attention to the impact of social structures and practices on individual behaviors. In fact, even our attempt to address the problem with programs such as affirmative action are hampered by a widespread societal belief that individual achievement is unrelated to social structures and practices; that blacks simply do not work hard enough or they lack ability.

At this point an objective observer would ask how this could happen. How is it possible for our best institutions and social and behavioral scientists to ignore the obvious?

First, it has happened because Americans are not proud of our history of slavery, repression, and denial of blacks, and an elaborate system of denial and avoidance has emerged as a result. Second, there is little apparent or immediate political, economic, social, or political advantage to be gained for most in exploring and coming to a full understanding of the implications of the experience. The reality, however, is that such an understanding is necessary before Afro-American and larger society attitudes and behavior can be changed in a way to facilitate the kinds of structural and policy changes and practices that will promote a higher level of positive mental health among all.

Fortunately, students of black mental health, blacks and others, have held the course. They continue to point to the role of sociocultural structures and practices and the behavior of black individuals and the community. And while this book discusses issues from illness to positive mental health, most of the authors look at the structures and practices that impinge on individual behavior. For this reason it is a valuable contribution not only to the literature of black mental health, but also to mental health in general. This work suggests that all social and behavioral scientists need to focus on both the individual and social structures and practices at every level.

PREFACE

The concepts of mental health and mental disorder are vague and difficult to define. There is little agreement among psychiatrists about how to define these concepts as well as how to diagnose and treat mental disorder. While the medical issues surrounding mental health and mental disorder are important, this book focuses on the social, structural, and cultural issues pertaining to the mental health status of black Americans. It approaches the concept of mental health from a broad theoretical perspective as opposed to a "mental disease" perspective. A broad perspective allows us to explore a wide range of psychological stressors that impact on the lives of black Americans. Very few research efforts have been focused on the impact of social structures and social conditions on the mental health functioning of this particular group of individuals. However, there is a general assumption among social scientists that poverty, unemployment, and discrimination all have a serious impact on their psychological well-being and functioning.

This book underscores the increasing interest in the problem by social and behavioral scientists. It represents a multidisciplinary approach, incorporating the works of sociologists, social workers, psychologists, psychiatrists, and mental health administrators. Theoreticians and researchers in the fields of psychology, psychiatry, and psychoparmacology have presented conceptualizations pertaining to the etiology, treatment, and outcome of mental disorder. However, these disciplines have consistently overlooked social conditions and structural processes and their significance to the study of mental disorder. Over the past decade, the sociology of mental disorder as a subdiscipline has grown enormously. Increased mental health funding has allowed social scientists to develop more sophisticated research techniques for the detection of psychological disorders in the general population. However, despite the increased funding and interests, epidemiological evidence pertaining to the extent of mental disorder within the black population remains somewhat sketchy and inconclusive.

Our goal is to engage students, professors, clinicians, and administrators. We hope that students will find our perspectives, ideas, and concepts useful in their efforts to provide sociological explanations to societal problems. We hope that professors will find the articles both interesting and informative. This volume provides an adequate amount of information on diagnosis and treatment which, we hope, will be beneficial to clinicians and administrators alike.

Dorothy S. Ruiz

INTRODUCTION

Dorothy S. Ruiz

Mental disorder is one of the illnesses that presents the greatest threat to the health of Americans. It is not possible to detect the exact number of people who suffer from mental disorder; however, according to the best estimates from the National Institute of Mental Health, about 33 million Americans, or 15 percent, are afflicted annually by a psychological disorder. This book attempts to shed some light on the broad array of social factors that contribute to both mental health and mental disorder among the black American population.

For our purpose, mental health is defined as the ability to function effectively in spite of social demands and expectations. On the other hand, mental disorder is defined as a state of the individual characterized by a set of symptoms that hamper or disrupt the ability to function effectively with respect to the social demands of society. Factors contributing to positive mental health include a healthy self-esteem, adequate shelter, a good education, a successful career, a good job, intelligence, access to good health care, and well-defined role responsibilities. These constitute the basic psychological and physical needs of every human being. Yet thousands of people in this country go to bed hungry, and thousands more sleep on city streets throughout urban America. Thus quality health care and quality education are not shared by all Americans. Factors contributing to poor mental health functioning are poverty, segregated and disorganized communities, low-quality education, few role responsibilities, unemployment, stereotyping, discrimination, and poor health care.

There is a need for a reorganization of the health care system in the United States; providing more comprehensive services to all citizens. However, as it stands, the inadequate health care system in addition to certain sociocultural factors contribute to a poor sense of self and maladaptive behavior for many Americans.

This book stresses the importance of the relationship between the individual and the social systems as well as the impact of social forces on behavior. The importance of social processes is generally acknowledged; however, models often address the individual personality as opposed to the impact of social and economic forces on the lives of people. An effective psychiatric model must integrate individual differences and the social structure in which the individual is involved.

Handbook of Mental Health and Mental Disorder among Black Americans consists of 15 original articles that present concepts, theories, and research pertaining to the mental health functioning of black Americans. Our aim for this book was to go beyond the conventional definition of what constitutes poor mental health functioning and to develop a perspective that would include the impact of environmental factors and social processes on the distribution, diagnosis, and treatment of mental disorder of this particular group.

In part I, Dorothy S. Ruiz and Alvin F. Poussaint discuss the mental health and social status of black Americans. Much of their discussions is centered around the influence of sociostructural factors and the social and health status of black Americans. Ruiz begins by looking at the relationship between racism, stereotyping, discrimination, and psychological well-being. The general health of black Americans, their mental health in particular, is closely linked to the way in which social and economic relationships are structured in this society. The social and health status of black Americans is not likely to change as long as Americans continue to believe in and practice stereotyping and racism. Americans, both black and white, need to be constantly reminded that differences are important elements in a society, but that differences do not make one individual better than or less than another. Americans need to be reminded that racism and discrimination take away from the moral quality and creative potential of the entire society. They not only influence the social and psychological well-being of the target group, they also have an impact on the psychological health of the perpetrator and ultimately reduce the health of the nation. Additional issues covered in chapter 1 include social and economic characteristics, geographic location, employment, education, the family, wealth, and poverty status.

The Poussaint chapter, "The Mental Health Status of Black Americans, 1983," presents a broad viewpoint of the mental health status of blacks. The Ruiz and Poussaint positions are supportive in the sense that both identify sociostructural factors as contributors to low positive mental health among blacks. Whereas structural factors, such as poverty and unemployment, may not lead to psychiatric disorder, they do induce a tremendous amount of stress, alienation, depression, low self-esteem, and self-hatred. These, in turn, lead to drug abuse, alcoholism, crime, mental disorder, suicide, and black-on-black homicide. Poverty and discrimination are risk factors for a variety of physical and mental problems. Poussaint provides a detailed analysis of the following problems in relation to the health of blacks: unemployment, physical health, the black child, the black family, child abuse and neglect, alcoholism, and drug abuse among others.

In part II, Harold W. Neighbors, Suzan Lumpkin, Diane Robinson Brown and Jacquelyne Johnson Jackson discuss epidemiological perspectives and issues. In the "Epidemiology of Mental Disorder in the Black Population," Neighbors and Lumpkin organize their discussion around five broad topics: (1) the impact of classification in psychiatric epidemiologic research on black Americans, (2) the prevalence of discrete disorders and the epidemiology of depressive symptomatology, (3) social support as a buffer against stress, (4) the impact of upward and downward social mobility on black mental health, and (5) the black family as a setting for intervention programs. Neighbors and Lumpkin argue that, in order to prevent the incidence of mental disorder among black Americans, a good epidemiological knowledge is needed. An overview of the literature shows that, while there has been a vast increase in epidemiological research, more is needed. The authors contend that racism and discrimination place blacks at risk for mental disorder.

"Depression among Blacks: An Epidemiological Perspective," by Brown, provides current epidemiological data on the impact of social and demographic factors. Community studies of noninstitutionalized groups show that approximately 30 percent of black Americans experience high levels of depression, and approximately 6 percent may be clinically diagnosed with a major depressive disorder. When high levels of depression are analyzed, prevalence rates are higher for blacks than for whites; however, recent findings from the National Institute of Mental Health's Epidemiologic Catchment Area study show no racial differences in prevalence rates for major depressive disorders, reports Brown. She identifies the various subgroups within the black population that are at greater risk for depression: the poor, black women, and low-socioeconomic status individuals. Individuals who are experiencing multiple negative problems are also at high risk for depression. Although depression has gained increased attention in recent years, researchers need to investigate the relationship between major depressive disorders and racial prejudice.

Jacquelyne Jackson analyzes the literature on "Suicide Trends of Blacks and Whites by Sex and Age, United States, 1967–1986." Her chapter compares trends between 1967 and 1986 in five-year annual averages of suicide rates of Americans, blacks and whites, by age and sex. She reviews demographic trends, suicide rates and all causes of death, suicide and homicide, marital status and mortality experience, and the insufficient explanations for black suicides.

In part III, Joycelyn Landrum-Brown and Patricia J. Dunston present the effects of cultural, structural, and social variables in relation to psychological functioning in their assessment of racism and mental health. In "Black Mental Health and Racism Oppression," Landrum-Brown views several ways in which racial oppression has influenced the mental health functioning of black Americans. Racism is viewed by the author as an infection of the belief system and interpreted by many scholars as a primary mental health problem in this society. Racism is considered a mental disorder in the sense that individuals' perceptions are distorted: denial of reality, delusions of grandeur, projections of blame, and phobic reactions to individual and group differences. The negative psychological effects of racism have been documented; however, it is important to emphasize that racism has negative consequences on the mental health functioning of both blacks and whites. Landrum-Brown charges that traditional Western mental health models are inadequate because they fail to accommodate the experience of black Americans. The author emphasizes the importance of a positive self-image through a cultural pro-African perspective. She contends that black people will never realize optimal psychological functioning and affirm their heritage and identity until they cease to respond culturally by way of an anti-African, anti-self perspective.

Patricia Dunston highlights theoretical and research problems in her chapter on "Stress, Coping, and Social Support: Their Effects on Black Women." She contends that little attention has been given to the mental health needs of black women. Because of the increasing cost of health care, combined with their economically disadvantaged status, black women are excluded from mental health treatment choices. Quality mental health care is largely inaccessible to black women, leaving their treatment needs unmet and placing them at a possible risk for various kinds of maladaptive behavior, such as chronic depression, child abuse, alcoholism, and drug abuse. Despite the impact of social structures and relationships on their daily lines, black women exhibit enormous adaptation to societal pressures. Research shows a direct relationship between stress, coping, social support, and psychological well-being; however, the direction of the relationship is not clear. Research in this area should address the relationships between gender, race, and stressful life events.

In part IV, on psychiatric diagnosis and treatment, James L. Collins, Eliot Sorel, Joseph Brent, and Clyde B. Mathura, in chapter 8, and Clyde Mathura and Melanie Baer, in chapter 9, discuss social and cultural factors in psychiatric diagnosis and treatment of black patients. "Ethnic and Cultural Factors in Psychiatric Diagnosis and Treatment" addresses the long-standing question frequently asked by mental health professionals: "Are blacks and other nonwhites more susceptible to mental disorders than whites?" There is no conclusive evidence to support this contention. Future research is needed in order to clarify the relationship among environmental, psychological, physiological, and cultural factors in relation to the onset of mental disorder among black Americans. Important issues emphasized by these authors are that blacks do not receive outpatient psychotherapy as frequently as white patients and that they are more likely to receive medication with only periodic medical follow-up and no psychotherapy at all. The shortage of black psychiatrists and the high cost of psychotherapy cause many black patients to receive their psychotherapy from white nonpsychiatric therapists in public and community mental health facilities. In order to make comprehensive psychiatric care available in public and community mental health facilities, Collins contends that white therapists must begin to understand the influence of race, socioeconomic status, and culture on the therapeutic process. Placing too much emphasis on color differences only increases the level of the already existing tension between the white therapist and the black patient. The issues raised in "Social Factors in Diagnosis and Treatment" support the notions in Collins' chapter. Mathura and Baer address the impact of oppression and discrimination on psychotherapy. They contend that the social and economic status of blacks places them at a clear disadvantage in the treatment setting, particularly with respect to language, family structures, mannerisms, and other basic characteristics of the black experience. The authors analyze a variety of social factors that emerge from the black/white therapeutic setting. Considerable emphasis was placed on the effects of race, social class, gender, and age. According to Mathura and Baer, the major problems that face the black patient in a black/white therapy situation are seen primarily in socioeconomic status differences. The dynamics of racism influence socioeconomic status and keep stereotypes and discrimination in place. Additional research needs to emphasize the role of cultural differences, sex roles, and other social factors in relation to their impact on effective therapy for blacks.

In part V, Linda James Myers uses optimal psychological theory to explain family violence in this society. She addresses the causes of anger and hostility within the black American family and their implications for black mental health and illness. The goal of her chapter, "Understanding Family Violence: An Afrocentric Analysis Based on Optimal Theory," is to explain three aspects of this perspective: (1) the framework of optimal theory; (2) the root cause of family violence and its meaning at the individual, community, and cultural levels; and (3) methods to reduce family violence. Myers contends that it would be difficult to understand and analyze violence in the black family without addressing the effects of racism and sexism. Myers explains her perspective by using a nonracist/ nonsexist optimal analysis. Culture and socialization are important aspects of an optimal analysis because they provide the basis for our values, ideals, perceptions, thought, and experience. As in many social problems, education seems to be the best method of addressing family violence in this country.

"Black-on-Black Homicide: The Implications for Black Community Health" analyzes a number of issues, including why this problem has gone largely unnoticed as far back as 1932. Even today, little is being done to ameliorate the problem. Carl C. Bell discusses a number of myths surrounding black-on-black homicide which encourage the community to become oblivious to the problem. Over the last 10 years, approximately 20,000 people have been killed each year by homicide, and, of these, about 9,000 each year were black. According to Bell, it is crucial to place some of the blame for black-on-black homicide on the community. Three out of every five, or 16 percent of murder victims in 1986, were related to or acquainted with their assailants. Bell contends, then, that murder is a societal problem over which law enforcement has little control. In order to understand black-on-black homicide, there is a need for an epidemiologic study of such variables as age, sex, race, circumstances, victim/offender relationship, and type of community. Bell has outlined several strategies for attacking the problem, but he adds that public awareness and education are required to solve this complex problem.

In part VI, Alice Gresham Bullock's chapter on "Legal Issues in Mental Health" reviews developments in mental health law from the beginning of reform to the transitional period of the 1980s. The impact of mental health as it pertains to blacks will be discussed where applicable; however, the literature shows that the impact of laws do not affect blacks any differently than any other racial or ethnic group. The author focuses on civil and criminal commitment issues, the right to treatment, deinstitutionalization, zoning, the homeless mentally ill, and the liability of health professionals and facilities.

Mary S. Harper addresses a series of issues pertaining to "Mental Health and Social Policy," including the prevalence of mental disorder, diagnosis and treatment, mental health services, patient rights, and chronically mentally ill women among others. She places considerable emphasis on the impact of cultural and social influences on psychopathology. According to Harper, the refusal to seek mental health services is due, in part, to stigma, acceptance of the disorder, lack of accurate diagnosis, access to mental health services, lack of transportation, and lack of resources. The psychological stressors experienced by blacks include single parenting, interpersonal relationships, living arrangements, racism, discrimination, and lack of access to quality health care. In conducting mental health research from a social policy perspective for blacks, Harper suggests that a heuristic model would be appropriate. Such a model would encompass the individual, family, and community as well as a redistribution of social, economic, and social welfare resources. Mental health research is needed in the following areas: (1) family policy, (2) family processes, and (3) the social and public policies pertaining to specific populations. Mental health and social policy concerns should include the following: (1) the impact of deinstitutionalization of the mentally ill and the mentally retarded, (2) delivery of mental health services, (3) access to quality care, (4) stigma, and (5) commitment laws.

In part VII, Louis P. Anderson, Chuck L. Eaddy, and Ernestine A. Williams examine internal, familial, and sociocultural factors in relation to psychosocial competence. Their belief is that traditional definitions of mental disorder have been narrowly defined and do not explain how black Americans are able to cope, adapt, and problem solve under stressful life circumstances. The authors provide a detailed analysis of the competency model and show how it may be applied to connect sociocultural and psychological dimensions of human existence. Their discussion of internal factors includes concept perception, coping, vigilance, self-esteem, and locus of control. Included in their discussion of familial and sociocultural factors are such concepts as the black family, the nuclear black family, the extended family, the friend network, the black church, and group identification. The authors conclude with the assumption that health is related to competence or one's ability to adapt adequately to the environment. The broader the worldview one has, the more capable one is likely to be in meeting needs for health functioning.

"Coping with Color: The Anatomy of Positive Mental Health" is an interesting analysis of how color has become a mark of oppression, a pathological obsession, and a method of evaluation for Afro-Americans. Barbara J. Shade explains how "skin color" by itself has no meaning; however, in this society, a symbolic meaning has been attached which represents inferior status for the racial group. Meanings associated with skin color have serious psychological consequences for Afro-Americans. Shade discusses the psychological consequences of skin color and provides five strategies for dealing with the problem: (1) a strong knowledge base, (2) a sense of self-identity, (3) an adaptive personality, (4) a social intelligence, and (5) a social responsibility. Positive mental health for Afro-Americans, says Shade, means developing competency, self-confidence, and an effective message. Progress of black Americans will not be determined by government handouts; the major task of educators and other socializating agents is to develop programs designed to enhance self-confidence, creativity, and social awareness.

Anderson J. Franklin and James S. Jackson have developed some interesting concepts around "Factors Contributing to Positive Mental Health among Black Americans." The authors define positive mental health as a psychological orientation toward life experiences with attributes of inner strength, resiliency, optimism, and a capacity for mastery. This chapter focuses on the pscyhological strengths of black Americans that constitute the basis of positive mental health. The authors place considerable emphasis on examining the strengths within black people. Several ideas are explored: epidemiological perspectives, the concept of positive mental health, self-concept and self-esteem, autonomy and control, perceptions of reality, and self-actualization. They, like most of the authors contributing to this book, emphasize the influence of poor economic conditions and discrimination on the mental health status and functioning of blacks. Models of positive mental health must be sensitive to internal as well as external sources of stress according to Anderson and Jackson.

RESEARCH CONSIDERATIONS

The dual health care delivery system remains a serious problem for black patients. Under this system, poor individuals, especially blacks, receive inferior health care. They often receive psychiatric treatment in public facilities which frequently are inferior to the facilities utilized by the more advantaged population. Black patients are often treated with drugs; little or no attention is directed toward interpersonal and personality development therapy.

There is a serious need to assess adequately the mental health needs of the black community and to redirect the mental health services. Previously, mental health professionals were more concerned with treating the individual after the onset of illness. Mental health facilities should emphasize preventive techniques, especially for the black community, since diagnosis and treatment of blacks have far more serious consequences than for more affluent individuals.

Another important issue facing the psychiatric community is that psychiatrists do not agree on etiology and definition of mental illness. Vague definitions lead to problems in diagnosis and treatment. Black mental health professionals therefore must become more involved in assessing the factors that contribute to mental disorder among blacks and develop programs that address the particular needs of blacks.

The argument centered around the misdiagnosis of black schizophrenic patients should be addressed among black psychiatrists and among professionals generally. Are black patients more schizophrenic than whites, or is this diagnosis a result of some other factor, such as a delay in seeking treatment? If blacks are more schizophrenic than whites, what are the common factors responsible for this difference? If this diagnosis is caused by a delay in seeking treatment for a disorder, how can mental health facilities educate the black population to recognize the early symptoms of mental disorder? Recognition of the early signs of depression is not easy. How can mental health facilities help individuals to recognize illness symptoms and to understand when they should seek professional help?

Some studies show that sociocultural factors are related, in some ways, to the onset of mental disorder. However, the particular social factors which are related to depression, schizophrenia, and other disorders among blacks are not clear. The findings of whites which emphasize pathology have been relied upon, while the societal conditions that predispose certain groups to different types of social and psychological behavior have been given little attention. Black mental health professionals must begin to take a more active role in determining the psychological well-being of the black community. This kind of involvement is necessary in order to develop programs that can address the particular psychological and social needs for blacks which obviously are different from those of their more affluent counterparts. Social and economic problems are related to mental health problems in the black community; however, how they are related is not known. Is there a direct relationship between life events and psychiatric disorders in the black community? Are specific sociocultural factors related to an increase in psychiatric symptomatology and subsequently psychopathology? These are among the research questions that deserve further attention.

Black mental health professionals must develop mental health research training programs so that they do not have to rely solely on the findings of white researchers. There is a paucity of research by black professionals which investigates epidemiological factors and mental disorder. Research of this nature is badly needed. An effective black mental health training program that will train clinicians to recognize cultural differences in expressing psychological disorder could be beneficial to the nonwhite population.

Schizophrenic disorders are widely present in the patient population. There is a critical need for further studies that address the epidemiological and etiological issues. In addition, research should be conducted in the area of genetics because often it is theorized that certain factors predispose some individuals to schizophrenic influences in the family structure. Finally, it is hoped that further studies of schizophrenia will show mental health professionals the need for critical examination of the implications of this elusive behavior and will enlighten them as well about the problem involved in the diagnosis and treatment of this disorder (Ruiz, 1983).

REFERENCE

Ruiz, D. (1983). Epidemiology of Schizophrenia: some diagnostic and sociocultural considerations. *Phylon*, *43*, 315–326.

PART I

HEALTH AND SOCIAL STATUS OF BLACK AMERICANS

SOCIAL AND ECONOMIC PROFILE OF BLACK AMERICANS, 1989

Dorothy S. Ruiz

The socioeconomic status of black Americans as a group looks uncertain as we approach the twenty-first century; however, for many blacks who are experiencing economic hardship, the economic situation looks especially bad. The issues and concerns of blacks today are basically the same as they were three decades ago; the most imminent ones center around achievement and advancement.

Although largely ignored in the social science literature and rejected by the general public, the primary sociostructural factors that have hampered the achievement and advancement of blacks are racism and discrimination. Majority group members reject the obvious explanation and are content to believe that blacks lag behind economically, socially, and politically simply because they do not work as hard as members of the other groups. This irrational belief—politically and economically advantageous for many Americans—is held primarily for the purpose of political and economic domination. Blacks work just as hard as the members of other ethnic groups, and their contributions to the historical development of this country are enormous. To believe otherwise, however, would mean to reduce the social distance, to share the wealth, and to share the power. "In our contemporary society, black families bear the blame of others as scapegoats, through the irrational hostility and guilt of whites" (Reynolds, 1984). In an essay, which appeared in *Look Magazine* in August 1964 and will be published in 1988 as part of his memoirs, George Leonard, a white southerner writes:

Up to now, we have skirted the truth. National leaders and experts have analyzed segregation and racial prejudice as a sociological phenomenon, a political gambit, and economic lever. In limited ways, it is all of those things. But we have got to go a step further. If we of the white race are to move effectively against the malady that cripples us, we must see it for what it is, and call it by its true name. Start with those glazed unseeing eyes. What you are looking at is not a political, sociological or economic phenomenon. It is dangerous, self-destructive madness.

Stereotyping plays a major role in the process of black/white relations in the United States. The social and economic status of black Americans is influenced by social structural factors and aggregated by the ways in which blacks respond and react to their social status. Stereotyping of American blacks is so pervasive and so deeply ingrained that many blacks actually believe the false images imputed onto them by majority group members. Believing these false images ultimately leads to self-rejection, which is the ultimate goal. Bruce Hare (1988) supports the notion that blacks are successfully socialized to internalize negative messages about themselves. Other blacks believe that what is said about the group is true, but they view themselves as exceptions.

The general health of black Americans and their mental health in particular is closely related to socioeconomic status. However, since the socioeconomic conditions of many black individuals are bad, their overall health and psychological well-being will be adversely affected. The social and economic status of black Americans will continue to be depressing, and the problems of race are not likely to disappear as long as Americans continue to believe in and practice the racial superiority of one race over another.

Racial discrimination results in decreased opportunities and cultural adaptations (Merton, 1968; Rank, 1988). This is evidenced by the disproportionately high incidence of poverty among black Americans. Contrary to popular beliefs, most of the persistently poor people in this country have economic problems that are not related to inherent ability or lack of motivation; instead, lack of opportunities, ill health, low wages, old age, and responsibility for young children are largely to blame for poverty in this country (Coser, Nock, Steffan, and Rhea, 1983). Another popular misconception is that poverty persists because of the personal inadequacies of the poor. There are many theories, but little consensus, about why people are poor. Poverty in the United States will not be eradicated until we cease to blame the victims for their problems. The myth of equal opportunity obscures the fact that true causes of inequality are not located within the individuals, but in the economic and social conditions that give the poor a less than equal chance to succeed. "The social and psychological consequences of job discrimination remain enormous both for the individuals and the relationships within the community and its families" (Hare, 1988). Although we would conclude that racism is a factor in inequality, it is not the only factor. William Wilson (1987) contends that, even if there were no racism, the situation would not change significantly unless some changes were also made in the economy and the ghetto communities.

The practice of racism, stereotyping, and discrimination has caused blacks to think that something is wrong with their blackness, often resulting in poor self-

Table 1.1
The Black Population at a Glance: 1980

Category	Number (in Millions)	Percent Black Population of Total Population
Under 18 years	9.4	14.7
18 years and over	17.1	10.5
65 years and over	2.1	8.2
Males	12.5	11.4
Females	14.0	12.0
College graduates (25 years and over)	1.1	5.1
High school graduates (25 years and over)	6.8	7.6
In labor force (16 years and over)	10.9	10.2
Single (15 years and over)	7.1	15.3
Married	7.3	7.3
Separated	1.4	34.9
Divorced	1.5	13.3
Widowed	1.6	12.1
Female householder, no husband present	2.3	27.2
Married-couple families	3.4	7.0

Source: U.S. Bureau of the Census, *We, the Black Americans*. No. 3 of 6, March 1986.

esteem and lack of self-respect. Too often, black children do not grow up with the understanding that it is all right to be different and that skin color is only one of the many ways in which people differ. Black children need to understand, at an early age, that skin color is not related to anything except in the minds of those individuals who are determined to use it to their own advantage. "Color is just color" writes E. Shils (1967); however, color is not just color as it is used in the American society. The symbolic significance of skin color has produced patterns of adaptation which include displaying psychosocial behavior as apathy, hostility, aggression, self-hate, and lack of fate control (Adam, 1978). Individual differences are important in our daily lives and Americans must learn to appreciate and value these differences.

CHARACTERISTICS OF THE BLACK POPULATION

Black Americans are the largest and one of the oldest ethnic groups in the United States. According to the 1980 Census report, blacks constituted 11.5 percent of the total population, making them the second largest racial group. The 1980 Census showed 26.5 million blacks, an increase of about 17 percent

Table 1.2
Total and Black Populations: 1900–1980 (Numbers in Millions)

Year	Total	Black	Percent Black
1900	76.2	8.8	12
1910	92.2	9.8	11
1920	106.0	10.5	10
1930	123.2	11.9	10
1940	132.2	12.9	10
1950	151.3	15.0	10
1960	179.3	18.9	11
1970	203.2	22.6	11
1980	226.5	26.5	12

Source: U.S. Bureau of the Census. *We, the Black Americans*. No. 3 of 6, March 1986.

over the 1970 Census. At age 15 and under, blacks constitute approximately 15 percent of the total population; however, by age 64, their relative proportion has decreased to 8 percent. In 1790, when the first census was taken, blacks numbered about 760,000 and represented about 19 percent of the U.S. population. By the start of the Civil War in 1860, the numbers had increased to 4.4 million, but the percentage of the U.S. total had dropped to 14.1 percent. Most blacks were slaves; only 488,000 were counted as freedmen. By 1900, the black population had doubled over the 1860 figure, reaching 8.8 million. The 15-million mark was passed in 1950, and the census counted 22.6 million blacks in 1970. By 1985, they numbered 28.2 million. See tables 1.1 and 1.2.

Geographic Location

In 1910, approximately 90 percent of the black population lived in the South. Influenced by the desire for job opportunities and better living conditions, blacks began leaving the South in large numbers. In the 1940 decade, about 1.6 million more blacks left the South than moved there. However, during the last half of the 1970s, spurred by improved opportunities in the region, more blacks moved back to the South than moved away. Currently, slightly over half of all blacks live in the South. About 60 percent of blacks lived in central cities of metropolitan areas in 1980. They moved to these places in search of better job opportunities. Some were able to improve their lifestyles. Many prospered and sent back "down home" for relatives and friends. In 1980, of the 100 cities with the largest black population, 17 cities had black populations of 50 percent or more. Blacks make up about 70 percent of the total population of Washington, D.C., the nation's capital, but the city with the highest proportion of blacks is East St. Louis, Illinois; almost 96 percent of its residents are black. Twenty-eight cities had black populations that exceeded 100,000: New York had the largest black population (1,784,337); second was Chicago (1,197,000); and then Detroit (758,939), Philadelphia (638,878), and Los Angeles (505,210). In recent years, blacks have been moving from the inner city to the suburbs. The percentages of blacks residing in suburbs grew by 43 percent between 1970 and 1980. Despite rapid suburban growth, blacks constitute only 6 percent of the nation's suburban population.

Income

In 1984, the median family money income for blacks was $15,430. In other words, half of the families received more and half received less than $15,430. Twenty-nine percent had incomes of $25,000 or more in 1984; more than half of the white families were in this income category. The median income was highest for those blacks who lived in the West ($19,210) and lowest for those who resided in the South ($14,860) and Midwest ($14,370). After adjusting for inflation, the median income of black families in 1984 was not significantly different from 1980—$15,430 versus $15,980. Black family median income was 56 percent of white family income in 1984. Stated another way, for every $100 a white family received, a black family received $56. Farley Reynolds (1984) concludes that the distribution of black family income has changed only slightly over the past 30 years. He contends that racial discrimination is a factor that contributes to the status of blacks.

Median incomes for black families have not improved partly because of the existence of a high proportion of black families with a female householder with no husband present and because of the low incomes received by these families. In 1984, 44 percent of black families were maintained by women alone compared with only 13 percent of white families. The 1984 median income of black families maintained by women was only $8,650,37 percent of the median of black married-couple families ($23,420). In white husband-wife families, the median income was $30,060 and $15,130 for families maintained by women with no husbands present. (U.S. Bureau of the Census, Current Population Reports, *Household Wealth and Asset Ownership: 1984*).

Employment

In 1980, 9.3 million blacks were employed. Though many blacks have moved into better paying jobs, their representation in the professions and in some high-skilled jobs is still small. For instance, blacks accounted for only 7 percent of all professionals and 8 percent of all technicians and related support workers in 1980. Blacks are still heavily concentrated in certain jobs. For example, blacks

Table 1.3
Selected Occupational Groups, by Race: 1980

Occupation	Black	White	Percent Black of Total
Professional Specialty	867,345	10,937,561	7.1
Executive, Admin. & Managers	510,776	9,547,471	4.9
Technicians and Related Support	258,213	2,547,471	8.4
Administrative Support including Clerical	1,762,420	15,113,627	10.0
Sales	533,475	9,410,609	5.2
Service	2,395,273	10,446,792	17.6
Private Household	256,132	333,244	40.6

Source: U.S. Bureau of the Census. *We, the Black Americans*. No. 3 of 6, March 1986.

accounted for more than half (54 percent) of private household cleaners and servants and about one-fourth of all postal clerks, and of all nurses' aides, orderlies, and attendants. There has been improvement in many areas. For example, the number of black airplane pilots and navigators jumped from 77 in 1970 to 678 in 1980. Between 1970 and 1980, the number of black judges rose from 297 to 1,683. Also noteworthy is the increase in the ranks of black lawyers; their numbers moved from 3,406 to 13,594 during the 1970s. In 1980, black women constituted almost one-third of all black lawyers in the country (see tables 1.3 and 1.4).

Black women have approximately the same rate of participation in the work force as nonminority women, but the rate for black men is slightly lower than that for nonminority men. Black women have a 39 percent greater chance of sustaining job-related disease and serious work-related injuries than nonminority women. Blacks in the work force are highly concentrated in three of the six major occupational groups: operators, fabricators, and laborers (27 percent); technical, sales, and administrative support (24 percent); and service occupations (23 percent). Blacks are consistently underrepresented in managerial and professional specialty occupations, where they constitute only 6 percent of the work force.

Education

Blacks continue to place a high value on education. Today, blacks are better educated and more are staying in school. For instance, the proportion of high

Table 1.4
Selected Occupations by Race and Sex: 1980

Occupation	Black		White	
	Male	Female	Male	Female
Lawyers	9,322	4,272	417,815	63,165
Judges	1,162	521	21,551	41,147
Dentists	2,715	480	110,425	7,171
Physicians	10,264	3,245	330,297	42,316
Registered Nurses	5,489	91,534	44,278	1,086,595
Chemistry Teachers	148	58	6,126	1,559
Airplane Pilots and Navigators	652	26	73,572	986
Hairdressers and Cosmetologists	4,445	33,623	60,340	437,933
Computer Operators	18,681	28,041	133,986	195,336
Plumbers, Pipe-fitters and Steamfitters Apprentices	32,746	983	446,313	5,313

Source: U.S. Bureau of the Census. *We, the Black Americans*. No. 3 of 6, March 1986.

school dropouts for blacks from 16 to 19 years old declined from 22 percent in 1970 to 12 percent in 1983. There has also been an improvement in the educational attainment of blacks. The proportion of blacks 25 years and over who have completed high school rose from 34 percent in 1970 to 57 percent in 1983. For blacks from 25 to 34 years old, 79 percent had completed high school in 1983 compared with 53 percent in 1970. The comparable figures for whites were 87 and 76 percent for those years. In 1983, 1.1 million blacks were enrolled in college, double the number in 1970. Blacks represented 10 percent of the college population between the ages of 18 and 34 in 1983, and black women in college (605,000) outnumbered black men (497,000).

The Family

A review of the family and behavior patterns of blacks reveals that among the black populations, kinship and family ties are extremely important. These ties often form the basis of a network of mutual support that can provide material, emotional, and social resources to family members in distress. Also, the church is a powerful source of emotional strength for many blacks and their families.

Folk beliefs about health and illness may have varying effects on how an individual reacts to the signs and symptoms of poor health; however, little is known about folk beliefs among blacks or the extent to which blacks rely on folk remedies. Research on the relationship between health beliefs and illness behavior suggests that such differences may help explain the patterns of health care for some minorities.

The median age of blacks is 24.9 years. The life expectancy in 1983 was 65 years for men and 74 years for women, contrasted to 72 years and 79 years for white men and women, respectively. The age-adjusted mortality rate per 1,000 population for blacks is 7.7; for whites, 5.3. Black families are on the average slightly larger than nonminority families; the average black family comprises 3.7 members. Although total birth rates among all groups have dropped since 1970, the overall rate of childbearing is still higher among black women than among the women of nonminority groups; currently it averages 2.3 births per black woman and 1.7 per nonminority woman. The percent of black households headed by women (37.7 percent) is more than three times higher than that of nonminority households headed by women (10.9 percent).

Black families are not as large as they used to be; more blacks are living alone, and more black marriages are being dissolved through divorce and separation. Even so, the number of black families increased from 4.9 million in 1970 to 6.5 million in 1983.

There were other findings for 1983:

- Separation and divorce rates were highest for blacks among all racial groups.
- About one-third of black women who maintained families had never been married.
- More than half of black children lived in one-parent homes.

Even though profound changes have occurred in black families, more than half (53 percent) of black families were still maintained by married couples in 1983. On the other hand, the proportion has declined from the 1970 level of 68 percent. Increased separation and divorce were part of a national trend during the late 1970s (U.S. Bureau of the Census, *We, the Black Americans, 1986*).

WEALTH DISPARITY IN THE UNITED STATES

Wealth and poverty are important societal issues that are of concern to economists and sociologists alike. However, despite the concern about wealth, it is difficult to determine just how wealthy the rich are in relation to the poor. Income differences are often researched, but until recently little was known about the actual disparity between the rich and poor in this country. According to 1984 statistics released by the Census Bureau, the net worth of the white American household in 1984 was 12 times greater than the net worth of the typical black household and 8 times greater than the net worth for a Hispanic household. Net worth is defined as the value of assets covered in the survey less any debts (either unsecured or secured by assets).[1] Assets included in the survey were stock-earning assets; liabilities included debts secured by any asset, credit card, store bills, bank loans, and other unsecured debts.[2] Overall, home equity constituted the largest share of net worth. Home ownership, reported by two-thirds of all households, accounted for 14 percent of net worth; other interest-earning assets made up 3 percent. Approximately 72 percent of households had interest-earning assets at financial institutions.

The survey showed that the median net worth of the nation's households in 1984 was $32,667. When wealth and race were analyzed, gross disparities were discovered. The median net household worth for white households was $39,135; for Black households, $3,397; and for Hispanic households, $4,910. The differentials by race, measured by the ratio of median values, were greater for wealth holdings than for income. For example, the ratio of the median net worth of white householders to that of black householders was 12, whereas the ratio of median incomes was 2. When income was held constant, white householders had higher levels of net worth than black householders. However, the relative differences in net worth were smaller for upper-income households than for households in general; the ratios of median net worth of white householders to that of black households with incomes of from $2,000 to $3,000 and $4,000 or over were 3 and 2, respectively. The differentials by race also declined when the types of households were considered. For example, for married-couple households, the white-to-black ratio of median net worth was 4. The white-to-black ratio was approximately the same for male-maintained households, but it was higher for female-maintained households.

Furthermore, the survey showed that 16.9 percent of white households had a net worth of from $100,000 to $249,999; 4.4 percent, from $250,000 to $499,000; and 2.1 percent, $500,000 or more. When blacks and Hispanics are compared, the findings of the same income intervals are as follows: 3.3 and 5.1 percent; 0.5 and 2.1 percent; and 0.1 and 1.0 percent, respectively. One-third of all black households and one-fourth of Hispanic households had no net assets and were in debt; fewer than one in ten whites had no assets or were in debt. The census figures revealed that 11 percent of all Americans (9 million households) have no assets or are in debt; 21 percent have assets worth less than $10,000; and 12 percent of the households surveyed had 38 percent of all the personal wealth in the nation. The wealth figures reveal much greater disparities in the economic welfare of blacks and whites and blacks and Hispanics than do annual income figures.

To the extent that these figures are reliable, the survey confirms that the rich are getting richer, and the poor are getting poorer. The survey shows that blacks have made only meager gains over the last few decades. Wealth accumulation among blacks has been modest. The small net wealth percentage of blacks is a reflection of their historically disadvantaged economic and social position. Disparities in income and wealth have accelerated in the past decade; however, this pattern is not a new phenomenon. The relevant question is what accounts for the enormous disparity in net wealth among Americans. Various explanations are required to account for this disparity. There is also much disagreement on who or what is responsible for wealth and poverty in this country. However, despite the disagreements, the differences in net wealth between groups in America are real.

Poverty

According to Census Report, Poverty in the U.S. (1985), blacks have made significant progress in several areas during the past decade, but inflation and a periodically recessionary economy have caused many to slip below the poverty level.

- The number of black persons below the poverty line rose from 8.6 million in 1980 to 9.5 million in 1984. Among whites, 23.0 million were poor in 1984.
- The black poverty rate was 33.8 percent in 1984, not significantly different from the 1980 rate of 32.5 percent. The poverty rate for whites was 11.5 percent in 1984.
- Black female householders accounted for 73 percent of all poor black families in 1984.

The federally defined poverty level does not include noncash benefits such as housing, food, and medical assistance. Two-fifths of the poor are children. Forty-nine percent of black children under six years of age lived in poverty last year compared to 17 percent of white children in the same age group. Income differs from family income in that it includes the income of all persons, whereas family income is restricted to the income of related persons living in households. Changes in family income do not, therefore, reflect the changes in income for other segments of the population, such as unrelated individuals, or the fact that the characteristics of families are changing. Changes in living arrangements, such as declines in average family size or decreases in the proportion of families maintained by married couples, can affect the measurement that includes all population segments, and that is less affected by changes in living arrangements.

Poverty Status

The number of persons in poverty was 32.4 million in 1986, and the poverty rate was 13.6 percent. The number of poor in 1986 was not statistically different from the 1985 figure, but it was below the recent peak of 35.3 million recorded in 1983. The 1986 poverty rate of 13.6 percent was lower than the 1985 rate of 14.0 percent at the 90-percent confidence level but not at the 95-percent level. The poverty rate was 15.2 percent in 1983. Poverty data using the official government definition were first tabulated for 1959. The poverty rate fell dramatically in the 1960s, decreasing from 22 percent to 12 percent in 1969. During the same period, the number of poor declined from 39.9 million to 24.1 million. During the period from 1970 to 1977, the size of the poverty population fluctuated between 23 and 26 million, and the poverty rate was in the 11-to-13-percent range. From 1978 to 1983, the number of persons in poverty increased by 44 percent, from 24.5 to 35.3 million, and the poverty rate rose from 11 to 15 percent. The poverty definition used here is that adopted for official government use by the Office of Management and Budget and consists of a set of money income thresholds that vary by family size and composition. Families or individuals with income below their appropriate thresholds are classified as below the poverty level. The poverty thresholds are updated every year to reflect changes in the Consumer Price Index. For example, the average poverty threshold for a family of four was $11,203 in 1986, $10,989 in 1985, and $10,609 in 1984 (U.S. Bureau of the Census, *Money Income and Poverty Status of Families and Persons in the United States*, 1986).

Whites represented 69 percent of the poor in 1986, blacks represented 28 percent, and the remainder were persons of other races. The poverty rate in 1986 was 11 percent for whites, 31 percent for blacks, and 16 percent for persons of other races. The poverty rate for persons of Hispanic origin (who may be of any race) was 27 percent in 1986. Neither the number of poor nor the poverty rate changed significantly for whites, blacks, or persons of other races between 1985 and 1986. Among Hispanics, the number in poverty did not change between 1985 and 1986, but their poverty rate declined from 29 percent to 27 percent. The poverty rate for whites had declined since 1983 (the rate in that year was 12 percent), but the 1986 rate was higher than the 1978 rate of 9 percent (1978 was a recent low point in the poverty rate). Among blacks, the 1986 poverty rate was lower than the 1983 figure of 36 percent and was at about the same level as the 1978 rate. The 1986 rate among persons of Hispanic origin was not statistically different from the 1983 rate, but it was well above the 1978 rate of 22 percent. The number of poor and the poverty rates in the Northeast and Midwest declined between 1985 and 1986, but there were no significant changes in the South or West. Each of the four regions had a 1986 poverty rate that was lower than the 1983 rate. The number of poor families in 1986 was about 7 million, not significantly different from the 1985 figure. About 44 percent of the poor families were composed of married-couple families, and 51 percent were composed of families with a female householder, no husband present. The number of poor married-couple families decreased from 3.4 to 3.1 million between 1985 and 1986, but the number of poor families maintained by a woman with no husband present did not change significantly. The number of poor families has decreased since 1983, when there were about 7.6 million, as has their poverty rate (12 percent in 1983; 11 percent in 1986). Similarly the number of married-couple families below the poverty level decreased during the 1983–1986 period, from 3.8 to 3.1 million, and their poverty rate dropped from 8 to 6 percent. The number of poor families with a female householder and no spouse present was about 3.6 million in both 1983 and 1986, and their poverty rate was about 35 percent in both years (U.S. Bureau of the Census, *Money Income and Poverty Status of Families and Persons in the United States*, 1986).

Persons in families represented 76 percent of the poor in 1986 and persons living alone or with nonrelatives represented 21 percent (persons in unrelated subfamilies made up the remainder of the poverty population). Between 1985 and 1986, the number of family members in poverty declined by about 1 million, but the number of poor unrelated individuals did not change significantly. Between 1983 and 1986, the number of poor family members declined by 3.2 million, but the number of poor unrelated individuals showed no statistically significant change.

The poverty rate in 1986 was about 20 percent for related children under 18 years old in families and 12 percent for persons 65 years and over. These rates were not statistically different from the 1985 rates, but they were lower than the 1983 rates (22 percent and 15 percent, respectively). The 1986 poverty rate was higher in central cities of metropolitan areas and in nonmetropolitan areas (both about 18 percent) than in suburban areas (about 8 percent). The poverty rate in central cities declined from 19 percent in 1985, but the rates for suburban and nonmetropolitan areas did not change significantly. The number of poor in central cities declined by about 900,000 between 1985 and 1986. One-half of the poor family householders worked at some time during 1986, and 17 percent worked year round, full time. Neither of these proportions changed between 1985 and 1986 (U.S. Bureau of the Census, *Money Income and Poverty Status of Families and Persons in the United States*, 1986).

The disadvantaged position of black Americans contributes to their overall health status, and it has an adverse effect on their mental health status in particular. The social and economic status of many blacks has improved somewhat over the last decade; however, a disproportionately larger number will experience a worsening of their economic and health status. Even a tentative solution to the problem requires the concern of the society at large. Negative attitudes about the poor must change, and there must be more of an effort not to blame individuals for their disadvantaged position. When large numbers of individuals suffer, it is everybody's problem. If we are to move toward a mentally healthy society, we must make efforts to address and solve the broader societal problems and issues concerning the masses. It is more expensive to maintain a sick society than to maintain an emotionally and socially healthy society.

NOTES

1. "Group quarters" are excluded from the results shown in this report. Group quarters are units which consist of unrelated individuals living together in housing units that have separate rooms but share common facilities such as dining halls. Individuals in group quarters would not normally share financial resources. The Universe also excludes persons in institutions and persons living in military barracks.

2. Interest-earning assets include regular savings accounts, money market deposit accounts, certificates of deposit, interest-earning checking accounts, money market funds, corporate or municipal bonds, U.S. Government securities, and other interest-bearing assets.

REFERENCES

Adam, Barry D. (1978). Interiorization and self esteem. *Social Psychology*, *41*; 47–53.

Coser, Lewis A., Nock, S., Steffan, P. A., & Rhea, B. (1983). *Introduction to sociology* (2d ed.). New York: Harcourt Brace Jovanovich, chap. 9.

Hare, Bruce. (1988). Black youth at risk. In Janet Deward (Ed.), *The state of black America 1988*. New York: National Urban League.

Leonard, George. (1964, August 11). A southern appeal. *Look Magazine*, pp. 7–26.

Merton, Robert K. (1968). *Social theory and social structure*. New York: Free Press, chaps. 6 and 7.

Noel, Davis L. (1968, Fall). A theory of the origin of ethnic stratification. *Social Problems*, *16*, 157–72.

Price, M. Cobbs, M.D. (1988). Perspectives on the psychology of race. In Janet Dward (Ed.), *The state of black America 1988* (pp. 61–70). New York: National Urban League.

Rank, Mark R. (1988, June). Racial differences in length of welfare use. *Social Forces*, *66* (4), 1080–1104.

Reynolds, Farley. (1984). *Blacks and whites*. Cambridge, MA: Howard University Press.

Shils, E. (1967). Color, the universal intellectual community and the Afro-Asian intellectual. *Color and Race*, *96*, 270–286.

U.S. Bureau of the Census. (1983). *Current population reports. General population characteristics, United States summary, 1980 census of the population*. Washington, D.C.: Government Printing Office.

U.S. Bureau of the Census. (1986, March). *We, the Black Americans*. (No. 3 in a series of 6). Washington, D.C.: U.S. Government Printing Office.

U.S. Bureau of the Census. (1986, July). *Current population reports. General population reports. Household wealth and asset ownership: 1984*. (Series P–70, No. 7). Washington, D.C.: U.S. Government Printing Office.

U.S. Bureau of the Census. (1987, March). *Current population reports. Money income and poverty status of families and persons in the United States: 1986*. (Series P–60, No. 157). Washington, D.C.: U.S. Government Printing Office.

U.S. Bureau of the Census. (1987, April). *Current population reports. Population profile of the United States 1984/85*. (Special Studies Series P–23, No. 150). Washington, D.C.: U.S. Government Printing Office.

U.S. Bureau of the Census. (1987, October). *Current population reports. Poverty in the United States 1985*. (Series P–60, No. 158). Washington, D.C.: U.S. Government Printing Office.

Wilson, William J. (1987). *The truly disadvantaged*. Chicago: The University of Chicago Press.

2

THE MENTAL HEALTH STATUS OF BLACK AMERICANS, 1983*

Alvin F. Poussaint

OVERVIEW

The outlook for the positive mental health of black Americans over the next several years is grim. Although many racial barriers have been broken down over the last decades, in view of a continuing white backlash and a slippage of black gains, the 1969 statement of the Joint Commission on Mental Health of Children is relevant to the plight of blacks today.

The racist attitude of Americans which causes and perpetuates tension is patently a most compelling health hazard. Its destructive effects severely cripple the growth and development of millions of our citizens, young and old alike. Yearly, it directly and indirectly causes more fatalities, disabilities and economic loss than any other factor. (Subcommittee to the President's Commission on Mental Health, 1978, p. 822)

The subpanel on the Mental Health of Black Americans of the President's Commission on Mental Health (1978) stated: "it is largely the environment created by institutional racism, rather than intrapsychic deficiencies in black Americans as a group, that is responsible for the overrepresentation of blacks among the mentally disabled" (p. 823).

Institutional racism includes those political and social forces that confine blacks to ghettos and racially isolated schools. In addition, these forces guarantee high rates of unemployment and poverty in the black community at the same time that blacks have limited access to health and social services. Some investigators

*This chapter originally appeared in *The State of Black America* (1983). New York: National Urban League.

believe that it is socioeconomic conditions and not racism per se that accounts for blacks' current predicament. Most social scientists agree, however, that both racism and poverty act synergistically to confound the black experience (Bass, Wyatt, & Powell, 1982; Jones & Korchin, 1982).

The United States Commission on Civil Rights, for instance, recently reported that persistent discrimination was the primary reason that blacks had experienced much higher rates of unemployment than whites (Robert Pear, "Bias Blamed for High Minority Jobless Rate," *New York Times*, November 24, 1982).

This high rate of black joblessness is certain to push more blacks of all classes into the ranks of the poor. H. F. Myers concluded: "By nature, poverty is an illness-inducing state because of the excessive and continuous pressures the person faces, because of the long-term consequences of the continuous exposure to pathogens and to endemic stressors (i.e., high vulnerability), and because of the chronic scarcity of services, resources and assets" (Myers, 1982, p. 119). If one adds racial discrimination to this equation, it is clear that black Americans, both poor and middle class, are at higher risk for mental disorder than the white majority.

MENTAL HEALTH: A BROAD PERSPECTIVE

In examining the mental health status of blacks, we are not solely concerned with mental disease, or the mentally ill, as defined in psychiatric nomenclature. Such a restriction in subject matter would severely misrepresent the true psychological stresses on black Americans. We must examine the environmental factors and conditions mentioned above that create low positive mental health in Afro-Americans (Pettigrew, 1964; Clark, 1965; Grier & Cobbs, 1968; Willie, Kramer, & Brown, 1973; Gary, 1978; Jones & Korchin, 1982). In American society, an unemployed poverty-stricken black man or woman experiences tremendous stresses which may not necessarily lead to a defined mental disease, but, nonetheless, may create feelings of depression, anger, low self-esteem, and powerlessness. In turn, these feelings and perceptions are likely to affect the life of the black person's entire family by leading to increased rates of alcoholism, drug abuse, mental illness, crime, child abuse, spouse batterings, suicide, and homicide within and without the black community (Clark, 1965; Curtis, 1975; Gary, 1978; Bass et al., 1982). Although poverty does not necessarily result in poor mental health, it is a significant contributing factor. Many individuals from low-income circumstances may gain strength from the experience and become successful adults. How an individual positively adapts to stress depends on a host of internal and external variables, the most important of which appear to be good physical endowment within a supportive family and community environment. Poverty and discrimination, nonetheless, place blacks at high risk for many physical and mental health problems.

Table 2.1 shows that, although there has been a decline in the percentages of persons living below the poverty level since 1959 (when these data were first

Table 2.1
Persons below the Poverty Level by Family Status and Race: 1959, 1969, 1977, and 1980

Family Status and Race	Poverty Rate			
	1980	1977	1969	1959
ALL RACES				
Total...........................	13.0	11.6	12.1	22.4
65 years old and older.........	15.7	14.1	25.3	35.2
Family members....................	11.5	10.2	10.4	20.8
Householders...................	10.3	9.3	9.7	18.5
Female, no husband present...	43.7	31.7	32.7	42.6
Other family members...........	7.1	3.9	7.2	15.9
Unrelated individuals............	22.9	22.6	34.0	46.1
WHITE				
Total...........................	10.2	8.9	9.5	18.1
65 years old and older.........	13.6	11.9	23.3	33.1
Family members....................	8.6	7.5	7.8	16.5
Householder	8.0	7.0	7.7	15.2
Female, no husband present...	36.8	24.0	25.7	34.8
Other family members...........	5.5	4.6	5.8	13.3
Unrelated individuals............	20.4	20.4	32.1	44.1
BLACK				
Total...........................	32.5	31.3	32.2	55.1
65 years old and older.........	38.1	36.3	50.2	62.5
Family members....................	31.1	30.5	30.9	54.9
Householder....................	28.9	28.2	27.9	48.1
Female, no husband present...	57.6	51.0	53.3	65.4
Other family members...........	19.5	17.4	20.0	44.1
Unrelated individuals............	41.0	37.0	46.7	57.0

Sources: U.S. Department of Health and Human Services. *The status of children, youth and families 1979*. August 1980. Exhibit 5.7, p. 124.

U.S. Bureau of the Census. *Current population reports*. Characteristics of the population below the poverty level: 1977, 1980. July 1982.

collected), there is still an enormous difference between the percentages of white and black persons living in poverty. Also, we have seen an increase in all categories of percentages of persons below the poverty level between 1977 and 1980. The current stagnant economy and record-breaking unemployment rates (10.8 percent of the general population and 20.2 percent for blacks) suggest that overall poverty rates have risen significantly since 1982 (*The New York Times*, December 4, 1982). Figure 2.1 illustrates the fact that the largest segment of the black families lives with very little income. About one-third of black families live below the poverty line; the rates for black elderly and female-headed house-

Figure 2.1
How Blacks Have Fared

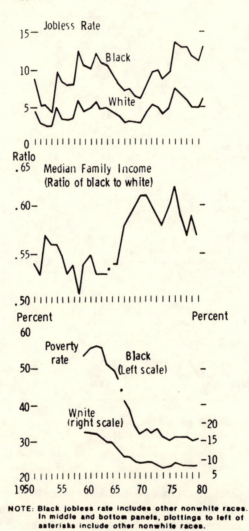

NOTE: Black jobless rate includes other nonwhite races.
In middle and bottom panels, plottings to left of
asterisks include other nonwhite races.

Shaded areas represent recessions as designated
by the National Bureau of Economic Research.

Source: Morgan Guaranty Trust Company of New York. (1981, August). Black America:
Progress and problems. *Morgan Guaranty Survey*. Used by permission of copyright owner,
J. P. Morgan & Co. Incorporated.

Figure 2.2
Distribution of Income in 1977 with Related Children under 18 Years Old, by Race

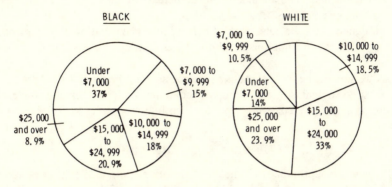

Source: U.S. Department of Health and Human Services. *The status of children, youth and families, 1979.* August 1980.

holds are particularly high. More blacks are currently living in poverty than they were in 1977. Figure 2.2 gives an overview of trends in the black economic situation since 1950.

UNEMPLOYMENT: ITS IMPACT

The skyrocketing unemployment rate among blacks is the most critical index of the deleterious effect our troubled economy is having on Afro-American mental health. M. H. Brenner (1977) has demonstrated a rise in admissions to mental hospitals during jumps in unemployment and a decrease in admissions during times of relative economic prosperity. The social costs of unemployment, inflation, and poverty become apparent in a dramatic increase in the levels of physical and mental instability and crime in a given community (Subcommittee to the President's Commission on Mental Health, 1978). Brenner has calculated that a 1-percent increase in unemployment (which represents nearly a million people) sustained for six years will lead to the following (based on 1970 census data):

- 36,887 deaths, including 20,240 from heart disease
- 920 suicides
- 648 homicides
- 495 deaths from cirrhosis of the liver (often related to chronic alcoholism)
- 4,227 state hospital admissions

These figures today would be higher. Brenner recently reported that authoritative studies have shown that every 1-percent increase in the unemployment rate is accompanied by a 2-percent increase in the mortality rate, about a 2-percent increase in cardiovascular deaths, a 5- to 6-percent increase in homicides, a 5-percent increase in imprisonment, a 3- to 4-percent increase in first admissions to mental hospitals, and about a 5-percent increase in infant mortality (*New York Times*, October 24, 1982).

With unemployment rates at 20.2 percent for blacks and over 45 percent for black youth, the potential outcome for blacks, particularly black males, is ominous.

As we review the current status of the mental well-being of Afro-Americans, we must do so against the backdrop of economic conditions that are worse than when most of these data were reported. The future becomes alarmingly bleak.

PHYSICAL HEALTH OF BLACK AMERICANS

Perhaps it is appropriate to begin an examination of the state of black American mental health with a look at the physical health status of black Americans. Here, the strain under which the average black person in our society lives can be seen clearly.

First, the life expectancy for black individuals is shorter than that of their white counterparts. According to the *Monthly Vital Statistics Report* published by the National Center for Health Statistics (NCHS) in September 1982, the life expectancy for black Americans in 1979 was about 68.3 years (a 4.2-year increase since 1969–1971). Whites can expect to live about 74.4 years (a 2.8-year increase since 1969–1971). Although the gap between them has narrowed (from 7.5 to 6.1 years), there is still a significant difference between the groups.

A look at the leading causes of death in the United States shows how blacks are most vulnerable. Among the 15 leading causes of death, there are only two for which the death rate is greater among whites. (Whites are 1.3 times more likely to die from chronic obstructive pulmonary and related diseases and 1.7 times as likely to commit suicide as blacks). The largest difference between the death rates of white and black Americans is in the category of homicide where the death rate is 6.3 times greater for blacks. Other significant differences are in the categories of diabetes, nephritis, septicemia, and chronic liver disease and cirrhosis (often related to alcoholism and for which the death rate is 1.9 times higher among blacks). Especially when homicide and cirrhosis are considered, it becomes clear that the strain on the physical health of black Americans is related to social and psychological stress (NCHS, September 1982).

The high death rates (as well as a lower general quality of life) for blacks also are affected by the health care delivery system to minorities and the poor. R. M. Russo, in a 1982 article entitled, "Poverty: A major deterrent to America's good health," discusses four stages of health care development, the highest of which is the personal intervention of a health care professional with ongoing delivery of medical services to individuals. Although Medicare and Medicaid have improved access to this kind of service for poor people and minorities, these groups are still less likely than whites and higher income groups to have a source of regular health care. About one in four blacks uses a hospital clinic or emergency department as compared to one in eight whites.

According to a recent article in *Medical World News*, the issue of inadequate services for the poor and minorities is complicated by the fact that federal government funding cutbacks instituted under the Reagan administration are beginning to have dramatic effects on the medical treatment received by the poor.

One of the areas most deeply affected by these cuts is maternal and child health, which received 23 percent less federal money this fiscal year than last. Dr. William B. Hope says that it should be no surprise, then, that the fetal death rate has actually gone up, from 10.0 to 12.2 per 1,000 from 1979 to 1981, and it is continuing to climb.

Also badly hurt by 38-percent cutbacks have been the combined alcohol, drug, and mental health programs. Based on Brenner's predictions, these cuts could not have come at a worse time, as we can anticipate a rising need for these services in the black community.

Once free clinic visits now typically cost anywhere from $2 to $15 on a sliding scale, and outreach services (such as lead screening and immunization vans) have been dropped from many health programs because of insufficient funding (*Medical World News*, December 6, 1982).

THE BLACK CHILD

A Portrait of Inequality (Edelman, 1980), published by the Children's Defense Fund, and recent mortality statistics clearly show how poverty conditions and inadequate health care affect the lives and development of poor black children. Others also have reported on the dreadful conditions under which black children must survive (Silverstein and Krate, 1975; Bass et al., 1982). It is generally agreed that black children and families are at a disadvantage when compared to whites in most areas of social, economic, and psychological well-being.

Table 2.2 shows that, although both have been declining over the years, the black infant mortality rate has remained consistently twice as high as that for whites. Figure 2.3 illustrates the major causes of infant mortality. Of these, disorders related to short gestation and unspecified low birth weight caused three times as many deaths for black as for white babies. The rate for pneumonia and influenza was 2.7 times as high among black as among white infants. The effects of maternal complications on the newborn accounted for 2.3 times as many deaths for blacks as for whites. Accidents and adverse effects and infections specific to the perinatal period also accounted for significantly more deaths for black babies (NCHS, September 1982).

Also, a black baby is four times more likely to have a mother who dies from causes associated with pregnancy, childbirth, and the puerperium than a white baby (NCHS, September 1982). A black child is twice as likely as a white child

Table 2.2
Infant, Neonatal, and Postnatal Mortality Rates, According to Race: United States, Selected Years, 1950–1977

Mortality Rate and Year	Race					
	Black	American Indian	Chinese-American	Japanese-American	White
Infant Mortality Rate[1]	Number of deaths per 1,000 live births					
1950..................	43.9	82.1	19.3	19.1	26.8
1960..................	44.3	49.3	14.7	15.3	22.9
1970[2]................	32.6	22.0	8.4	10.6	17.8
1977[2]................	23.6	15.6	5.9	6.6	12.3
Neonatal mortality rate[3]					
1970[2]................	22.8	10.6	5.4	8.4	13.8
1977[2]................	16.1	8.3	4.2	5.1	8.7
Postneonatal mortality rate[4]					
1970[2]................	9.9	11.4	3.1	2.2	4.0
1977[2]................	7.6	7.3	1.7	1.5	3.6

[1]Infant mortality rate is the number of deaths for infants under 1 year of age per 1,000 live births.

[2]Excludes deaths of nonresidents of the United States.

[3]Neonatal mortality rate is the number of deaths for infants within 28 days of birth per 1,000 live births.

[4]Postneonatal mortality rate is the number of deaths for infants within 28 days to 365 days of birth per 1,000 live births.

Source: U.S. Department of Health and Human Services. *The status of children, youth and families, 1979*. August 1980.

Figure 2.3
Major Causes of Infant Mortality: United States, 1976

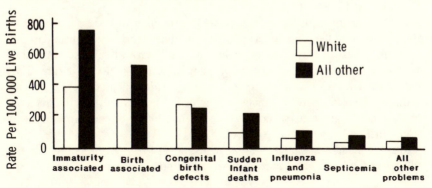

Source: U.S. Department of Health and Human Services. *The status of children, youth and families, 1979*. August 1980.

Table 2.3
Percentages of Children Born to Unmarried Mothers, by Race, 1970, 1975, 1977, and 1980

YEAR	1970	1975	1977	1980
Black	37.6	48.8	51.2	55.3
White	5.7	7.3	8.2	11.0

Sources: National Center for Health Statistics. *Vital statistics of the U.S.*, vol. 1, Natality, 1977 (for 1970, 1975, and 1977).

National Center for Health Statistics. *Data from advance report of final natality statistics*, 1980 (for 1980).

to be born to a mother who has had no prenatal care, or only minimal care. The chances are also greater that the mother will be poor and inadequately nourished. We can anticipate, therefore, that such children are at higher risk for birth defects, including mental retardation and learning disabilities. Children who need specialized care while they are growing up often live in situations of poverty where there are limited social and economic resources and where community services are woefully inadequate to meet the great needs.

Table 2.3 shows that over 50 percent of black babies born in recent years were born out of wedlock. This rate has been rising steadily in the last decade. Most of the mothers of these children are teenagers. Currently, about 45 percent of black children live in single-parent households. Thus, it is no surprise that a black child has a one in two chance of living in poverty and run-down housing. Black children have a very high rate of sickness and mental disorder because they are poor and live in environments which are hazardous to their health, thereby increasing their chances of becoming ill or of dying from accidents, lead poisoning, and even rat bites.

Black mothers in one-parent households struggling to cope are victims of discrimination in the job market. Many cannot find or afford adequate day care and some in despair may abuse or neglect their children. Although some children from such environments may succeed, many more face a gloomy future. They are expelled from or drop out of school, lag behind in grade level, and are frequently labeled "educable mentally retarded." In addition, one in three children is in a segregated school, and many face other direct forms of racial discrimination while attending school.

Russo concludes his article with an assessment of how recent political trends will affect the lives, and futures, of America's poor:

If poverty contributes, as it does, to the risk of disease, then the remedies for certain ills are socioeconomic and political, not medical. The current climate in Washington would appear to reflect a turning away from the task—perhaps to newer methods of paying the bill; perhaps not. There is, after all, a large price to health and it will be society's task to determine how that price will be paid. The alternative of not paying is indeed grim. (Russo, 1982, p. 47)

THE BLACK FAMILY AND HEALTH

The black family, although it has frequently been maligned, has been the key buffer and support that has enabled many black children to grow into healthy adulthoods (Billingsley, 1968; Hill, 1972; Bass et al., 1982). Although, in many ways, the survival of the black family depends upon the flexibility of the family structure, that flexibility also causes some problems which are aggravated by social and economic burdens. One of the most serious of these problems is the high divorce rate among black American couples. This, coupled with the high percentages of black children born out of wedlock, has led to a very large number of black households headed by single women. The black divorce rate has increased rapidly in the past decades. The increase in only one year, from 1980 to 1981, about 15 percent, is ominous for the well-being of the black community (see table 2.4).

Most single-parent homes in the black middle-class community are the result of divorce, although a small number of black middle-class women are bearing children out of wedlock. It is also evident that the divorce rate among the black middle class is increasing at a faster rate than in any other class. More children are victims of dissolved marriages now than in earlier years. Children from divorced families are at a higher risk for emotional difficulty and behavior disorders. The profound impact of divorce upon children is now receiving renewed interest. Fortunately, a high percentage of divorced blacks remarry. Still, divorced black women outnumber divorced black men by a ratio of three to one

Table 2.4
Number of Divorces per 1,000 Married Persons (Spouse Present) by Race, 1970, 1980, and 1981

YEAR	1970	1980	1981
Black	83	203	233
White	44	92	100

Source: U.S. Bureau of the Census. *Current population reports*. Marital status and living arrangements: 1981. 1982. Series P–20, no. 372.

Figure 2.4
Living Arrangements of Children under 14 Years of Age by Race, March 1978 (Numbers in Thousands)

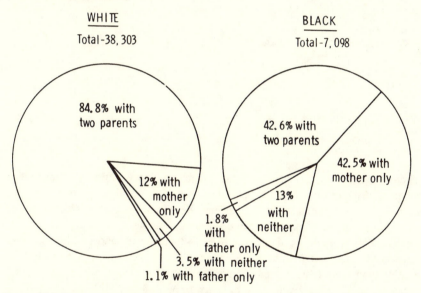

Source: U.S. Department of Health and Human Services. *The status of children, youth and families, 1979*. August 1980.

because of higher male remarriage rates. This is another contributing factor to the high number of black single-parent households headed by women (Staples, 1981).

Needless to say, the increasing flexibility in black family structures has a definite effect on the children growing up in them. Black children are much less likely than their white peers to live with two parents. Approximately 84.8 percent of white children live with both of their parents as opposed to only 42.6 percent of black children. About 42.5 percent of these children live with only their mothers. For white children, that figure is only 12 percent (see figure 2.4).

Table 2.5

Children in Families below the Poverty Level by Head of Household, Race, and Spanish Origin: 1977

	Number of children under 18 years below poverty level	Percent of children under 18 years below poverty level
All types of families		
All children	10,028	16.0%
White	5,943	11.4%
Black	3,850	41.6%
Spanish Origin	1,402	28.6%
Children in families with male head		
All children	4,371	8.5%
White	3,250	7.1%
Black	965	19.3%
Spanish Origin	716	17.9%
Children in families with female head		
All children	5,658	50.3%
White	2,693	40.3%
Black	2,885	65.7%
Spanish Origin	686	68.6%

Source: U.S. Department of Health and Human Services. *The status of children, youth and families, 1979*. August 1980.

There is also some evidence that the number of black children living with a member of the extended family (a relative) has declined slightly from 16 percent in 1975 to 13 percent in 1978 (National Research Council, 1976). A strong extended family is a major resource for single-parent households, and erosion of that support could be damaging to both the mothers and children in those households, but current trends are unclear. Economic hardships and high unemployment would suggest more interdependence among family members and relatives for sheer survival (Taylor, Jackson, & Quick, 1982).

The major burden of single-parent families is that, among all racial groups, the largest percentages of children below the poverty level are those living with female household heads (50.3 percent), but this is particularly evident in black families where 65.7 percent of children living only with their mothers are below the poverty level (see table 2.5).

Perhaps one of the clearest indicators of family poverty is the receipt of Aid for Families with Dependent Children (AFDC) support. Statistics show that blacks are very overrepresented among AFDC recipients. In 1979, they collected about 43.1 percent of the money distributed by AFDC, although they account for only about 12 percent of the population of the United States. White persons, on the other hand, who make up about 84 percent of the U.S. population, received

Figure 2.5
Major Causes of Death for Ages 1–14 Years: United States, 1976

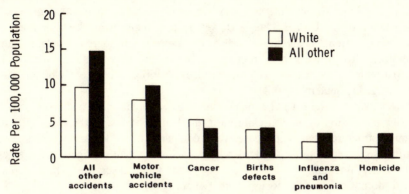

Source: U.S. Department of Health and Human Services. *The status of children, youth and families, 1979.* August 1980.

about 40.4 percent of the AFDC funds. Households headed by women also are overrepresented among AFDC recipients (Duvall, Goudreau, and Marsh, 1982).

Once past infancy, it is clear from figure 2.5 (where blacks represent approximately 90 percent of the nonwhite category) that children growing up in white homes have a better chance of surviving to their teenage years than do minority children. High death rates due to accidents, birth defects, influenza, pneumonia, and homicide point to inadequate health care (including prenatal), unsatisfactory living conditions, and the stress brought on by such conditions.

CHILD ABUSE AND NEGLECT

Some very interesting statistics have been gathered regarding child abuse and neglect in white and minority families. First, all forms of abuse (physical, sexual, other) and neglect (emotional, educational, other) are found at all income levels and in all races. Low-income children, however, are more likely to experience maltreatment than their higher income peers, which supports the hypothesis that various environmental stresses contribute to the incidence of child abuse and neglect.

What is somewhat surprising, however, in light of evidence that social stresses on blacks are different and often more severe than those on whites, is that the incidence of recognized maltreatment of children is nearly identical across races. Of the known cases, about 10.5 per 1,000 are white children and about 11.5 per 1,000 are black. In families with incomes under $15,000 per year, the incidence among whites is actually greater than among nonwhites for all forms of maltreatment except educational neglect. Generally speaking, all forms of neglect are more prevalent in low-income families than in higher income minority families. Abuse is close to constant, and relatively low, in these groups.

In overall categories, black children experience abuse and neglect at a rate that about equals their representation in the general population. (Their rate of abuse is about 16 percent, and they constitute about 15 percent of the child population of the United States.) However, 27 percent of black children experience educational neglect, and, when that figure is considered, blacks are un-underrepresented in the general population for other forms of maltreatment (U.S. Department of Health and Human Services, National Center on Child Abuse and Neglect, September 1981).

There seem to be several explanations as to why blacks are underrepresented in the population of abused children in the United States. Perhaps, in spite of family structures that seem loose when compared to white families, there are strong social and family supports which, to some extent, mitigate the stresses of poverty, unemployment, and poor social and medical services. The children, then, do not become the focus of adult anger and frustration.

Another possible explanation is that child abuse and neglect do occur at high rates among minority and lower income families, but they are underreported. The national study cited above stated that most reporting is done by schools and by social service, mental health, and court-related agencies. If these institutions are nonexistent or inadequate to meet the needs of minority communities, then it is quite possible that much of the maltreatment of children in poor and minority families will go undetected.

THE BLACK YOUNG ADULT

As black children become young adults, they continue to experience the stresses they have known from childhood, as well as new difficulties inherent in growing older. Figure 2.6 shows that, by far, the leading cause of death for black youths from 15 to 24 years old is homicide. Approximately 42 per 100,000 black youths die from homicide as compared to approximately 8 per 100,000 white youths.

Unemployment

One problem which has recently become increasingly difficult for youth, and especially minority youth, is unemployment. Trends indicate that when the economy is strong, youth employment improves slightly more than adult employment, but when the economy is weak, youth tend to fare a bit worse than the rest of the work force. In the early 1980s, with our faltering economy, young people found it especially difficult to get jobs. The unemployment rates as of December 4, 1982, were 10.4 percent for the overall labor force, 20.2 percent among blacks, and over 45 percent for black youths. Table 2.6 shows clearly that those having the most difficulty in the job market at present are nonwhite youths, of whom approximately 90 percent are black.

In February 1982, the Congressional Budget Office, in *Improving youth em-*

Figure 2.6
Major Causes of Death for Ages 15 to 24 Years: United States, 1978

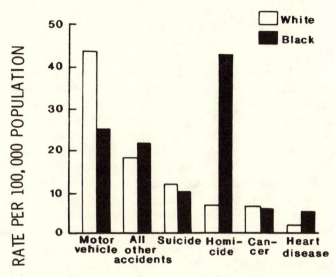

Source: U.S. Department of Health and Human Services. *The status of children, youth and families, 1979*. August 1980.

Table 2.6
Unemployment Rates in the Civilian Population, by Age, Race, and Sex: 1981 (In Percentages)

	Youths (16-19)	Youths (20-24)	Youths (25-54)
All Males	20.1	13.2	5.4
White males	17.9	11.6	4.9
Nonwhite males	38.3	24.9	10.3
All Females	19.0	11.1	6.3
White females	16.6	9.1	5.5
Nonwhite females	38.6	24.5	10.8

Source: Congressional Budget Office. *Improving youth employment prospects: Issues and options*. February 1982.

ployment prospects, stated: "Nearly two-thirds of measured youth unemployment in 1978 was experienced by the 10 percent of the youth labor force that was unemployed for 15 weeks or longer. This group is disproportionately black and poor, and many of them lack basic academic skills" (p. x). The report states further that these are precisely the individuals who will face chronic unemployment problems. They will continue to need help to overcome economic and educational handicaps to become productive and consistent workers. The tightening job market comes at a time when government programs (such as the Comprehensive Employment and Training Act and Targeted Jobs Tax Credit) are expiring or undergoing changes, making necessary assistance unavailable.

The study states that the individuals who are at greatest risk for unemployment are high school dropouts from low-income families. We have already discussed the poverty cycle and how black children are more likely to grow up in low-income households than are white children. Black children are also likely to come out of school with less education. A 1975 study showed that only 58 percent of 17-year-old blacks in school could meet the standard of functional literacy, compared to 92 percent of white enrolled 17 year olds. Needless to say, for dropouts, the percentages would be lower. Lack of academic skills makes getting a job more difficult, especially now, when the proportion of unskilled jobs in the United States is shrinking, and when the military (a major employer of unskilled youth) is also dwindling in size.

America's sluggish economy, government cutbacks to job programs, a smaller market for unskilled labor, and inadequate educational preparation all combine to make black youths, especially, vulnerable to unemployment. Compared to the total population aged from 16 to 21, those experiencing long-term unemployment are 1.4 times as likely to be from the inner city, 1.6 times as likely to come from low-income families, and 1.8 times as likely to be high school dropouts. Considering the social and educational circumstances surrounding black young people, it is not surprising, then, that unemployed youths are 2.1 times as likely to be black.

A recent development under the economic conditions of the 1980s is that the black youth's opportunities for college or professional education may be much more limited than it once was. In 1982, the United Negro College Fund reported a significant decrease in the number of black college freshmen. Many potential students are turning away from college because of financial hardship. Others are victims of inferior secondary school education, and some are being rejected because of a serious slackening in affirmative action programs (Edward B. Fiske, "Colleges Report Large Decline in Black Freshmen," *New York Times*, November 28, 1982).

If a poor black child makes it through the early years, he or she faces a new set of difficulties as a teenager or young adult. A black adolescent has a high probability of getting into trouble with the law and is seven times as likely to be involved in violent crimes as his or her more affluent white peers. Many black youths die as a result of black-on-black homicide, which has now become

Table 2.7
Comparisons of Percentages of Black and White Persons under 18 Arrested for Selected Crimes

CRIME	Black	White
Murder and non-negligent manslaughter	44.1	51.5
Forcible rape	54.5	43.2
Robbery	62.5	35.0
Aggravated assault	43.6	63.4
Burglary	25.9	72.1
Violent crime	49.0	48.7
Property crime	26.3	71.2

Source: U.S. Department of Justice, Bureau of Justice Statistics. *Sourcebook of criminal justice statistics: 1981*. 1982.

Note: Some figures may not total 100 percent because of small percentages of other minority youths arrested.

the leading cause of death among young black men (Reynolds, 1980). And, not too surprisingly, the suicide rate among black males has increased dramatically in the past several decades. In 1960, the rate was 7.8 per 100,000 of the black population; by 1978, it had increased to 12.1 per 100,000. This rise was mainly attributable to a dramatic increase among young black males. The suicide rate for black women remains relatively low, but it does show some increase, from 1.9 to 3.0 per 100,000 between 1960 and 1978 (U.S. Department of Health and Human Services, 1981).

Incarceration

If a black teenager avoids dying at a very early age, he is at a shockingly high risk of being incarcerated. Today 46 percent of inmates in federal, state, and local prisons are black males (Gary, 1981). Their opportunities for rehabilitation and positive mental health are severely damaged when they are released. Many black teenagers, particularly male, do not survive this treadmill without serious psychological damage and behavioral disorders. It is also becoming increasingly clear that the black male is at higher risk for certain forms of maladaptation, whereas the black female is at higher risk for others.

Table 2.7 shows some comparisons of percentages of black and white persons under 18 who were arrested for selected crimes. Considering that blacks constitute about 12 percent of the total population of the United States, it is clear that they are overrepresented in all of the above categories, and that there is a dramatic

Figure 2.7
Arrests for Property Crimes, by Offense Charged and Race, United States, 1979

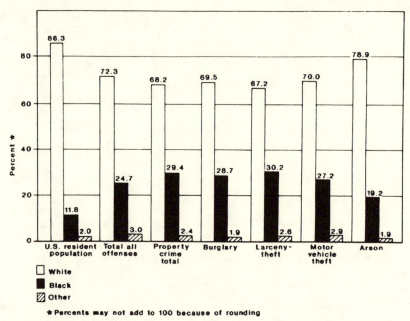

Source: U.S. Department of Justice, Bureau of Justice Statistics. *Sourcebook of criminal justice statistics: 1981*. 1982.

difference in the percentages of violent crimes as opposed to property crimes committed by black youths, primarily males. Almost twice as many arrests of black youths are made for violent crimes.

The fact that crime is a significant problem in the black community, for adults as well as youths, is underscored by the high proportions of blacks in state and federal prisons. Whereas 51 percent, a bare majority, of prison inmates are white, 46 percent are black. This is nearly four times their representation in the population of the United States. Figures 2.7 and 2.8 compare the rates of arrest of black and white persons for selected property and violent crimes.

Blacks are overrepresented as victims as well as offenders. The phenomenally high proportion of black homicide victims, especially between the ages of 25 and 44 years, has already been discussed. For nearly all age groups, the numbers of black and white murder victims are nearly equal, even though there are considerably fewer blacks in America than whites (see table 2.8). There are other kinds of crime to which blacks seem particularly vulnerable, for example, robbery and assault, where black victims actually outnumber white victims (see table 2.9).

What does a black person do who grows up without hope? Criminal activity is only one option. Many others turn to alcohol and drug abuse.

Figure 2.8
Arrests for Violent Crimes, by Offense Charged and Race, United States, 1979

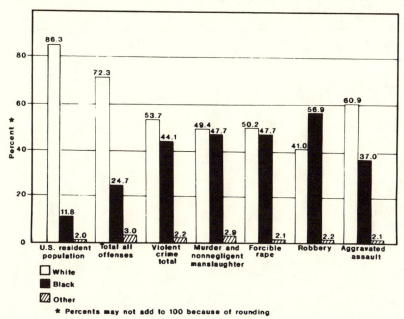

Source: U.S. Department of Justice, Bureau of Justice Statistics. *Sourcebook of criminal justice statistics: 1981*. 1982.

ALCOHOLISM

Alcoholism is one of the most serious mental health issues facing the black community (Harper, 1976). Three times as many blacks die from alcoholism as whites. Just as significant, alcohol abuse is associated with over 50 percent of the deaths from accidents, and it is connected with more than 50 percent of black-on-black homicides, which have reached epidemic proportions. Alcohol is both a depressive drug and one that releases inhibitions. Therefore, it is closely linked to violent behaviors—rape, child abuse, and spouse battering. As a result, alcohol abuse is tied to criminal arrest rates. It also takes its toll because of associated health problems such as cirrhosis of the liver, cancer, heart disease, stroke, and neurological and brain deterioration (Harper, 1981). The abuse of alcohol is a key element in the breakdown of family life, and it frequently leads to neglected children and divorce. Sadly, alcohol abuse during pregnancy leads to fetal alcohol syndrome which results in children who are retarded in physical growth and intellect.

It is clear that, although blacks may use alcohol to cope with the stress of living, abuse invariably leads to more social, economic, and psychological stress.

Table 2.8
Murders and Non-Negligent Manslaughters Known to Police, by Race and Age of Victim, United States, 1979

AGE OF VICTIM	White	Black
Total	11,154	8,934
Percent	54.2	43.4
Infant (under 1)	87	70
1 to 4	194	130
5 to 9	109	61
10 to 14	124	77
15 to 19	1,098	728
20 to 24	1,842	1,545
25 to 29	1,645	1,620
30 to 34	1,253	1,217
35 to 39	925	857
40 to 44	740	631
45 to 49	699	505
50 to 54	578	442
55 to 59	453	333
60 to 64	364	229
65 to 69	308	154
70 to 74	221	85
75 and older	322	119
Unknown	192	131

Source: U.S. Department of Justice, Bureau of Justice Statistics. *Sourcebook of criminal justice statistics: 1981.* 1982.

The number of liquor stores and bars in black residential neighborhoods attests to the popularity of alcohol indulgence and its ready availability.

The number of deaths from cirrhosis of the liver, which is frequently, but not always, associated with alcoholism, highlights the magnitude of the alcohol problem in the black community. From 1950 to 1975, the age-adjusted death rate of cirrhosis for whites increased by 50 percent; however, for nonwhites, the increase was over 200 percent. Black males die from cirrhosis at twice the rate of black females (U.S. Department of Health, Education and Welfare, Public Health Service, 1979). The death rate of cirrhosis for minorities is now over twice that for whites.

It is of interest that surveys show that a greater proportion of people at lower socioeconomic levels are abstainers than at higher class levels. Moderate and severe drinking increase as class level rises. Middle-class blacks have significant rates of alcoholism. The higher rate of cirrhosis among low-income groups may be related to poor nutrition and a greater incidence of hepatitis, both of which contribute to the disease (U.S. Department of Health, Education and Welfare, Public Health Service, 1979).

Table 2.9

Estimated Rate (Per 100,000 Persons 12 Years of Age or Older) of Personal Victimization, by Race of Victim and Type of Victimization, United States, 1979*

Type of Victimization	Race of Victim	
	White	Black and Other Races
Base	155,539,091	22,703,914
Rape and attempted rape	102	143
Robbery	548	1,161
Robbery with injury	193	360
Serious assault	96	237
Minor assault	96	123
Robbery without injury	214	608
Attempted robbery without injury	141	193
Assault	2,710	2,780
Aggravated assault	949	1,291
With injury	302	571
Attempted assault with weapon	647	720
Simple assault	1,761	1,489
With injury	458	365
Attempted assault without weapon	1,303	1,124
Personal larceny with contact	251	532
Purse snatching	53	165
Attempted purse snatching	26	25
Pocket picking	172	342
Personal larceny without contact	9,003	8,182

*Subcategories may not sum to total because of rounding.

Source: U.S. Department of Justice, Bureau of Justice Statistics. *Sourcebook of criminal justice statistics: 1981*. 1982.

As in other communities, alcohol abuse has become interwoven with social activities and other cultural norms. Therefore, a major obstacle in treating the black alcoholic is his or her acceptance and recognition of the disease of alcoholism. Many persons who are clearly alcoholic to observers may brag that they can "hold" their liquor. Alcohol abuse may therefore become the norm among black men and women who are trying to convey a "macho" image. As a result of their refusal to admit an alcohol addiction, many either do not seek or refuse treatment. Blacks are particularly reluctant to join such groups as Alcoholics Anonymous, and other sources of help are frequently not available in their communities (Christmas, 1978; Harper, 1981). One study (Lowe and Hodges, 1972) states that race has a definite effect on the quality of treatment a black alcoholic will receive.

The black community and its institutions must become more concerned with alcoholism and the discouragement of heavy drinking. It must also make political

Figure 2.9
Drug Abuse: Utilization of Federally Funded Drug Abuse Clinics

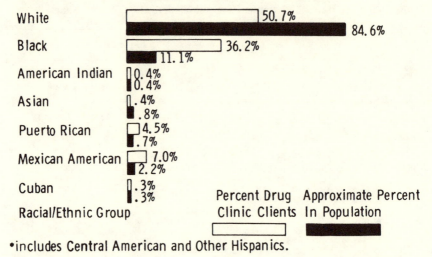

White   50.7%
                                                              84.6%
Black   36.2%
                                        11.1%
American Indian   0.4%
                         0.4%
Asian   .4%
                         .8%
Puerto Rican   4.5%
                         .7%
Mexican American   7.0%
                         2.2%
Cuban   .3%   Percent Drug   Approximate Percent
                         .3%   Clinic Clients In Population
Racial/Ethnic Group

•includes Central American and Other Hispanics.

Source: U.S. Department of Health, Education, and Welfare, Public Health Service *Health Status of Minorities and Low-Income Groups, 1979.*

and economic demands for more local treatment facilities for substance abuse in general.

DRUG ABUSE

Drug abuse has been an important problem in the black community for many decades. It has been used as a major form of psychological escape from the pressures of black life. In the 1940s and 1950s, many teenaged black youth in the Harlems of the country were smoking marijuana and becoming addicted to heroin. By the 1960s, the popularity of these drugs had spread to the white community as well; the drugs were even more widely used among blacks. The 1960s also ushered in other drugs, including the hallucinogens and more wide-spread use of stimulants (''speed'') and sedatives (''downers'') as well as various tranquilizers such as librium and valium. A drug that has gained recent popularity is cocaine, which is used extensively in the entertainment industry, but has also spread to the general public. It is an extremely expensive drug, which limits its use to some degree, but it is not uncommon for the poor and students to spend enormous sums of money to obtain cocaine, which is not actually a narcotic, but a stimulant drug.

It is difficult to estimate the exact toll of drug abuse on the black community. Figure 2.9 indicates clinic utilization rates, which are proportionately high for blacks.

Table 2.10 shows the percentages of blacks and whites of different age groups admitted to federally funded drug treatment programs by their primary drug of abuse at admission. This seems to show that heroin use is considerably higher for blacks than for whites of all age groups, but it is difficult to estimate the exact prevalence in the black community. An unknown number of addicts die of drug overdoses per year, and of this group, a large percentage is black. Black males die more frequently of heroin overdoses than do black females. But many become a mere death statistic because of the crime and violence associated with drug addiction. "Junkies" must get money one way or the other. Most steal; many females turn to prostitution to support their habits.

The toll of crime and family disruption due to drug addiction is not recognized sufficiently by the public—the social costs are enormous.

Also insufficiently recognized is the price one pays for the abuse of marijuana. Besides physical health risks, marijuana ingestion can lead to acute paranoid episodes as well as a loss of interest in the environment. Because of its disorienting and disruptive effect on memory, students who smoke "pot" frequently are unable to concentrate or perform their studies. Similar results occur with the abuse of stimulants, including cocaine and sedatives. In addition, "speed" and cocaine abuse can produce a schizophrenic-like psychosis and a general deterioration of mental and physical health (Kaplan, Freedman, & Sadock, 1980).

Unfortunately, despite these ill effects, drug abuse has become a norm among some of our youth, even on the elementary school level. It can be a significant contributing factor to the lack of achievement of our youth at both the secondary school and college levels. Though it is difficult to measure the long-range effects on the black community, it can be extrapolated that they are considerable and that they contribute to the increased vulnerability to mental disorder of black citizens. More research on the general social and psychological effects on the black family is desperately needed.

Drug treatment programs overall have not been successful. Methadone treatment programs have been abused and have often even contributed additional problems. There are still insufficient treatment facilities and social commitment to handle this drug abuse problem. Local community clinics with innovative approaches are required, but reduced state and federal funds will undoubtedly hamper efforts of this sort (U.S. Department of Health, Education and Welfare, December 1977).

As we proceed with an examination of the mental health status of black Americans, the reader should be ever mindful of black male and female differences in the nature and extent of various problems (such as drug and alcohol abuse, homicide, suicide, and incarceration). This must influence the strategies and policy approaches designed to alleviate many of the institutional barriers to positive black mental health. Although all of these issues cannot be addressed here, some examples of the types of questions which must be studied are: (1) What are the implications of the socialization process of male and female children in female-headed households? (2) How does institutional racism impact differ-

Table 2.10
Drug Users Admitted to Federally Funded Drug Abuse Treatment Programs, by Ethnicity, Sex, Age at Admission, and Primary Drug of Abuse at Admission, United States, 1979

| | Total Admission | | Heroin |
	Number	Percent	
Total	235,414	100.0	40.4
White Male	95,514	100.0	23.9
Under 18 Yrs.	13,737	100.0	0.4
18 to 19 Yrs.	8,689	100.0	2.7
20 to 24 Yrs.	23,458	100.0	17.4
25 to 29 Yrs.	22,704	100.0	40.8
30 Yrs. and Older	23,936	100.0	35.4
White Female	40,975	100.0	24.5
Under 18 Yrs.	8,602	100.0	0.8
18 to 19 Yrs.	3,467	100.0	8.9
20 to 24 Yrs.	10,572	100.0	32.7
25 to 29 Yrs.	9,299	100.0	43.0
30 Yrs. and Older	9,035	100.0	24.5
Black Male	50,466	100.0	62.9
Under 18 Yrs.	2,800	100.0	1.2
18 to 19 Yrs.	1,973	100.0	8.8
20 to 24 Yrs.	8,634	100.0	45.2
25 to 29 Yrs.	15,643	100.0	73.4
30 Yrs. and Older	21,416	100.0	75.6
Black Female	17,239	100.0	64.3
Under 18 Yrs.	1,311	100.0	2.3
18 to 19 Yrs.	816	100.0	15.8
20 to 24 Yrs.	4,070	100.0	61.0
25 to 29 Yrs.	5,950	100.0	78.1
30 Yrs. and Older	5,092	100.0	74.5

Table 2.10 (continued)

Other Opiates	Marihuana	Barbiturates	Amphetamines
7.5	16.2	3.9	6.5
9.8	21.0	5.2	8.4
0.8	58.6	4.1	7.3
2.6	38.4	6.8	11.0
8.7	20.3	7.5	11.3
15.5	8.9	4.8	8.0
13.3	5.1	3.4	5.7
10.8	18.5	6.0	11.0
1.2	49.7	5.3	12.0
5.2	27.0	7.8	17.8
12.3	11.3	6.9	12.6
17.0	7.1	5.2	8.9
14.1	5.9	6.0	7.5
4.0	9.9	1.5	3.4
0.5	62.0	2.1	2.4
2.5	44.1	3.5	3.9
3.8	14.4	3.0	5.8
4.8	4.2	1.2	3.8
4.2	2.3	0.9	2.3
5.3	9.7	2.4	2.9
1.2	63.5	3.7	3.9
3.3	36.9	4.7	5.6
5.2	7.6	3.0	4.2
5.9	2.2	1.9	2.5
6.3	2.0	1.9	1.6

Table 2.10 (continued)

	Alcohol	Cocaine	Hallucinogens
Total	7.5	3.8	2.7
White Male	11.8	4.3	4.3
Under 18 Yrs.	5.1	2.4	7.4
18 to 19 Yrs.	7.2	4.8	10.0
20 to 24 Yrs.	7.3	6.6	6.1
25 to 29 Yrs.	7.5	4.3	2.2
30 Yrs. and Older	25.6	2.9	0.9
White Female	5.3	3.3	3.4
Under 18 Yrs.	4.9	2.8	7.7
18 to 19 Yrs.	4.2	5.6	7.2
20 to 24 Yrs.	3.3	4.8	3.1
25 to 29 Yrs.	2.9	2.9	1.3
30 Yrs. and Older	11.0	1.7	0.6
Black Male	5.6	4.4	0.9
Under 18 Yrs.	5.4	5.3	3.3
18 to 19 Yrs.	4.9	8.1	2.9
20 to 24 Yrs.	3.8	6.8	2.0
25 to 29 Yrs.	3.1	4.2	0.6
30 Yrs. and Older	8.3	3.1	0.2
Black Female	3.2	3.4	0.8
Under 18 Yrs.	4.9	4.7	2.1
18 to 19 Yrs.	2.1	10.9	3.3
20 to 24 Yrs.	1.9	4.6	1.1
25 to 29 Yrs.	1.9	2.4	0.3
30 Yrs. and Older	5.4	2.1	0.3

Table 2.10 (continued)

Primary Drug of Abuse at Admission

PCP	Tranquilizers	Other Sedatives	Other
3.5	3.1	2.4	2.4
3.3	3.0	2.9	2.2
3.4	2.4	4.0	4.1
5.6	3.4	4.3	3.2
6.2	3.1	3.3	2.3
2.0	2.4	2.1	1.6
0.7	3.9	2.0	1.2
2.5	8.0	4.4	2.1
3.5	4.3	5.0	2.9
5.9	4.5	4.0	2.0
3.5	4.7	3.5	1.3
1.0	6.0	3.4	1.4
0.5	19.0	6.2	3.0
4.2	0.8	1.0	1.2
4.0	1.7	8.5	3.7
12.6	3.0	3.5	2.3
11.5	1.3	1.0	1.4
2.9	0.5	0.3	1.0
1.4	0.5	0.4	0.9
4.2	1.6	1.0	1.2
3.6	2.7	4.5	2.8
12.6	1.3	2.7	0.7
8.2	1.4	0.7	1.0
2.7	1.1	0.4	0.8
1.6	2.1	0.7	1.6

Note: This table is based on data that were reported to the Client Oriented Data Acquisition Process (CODAP), an information system operated by the National Institute on Drug Abuse (NIDA) that collects admission and discharge reports on each client admitted to federally funded drug abuse treatment programs in the United States and each of its territories. To assure the quality of the data, NIDA has developed quality-control procedures that include manual edits at the state and national levels, as well as computer edits that test the internal consistency of information reported in individual forms. The number of cases for each table may vary because of missing values in different categories. Clients for whom no primary drug was reported and transfer admissions between CODAP clinics are not included in these data. The "primary drug of abuse at admission" is the drug type causing the most dysfunction at the time of admission to treatment. The subtotals of each category do not sum to the total due to the exclusion of cases with missing data on one or more of these attributes.

Source: U.S. Department of Justice, Bureau of Justice Statistics. *Sourcebook of criminal justice statistics, 1981*. 1982.

entially on black males and females? (3) What is the influence of peer pressure relative to black male and female adaptations? It has been well established that black mental illness must be examined in the context of black cultural patterns (Thomas & Comer, 1973; Jones & Korchin, 1982; Jackson, 1981).

BLACK MENTAL HEALTH AND CULTURAL BIAS

The status of black mental health is strongly related to the effects of cultural influences on behavior and its classification. These cultural influences have similarities for all citizens, but they differ in their impact depending on one's ethnic background and sex. One should recognize that blacks are not a homogeneous group and that there are many class and intraethnic cultural variations. Yet blacks of all classes have a common colored skin and the experience of institutional racism. Traditional models of mental health cannot be legitimately applied a priori to many black Americans. Numerous mental health workers in recent years have criticized mental health theory and practice because of racist and sexist approaches (Thomas & Sillen, 1972; Willie et al., 1973; Comer, 1972; Pinderhughes, 1973). The mental health of any black individual must be viewed in the context of his or her socioeconomic and cultural background, particularly as this context is shaped and influenced by a society pervaded to some degree by institutional racism. Mental health or illness does not exist in a social-political vacuum that can be analyzed free of the danger of subjectivity and cultural biases.

Perhaps the most dramatic example of psychological theory used in a politically abusive and repressive way against blacks is represented during the time of slavery in the work of Dr. S. A. Cartwright. This example is reported here because it underscores the subtle and invidious nature of cultural and political bias that is often inherent in the theory and practice of psychology and psychiatry.

Dr. Cartwright was a surgeon and psychologist who was summoned to a Louisiana plantation in 1851 to investigate the causes for the high percentage of slave runaways (Cartwright, 1851). After many weeks of study, he wrote a long report which concluded that the slaves who ran away to freedom were suffering from a mental disease he dubbed ''draptomania,'' which, translated, means runaway mania. This illustration is germane to blacks' current predicament because Dr. Cartwright, as probably most whites of the time, accepted slavery as ''normal'' and considered it an acceptable social system arrangement for Afro-Americans. Black rejection of this norm was viewed as pathological. Cartwright's tactic (perhaps unknowingly) was to use psychology, with the trappings of objective scientific research, not only to justify and condone slavery, but also to indoctrinate the slaves into believing that mental health for them was being happy on the plantation. Any slave, of course, who accepted the ''scientific'' theories of Cartwright was an accomplice in his or her own oppression.

Although the above example would be viewed as an extreme, many related and similar circumstances exist today, and they are relevant to the mental health status of blacks as they enter the decade of the 1980s, 120 years removed from the Emancipation Proclamation. Most people will agree that blacks have progressed substantially since the Civil War. Sometimes, that progress has been slow, and much of it was the result of the active struggle and sacrifice of dedicated black and white Americans. Still, the current mental health status of black Americans, which cannot be examined apart from the predominantly white culture in which they live, shows clearly that we still have a long way to go.

Numerous studies of black mental health in the past have reflected such biases and have distorted the picture of the status of black mental health. Blacks were generally measured against white middle-class norms. This continued to be a problem in clinical diagnosis and the use of psychological and intellectual assessment tests (Bass et al., 1982; Jones, 1972). Evaluated against such norms, blacks have frequently been pictured as deviant or deficient. In many instances, so-called black pathology was a manifestation of cultural and class differences from the normative reference group. White mental health professionals have demonstrated biases and have harbored racial stereotypes similar to other whites in America (Thomas & Sillen, 1972; Willie et al., 1973; Comer, 1972; Spurlock, 1975). The Task Panel of the President's Commission on Mental Health has recommended that all mental health professionals be exposed to cross-cultural curricula in their training programs. It also recommended as a high priority the training of more minority mental health professionals, who currently represent only from 1.5 to 3 percent of such workers. Minorities must function at all levels of the system—clinicians, administrators, and researchers—to prevent biased practices toward blacks.

For instance, many studies have reported a low incidence of depression among blacks partly as a result of bias on the part of white researchers who have preconceived impressions of blacks as "happy-go-lucky." As a result, reports show that whites with serious mental disorders are likely to be diagnosed as having depressive disorders while blacks are more likely to be diagnosed as schizophrenic (Cannon and Locke, 1977; Collins, Rickman, & Mathura, 1980; Jones, Gray, & Parson, 1981; Adebimpe, 1981; Bell & Mehta, 1981). It has also been widely believed by some investigators that depression is low in blacks because for many decades the suicide rate for blacks was reported to be only one half the rate of whites. But one has to question whether there was a bias against recording a black death as a suicide if physicians generally believed blacks were "happy" and did not have such tendencies. Today, however, as already mentioned, the black suicide rate is rising, particularly among young black males whose rate has risen to the level of their white peers.

Mental Disorders

Overall, recent reports show increasing instances of serious (nonclinical) psychological depression among all segments of the black population, but particularly among those with broken marriages, those not employed outside the home, those with lower incomes, and the less well educated (Roberts, Stevenson, & Breslow, 1981).

However, it is difficult to determine whether blacks are being properly diagnosed and treated. Some investigators postulate that blacks are more likely than whites to be diagnosed as schizophrenic because of problems of communication with white therapists who are fearful of blacks (particularly angry blacks) and who are therefore more likely to diagnose them as paranoid schizophrenic (Adebimpe, 1981).

There is still much controversy about the degree of paranoia and paranoid schizophrenia among blacks (Collins et al., 1980; Jones et al., 1981). Many have suggested that black paranoia is adaptive and healthy (Grier and Cobbs, 1968; Kardiner and Ovesey, 1951). However, a legitimate diagnosis of paranoia or paranoid schizophrenia depicts an individual who is seriously anxious, suspicious, and unable to function with his or her environment because of severe loss of contact with reality, often manifested by delusions and hallucinations. Nonetheless, standards of deviant behavior are relative and depend upon the cultural situation as to their acceptability or rejection as a mental illness.

There is insufficient data on the exact percentage of blacks with psychotic (severe loss of contact with reality) disorders. One can examine, however, the percentage of distributions of this diagnosis for blacks from outpatient clinics. From 1961 to 1969, the percentage of psychotic disorders at hospital and clinic termination for black males rose from 17 percent to 19 percent and for black females from 25 percent to 40 percent (U.S. Department of Health, Education and Welfare, Public Health Service, 1979). Blacks use federally funded drug abuse centers at a rate that is over three times their representation in the population. Inpatient admissions to state and county hospitals seem to be significantly higher for blacks than for whites (table 2.11), but the race differential is not so great for outpatient clinic admissions (table 2.12). Utilization rates, however, are not an accurate measure of the incidence of disorders. This makes white-black comparisons unreliable. Nonetheless, it is clear from these two tables that blacks have high rates of admissions to mental facilities and that the rates for black males is alarmingly high.

Although the overall number of patients in mental hospitals has declined dramatically since 1950, the percentage drop for whites has been significantly greater (U.S. Department of Health, Education and Welfare, Public Health Service, 1979). Blacks often have fewer financial and social supports available for a return to the community. Halfway houses are overcrowded and finding living quarters for often marginally functioning mental patients who are barely self-supporting is difficult.

So-called deinstitutionalization programs have had mixed results and have often contributed to the social burdens within the black community. Often prematurely discharged mental patients are unable to survive without social service supports. Many have become sad figures among the rising number of the homeless who sleep on our city streets. Follow-up care for discharged patients has often

Table 2.11
Age-Specific and Age-Adjusted Rates per 100,000 Population of Inpatient Admissions to State and County Mental Hospitals by Race, Sex, and Age, 1975

Age on Admission	White			Black		
	Both Sexes	Male	Female	Both Sexes	Male	Female
Total Admission	296,151	190,788	105,363	83,367	53,646	29,721
	RATES PER 100,000 POPULATION					
All Ages	161.1	214.2	111.2	344.2	469.5	232.2
Under 18 years	31.6	39.3	23.6	77.8	103.1	52.2
18-24 years	234.0	343.9	129.4	539.6	892.1	241.8
25-44 years	270.2	349.3	194.2	688.3	1032.7	406.3
45-64 years	213.4	276.0	155.7	414.1	414.2	413.9
65 years plus	85.3	130.9	54.0	171.9	210.8	143.7
Median age	35.2	34.3	37.3	32.1	30.0	38.0
Age adjusted rates*	159.7	213.2	110.0	367.3	509.4	248.5

*Adjustment based on distribution of U.S. Civilian Population – July 1, 1975.

Source: Subcommittee to the President's Commission on Mental Health. *Task panel reports,* vol. 3. 1978.

Table 2.12
Age-Specific and Age-Adjusted Rates per 100,000 Population of Outpatient Clinic Admissions by Race and Sex, United States: 1975

Age on Admission	White			Black		
	Both Sexes	Male	Female	Both Sexes	Male	Female
Total Admissions	1,171,196	528,794	642,402	198,965	90,082	108,883
	RATES PER 100,000 POPULATION					
Under 18	505.6	620.7	386.4	715.1	947.3	480.4
18-24 years	883.9	798.3	985.5	782.6	881.3	699.0
25-44 years	1022.1	810.3	1225.4	1407.4	931.7	1795.5
45-64 years	444.4	376.1	507.5	431.7	371.8	483.0
65 years and over	217.9	129.2	278.9	480.9	132.9	735.0
Median Age	28.5	25.0	30.7	26.1	17.8	30.0
Age Adjusted Rates*	639.2	587.7	682.7	813.4	730.5	865.9

*Adjustment based on distribution of U.S. Civilian Population – July 1975.

Source: Subcommittee to the President's Commission on Mental Health. *Task panel reports*, vol. 3. 1978.

been poor or financially poorly supported. Without a strong extended family, the impaired and infirm will have more and more difficulty surviving. This is particularly true of the black elderly.

Black Elderly

Life expectancy has increased recently for black Americans to about 63 years for black men and 72 years for black women; therefore, they are now more susceptible to both chronic and mental conditions that require health and social supports. Many of the black elderly are falling below the poverty line. Housing is more difficult to find, and many become the ready victims of crime and violence. Major attention must be given to support the black elderly as a vital resource to the community and the family.

SUMMARY

It is clear from this discussion that black Americans are at high risk for maladaptation, behavioral disabilities, and mental illness throughout their life cycles. There appear to be no safety nets that protect the health or psyche of the Afro-American from institutional racism, poverty, high unemployment, and a stagnant economy.

RECOMMENDATIONS

It is clear from this analysis that the socioeconomic and racial conditions under which blacks live are the major contributors to rising rates of mental disorder, crime, and family and community breakdown. Therefore, we endorse the four primary recommendations of the subpanel on black Americans of the President's Task Force on Mental Health:

1. Full employment achieved through the initiatives of the public and private sectors, and equal access to jobs assured by continuation of affirmative action legislation.
2. Affirmative action in the distribution of housing funds and opportunities for adequate housing.
3. Redistribution of health care facilities,with particular attention to (1) primary prevention, and (2) improving access to the quality of health care.
4. Implementation of public welfare services that concentrate on the elimination of poverty and which support and supplement the initiatives of individuals to be participants in American society. (Subcommittee to the President's Commission on Mental Health, 1978, vol. 3, p. 827)

In addition, government cutbacks in social and health programs which further threaten the health and mental health status of the poor and minorities should be halted, and these programs should be restored through new or old mechanisms.

Black families and children are at high risk, and all efforts by private, public, humanitarian, and community organizations should be directed to providing resources and support to black families. Civil rights groups should include the restoration of family supports and resources as a primary target for action. There should be a special focus on family planning and effective parenting.

The mental health care system should provide greater and more innovative care to the black community based on the elimination of racial prejudice and a development of cross-cultural perspectives which should be included in all training programs. The numbers of minority health care professionals must be increased dramatically from the current meager 2 or 3 percent through affirmative action programs.

Finally, we recommend that the National Urban League, together with other organizations, quickly convene a task force of elected officials, government experts, professionals, and community representatives to develop programs and strategies to ameliorate the rapidly deteriorating positive mental health of Afro-Americans.

REFERENCES

Adebimpe, V. R. (1981, March). Overview: White norms and psychiatric diagnosis of black patients. *American Journal of Psychiatry, 138*(3), 279–285.

Bass, B. A., Wyatt, G. E., & Powell, G. J. (Eds.) (1982). *The Afro-American family: Assessment, research and treatment issues.* New York: Grune and Straton.

Bell, C. C., & Mehta, H. (1981, February). Misdiagnosis of black patients with manic depressive illness: Second in a series. *Journal of the National Medical Association, 73*(2), 101–107.

Benjamin, R., & Benjamin, M. (1981, January). Sociocultural correlates to black drinking. *Journal of Studies on Alcohol, 9,* 241–245.

Billingsley, A. (1968). *Black families in white America.* Englewood Cliffs, NJ: Prentice-Hall.

Brenner, M. H. (1977, May/June). Personal stability and economic security. *Social Policy, 8*(1), 2–4.

Cannon, M. S., & Locke, B. Z. (1977). Being black is detrimental to one's mental health: Myth or reality? *Phylon, 38*(4), 408–428.

Cartwright, S. A. (1851). Report on the diseases and physical peculiarities of the Negro race. *New Orleans Medical and Surgical Journal, 7,* 691.

Christmas, J. J. (1978, Spring). Alcoholism services for minorities: Training issues and concerns. *Alcohol Health and Research World,* pp. 20–27.

Clark, Kenneth B. (1965). *Dark ghetto: Dilemmas of social power.* New York: Harper and Row.

Collins, J. L., Rickman, L. E., & Mathura, C. B. (1980). Frequency of schizophrenia and depression in a black inpatient population. *Journal of the National Medical Association, 72*(9), 851–856.

Comer, J. P. (1972). *Beyond black and white.* New York: Quadrangle Books.

Congressional Budget Office. (1982, February). *Improving youth employment prospects: issues and options.* Washington, DC: U.S. Government Printing Office.

Curtis, L. A. (1975). *Violence, race and culture*. Lexington, MA: D. C. Heath and Company.

Duvall, H. J., Goudreau, K. W., & Marsh, R. E. (1982, April). Aid to families with dependent children: Characteristics of recipients, 1979. *Social Security Bulletin, 45*(4).

Edelman, M. W. (1980). *Portrait of inequality: Black and white children in America*. Washington, DC: The Children's Defense Fund.

Gary, L. E. (Ed.). (1978). *Mental health: A challenge to the black community*. Philadelphia: Dorrance and Company.

Gary, L. E. (Ed.) (1981). *Black men*. Beverly Hills, CA: Sage Publications.

Grier, W. H., & Cobbs, P. M. (1968). *Black rage*. New York: Basic Books.

Harper, F. (Ed.). (1976). *Alcohol abuse and black America*. Alexandria, VA: Douglass.

Harper, F. (1981). Alcohol and its abuse. In L. Gary (Ed.), *Black men*. Beverly Hills, CA: Sage Publications.

Hill, R. B. (1972). *The strengths of black families*. New York: Emerson Hall Publishers.

Jackson, J. (1981). Urban black Americans. In A. Harwood (Ed.), *Ethnicity and medical care*. Cambridge, MA: Harvard University Press.

Jones, B. E., Gray, B. A., & Parson, E. B. (1981, May). Manic depressive illness among poor urban blacks. *American Journal of Psychiatry, 138*(5), 654–657.

Jones, E. E., & Korchin, S. J. (Eds.). (1982). *Minority mental health*. New York: Praeger Publishers.

Jones, R. L. (Ed.). (1972). *Black psychology*. New York: Harper and Row.

Kaplan, H. I., Freedman, A. M., & Sadock, B. J. (Eds.). (1980). *Comprehensive textbook of psychiatry, III*, vol. 3. Baltimore: Williams and Wilkins.

Kardiner, A., & Ovesey, L. (1951). *The mark of oppression*. Cleveland: The World Publishing Company.

Lowe, G. D., & Hodges, H. E. (1972). Race and the treatment of alcoholism in a southern state. *Social Problems, 20*, 240–252.

Morgan Guaranty Trust Company of New York. (1981, August). *The Morgan Guaranty Survey*.

Medical World News. (1982). With less federal money, clinics cut back on health care for the poor. *23*(25), 20–21.

Myers, H. F. (1982). Stress, ethnicity and social class: A model for research with black populations. In Jones and Korchin (Eds.), *Minority mental health*. New York: Praeger Publishers.

National Center for Health Statistics. (1977). *Vital statistics of the U.S.*, vol. 1, *Natality*. Washington, DC: U.S. Government Printing Office.

National Center for Health Statistics. (1980). *Data from advance report of final natality statistics*. Washington, DC: U.S. Government Printing Office.

National Center for Health Statistics. (1982, September 30). *Monthly vital statistics report. Advance report of final mortality statistics, 1979*, 31(6).

National Research Council. Advisory Committee on Child Development. (1976). *Toward a national policy for children and families*. Washington, DC: National Academy of Sciences.

Pettigrew, T. F. (1964). *A profile of the negro American*. Princeton, NJ: D. Van Nostrand Company.

Pinderhughes, C. A. (1973). Racism and psychotherapy. In Willie, Kramer, and Brown (Eds.), *Racism and mental health*. Pittsburgh: University of Pittsburgh Press.

Reynolds, F. (1980, May). Homicide trends in the United States. *Demography, 17*(2), 177–188.

Roberts, R. E., Stevenson, J. M., and Breslow, L. (1981, December). Symptoms of depression among blacks and whites in an urban community. *Journal of Nervous and Mental Disease, 169*(12), 774–779.

Russo, R. M. (1982, July). Poverty: A major deterrent to America's good health. *Urban Health*, pp. 45–48.

Silverstein, B., & Krate, R. (1975). *Children of the dark ghetto: A developmental psychology.* New York: Praeger Publishers.

Spurlock, J. (1975). Psychiatric states. In R. A. Williams (Ed.), *Textbook of black-related diseases.* New York: McGraw-Hill.

Staples, R. (1981). *The world of black singles.* Westport, CT: Greenwood Press.

Subcommittee to the President's Commission on Mental Health. (1978). *Task panel reports*, vol. 3. Washington, DC: U.S. Government Printing Office.

Taylor, R. J., Jackson, J. S., & Quick, A. D. (1982). The frequency of social support among black Americans: Preliminary findings from the National Survey of Black Americans. *Urban Research Review, 8*(2), 1–4.

Thomas, A., & Sillen, S. (1972). *Racism and psychiatry.* New York: Brunner/Mazel.

Thomas, C. S., & Comer, J. P. (1973). Racism and mental health services. In Willie, Kramer, and Brown (Eds.), *Racism and mental health.* Pittsburgh: University of Pittsburgh Press.

U.S. Bureau of the Census. (1982). *Current population reports. Marital status and living arrangements: 1981.* (Series P–20, No. 372). Washington, DC: U.S. Government Printing Office.

U.S. Bureau of the Census. (1982, July). *Current population reports. Characteristics of the population below the poverty level: 1980.* (Series P–60, No. 133). Washington, DC: U.S. Government Printing Office.

U.S. Department of Health and Human Services. (1980, August). *The status of children, youth and families: 1979.* (DHHS Publication No. ODHS 80–30274). Washington, DC: U.S. Government Printing Office.

U.S. Department of Health and Human Services, National Center on Child Abuse and Neglect. (1981, September). *Study findings: National study on the incidence and severity of child abuse and neglect.* Washington, DC: U.S. Government Printing Office.

U.S. Department of Health and Human Services. (1981, December). *Health: United States, 1981.* (DHHS Publication No. PHS 82–1232). Washington, DC: U.S. Government Printing Office.

U.S. Department of Health, Education, and Welfare, National Institute of Drug Abuse. (1977, December). *Drugs and minorities.* (DHEW Publication No. ADM 78–507). Washington, DC: U.S. Government Printing Office.

U.S. Department of Health, Education, and Welfare, Public Health Service. (1979). *Health status of minorities and low-income groups.* (DHEW Publication No. HRA 79–627). Washington, DC: U.S. Government Printing Office.

U.S. Department of Justice, Bureau of Justice Statistics. (1982). *Sourcebook of criminal justice statistics: 1981.* Washington, DC: U.S. Government Printing Office.

Willie, C. V., Kramer, B. M., & Brown, B. S. (Eds.). (1973). *Racism and mental health.* Pittsburgh: University of Pittsburgh Press.

PART II

EPIDEMIOLOGICAL PERSPECTIVES AND ISSUES

3

THE EPIDEMIOLOGY OF MENTAL DISORDER IN THE BLACK POPULATION

Harold W. Neighbors and Suzan Lumpkin

Over the years, it has become evident that reliance solely upon a treatment mode of mental health intervention will not be enough to meet the needs of hard-to-reach ethnic minorities (Snowden, 1982). As a result, there is a need to move toward a public health model with an emphasis on the prevention of serious emotional difficulties (Hilliard, 1981). The promise of a public health approach lies in its emphasis on early intervention with groups rather than individuals. In order to develop and implement a public health model of prevention with blacks, however, the epidemiologic knowledge upon which to base those prevention efforts must be obtained. Thus, the purpose of this chapter is to review some of the most recent research on the epidemiology of mental disorder in black Americans.

While much of what is known about the epidemiology of mental disorder among black Americans comes from agency statistics, it is clear that no firm conclusions about black mental health can be made on the basis of treatment rate studies (Fischer, 1969). It is also apparent that community surveys fall short of answering important questions about black mental health because they focus only upon demographic variables (ignoring important risk factors) and do not compile rates of discrete (e.g., DSM-III-R) mental disorders (Neighbors, 1984). Epidemiologic research on black Americans should generate race-specific stress-coping hypotheses by measuring the multivariate relationships among race, class, stress, and other variables, such as social support and locus of control. These hypotheses will be useful in focusing attention on possible etiologic processes and important risk factors. Finally, there is a need to use etiologic and risk-factor information to design intervention programs which would have a preventive impact on the incidence of psychopathology in the black population.

In the past few years, a number of research projects have begun work on these areas. Below, we review the progress that has been made in these directions. The chapter is organized into five sections. First, the methodologic problem of classification in psychiatric epidemiologic research on blacks is reviewed. Next, the discussion focuses on the prevalence of discrete disorders and the epidemiology of depressive symptomatology. Third, social support as a potential buffer against stress is investigated. Fourth, the impact of upward and downward social mobility on black mental health is discussed. The chapter concludes by looking at the black family as a setting for intervention programs.

METHODOLOGIC ISSUES: DIAGNOSTIC CLASSIFICATION

Methodological problems vary with the nature of the disease and its mode of occurrence in the population under study. The basic aims of epidemiologic studies are to determine incidence and prevalence and to test for variation in those rates among subgroups of the population at risk. This includes such steps as defining the population to be studied and obtaining a representative sample, establishing a definition of caseness, creating a methodology for locating and identifying all cases of the mental disorder, expressing results in a form which will allow for comparison with other surveys, and describing possible causes of disorders.

Incidence and prevalence are the two major frequency indicators used in epidemiologic studies. Both have inherent difficulties associated with the source of the data to be used. For example, it cannot be assumed that admission to treatment is equivalent to the onset of illness, and incidence cannot be generalized to prevalence (Fischer, 1969). The "true prevalence" measure attempts to establish the total number of people in a community who are psychiatrically impaired, irrespective of treatment. This measure has been employed in the majority of epidemiologic community surveys focusing on blacks (Kessler & Neighbors, 1983).

Many concerns have been raised about the validity of survey research on minority communities (Jackson, Tucker, & Bowman, 1982). Perhaps the most difficult methodologic problem facing community surveys in psychiatric epidemiology is how to measure the dependent variable—mental disorder. Establishing the definition of caseness for mental disorders can be especially problematic when making assessments in terms of social class and culture (Adebimpe, 1981, 1982). A "case" refers to a particular instance of disease to be included in the field of investigation, the selection being made in accordance with the specific criteria indicating the presence of the pathological phenomenon. Uniformity of definition is difficult to achieve in samples investigating mental disorders, and it may vary from investigation to investigation as well as among individuals within a single survey. Clear definitions of caseness and the subgroup to be studied are imperative, along with the use of standardized scales to allow for comparison and replication.

In their classic review of race and psychiatric epidemiology, M. Kramer, B. Rosen, and E. Willis (1973) concluded that it was impossible to provide a precise description of the frequency or occurrence of the mental disorders by race due to a variety of methodologic problems in the measurement of mental illness in community surveys. Fortunately, this situation has changed over the intervening years. There is still much more to be done, however. Despite the progress that has been made as a result of the development of the Diagnostic Interview Schedule (DIS) (Robins, Helzer, Crougham, & Ratcliff, 1981), we are still unsure about its reliability and validity (Anthony, Folstein, Romanoski, et al., 1985; Robins, 1985; Hendricks, Brayton, et al., 1983; Aneshensel, Estrada, Hansell, & Clark, 1987; Parker, 1987). This is unfortunate because epidemiologic progress is greatly affected by the accuracy of its classification technology.

M. Weissman and G. Klerman (1978) argued that the same diagnostic procedures used for patients in clinical settings could also be applied to case finding in epidemiologic community surveys. But researchers have argued for quite some time that, for blacks, psychiatric diagnostic inference is prone to error and misdiagnosis (Bell & Mehta, 1980, 1981; Jones & Gray, 1986). If this is true, then the degree to which these diagnostic procedures are applied directly to epidemiologic case-finding technology raises the possibility that the same diagnostic errors that are occurring in clinics could be occurring in epidemiologic surveys. As a result, there is a need to conduct more systematic, cross-racial research on clinical diagnostic inference as well as on the newly developed epidemiologic case-finding methods. To argue that progress in the field of psychiatric epidemiology depends upon accurate, valid classification and meaningful comparison across population subgroups and yet continue to ignore the issue of cultural differences in the expression and classification of psychiatric symptoms would be negligent.

Given that verbal and behavioral indicators used to hypothesize about the presence of mental disorder are empirically derived within a particular social context, they will vary depending upon the cultural frame of reference within which the person was socialized. Similarly, the person defining the deviance as "ill," "sick," or "criminal" will also view these actions within a particular framework or perspective. Problems of definition can arise when one group relies too heavily on diagnostic norms derived from their own group and attempts to use them as the yardstick with which to measure psychopathology in all other groups (Good & Good, 1986). When ethnocentric assumptions underlie medical classification, diagnostic errors can result.

Despite much attention, it has not been unequivocally demonstrated that widespread misdiagnosis of blacks is occurring (Adebimpe, 1981). Addressing this issue will involve a more rigorous race-comparative research strategy than has been employed thus far. To assess the degree to which norms developed on white samples are also appropriate for blacks, we must evaluate the clinical expression of psychiatric morbidity and psychopathology of one group within the context of the other. Given the new diagnostic technology that has become available since the mid–1980s (e.g., the Diagnostic Interview Schedule, the Structured and Clinical Interview for DSM-III-R), there are significant methodological improvements that can be made in the research designs employed in previous studies (see Neighbors, Jackson, Campbell, & Williams, 1988, for a more detailed discussion).

Despite the qualifications raised above, it is a reality that the National Institute of Mental Health (NIMH) Epidemiologic Catchment Area (ECA) Program has fostered widespread use of the Diagnostic Interview Schedule. As a result, findings on race and discrete mental disorder are starting to appear (Robins, Helzer, Weissman, et al., 1984; Sussman, Robins, & Earls, 1987). In the next section, we review some of those results in order to summarize what is known about the epidemiology of specific mental disorders. The reader should keep in mind, however, that important questions remain about the accuracy and validity of the Diagnostic Interview Schedule (Hendricks et al., 1983).

DISCRETE MENTAL DISORDERS

There have been numerous studies conducted on race differences in global distress, but not many on the distribution of discrete psychiatric disorders (Neighbors, 1984). Until recently, we have had to use treatment rate studies for information on specific diagnoses. Currently these statistics provide some of the best estimates we have, but they cannot be generalized to the entire population. Community surveys of discrete disorders, specifically, the ECA program results, should help to clarify relative rates of depression and schizophrenia among blacks and whites. With respect to lifetime prevalence rates, the ECA program found that race differences were modest and rarely were statistically significant (Robins et al., 1984, p. 955). Furthermore, simple phobia was the only disorder to show replication across the ECA sites. Blacks had higher simple phobia rates in Baltimore, Maryland, and in St. Louis, Missouri, but not in New Haven, Connecticut. Blacks were more likely to have agoraphobia in Baltimore, but there were no differences in the other two ECA sites.

Agency statistics show that blacks are more likely to be diagnosed as schizophrenic and less likely to receive a diagnosis of depression (Kramer et al., 1973; Cannon & Locke, 1977; Ruiz, 1983). H. Neighbors (1984) argued that one advantage of the ECA study would be to clarify whether such findings are the result of differences in true prevalence, help-seeking behavior, or diagnostic practice. Thus, it is important to note that blacks had a higher rate of schizophrenia in Baltimore (2.4 percent vs. 1.2 percent) but not in New Haven nor St. Louis. There were no differences in major depressive episode nor dysthymia in any of the three sites. These results cast doubt on the true prevalence explanation for agency statistics on race and diagnosis.

Only one article has been published on race and help seeking from the ECA data. L. Sussman, L. Robins, and F. Earls (1987) analyzed the data from the St. Louis site and found that fewer blacks than whites sought professional help for depression. Whereas nearly three quarters of the depressed whites (74.3 percent) had sought help, fewer than half of the depressed blacks (49.3 percent) did so. When the severity of the depression was taken into account, Sussman et al. (1987) found that the whites were more likely to seek professional help for the least severe problems only. Whites did not exceed blacks in seeking care when depressive episodes were long lasting, severe, or frequent (Sussman et al., 1987, p. 6). Further analyses revealed that attitudes about psychiatric treatment, a tendency to consult informal helpers, and practical problems, such as the lack of time, were impediments to professional help seeking among blacks.

Although not from the ECA, an earlier investigation by S. Vernon and R. Roberts (1982) is consistent with the findings in Sussman et al. (1987). Using the Research Diagnostic Criteria (RDC) in conjunction with the Schedule for Affective Disorders and Schizophrenia (SADS), Vernon and Roberts (1982) found that while blacks and whites did not differ dramatically in the total prevalence of depression, whites were significantly more likely than blacks (58.3 percent vs. 21.4 percent) to seek professional help for depression. The articles by Vernon and Roberts (1982) and Sussman et al. (1987) lend support to the hypotheses that agency statistics on diagnostic rates may be reflective of differential selection into treatment.

D. Brown and W. Eaton (1986) took a closer look at racial differences in phobic disorders, using the St. Louis and Baltimore ECA data. When responses to specific fears for agoraphobia (Baltimore site) were examined, blacks reported greater fear of tunnels and bridges, of being in a crowd, and of public transportation. In St. Louis, blacks were more likely to be afraid of being in a crowd. The St. Louis data showed no significant race differences in specific fears for social phobia. In Baltimore, however, blacks showed greater fear of eating in front of others and interacting with strangers. Finally, for simple phobia, blacks were more likely than whites to show fear on every individual indicator (closed places, storms, water, bugs, harmless animals, and heights). This was true for both the St. Louis and Baltimore sites. Blacks were also more likely than whites, regardless of site, to have experienced a phobia within the past month.

Depressive Symptoms

A number of studies on discrete mental disorders among blacks have focused on depression. Unfortunately, a blurring of the distinction between depressive symptoms and clinical depression has resulted in a certain lack of clarity among studies. Many studies on depressive symptoms employ scales such as the Center for Epidemiologic Studies Depression Scale (CES-D), which can miss some of those who would be classified by DSM-III criteria for major depression (Radloff & Locke, 1986). Most studies report that blacks have more depressive symptoms than whites, but when age, income, education, and gender are taken into account, the differences are practically negligible.

Since chapter 4 examines in detail the correlates of depression within the black community, we will provide only a brief summary. Depression rates are highest among blacks who are separated and divorced, followed by blacks who are married and widowed, and least for blacks who have never married (Eaton & Kessler, 1981). G. Warheit, C. Holzer, and S. Arey (1973) found blacks with less than a fourth grade education had the highest rate of depressive symptoms and those with a college education the lowest. W. Eaton and L. Kessler (1981) and G. Comstock and K. Helsing (1976) found, however, that blacks with less than a seventh grade education had lower CES-D scores than those with at least some high school. With respect to age, Warheit et al. (1973) found that blacks under 19 years of age had the lowest depressive scores; the rates increased until age 69 and decreased slightly after age 70. Eaton and Kessler (1981) found, however, that the highest rate of depression was among blacks between the ages of 25 and 44 and that the rate declined after 44 years of age. Studies on gender also reveal conflicting results. Some studies show black females tend to have higher rates of depressive symptoms than black males (Eaton & Kessler, 1981; Warheit et al., 1973). Others find that black males have higher rates or that there are no gender differences at all (Comstock & Helsing, 1976; Roberts, Stevenson, & Breslow, 1981).

We agree with D. Brown, who concludes that more research on the distribution and causes of depression among blacks needs to be conducted. Currently, the Program for Research on Black Americans at the University of Michigan is conducting a follow-up study to the National Survey of Black Americans in which a modification of the DIS depression section is being used. The Institute for Urban Affairs and Research at Howard University is also conducting research on depression using the DIS (Milburn, Booth, Brown, & Gary, 1987). As the results from these studies begin to appear, we are confident that our understanding of the factors that contribute to the incidence and prevalence of depression among blacks will be increased.

SOCIAL SUPPORT AS A BUFFER

Environmental factors can be thought of as resources or stressors (Milburn, Brown, & Gary, 1985). Social support networks are thought to decrease the risk of depressive symptoms by offsetting the impact of stressful life events. Research shows that blacks have extensive social networks and that the family plays a particularly important role (McAdoo, 1981). Blacks also prefer to use informal rather than formal sources of help or assistance (Neighbors & Jackson, 1984).

Environmental resources, structural characteristics of the social support network, and environmental stressors are related to depressive symptoms (Milburn et al., 1985). Proximity of friends and relatives has also been found to be related to depressive symptoms (Warheit, Vega, Shimizu, & Meinherdt, 1982). Blacks with non-dense networks consisting of many close friends and relatives nearby report fewer depressive symptoms, as do women with friends and relatives nearby, confidants, and perceived social support (Milburn et al., 1985). In general, empirical evidence on the relationship between social support and psychological distress in blacks is contradictory, owing partly to inconsistencies in methodology.

G. Warheit, W. Vega, D. Shimizu, and K. Meinherdt (1982) analyzed three related psychiatric epidemiologic studies conducted in six counties in Florida and California (n = 5,174, including 609 blacks). Five different symptomatology scales were used to assess mental health. Blacks were more likely than whites to have relatives living in the vicinity of their homes. Furthermore, for blacks, the presence or absence of relatives made no difference in symptomatology. For both blacks and whites, seeking help from relatives was associated with higher levels of psychotherapy. In short, the presence of relatives was not associated with lower symptom scores, which Warheit et al. (1982) suggested raises questions about the role of the family as a source of social support (pp. 322–23). Because this study did not include a measure of stress, it did not actually test the stress-buffering hypothesis.

One of the first multivariate analyses of the buffering hypothesis conducted on an all-black sample was undertaken by W. Dressler (1985). This research examined the impact of stress and social support on depressive symptomatology in a sample of 285 blacks (age 17 and above) in a small southern city. An analysis carried out separately by sex showed that the stress process operated differently for black men than for black women. For males, social support (as measured by extended kin relationships) lowered the impact of stress on mental health. Support from non-kin, on the other hand, did not buffer the effects of stress. No buffering effects of stress on health were found for black women. In fact, among women age 17 to 34, neither type of support (kin, no-kin) lowered depressive symptomatology. Dressler hypothesized that the traditional social organization of the black community placed additional "psychological costs" on black women.

D. Brown and L. Gary (1987) tested the impact of stress and social support on depressive symptoms in an urban sample of 451 adult blacks (age 18 and over) in Richmond, Virginia. These authors made an important distinction between the social support network (relationships with other people) and perceived social support (the extent to which a person feels his or her needs are fulfilled— a by-product of interactions taking place within the social network). Religiosity (as measured by a 13-item scale of participation in religious and church activities) was conceptualized as a measure of perceived social support. Brown and Gary (1987) found buffering effects for perceived social support among females but not among males. This is an apparent contradiction of Dressler's (1985) results, although it should be noted that Dressler measured kin network availability whereas Brown and Gary assessed the perception of the degree to which networks met individual needs.

H. Myers, L. Adams, R. Miles, and J. Williams (1987a) explored the impact of role stress and social support on depressive symptoms in a sample of 150 (122 females, 28 males) working-class, black adults taken from 111 families who volunteered to participate in a study of stress and health. A one-way analysis of variance was used to test for gender and class differences, and buffering effects were assessed using regression with interaction terms. Family role stress was significantly and positively related to depressive symptomatology. This relationship was stronger among the lower socioeconomic respondents; parental stress was the most stressful among the low-income group. Social support was not related to depressive symptoms, nor was support found to buffer the impact of stress on mental health.

Data from the National Survey of Black Americans (NSBA) (Jackson, in press) are beginning to accumulate to the point where statements about the impact of informal networks and social support on mental health can be made. The NSBA took a problem-specific approach to mental health assessment. As a result, most analyses of stress on health from the NSBA have been within the context of a particular type of stressor (i.e., economic, interpersonal, physical, or death-related). Thus, Neighbors (1986) demonstrated that, for black adults, the relationship between socioeconomic status and psychological distress was conditional upon the type of stressor being confronted. Specifically, it was only among those respondents who were faced with physical health or economic problems where being poor increased symptoms. For other types of problems, there was no relationship between socioeconomic status and mental health.

H. Neighbors and T. LaVeist (in press) conducted a more detailed analysis of coping among NSBA respondents facing an economic stressor. The authors hypothesized that, since economic stress stemmed from the fact that respondents did not have enough money to meet financial commitments, those who were successful in obtaining material aid would evidence a lower rate of distress than those who were unable to obtain financial help. Results indicated that the vast majority (93.5 percent) of respondents sought either informal or professional help in response to their economic problem, but that only about one in five were able to obtain some type of financial assistance as a result of seeking help. The poor and non-poor were equally likely to obtain money from outside helpers. Furthermore, practically all respondents who were able to secure some financial assistance received it from members of their informal networks. Multivariate analyses revealed that receipt of financial aid reduced the level of distress, especially among those with the most severe economic problems. In other words, the ability to obtain financial help during an economic crisis buffered the impact of stress on psychological symptoms.

The above review is representative of the state of our knowledge with respect to multivariate analyses of stress, support, and mental health. Because there are so few studies and because they vary widely in terms of samples, response rates, geographical location, and measures of mental health, stress, and social support, it is difficult to make generalizations. It is clear that more research into the relationships among stress, coping, and black mental health is needed.

THE IMPACT OF SOCIAL MOBILITY

Epidemiologic studies frequently aid in the determination of the factors that may be significant to the etiology of a disorder. Studies on etiologic factors of mental disorders in the black community have focused particularly on the effects of socioeconomic status, stress, and other sociocultural factors. Using an additive linear regression analytic technique, these studies found that, when socioeconomic status is controlled, blacks and whites did not differ in levels of psychological distress (Warheit, Holzer, & Schwab, 1975). These results contradict the assumptions underlying the theory of social causation which was so fundamental to the thinking behind the Community Mental Health Movement (Wagenfeld & Jacobs, 1982). They also contradict the minority status argument which predicts a direct effect of race on mental health, regardless of socioeconomic status (Mirowsky & Ross, 1980; Kessler & Neighbors, 1986).

Studies of southern communities since the civil rights era of the 1960s have noted that blacks living in metropolitan areas have greater opportunities for education and employment and experience less discrimination than blacks residing in rural communities (Linn & Husaini, 1987). Linn and Husaini (1987) assumed that differential opportunities and discrimination would be reflected in the relationships between race and mental health for rural and urban areas of the South. Specifically, they tested the effects of race on psychological distress while controlling for social class. Results showed that race had both a direct and an indirect effect on depressive symptoms, but only in rural communities. Blacks living in rural Tennessee were more depressed than whites, and low-socioeconomic status exacerbated the racial differences in depression.

The assumptions underlying the Linn and Husaini (1987) study (e.g., the impact of discrimination on opportunity) indicate the potential importance of social mobility patterns in the mental health of black Americans. Specifically, the racism argument implies that it is more difficult for hard-working, talented, lower class blacks to move up than it is for similar whites. As a result, we might expect that the discrepancies between aspirations and actual achievement to be wider among blacks than whites. Such discrepancies are assumed to be stressful and, thus, to impact on mental health (House & Harkins, 1975; Kleiner & Parker, 1963). Dressler (1988) studied the relationship between status inconsistency and depressive symptomatology in a sample of black adults residing in a southern city, calculating three different measures of social consistency. His results indicated that younger people whose life-style, as assessed by material consumption, exceeded their socioeconomic standing showed the highest rate of symptomatology.

The limited research that has been conducted on this topic shows that the benefits for blacks of moving up the socioeconomic status scale outweigh the costs of moving down (Isaacs, 1984), but we are only in the early stages of understanding how black mobility striving is related to such personal coping factors as locus of control, expectancies, self-esteem, fatalism, and group consciousness. Some researchers argue that it is more adaptive to cope by reducing mobility strivings in order to bring aspirations more in line with the realities of a discriminatory opportunity structure (Parker & Kleiner, 1966). Others feel that black mental health will benefit from challenging and then changing the system (Gurin, Gurin, & Morrison, 1978). No doubt, the manner in which black Americans cope with the failure to rise or the inability to maintain a middle-class lifestyle will have important implications for mental health.

These important issues badly need resolution. For example, McAdoo (1981), in a study of 178 urban and suburban middle-class black families, found that there was a status decline in the third generation of middle-class families (p. 166). McAdoo (1981) hypothesized that it may be extremely difficult for successfully upwardly mobile blacks to maintain that status over successive generations because of downward social pressure, lack of parental involvement with children, decreases in achievement striving, and an unwillingness to sacrifice within the context of a comfortable middle-class life-style. Neighbors (1987) argued that, because schools and employment training programs are instrumental for black social mobility patterns, they are useful settings for preventive intervention programs. But as McAdoo's (1981) results imply, the family represents another important area for intervention.

INTERVENTION PROGRAMS: THE BLACK FAMILY

There can be no doubt that the black family is the most important source of values in regard to achievement and social advancement. Recent studies in this area have been focused on the role of family in moderating risk for social problems like substance abuse and juvenile delinquency in black children (Myers, 1982). Such studies are based on the assumption that a black child's future health and well-being involve a complex combination of sociocultural variables (e.g., poverty, racial discrimination), parent variables (parent's substance use, personality, and child rearing), child variables (child's personality, social and academic status), and family variables (family structure and stresses). A 10-year longitudinal study conducted by S. Kellam, H. Brown, B. Rubin, and M. Ensminger (1983) showed that certain social, psychological, and academic characteristics of first grade children, and certain family characteristics, were related to substance use ten years later. For example, isolation and aloneness in female-headed, single-parent families were related to teenage substance use.

Other retrospective and prospective studies have found that lack of parental warmth, poor rule enforcement, parental substance use, parental depression, as well as a variety of family and life stresses, were risk factors for teenage substance use (Gorsuch and Butler, 1976; Huba, Wingard, & Bentler, 1980; Newcomb,

Huba, & Bentler, 1983). A three-year study aimed at testing a behavioral child management program adapted to make it more relevant to the life of low-income black families, is being conducted by K. Alvy of the Center for Improvement in Child Caring (Alvy & Rubin, 1981; U.S. Department of Health and Human Services, 1985). Three hundred black parents and their first grade children are being studied as a possible method of preventing drug abuse. Many of the risk factors to be impacted by the adapted program have also been shown to be significant in the development of mental health problems.

Another study, "Socio-Familial Context of Black Drug Use and Delinquency," proposed by H. Myers and his associates, will investigate the role of family attributes in enhancing or moderating the risk for substance use and juvenile delinquency in inner-city black children. Because the study focuses on families of young black children, an etiologic model is proposed that looks at family factors as predictors of teen substance use and delinquency. The proposed model distinguishes between family contextual attributes (those that are believed to contribute to contextual risk such as family social status, resources, and stress) and family relational attributes (parent-child relationship variables that are believed to mediate contextual risk). Attributes of the parents that influence the impact of both family context and the relational factors on the child are also being considered. Myers (1982) is interested in those early childhood behaviors previously identified as precursors of teen substance use and delinquency such as behavioral problems at home, school academic difficulty, and early exposure to the use of illegal substances.

A study recently completed by Myers et al. (1987b) investigated the effectiveness of culturally adapted, behaviorally oriented parent training, the Effective Black Parenting Program (EBPP), on a sample of inner-city black parents. The study also looked at program effects on the parent-child relationship, parenting practices, parental mental health, and perceived family role stress. Most parents were in sizable, family-based social networks with a small number of close friends and significant involvement in the church. Parents who completed the EBPP reported significant decreases in aggressive and hostile feelings toward their children, decreases in the use of aggressive or hostile parenting practices, and increases in the use of praise. Those who completed the test also reported significantly greater reductions in obsessive-compulsive symptoms and reductions in depressive symptoms but no significant changes in perceived parental role stress. The EBPP parents reported improvement in relationships with the target child, other children, family members, and spouses. Thus, preliminary findings indicate that the EBPP produces generally positive results with the sample black parents who completed a significant percentage of the classes.

Such programs can serve to influence parents' child rearing, parental affective states, and the capacity to deal with environmental stress through serving as both a support group and a teacher of skills that can be helpful in dealing with relationships. Given that the program orients the parents to respond to their children in ways that are believed to promote self-esteem and emotional stability, the program may aid parents in dealing with social environmental stress which may affect their coping behavior and child rearing.

Studies of this nature can be of great assistance in the detection of early outcomes and risks of disorder, as well as in the identification of the individuals most in need of interventions. Studies on the influence of family on mental disorders are very important in the effort to prevent psychological problems by enhancing the coping skills of black children. These studies have also recognized the need for socioculturally adapted programs, reemphasizing the importance of ethnicity and its effects on mental health.

CONCLUSIONS

Much of our epidemiologic knowledge will come from close scrutiny of discrete mental disorders in the black community, and this will take a multidisciplinary effort. With this knowledge we should attempt to target high-risk individuals for preventive programs in order to eliminate the development of clinically significant mental disorder. This chapter has argued that a solid epidemiologic knowledge base is necessary in order to prevent the occurrence of mental disorder among black Americans. The literature on what is currently known about the epidemiology of mental disorder was reviewed, and it was concluded that while much has been learned over the past 25 years, more work remains to be done. Specifically, more research is needed on race and diagnostic inference, social support as a buffer against stress, and the impact of social mobility. The chapter concluded with some examples of how the black family is a particularly important setting for intervention research. Intervention programs such as the Effective Black Parenting Program remind us of the strong influence that family relationships have on the degree of vulnerability to stress possessed by members of the black community.

The increased interest in epidemiologic studies of mental disorders in recent years demonstrates the great distance we have come in identifying and describing the prevalence, distribution, and etiology of mental disorders. There is much more to be done, however. Evaluations of present and future epidemiologic techniques must persist in order to ensure they are sensitive to the sociocultural processes of the black community. Because current trends in psychiatric epidemiology are focused on developing techniques for estimating the true prevalence of specific (e.g., DSM-III-R) mental disorders, more work needs to focus on how racial factors influence the psychiatric diagnostic process. We also need to know more about just how reliable and valid these new epidemiologic techniques are. Because of the importance of the NIMH Epidemiologic Catchment Area Program, the Diagnostic Interview Schedule should command much of our attention.

Much has been written about the importance of informal social networks in the survival of blacks. But the reality is that the stress-buffering role of social support has not been adequately studied from the psychiatric epidemiologic risk-factor perspective. This review uncovered only a handful of studies on blacks which have simultaneously measured stress, social support, and psychological distress. The results of these studies are contradictory, and, until more work is conducted to resolve the empirical discrepancies, the potential mental health–enhancing role of black informal helpers will remain unclear.

It almost goes without saying that racism, discrimination, and blocked opportunities for advancement place blacks at a disproportionate risk for mental health problems. But the crucial processes by which blacks maintain their mental health by coping with the status inconsistencies which result from differential treatment have not been documented. The result is that the literature is full of provocative hypotheses about stress and coping which are begging to be put to the empirical test. In so doing, researchers will clarify black survival mechanisms and, at the same time, provide a deeper understanding of the more general stress-adaptation process.

REFERENCES

Adebimpe, V. (1981). Overview: White norms and psychiatric diagnosis of black patients. *American Journal of Psychiatry, 138*, 279–285.

Adebimpe, V. (1982). Psychiatric symptoms in black patients. In S. Turner (Ed.), *Behavior modification in black populations: Psychosocial issues and empirical findings.* New York: Plenum.

Alvy, K., & Rubin, H. (1981). Parent training and the training of parent trainers. *Journal of Community Psychology, 9*, 53–66.

Aneshensel, C., Estrada, A., Hansell, M., & Clark, V. (1987). Social psychological aspects of reporting behavior: Lifetime depressive episode reports. *Journal of Health and Social Behavior, 28*, 232–246.

Anthony, J., Folstein, M., Romanoski, A., et al. (1985). Comparison of the lay Diagnostic Interview Schedule and a standardized psychiatric diagnosis. *Archives of General Psychiatry, 42*, 667–675.

Bell, C., & Mehta, H. (1980). The misdiagnosis of black patients with manic depressive illness. *Journal of the National Medical Association, 72*, 141–145.

Bell, C., & Mehta, H. (1981). Misdiagnosis of black patients with manic depressive illness: Second in a series. *Journal of the National Medical Association, 73*, 101–107.

Bell, R., Leroy, J., Lin, E., & Schwab, J. (1981). Change and psychopathology: Epidemiologic considerations. *Community Mental Health Journal, 17*, 203–213.

Brown, D. (1988). Depression among blacks: An epidemiologic perspective. In D. Smith-Ruiz (Ed.), *Mental health and mental illness.* Westport, CT: Greenwood Press.

Brown, D., & Eaton, W. (1986). *Racial differences in risk factors for phobic disorders.* Paper presented at the Black Health Caucus for the 114th annual meeting of the American Public Health Association, Las Vegas, NV.

Brown, D., & Gary L. (1987). Stressful life events, social support networks and the physical and mental health of urban black adults. *Journal of Human Stress, 13*, 165–174.

Cannon, M., & Locke, B. (1977). Being black is detrimental to one's mental health: Myth or reality? *Phylon, 38*, 408–428.

Comstock, G., & Helsing, K. (1976). Symptoms of depression in two communities. *Psychological Medicine, 6*, 551–563.

Dressler, W. (1985). Extended family relationships, social support and mental health in a southern black community. *Journal of Health and Social Behavior, 26*, 39–48.

Dressler, W. (1988). Social consistency and psychological distress. *Journal of Health and Social Behavior, 29*, 79–91.

Eaton, W., & Kessler, L. (1981). Rates of symptoms of depression in a national sample. *American Journal of Epidemiology, 113*, 528–538.

Fischer, J. (1969). Negroes and whites and rates of mental illness: Reconsideration of a myth. *Psychiatry, 32*, 428–446.

Good, B., & Good, M. (1986). The cultural context of diagnosis and therapy: A view from medical anthropology. In M. Miranda & H. Kitano (Eds.), *Mental health research and practice in minority communities: Development of culturally sensitive training programs*. (DHHS Publication No. ADM 86–1466). Washington, DC: U.S. Government Printing Office.

Gorsuch, R., & Butler, M. (1976). Initial drug abuse: A review of predisposing social psychological factors. *Psychological Bulletin, 83*, 120–137.

Gurin, P., Gurin, G., & Morrison, B. (1978). Personal and ideological aspects of internal and external control. *Social Psychology, 41*, 275–296.

Hendricks, L., Bayton, J., & et al. (1983). The NIMH's Diagnostic Interview Schedule: A test of its concurrent validity in a population of black adults. *Journal of the National Medical Association, 7*, 667–671.

Hilliard, T. (1981). Political and social action in the prevention of psychopathology of blacks: A mental health strategy for oppressed people. In J. Joffee & G. Albee (Eds.), *Primary prevention of psychopathology: Prevention through political action and social change*. Hanover, NH: University Press of New England.

House, J., & Harkins, E. (1975). Why and when is status inconsistency stressful? *American Journal of Sociology, 81*, 395–412.

Huba, G., Wingard, J., & Bentler, P. (1980). Longitudinal analysis of the role of peer support, adult models and peer subcultures in beginning adolescent substance use: An application of stepwise canonical methods. *Multivariate Behavior Research, 15*, 259–280.

Isaacs, M. (1984). *The determinants and consequences of intergenerational mobility among black American males*. Unpublished doctoral dissertation, Brandeis University, The Heller School for Advanced Studies in Social Welfare, Waltham, MA.

Jackson, J. (in press). The program for research on black Americans. In R. Jones (Ed.), *Advances in black psychology*. Richmond, CA: Cobb and Henry Publishers.

Jackson, J., Tucker, M. B., & Bowman, P. (1982). Conceptual and methodological problems in survey research on black Americans. In W. Liu (Ed.), *Methodological problems in minority research*. Chicago: Pacific/Asian American Mental Health Research Center.

Jones, B., & Gray, B. (1986). Problems in diagnosing schizophrenia and affective disorders among blacks. *Hospital and Community Psychiatry, 37*, 61–65.

Kellam, S., Brown, H., Rubin, B., & Ensminger, M. (1983). Paths leading to teenage psychiatric symptoms and substance use: Developmental epidemiological studies in Woodlawn. In S. Guze, F. Earls, & J. Barrett (Eds.), *Childhood psychopathology and development* (pp. 17–51). New York: Raven Press.

Kessler, R., & Neighbors, H. (1983). Special issues related to racial and ethnic minorities in the U.S. Position paper written for the NIMH consultant panel to review behavioral sciences research into mental health.

Kessler, R., & Neighbors, H. (1986). A new perspective on the relationships among race, social class and psychological distress. *Journal of Health and Social Behavior, 27,* 107–115.

Kleiner, R., & Parker, S. (1963). Goal striving, social status and mental disorder: A research review. *American Sociological Review, 28,* 189–203.

Kramer, M., Rosen, B., & Willis, E. (1973). Definitions and distributions of mental disorders in a racist society. In C. Willie, M. Kramer, & B. Brown (Eds.), *Racism and mental health.* Pittsburgh: University of Pittsburgh Press.

Linn, J. G., & Husaini, B. (1987). *Community satisfaction, life stress, social support, and mental health in rural and urban southern black communities.* Unpublished manuscript, Center for Health Research, Tennessee State University, Nashville.

McAdoo, H. (1981). Patterns of upward mobility in black families. In H. P. McAdoo (Ed.), *Black families.* Beverly Hills, CA: Sage.

Milburn, N., Brown, D., & Gary, L. (1985). Epidemiological research on blacks and depression: A sociocultural perspective. Paper presented at the 113th annual meeting of the American Public Health Association, Washington, DC.

Milburn, N., Booth, J., Brown, D., & Gary, L. (1987). Conducting epidemiologic research in a minority community: Methodological issues. Paper presented at the 33rd annual meeting of the Southeastern Psychological Association, Atlanta, GA.

Mirowsky, J., & Ross, C. (1980). Minority status, ethnic culture and distress: A comparison of blacks, whites, Mexicans and Mexican Americans. *American Journal of Sociology, 86,* 479–495.

Myers, H. (1982). Research on the Afro-American family: A critical review. In B. Bass, G. Wyatt, & G. Powell (Eds.), *The Afro-American family: Assessment, treatment and research issues.* New York: Grune & Stratton.

Myers, H., Adams, L., Miles, R., & Williams, J. (1987a). *Role strains, social supports and depression in black adults: The role of gender and social class.* Unpublished manuscript, University of California, Los Angeles.

Myers, H., Alvy, K., Arrington, A., et al. (1987b). *Effective black parenting: Preliminary results.* Unpublished manuscript, Center for the Improvement of Child Caring, Fanon Research and Development Center, Charles Drew Medical School, Los Angeles, CA.

Neighbors, H. (1984). The distribution of psychiatric morbidity: A review and suggestions for research. *Community Mental Health Journal, 20,* 5–18.

Neighbors, H. (1986). Socioeconomic status and psychologic distress in black Americans. *American Journal of Epidemiology, 124,* 779–793.

Neighbors, H. (1987). Improving the mental health of black Americans: Lessons from the community mental health movement. *Milbank Memorial Fund Quarterly, 65*(2), 348–380.

Neighbors, H., & Jackson, J. (1984). The use of informal and formal help: Four patterns of illness behavior in the black community. *American Journal of Community Psychology, 12,* 629–644.

Neighbors, H., Jackson, J., Campbell, L., & Williams, D. (1988). *The influence of racial factors on psychiatric diagnosis: A review and suggestions for research.* Community Mental Health Journal, 25(4), 301–311.

Neighbors, H., & LaVeist, T. (1989). Socioeconomic status and psychological distress: The impact of material aid on economic problem severity. *Journal of Primary Prevention, 10*(2), 149–165.

Newcomb, M., Huba, G., & Bentler, P. (1983). Mother's influence on the drug use of their children. *Developmental Psychology, 19*, 714–726.

Parker, G. (1987). Are the lifetime prevalence estimates in the ECA accurate? *Psychological Medicine, 17*, 275–282.

Parker, S., & Kleiner, R. (1966). *Mental illness in the urban Negro community.* New York: The Free Press.

Radloff, L., & Locke, B. (1986). The Community Mental Health Assessment Survey and the CES-D Scale. In M. Weissman & J. Myers (Eds.), *Community surveys of psychiatric disorders.* New Brunswick, NJ: Rutgers University Press.

Roberts, R., Stevenson, J., & Breslow, L. (1981). Symptoms of depression among blacks and whites in an urban community. *Journal of Nervous and Mental Disease, 169*, 774–779.

Robins, L. (1985). Epidemiology: Reflections on testing the validity of psychiatric interviews. *Archives of General Psychiatry, 42*, 918–924.

Robins, L., Helzer, J., Crougham, J., & Ratcliff, K. (1981). National Institute of Mental Health Diagnostic Interview Schedule: Its history, characteristics and validity. *Archives of General Psychiatry, 38*, 381–389.

Robins, L., Helzer, J., Weissman, M., et al. (1984). Lifetime prevalence of specific psychiatric disorders in three sites. *Archives of General Psychiatry, 41*, 949–958.

Ruiz, D. (1983). Epidemiology of schizophrenia: Some diagnostic and sociocultural considerations. *Phylon, 43*, 315–326.

Snowden, L. (1982). *Reaching the undeserved.* Beverly Hills, CA: Sage.

Sussman, L., Robins, L., & Earls, F. (1987). Treatment-seeking for depression by black and white Americans. *Social Science and Medicine, 24*, 187–196.

U.S. Department of Health and Human Services. (1985). Black parenting. *ADAMHA News*, 11(10).

Vernon, S., & Roberts, R. (1982). Prevalence of treated and untreated psychiatric disorders in three ethnic groups. *Social Science and Medicine, 16*, 1575–1582.

Wagenfeld, M., & Jacobs, J. (1982). The community mental health movement: Its origins and growth. In M. Wagenfeld, P. Lemkau, & B. Justice (Eds.), *Public mental health.* Beverly Hills, CA: Sage.

Warheit, G., Holzer, C., & Arey, S. (1973). An analysis of social class and racial differences in depressive symptomatology. *Journal of Health and Social Behavior, 14*, 291–299.

Warheit, G., Holzer, C., & Schwab, J. (1975). Race and mental illness: An epidemiologic update. *Journal of Health and Social Behavior, 16*, 243–256.

Warheit, G., Vega, W., Shimizu, D., & Meinherdt, K. (1982). Interpersonal coping networks and mental health problems among four race-ethnic groups. *Journal of Community Psychology, 10*, 312–324.

Weissman, M., & Klerman, G. (1978). Epidemiology of mental disorder: Emerging trends in the United States. *Archives of General Psychiatry, 35*, 705–712.

4

DEPRESSION AMONG BLACKS: AN EPIDEMIOLOGIC PERSPECTIVE

Diane Robinson Brown

INTRODUCTION

With the advent of new research findings on psychiatric morbidity among blacks as well as improvements in sampling and data-gathering methodologies, depression among black Americans has recently gained increased interest and concern among mental health practitioners and researchers. Recognizably, sadness or melancholia has been well documented throughout time and in many cultures, but the American tradition with its roots in European psychiatry has generally associated depression with middle- and upper-income persons. Consequently, the clustering of blacks in the lower socioeconomic strata of American society has historically rendered them less likely to be diagnosed as having depression than whites. Instead, black Americans have traditionally been more likely to be diagnosed by white clinicians as having psychoses, paranoia, schizophrenia, and other antisocial disorders (Pasamanick, 1962). In addition, many of the earlier studies that included black respondents utilized hospital admissions data in lieu of data from community-based field studies to determine the rates of disorders by race. These findings, however, were distorted by the greater likelihood of those with schizophrenia and other psychoses being admitted for hospitalization than those with depression.

Moving beyond the research based on persons in psychiatric treatment, community-based field studies were initiated in an attempt to ascertain the extent of psychopathology and depression in the noninstitutionalized general population. Often with small subsamples of blacks, these studies also reported blacks and persons of low socioeconomic status as being less likely to have depression and as being more prone to psychoses than persons of higher socioeconomic status (Faris & Dunham, 1939; Hollingshead & Redlich, 1958; Noyes & Kolb, 1958; Parker, 1959). However, subsequent community-based field studies of the 1960s began to find higher rates of depression among blacks than whites (Srole, Langner, Michael, Opler, & Rennie, 1962; Langner & Michael, 1963; Prange & Vitols, 1962). Nonetheless, these studies did not provide conclusive determination of higher rates of depression among blacks; in their 1969 study, B. P. Dohrenwend and B. S. Dohrenwend noted substantial contradictory findings in their review of eight field studies.

To obtain good epidemiologic baseline data on psychiatric illness in the population, epidemiologic field studies were initiated which included larger numbers of blacks and which also addressed some of the methodological concerns of earlier studies. These more recent studies provide greater understanding of the distribution of depression among blacks and some of the factors associated with risks for depression. This chapter examines current epidemiologic data on depression among black Americans and looks not only at traditional demographic factors, but also at stress and social factors influenced by the experiences of blacks in American society.

DEFINING DEPRESSION

Given its widespread usage in popular as well as medical literature, depression is often loosely defined. In general, depression is viewed as an affective disorder characterized by disturbances of mood. It includes negative perceptions of self, such as self-blame, self-degradation, unworthiness, helplessness, and hopelessness; not infrequently it includes thoughts of death or suicide (Radloff, 1980; Klerman & Weissman, 1980). It also may encompass a vegetative dimension, accompanied by loss of energy, fatigue, and impairment of bodily functioning, as reflected in disturbance of sleep, appetite, sexual interest, and gastrointestinal activity (Klerman & Weissman, 1980). Overall, it may result in a reduced desire and ability to execute expected roles in the family, at work, in marriage, or in school.

Three meanings are generally given to the term depression, including a mood, a symptom, and a syndrome. Depression, can consist of a mood which is a part of normal sadness stemming from the general vicissitudes of life. In this case, impairment is apt to be short-lived, and psychiatric treatment is rarely sought. On the other hand, depression can be viewed in terms of specific symptomatology such as feeling ''sad'' or ''blue.'' Furthermore, depression can be viewed as a syndrome around which a clustering of particular symptoms forms the basis for a diagnosis of major affective disorder (Klerman & Weissman, 1980).

As the most severe form of depression, the syndrome is usually diagnosed by a clinician after a psychiatric assessment based upon predetermined criteria such as those established by the American Psychiatric Association's Diagnostic and Statistical Manual of Mental Disorders (DSM-III-R). In addition to the diagnosis of major depression, the DSM-III also includes bipolar disorder under the category of major affective disorders. Bipolar disorder encompasses major depression when one or more episodes of mania have occurred. Generally, those with major affective disorders obtain outpatient treatment or are hospitalized. Somewhat less severe, although with considerable impairment, is dysthymia. The depressed mood is relatively persistent but is separated by periods of normal mood. Because of the chronicity of this order, there may be a greater likelihood of the development of substance abuse (American Psychiatric Association, 1980).

In the past, community-based field studies have used instruments which detect depressive mood or symptomatology but not syndrome. Included among these are the Center for Epidemiologic Studies Depression Scale (CES-D), the Beck Depressive Inventory, the Hopkins Symptom Checklist, or the Zung Self-Rating Depression Scale. To varying degrees, most of these have been used with the black population, although reports of the validity of use with blacks have often been lacking. Most recently however, the development of the fully structured Diagnostic Interview Schedule (DIS) has allowed the diagnosis of major depressive disorder by lay persons in a community setting (Robins, Helzer, Croughan, & Ratcliff, 1981). The following section reviews the findings from community studies specifically related to blacks.

RATES OF DEPRESSION AMONG BLACKS

The epidemiologic approach is generally concerned with patterns of disease in the population and factors that influence these patterns (Lilienfeld & Lilienfeld, 1980). Epidemiologic analysis relies on gathering data from a community sample of noninstitutionalized persons in order to determine the rates of a disorder in the general population. It involves taking a random sample of persons to determine the incidence and prevalence rates of depression and other disorders. Table 4.1 presents rates for blacks obtained from several community-based surveys, including national and area-specific data. The first part of table 4.1 lists surveys detecting depressive symptomatology, followed by studies focusing on clinical diagnoses. Despite improvements in methodology, comparability of findings across studies is still difficult, given the different measures of depression and the different methodologies used.

Depressive Symptomatology

Estimates of prevalence rates for depressive symptomatology vary considerably. Seven of these nine studies used the CES-D, but there is no overall accord on prevalence rates. The range of prevalence rates of depressive symptoms from these studies vary from 20 to 30 percent. The divergence of findings is due to considerable variation in sample sizes and sampling strategies, as well as different populations of blacks and different operational definitions of depression. For example, most of the studies are area specific, and two focus solely on elderly populations, suggesting that different populations of blacks were used in each study. With regard to different thresholds for defining high levels of depressive symptomatology, a cutoff score of 16 or above on the CES-D is frequently used (Radloff, 1977);

Table 4.1
Community Surveys of Depression with Black Samples

Investigators	Population	No. of Blacks	Instrument	Findings
Depressive Symptomatology				
Warheit, Holzer & Schwab (1973)	Florida County	N = 366	18 item inventory	29.2 percent scores 25+
Comstock & Helsing (1976)	Kansas City, Missouri	N = 295	CES-D	26 percent of Blacks with scores 25+
Eaton & Kessler (1981)	United States 25-74 years	N = 242	CES-D	28.5 percent scores 16+; 10.8 percent of males and 20.8 percent of females with scores 16+
Frerichs, Aneshensel	Los Angeles	N = 124	CES-D	21.8 percent with scores 16+
Roberts, Stevenson & Breslow (1981)	Alameda County, CA	N = 382	40 item inventory	18.1 percent for males and 26.9 percent for males
Neff & Husaini (1982)	Rural Tennessee	N = 67	CES-D	x = 9.1

Study	Location	N	Instrument	Findings
Murrell, Himmelfarb, & Wright (1983)	Kentucky, 55 yrs. +	N = 169	CES-D	12.8 percent of males and 23.4 percent of females with scores 20+
Gary, Brown, Milburn Thomas & Lockley (1983)	Richmond, VA 18 yrs. +	N = 451	CES-D	24.2 percent with scores 16+ 15.8 percent for males; 28.1 percent for females
Berkman et al. (1986)	New Haven 65 yrs. +	Actual N not reported	CES-D	16.7 with scores 16+

Major Depressive Disorder

Study	Location	N	Instrument	Findings
Jones, Gray & Parson (1981)	New York City	N = 117	DSM-III Diagnostic Criteria	15 percent diagnosed as manic depressive
Robins et al. (1984)	Baltimore New Haven St. Louis	N = 1,181 N = 334 N = 1,158	Diagnostic Interview Schedule	Lifetime prevalence rates were 3.7 Baltimore; 5.9 for New Haven; and 4.9 percent for St. Louis

however, one study (Murrell, Himmelfarb, & Wright, 1983) established a cutoff score of 20, based upon their pretest findings with elderly respondents.

In six studies, crude prevalence rates for high levels of depressive symptoms are greater for blacks than whites (Comstock & Helsing, 1976; Warheit, Holzer, & Schwab, 1973; Eaton & Kessler, 1981; Frerichs, Aneshensel, & Clark, 1981; Roberts, Stevenson, & Breslow, 1981; Berkman et al., 1986). J. A. Neff and B. A. Husaini (1982) do not report crude prevalence rates, although nonwhites ($X = 9.1$) have significantly higher mean CES-D scores than whites ($X = 6.4$, $p = 0.05$); and L. E. Gary, D. R. Brown, N. G. Milburn, V. G. Thomas, and D. S. Lockley (1985) gathered data solely on blacks. The only study with higher crude prevalence rates for whites than blacks was conducted by Murrell and his colleagues (1983), and they used an operational definition of high depressive symptomatology for the CES-D that differed from the other investigators. They find elderly blacks (12.8 percent) with a slightly lower prevalence rate of high depressive symptoms than whites (13.7 percent). However, the mean CES-D score was significantly higher among elderly blacks ($X = 10.4$) than whites ($X = 9.3$), suggesting a lower threshold may be needed for examining high levels of depression among older blacks.

In making racial comparisons, some studies have also taken selected demographic background variables to adjust prevalence rates for depression. After adjusting for these variables (most often socioeconomic status), some find no significant racial differences in depressive symptomatology (Comstock & Helsing, 1976; Roberts, Stevenson, & Breslow, 1981; Frerichs, Aneshensel, & Clark, 1981). On the other hand, W. W. Eaton and L. G. Kessler (1981) found that blacks are still at greater risk for depression, even when selected demographic variables are controlled.

A note of caution is offered with regard to the use of statistical adjustments for racial comparisons. Not infrequently, the factors that are used to make adjustments in rates are also those in which blacks and whites are most likely to differ. Specifically, caution is urged when socioeconomic status is controlled and no racial differences are found. The preponderance of research evidence shows an inverse relationship between depression and socioeconomic status. With blacks disproportionately more likely than whites to be in the lower socioeconomic groups, they are also at greater risk for depression irrespective of statistical controls that obviate differences.

Major Depressive Disorders

Having a major depressive illness is a much rarer occurrence in the population than having depressive symptoms. Furthermore, there is a noticeable paucity of data on prevalence rates among blacks for major depression. It is estimated that as much as 50 percent of those with high scores on the CES-D may also have major depression (Link & Dohrenwend, 1980), but additional research is needed to be conclusive.

In an effort to gather data on clinically diagnosed depression among blacks, B. E. Jones, B. A. Gray, and E. B. Parson (1981) reviewed the hospital charts of 117 patients. They determined that 15 percent were manic-depressives, which was more than four times the national admissions rate. Their findings, however, are based upon treatment data from a short-term emergency care unit of a municipal hospital, and they cannot be used to provide prevalence rates of major depression.

To address the need to have estimates of specific mental disorders in the treated as well as untreated population, the National Institute of Mental Health implemented its Epidemiologic Catchment Area (ECA) Study (Regier et al., 1984). Using the DIS, ECA findings show a lifetime prevalence rate for major depression among blacks that varies from a high of 5.9 percent in New Haven, Connecticut, to 4.9 percent in St. Louis, Missouri, and 3.7 percent in the Baltimore, Maryland, catchment areas (Robins et al., 1984). Again, there is variation by ECA site in the demographic characteristics of the black populations included in the study. To be noted, no racial differences emerged with regard to major affective disorders; blacks were not more likely than whites to have had a major depressive disorder or dysthymia over their lifetime.

Origins of Depression

Recognizably, numerous explanations have been put forth to understand the occurrence and etiology of depression. These include explanations based upon biological, chemical, and genetic factors (Bunney & Davis, 1965; Shore & Brodie, 1957; Depue & Evans, 1976; Beck, 1967) as well as those focusing on personality and psychological factors. For example, depression is purported to occur in response to loss or separation (Brown, Harris, & Copeland, 1977), or depression can result from learned helplessness associated with being unable to control or predict life events (Seligman, 1975; Loeb, Beck, & Diggory, 1971). Traditionally, the epidemiologic approach has utilized demographic background factors such as age, race, education, and marital status, as well as behavioral life-style factors affecting health. These factors help to determine which subgroups of the population are at greater risk for depression than others. The following section examines findings related to selected demographic background factors and depression among blacks.

DEPRESSIVE SYMPTOMATOLOGY AND DEMOGRAPHIC FACTORS

Gender

A consistent finding in the literature based upon research of the general population is that women report more depression than men (Weissman & Klerman,

1977). Studies which have included blacks have also confirmed this gender difference (Srole et al., 1962; Eaton & Kessler, 1981; Warheit et al., 1973; Gary et al., 1985). However, when crude rates are adjusted, the status of gender differences in depression is not conclusive. Whereas some found black males to have higher rates than females (Comstock & Helsing, 1976), others found no gender differences (Roberts et al., 1981).

Considerable controversy surrounds the explanations for gender differences in depression. Primarily from data on white respondents, gender differences in depression are most often attributed to the social roles of men and women (Gove & Tudor, 1973; Weissman & Klerman, 1977).

Additional research on gender differences in depression among blacks, however, is needed given that historical patterns of racial discrimination have encouraged egalitarian roles and economic parity among black males and females. In other words, the explanations given for gender differences among whites may not be completely applicable to accounting for higher crude rates of depressive symptoms for black females in comparison to black males. For example, D. R. Brown and L. E. Gary (1985) found no gender differences among black adults who were unemployed. Black women have traditionally worked, even while child rearing, in order to bolster the economic viability of their families. Consequently, it is concluded that unemployed black females were just as vulnerable to depression as were unemployed black males.

Income

Again, one of the most consistently documented findings in the literature is that depression is inversely related to income (Warheit et al., 1973; Comstock & Helsing, 1976; Steele, 1978; Eaton & Kessler, 1981; Frerichs et al., 1981). As indicated in table 4.2, Gary and his colleagues report the highest mean level of depressive symptomatology ($X = 14.4$) among those of the lowest income category of $6,000 a year or less. In terms of prevalence rates of depressive symptoms, Comstock and Helsing (1976) earlier found that approximately one-third of the blacks with the lowest incomes had high CES-D scores above the cutoff point of 16; Eaton and Kessler (1981) noted that nearly 50 percent of the lowest income black adults evidenced high levels of depressive symptomatology.

Age

Although some studies report slightly different results (Sayetta & Johnson, 1980; Roberts et al., 1981; Murrell et al., 1983), the relationship between age and depression appears to be a curvilinear one among blacks as supported by Eaton and Kessler (1981) and findings from Gary and his colleagues (1985). The highest rates of depression, as measured by the CES-D, occur for the youngest adult age groups, that is persons under 45 years of age. Middle-age black adults, from 45 to 64 years of age, report the lowest depressive symptom-

Table 4.2
CES-D Scores by Demographic Variables for Black Males and Females

		Females			Males	
	n	X	(sd)	n	X	(sd)
Household Income						
Less than $6,000	68	14.41	(10.1)	29	13.66	(9.9)
$6,000-$11,999	55	11.00	(8.1)	24	10.21	(6.8)
$12,000-$24,999	63	10.40	(8.2)	52	7.81	(7.8)
$25,000 or more	27	9.96	(8.8)	35	6.71	(4.5)
Age						
18-30	93	14.29	(8.9)	67	11.13	(7.7)
31-45	65	12.51	(9.9)	39	9.23	(8.4)
46-65	65	9.00	(7.7)	37	7.51	(8.0)
over 65	41	9.63	(7.9)	28	10.82	(7.9)
Education						
Less than high school	133	12.14	(8.9)	88	12.39	(8.6)
Some high school	65	12.92	(10.6)	44	7.30	(6.7)
High school graduate	38	11.82	(7.9)	25	6.00	(4.9)
Some college	19	6.79	(5.7)	6	10.33	(4.9)
College graduate +	10	8.70	(5.4)	4	5.25	(4.8)
Marital Status						
Never married	83	12.84	(8.8)	63	11.78	(8.6)
Married	89	9.83	(8.1)	70	7.76	(6.8)
Widowed	40	10.73	(8.2)	11	13.55	(7.9)
Divorced/Separated	55	14.15	(10.3)	27	9.37	(8.2)
Employment Status						
Employed	141	10.51	(8.3)	102	8.32	(7.3)
Not employed	84	13.82	(9.7)	39	14.00	(8.6)
Minor Children in Household						
Yes	132	13.83	(9.5)	68	9.48	(6.8)
No	130	9.83	(7.3)	103	10.12	(8.6)

Source: Gary, Brown, Milburn, Thomas, and Lockley. *Pathways: A study of black informal support networks*. Washington, D.C.: Institute for Urban Affairs and Research, Howard University. (1985).

atology. The gender difference remains, however, with decreasing depressive symptomatology being more strongly associated with increasing age for black females than males (Gary et al., 1985). After age 65, there is an increase in reported depressive symptomatology.

Education

Among whites, depressive symptoms appear to decrease with high levels of education (Eaton & Kessler, 1981), whereas among blacks, the association between education and depression is not consistent. Several studies (Warheit et al., 1973; Roberts et al., 1981) find that the rates of depressive symptoms decrease with increasing educational attainment for blacks; those of the lowest educational levels report the highest depressive symptoms, and those with a college education report the least. On the other hand, other studies have found that blacks with less than an eighth grade education have lower CES-D scores than those with at least some high school education (Comstock & Helsing, 1976; Eaton & Kessler, 1981). In addition, Comstock and Helsing report that blacks with a college education were as likely to report high levels of depressive symptoms as were those with less education.

Employment Status and Occupation

Unemployment is associated with higher levels of depressive symptomatology as evidenced in the findings of numerous epidemiologic studies (Eaton & Kessler, 1981; Frerichs et al., 1981, Radloff, 1980; Gary et al., 1985). Specifically, employed black adults have a lower prevalence rate of depressive symptoms than those who are not employed (Brown & Gary, 1985; Gary et al., 1985). Further, in an effort to elucidate differences among women, Brown and Gary (1988) compared unemployed women to homemakers, noting a significantly higher level of depression amount the unemployed. Black homemakers were similar to employed black women, with considerably lower levels of depressive symptoms than the unemployed.

With regard to occupational status and depression, very little data have been reported on blacks. For the general population, R. B. Sayetta and D. P. Johnson (1980) indicate that household workers (mostly females) and farm laborers and foremen (mostly males) have the highest rates of depressive symptoms. For both males and females, the lowest scores are found for professional, technical, managerial, and administrative workers.

Marital Status

The relationship between depression and marital status for blacks varies somewhat from the patterns noted for the general population. Similar to the findings for whites, Gary et al. (1985) find that blacks who are married report the lowest depressive symptomatology, followed by the widowed and the never-married. Separated and divorced persons report the highest level. Although Eaton and Kessler (1981) report the highest rates for the separated and divorced, they find that never-married blacks have the lowest rate, followed by the widowed and then the married.

Considerable gender differences in the relationship between marital status and depression have been found. In his study of black men, Gary (1985) reports that formerly married black men, primarily divorced and separated, had the least depressive symptomatology, followed by the married and then the never-married. The differences, however, were not statistically significant. On the other hand, the findings shown in table 4.2, (Gary et al., 1985) indicate that widowed black males encounter the highest depressive symptomatology, followed by the never-married, and then those who are divorced or separated. Married black men have the lowest level of depressive symptoms. Similarly, married black women report the least depression; higher levels of symptomatology are associated with the widowed and never-married. Separated and divorced black females are the most depressed of all. With the exception of the widowed, black females report more depressive symptomatology than males across marital status categories.

Children in the Household

The presence of children under 18 years of age in the household is associated with increased strain and concomitantly greater vulnerability to depression (Gurin, Veroff, & Feld, 1960; Campbell, 1980). These studies, however, are generally based upon research with women, to the exclusion of gender comparisons. The data in table 4.2 support a finding of greater levels of depressive symptomatology among black women with children in the household, in contrast to women with no minor children. This finding for black women is not surprising as many are apt to work while child rearing. Working married mothers with the lowest family income are at the greatest risk for depressive symptomatology (Pearlin & Johnson, 1977; Cleary & Mechanic, 1983). The data in table 4.2 indicate the reverse for black males. Those with no minor children in the household report higher levels of depression, whereas fewer symptoms are reported by those with young children in the household. It is possible that black males with no young children in the household are also likely to be widowed or never-married, and to be in the youngest and oldest age categories where vulnerability to depression increases.

MAJOR DEPRESSIVE DISORDERS AND DEMOGRAPHIC FACTORS

With regard to major depressive disorders, data from clinical studies have traditionally been used to assess which subgroups of the population have the greatest vulnerability to depression. Again, these findings from a treatment population are very limited in their ability to generalize. However, they generally point out significantly higher rates among females than males (American Psychiatric Association, 1980) and among those in the lower socioeconomic strata (Jones, Gray, & Parson, 1981).

Findings from the ECA study, in particular the eastern Baltimore site, provide additional insight into how prevalence rates of major depression are distributed among blacks, according to selected demographic factors. As shown in table 4.3, six-month prevalence rates are significantly higher for black females than males. In terms of income, the relationship is not linear, as might be expected. Persons of the lowest income group, $4,999 or less, have the highest prevalence

Table 4.3
Six-Month Prevalence Rates of Major Depression by Selected Demographic Factors

	(Weighted Data) N=1,182	
Household Income		
$ 5,999 and less	4.2	
$ 5,999-10,999	3.5	
11,000-14,999	3.2	X^2=485.1
15,000-19,999	3.3	df=5
20,000-24,999	4.0	p=.001
25,000 and over	1.4	
Age		
18-24	2.6	X^2=607.4
25-44	4.1	df=3
45-64	3.2	p=.001
65+	1.1	
Marital Status		
Married	2.6	X^2=560.8
Widowed	2.8	df=3
Separated/divorced	5.4	p=.001
Never maried	2.6	
Education		
Less than high school	2.6	X^2=314.1
Some high school	4.2	df=3
High school graduate	2.8	p=.001
Some college +	2.3	
Sex		
Male	1.8	X^2=690.8
Female	4.1	df=1
		p=.001
Employment Status		
Employed	2.4	X^2=643.5
Not employed	3.9	p=.001
Children in Household		
Yes	4.1	X^2=344.5
No	2.1	df=1
		p=.001

Source: Eastern Baltimore Epidemiologic Catchment Area Study.

rate (4.2 percent), but persons with incomes between $20,000 and $24,999 are also among those with the highest rate (4.0 percent). Similar to findings for depressive symptoms, a major depressive episode is most likely to occur among young black adults, from 25 to 44 years of age, and decrease thereafter. Married, widowed, and never-married persons do not differ significantly in prevalence rates for major depression within the past six months. On the other hand, separated and divorced persons report the highest risk with a six-month prevalence rate of 5.4 percent.

When educational level is considered, blacks with only some high school education reported the highest six-month rate of 4.2 percent. And, as would be expected, unemployed blacks and those with minor children in the household are at greater risk for a major depressive episode in comparison to employed blacks and those with no children in their household.

STRESS AND SOCIOCULTURAL FACTORS IN DEPRESSION

Over the past two decades, increasing attention has been directed to social and environmental factors which affect depression. Of particular interest to blacks are the stress and sociocultural factors that take into consideration the experiences of being black in American society and how this influences mental health, specifically depression. For the most part, the epidemiologic studies of depression have not included extensive sociocultural or stress-related factors with research on blacks.

Stress and Depression

Evidence from numerous studies indicate that stress increases vulnerability to depression (Neff & Husaini, 1982; Hirschfeld & Cross, 1983; Mueller, 1980; Kaplan, Roberts, Camacho, & Coyne, 1987). Furthermore, being black in American society places one at higher risk for stress and also depression. There are two explanations for the increased risk for stress-related depression among blacks (Mirowsky & Ross, 1980). One explanation purports that the prejudice and discrimination faced by blacks are themselves stressful since feelings of frustration and powerlessness may result from denigrating experiences. Similarly, being a member of a minority group in American society is generally associated with a greater likelihood of being poor and in the lower socioeconomic strata, despite capability and effort. Moreover, research has consistently reported higher rates of depression and psychological distress among persons of lower socioeconomic status (Kessler & Neighbors, 1986; Eaton & Kessler, 1981; Srole et al., 1962; Mirowsky & Ross, 1980; Frerichs et al., 1981).

Although the relationship between stress and depression has been well documented, studies including blacks have been few. In an effort to further understand stresses experienced by blacks and their relationship to depression, Gary et al. (1985) used a modified version of the Social Readjustment Rating Scale (Holmes & Rahe, 1967) in their community sample of 451 black adults. Their findings indicate that, on the average, 2.9 stressful life events had been experienced within the past year. Financial problems were the most frequently cited source of stress, followed by the death of a close family member and family members quarreling among themselves. Significantly more stressful life events were reported by women than men, by those who were divorced and separated, and by younger individuals aged from 18 to 30 years. Recognizably, these are also characteristics of persons at higher risk for depression. The relationship between the number of stressful life events and depressive symptoms was strong, with a Pearson's correlation of .33, p $<$.01.

Much of the literature on stress and depression has focused on stressful life events. Although blacks have greater vulnerability than whites to stressful life crises which may result in depression (Liem & Rayman, 1982), only recently has considerable attention been directed toward the chronic daily stresses of life that may also contribute to depression (Kanner, Coyne, Schaefer, & Lazarus, 1981). These include ongoing conditions or daily hassles such as those related to family role obligations, having enough money for necessities, the irritations of traffic and transportation, or problems with home maintenance. In particular for blacks, chronic daily stress may include a range of financially related considerations as well as regular experiences of unfair treatment because of their race. In addition, it is important to note that some researchers have projected that there is a significant relationship between chronic stress and stressful life events (Pearlin, Lieberman, Menaghan, & Mullan, 1981; Brown & Harris, 1978; Thoits, 1982). For example, loss of a job may exacerbate already existing chronic financial problems. Further investigations, however, are needed in general, and among black Americans in particular, relative to the relationship between depression, life crises, and chronic stresses.

Sociocultural Factors

Recent years have witnessed emerging concerns for the inclusion of sociocultural factors in research on mental health. Demographic factors alone are not sufficient to explain depression. Admittedly, the term "sociocultural" has been widely used, but for the purpose of this discussion it pertains to social and cultural values and patterns of behavior in particular communities. Given that research in this area is still developing, it is not totally understood how sociocultural factors are associated with depression. In some instances, sociocultural factors appear to diminish depressive symptoms (Dressler, 1985), whereas in others, it may increase risk to illness (U.S. Public Health Service, 1979). Furthermore, the relationships between sociocultural factors and depression may be quite complex as some sociocultural factors may have a direct effect on depression, whereas others may have an indirect or moderating effect (Lin, Ensel, Simeone, & Kuo, 1979; Brown & Gary, 1988).

Among black Americans, a number of distinctive sociocultural patterns have been documented, and many of these may have ramifications for the etiology of depression. Included among these are patterns of religious involvement, social participation, and social support.

Involvement in religious activities, particularly around the black church, has traditionally taken a unique sociocultural form in black communities (Mydral, 1944; Brown, 1982). The black church has provided not only opportunities for spiritual fulfillment, but also a range of social, psychological, economic, and political functions (Frazier, 1964; Gary, 1981).

Table 4.4

Sociocultural Factors and Depressive Symptoms among Black Males and Females

	Females			Males		
	n	X	(sd)	n	X	(sd)
Religiosity						
Low	49	14.18	(10.2)	42	12.31	(8.5)
Medium	170	11.59	(8.7)	108	9.57	(7.9)
High	44	9.77	(8.1)	20	6.53	(5.7)
Perceived Social Support						
Low	31	16.94	(11.9)	20	10.45	(8.8)
High	217	10.97	(8.3)	129	9.18	(7.1)
Family Structure						
Nuclear	122	11.57	(8.9)	81	8.53	(7.1)
Extended	75	13.77	(9.7)	47	11.34	(8.0)
Augmented & Other	23	11.80	(2.6)	19	7.00	(8.3)
Community Participation						
No	128	13.15	(9.7)	83	11.83	(8.9)
Yes	139	10.54	(8.0)	88	8.01	(6.5)

Source: Gary, Brown, Milburn, Thomas, and Lockley. *Pathways: A study of black informal support networks*. Washington, D.C.: Institute for Urban Affairs and Research, Howard University. (1985).

In particular, research on black Americans has given further support to the importance of religiosity to mental health. As shown in table 4.4, Gary et al. (1985) found that the highest depressive symptom scores occur among males and females reporting the lowest levels of religiosity. Moreover, depressive symptoms decrease as participation in religious activities increases. Similarly, Neff and Husaini (1982) reported that stress from life events was most strongly related to depressive symptoms among the least religious. On the other hand, the relationship between depression and stress was considerably weaker among the highly religious.

Social participation, especially involvement in a variety of voluntary organizations, has also been documented as a characteristic of black communities (Klobus-Edwards, Edwards, & Klemmack, 1978; Brown, 1982; Drake & Cayton, 1945), and social participation has been positively associated with global happiness and mental well-being (Bradburn, 1969; Phillips, 1967). Furthermore, Gary et al. (1985) found a statistically significant difference in depressive symptoms according to the level of social participation. As shown in table 4.3, both males and females who participated in community activities evidenced fewer depressive symptoms than those who did not.

A considerable effort in recent years has been given to investigating the relationship between social support and depression. Specifically, it is argued that social support buffers or moderates the effects of stressful life events and conditions on health, thereby decreasing vulnerability to depression (Cobb, 1976; Lin et al., 1979). Social support includes instrumental or informational assistance as well as emotional assurance or appraisal by family members, friends, co-workers, neighbors, and others (Leavy, 1983).

The supportive nature of family and friendship ties among black Americans has received considerable documentation in recent years (Billingsley, 1968; McAdoo, 1978, 1982; Stack, 1974; Martineau, 1977). Moreover, their link to mental health and, specifically, depression has been studied (Dressler, 1985; Slater & Depue, 1981; Gore, 1978). Although a variety of different social support measures are used, these studies generally indicate that depressive symptoms tend to be fewer among persons who are socially supported by family members and friends.

Gary et al. (1985) also examined depressive symptomatology in light of se-lected social support characteristics. Among black males and females who per-ceived high levels of satisfaction with social support, there were significantly fewer depressive symptoms than among those having low satisfaction with social support. On the other hand, when family structure was examined using a modified version of Billingsley's typology (1968), somewhat unexpected findings were noted. For both black males and females, living in extended family households was associated with the highest mean level of depressive symptoms. In contrast to black adults in nuclear family households, it is possible that blacks in extended families also have other characteristics of persons at high risk for depression. Specifically, they are apt not to be married, to be young, to have few personal economic resources, and perhaps to be unemployed.

Health Behavior

Among other sociocultural patterns with ramifications for depression among black Americans are health behaviors and life-styles. In particular, those related to substance abuse are of concern, given their devastating impact on many black families and communities. It is suggested that patterns of alcohol use, cigarette smoking, and use of other drugs are strongly related to depression (Taylor, 1981). The relationships between alcohol use patterns remain to be thoroughly investigated, although numerous researchers have suggested that alcohol use among blacks, particulary black males, is a mechanism to alleviate the stresses of poverty, discrimination, and deprivation (Harper, 1981; Cahalan & Cisin, 1968; Neff & Husaini, 1982). Research by R. E. Steer et al. (1977) using the Beck Depressive Inventory with 103 black males found dimensions of depression in alcoholic males to be similar to those with a primary diagnosis of depression. On the other hand, in a study of noninstitutionalized black males, Gary (1982) reports no significant direct relationship between alcohol use and depressive symptoms. Moderate drinkers reported lower depressive scores on the CES-D than did those who were heavy drinkers. Similarly, Neff and Husaini (1982) report that moderate drinking serves to minimize the effects of stress on depressive symptomatology. Among heavy drinkers as well as abstainers, the effects of stress were more severely experienced.

With regard to cigarette smoking, researchers have only begun to explore its relationship to mental health in the general population. Among blacks, it is a matter of considerable concern given the high rates of morbidity and mortality from smoking-related cancers. Findings from one of the few studies on cigarette smoking and depression indicate that smokers report significantly higher levels of depression than nonsmokers as measured by the CES-D. These findings were not analyzed by race, although blacks were included in the study (Frerichs, Aneshensel, Clark, & Yokopenic, 1981). It was hypothesized that smokers were more depressed than nonsmokers because of the negative image of smoking behavior developed by the media. Also, smoking is self-destructive behavior assumed to be indicative of a negative image of self. Additional research, however, is needed among blacks to examine anxiety, as well as depression, and their relationship to cigarette smoking and alcohol use.

SUMMARY AND IMPLICATIONS FOR BLACK AMERICANS

Overall, much remains to be learned about the distribution and etiology of depression among black Americans. With concern for getting better epidemiologic data emerging within the past decade, community-based field studies of noninstitutionalized populations have indicated that between 20 and 30 percent of black Americans experience high levels of depressive symptoms. From 4 to 6 percent of black Americans can be clinically diagnosed as having a major depressive disorder. For high levels of depressive symptoms, prevalence rates among blacks are higher than for whites. Recent findings from the National Institute of Mental Health's Epidemiologic Catchment Area Study support no racial differences in prevalence rates for major depressive disorders.

These studies also provide evidence that there are subgroups within black populations that are at greater risk to depression than others. Foremost are the poor and those at the bottom of the socioeconomic strata. Also included at high risk are black females, although depression among black males may be masked by alcohol use, cigarette smoking, and substance abuse. This is an area warranting further investigation. Young blacks between the ages of 18 and 44 years appear to be especially vulnerable to depression, as well as blacks who are unemployed. Black women with some high school education or less and black men who did not enter high school are at considerable risk for high levels of depression. Also, black men with an incomplete college education are more likely than others to be depressed. Having minor children in the household enhances risk for depression among black females, but not black males. Married persons are least likely to be depressed. Separated and divorced black females have the greatest vulnerability for depression, along with widowed black males.

Research has also consistently demonstrated that those experiencing stressful life crises are at greater risk for depression than others. Furthermore, black

Americans, because of their greater likelihood of being in the lower socioeconomic strata than whites, are also more likely to experience stressful life events, followed by the onset of depression. These studies, however, tend to focus soley on stressful life events, and not on the daily stressful conditions that many blacks face. More research is needed on chronic stresses and, particularly, those related to racial discrimination and prejudice.

At some point in their lives, most persons experience a condition or crisis that increases their vulnerability to depression. Of utmost concern to black Americans is that many will disproportionately be at greater risk because of the convergence of multiple conditions or experiences which occur at the same point in time. For example, at great risk are young, black females who are separated, divorced, or never-married, who have young children in the household. Many are also likely to have limited educational attainment and job skills, along with conditions of low income. The likelihood of their experiencing depression is high, which in turn may affect their ability to cope with parenting and other aspects of their circumstances.

Another high risk group among blacks are young males, particularly those who are unemployed, with less than a high school education. Impairment from depression may impede their ability to improve their education and job skills. In addition, depression may increase their vulnerability to utilizing mechanisms designed to alleviate pain, anxiety, and oppression.

Recognizably, not all black Americans who find themselves in situations conducive to depression actually evidence high levels of symptomatology. For some, there are sociocultural factors such as religiosity, community participation, and social support which help to minimize depressive symptoms. Subsequent studies, particularly of a longitudinal nature need to be implemented to ascertain the importance of sociocultural factors to determine their relationship to mental health in general and depression, in particular. In addition, there are other demographic, stress-related, and psychosocial factors to be explored in an effort to elucidate the epidemiology of depression among black Americans.

REFERENCES

Appreciation is extended to Dr. Lawrence E. Gary for use of his data. The author also thanks Dr. Samuel C. Ndubuisi, Dr. Norweeta G. Milburn and Mrs. Gearldine Davis for their invaluable assistance.

Adebimpe, V. (1981). Overview: White norms and psychiatric diagnoses of black patients. *American Journal of Psychiatry, 138,* 279–85.

American Psychiatric Association. (1980). *Diagnostic and statistical manual of mental disorders.* (3rd ed.). Washington, DC.

Beck, A. (1967). *Depression: Causes and treatment.* Philadelphia: University of Pennsylvania Press.

Berkman, L. F., Berkman, C., Kasl, S., Freeman, J., Daniel, H., Leo, L., Ostfeld, A., Cornoni-Huntley, J., & Roady, J. A. (1986). Depressive symptoms in relation to physical health and functioning in the elderly. *American Journal of Epidemiology, 124*(3), 372–388.

Billingsley, A. (1968). *Black families in white America*. Englewood Cliffs, NJ: Prentice-Hall.

Bradburn, N. (1969). *The structure of psychological well-being*. Chicago: Academic Press.

Brown, D. R. (1982). *The church as a predictor of black social participation in voluntary associations*. Occasional paper, No. 19, Washington, DC: Mental Health Research and Development Center, Howard University.

Brown, D. R. & Gary, L. E. (1985). Predictors of depressive symptoms among unemployed urban black adults. *Journal of Sociology and Social Welfare, 12*(4), 736–754.

Brown, D. R. & Gary, L. E. (1988). Unemployment and psychological distress among black American women. *Sociological Focus, 21*(3), 209–221.

Brown, G. W., Harris, T. O. (1978). *Social origins of depression: A study of psychiatric disorder in women*. New York: Free Press.

Brown, G. W., Harris, T. O., & Copeland, J. R. (1977). Depression and loss. *British Journal of Psychiatry, 130*, 1–18.

Bunney, W. E., & Davis, J. M. (1965). Norepinephrine and depressive reactions: A review. *Archives of General Psychiatry, 13*, 483–494.

Cahalan, D., & Cisin, I. (1968). American drinking practices: Summary of findings from a national probability sample. *Quarterly Journal of Studies on Alcohol, 29*, 130–151.

Cardoret, R. J., Winokur, G., Dorzab, J., & Baker, M. (1972). Depressive disease: Life events and the onset of illness. *Archives of General Psychiatry, 26*, 133–136.

Campbell, A. (1980). *Sense of well-being in America: Recent patterns and trends*. New York: McGraw Hill.

Cannon, M., & Locke, B. (1976). *Being black is detrimental to one's mental health*. Paper presented at the W. E. B. Dubois Conference on the Health of Black Populations, Atlanta, GA.

Cleary, P. D., & Mechanic, D. (1983). Sex differences in psychological distress among married people. *Journal of Health and Social Behavior, 24*, 111–121.

Cobb, S. (1976). Social support as a moderator of life stress. *Psychosomatic Medicine, 38*(5), 300–314.

Comstock, G. W., & Helsing, K. J. (1976). Symptoms of depression in two communities. *Psychological Medicine, 133*(6), 551–563.

Coyne, J. C., Aldwin, C., & Lazarus, R. S. (1981). Depression and coping in stressful episodes. *Journal of Abnormal Psychology, 90*(50), 439–447.

Dohrenwend, B. P., & Dohrenwend, B. S. (1969). *Social status and psychological disorder*. New York: Wiley.

Dohrenwend, B. P., & Dohrenwend, B. S. (1974). *Stressful life events: Their nature and effects*. New York: John Wiley and Sons, Inc.

Dohrenwend, B. S. (1973). Life events as stressors: A methodological inquiry. *Journal of Health and Social Behavior, 14*, 167–175.

Drake, S., & Cayton, H. R. (1945). *Black metropolis*. New York: Harcourt, Brace.

Dressler, W. W. (1985). Extended family relationships, social support and mental health in a southern black community. *Journal of Health and Social Behavior, 26*(1), 39–48.

Dupue, R. A., & Evans, R. (1976). The psychobiology of depressive disorders. In B. H.

Maher (Ed.), *Progress in experimental personality research*. Vol. 8. New York: Academic Press.

Eaton, W. W., & Kessler, L. G. (1981). Rates of symptoms of depression in a national sample. *American Journal of Epidemiology, 114*(4), 528–538.

Faris, R., & Dunham, H. (1939). *Mental health disorders in urban areas: An ecological study of schizophrenia and other psychoses*. Chicago: University of Chicago Press.

Frazier, E. F. (1964). *The Negro church in America*. New York: Schocken Books.

Frerichs, R. R., Aneshensel, C. S., & Clark, V. A. (1981). Prevalence of depression in Los Angeles County. *American Journal of Epidemiology, 113*, 691–699.

Frerichs, R. R., Aneshensel, C. S., Clark, V. A., & Yokopenic, P. A. (1981). Smoking and depression: A community survey. *American Journal of Public Health, 71*(6), 637–640.

Gary, L. E. (1982). *Substance abuse, homicide, and the black male. Black Caucus Journal, 13*, 13–18.

Gary, L. E. (1981). *Religion and mental health*. Paper presented at Conference on Mental Health Services to Blacks: Alternative Solutions, Houston, TX.

Gary, L. E. (1985). Correlates of depressive symptoms among a selected population of black men. *American Journal of Public Health, 75*(10), 1220–1222.

Gary, L. E., Brown, D. R., Milburn, N. G., Thomas, V. G., & Lockley, D. S. (1985). Pathways: A study of black informal support networks. Washington, DC: Institute for Urban Affairs and Research, Howard University.

Gore, S. (1978). The effect of social support in moderating the health consequences of the unemployed. *Journal of Health and Social Behavior, 19*(2), 157–158.

Gove, W., & Tudor, J. (1973). Adult sex roles and mental illness. *American Journal of Sociology, 78*, 812–835.

Gurin, G., Veroff, J., & Feld, S. C. (1960). *Americans view their mental health*. New York: Basic Books.

Harper, F. D. (1981). Alcohol use and abuse. In L. E. Gary (Ed.), *Black men*. Beverly Hills, CA: Sage Publications.

Hirschfeld, R. M. A., & Cross, C. K. (1983). Epidemiology of affective disorders: Psychosocial risk factors. *Archives of General Psychiatry, 39*, 35–46.

Hollingshead, A., & Redlich, F. (1958). *Social class and mental illness: A community study*. New York: Norton.

Holmes, T. H. & Rahe, R. H. (1967). The social readjustment rating scale. *Journal of Psychomatic Research, 11*, 213–218.

Ilfeld, F. (1977). Current social stressors and symptoms of depression. *American Journal of Psychiatry, 134*, 161–166.

Jones, B. E., Gray, B. A., & Parson, E. B. (1981). Manic-depressive illness among poor urban blacks. *American Journal of Psychiatry, 138*(5), 654–657.

Kanner, A. D., Coyne, S. C., Schaefer, C., & Lazarus, R. (1981). Comparison of two modes of stress measurement: Daily hassles and uplifts versus major life events. *Journal of Behavioral Medicine, 4*, 1–39.

Kaplan, G. A., Roberts, R. E., Camacho, T. C., & Coyne, J. C. (1987). Psychosocial predictors of depression: Prospective evidence from the Human Population Laboratory Studies. *American Journal of Epidemiology, 125*(2), 206–220.

Kessler, R. C. (1979). Stress, social status, and psychological distress. *Journal of Health and Social Behavior, 20*, 259–272.

Kessler, R. C., & Cleary, P. D. (1980). Social class and psychological distress. *American Sociological Review, 45*, 63–78.

Kessler, R. C., & Neighbors H. W. (1986). A new perspective on the relationships among race, social class and psychological distress. *Journal of Health and Social Behavior, 27*, 107–115.

Klerman, G., & Weissman, M. (1980). Depressions among women: Their nature and causes. In M. Gutentag, S. Salasin, & E. Belle (Eds.), *The mental health of women.* New York: Academic Press.

Klobus-Edwards, P., Edwards, J. N., & Klemmack, D. L. (1978). Differences in social participation: Blacks and whites. *Social Forces, 65*(4), 1035–1054.

Langner, T., & Michael, S. (1963). *Life stress and mental health.* New York: The Free Press of Glencoe.

Leavy, R. L. (1983). Social support and psychological disorder: A review. *Journal of Community Psychology, 11*, 3–21.

Liem, R., & Rayman, P. (1982). Health and social costs of unemployment. *American Psychologist, 37*, 1116–1123.

Lilienfeld, A., & Lilienfeld, D. E. (1980). *Foundations of epidemiology.* New York: Oxford University Press.

Lin, N., & Ensel, W. M. (1984). Depression mobility and its social etiology: The role of life events and social support. *Journal of Health and Social Behavior, 25*, 176–188.

Lin, N., Ensel, W., Simeone, R., & Kuo, W. (1979). Social support, stressful life events, and illness: A model and empirical test. *Journal of Health and Social Behavior, 20*, 108–119.

Link, B. G., & Dohrenwend, B. P. (1980). Formulation of hypotheses about the true prevalence of demoralization in the United States. In B. P. Dohrenwend, B. S. Dohrenwend, M. S. Gould, B. Link, R. Nuegebauer, & R. Wunsch-Hitzig, (Eds.), *Mental illness in the United States: Epidemiological estimates* (pp. 114–32). New York: Praeger.

Loeb, A., Beck, A. T., & Diggory, J. (1971). Differential effects of success and failure on depressed and non-depressed patients. *Journal of Nervous and Mental Disease, 152*, 106–114.

Martineau, W. (1977). Informal social ties among urban black Americans: Some new data and a review of one problem. *Journal of Black Studies, 8*, 83–105.

McAdoo, H. (1978). *The impact of extended family variables upon the upward mobility of black families.* Washington, DC: U.S. DHEW, Office of Child Development.

McAdoo, H. P. (1982). Stress absorbing systems in black families. *Family Relations, 31*, 479–488.

Mirowsky, J., & Ross, C. D. (1980). Minority status, ethnic culture, and distress: A comparison of blacks, whites, Mexicans, and Mexican-Americans. *American Journal of Sociology, 86*(1), 479–495.

Mitchell, R. E., & Moos, R. H. (1984). Differences in social support among depressed patients: Antecedents or consequences of stress. *Journal of Health and Social Behavior, 25*(4), 424–437.

Mueller, D. P. (1980). Social networks: A promising direction for research on the relationship of the social environment to psychiatric disorder. *Social Science and Medicine, 14a*, 147–161.

Murrell, S., Himmelfarb, S., & Wright, K. (1983). Prevalence of depression and its correlates in older adults. *American Journal of Epidemiology, 117*(2), 173–185.

Myrdal, G. (1944). *An American dilemma*. New York: Harper Brothers.

Neff, J. A., & Husaini, B. A. (1980). Socio-economic status and psychiatric impairment: A research note. *Journal of Community Psychology, 8*, 16–19.

Neff, J. A., & Husaini, B. A. (1982). Life events, drinking patterns and depressive symptomatology: The stress-buffering role of alcohol consumption. *Journal of Studies on Alcohol, 43*(3), 301–317.

Neighbors, H. W. (1984). The distribution of psychiatric morbidity in black Americans: A review and suggestions for research. *Community Mental Health Journal 20*(3), 169–81.

Newman, J. P. (1986). Gender, life strains and depression. *Journal of Health and Social Behavior, 27*(2), 161–178.

Noyes, A., & Kolb, L. (1958). *Modern clinical psychiatry* Philadelphia: W. B. Saunders.

Parker, J. (1959). Factors in manic-depressive reactions. *Disease of the Nervous System, 20*(11), 505–511.

Pasamanick, B. (1962). A survey of mental disease in an urban population. An approach to total prevalence by race. *American Journal of Psychiatry, 119*, 304.

Paykel, E. S., Emms, E. M., Fletcher, J., et al. (1980). Life events and social supports in perpetual depression. *British Journal of Psychiatry, 136*, 339–346.

Pearlin, L., & Johnson, J. (1977). Marital status, life strains and depression. *American Sociological Review, 42*, 704–715.

Pearlin, L., Lieberman, M., Menaghan, E., & Mullan, J. (1981). The stress process. *Journal of Health and Social Behavior, 22*, 337–356.

Phillips, D. (1967). Social participation and happiness. *American Journal of Sociology, 72*, 478–488.

Prange, A., & Vitols, M. M. (1962). Cultural aspects of the relatively low incidence of depression in southern Negroes. *International Journal of Social Psychiatry, 8*, 104–112.

Radloff, L. S. (1977). The CES-D scale: A self-report depression scale for research in the general population. *Applied Psychological Measurement, 3*, 385–401.

Radloff, L. S. (1980). Risk factors for depression: What do we learn from them? In *Health United States, 1980, with Prevention Profile* (DHHS Publication No. PHS 81–1232). Hyattsville, MD.

Regier, D. A., Myers, J. K., Kramer, M., Robins, L. N., Blazer, D. G., Hough, R. L., Eaton, W. W., & Locke, B. Z. (1984). The NIMH epidemiologic catchment area program. *Archives of General Psychiatry, 41*, 934–941.

Roberts, E., Stevenson, M. A., & Breslow, L. (1981). Symptoms of depression among blacks and whites in an urban community. *The Journal of Nervous and Mental Disease, 169*(12), 774–779.

Robins, L. N., Helzer, J. E., Croughan, J. R., Ratcliff, K. (1981). National Institute of Mental Health Diagnostic Interview Schedule: Its history, characteristics and validity. *Archives of General Psychiatry, 38*, 381–389.

Robins, L. N., Helzer, J. E., Weissman, M. M., Orvaschel, H., Gruenberz, E., Burke, J. D., & Regier, D. (1984). Lifetime prevalence of specific psychiatric disorders in three sites. *Archives of General Psychiatry, 41*, 919–958.

Sayetta, R. B., & Johnson, D. P. (1980 April). National Center for Health Statistics: Basic data on depressive symptomatology, United States, 1974–1975. *Vital and*

Health Statistics, Series 1, No. 216. (DHEW Publication No. PHS 80–1666). Public Health Service. Washington, DC: U.S. Government Printing Office.

Seligman, M. (1975). *Helplessness: On depression, development and death.* San Francisco: W. H. Freeman.

Shore, P. A., & Brodie, B. B. (1957). Influence of various drugs on serotonin and norepinephrine in the brain. In S. Garattini, & V. Ghetti (Eds.), *Psychotropic Drugs.* Amsterdam: Elsevier.

Silverman, C. (1968). The epidemiology of depression: A review. *American Journal of Psychiatry, 124,* 883–891.

Slater, J., & Depue, R. A. (1981). The contributions of environmental events and social support to serious suicide attempts in primary depression disorder. *Journal of Abnormal Psychology, 90,* 275–285.

Srole, L., Langner, T. S., Michael, S. T., Opler, M. K., & Rennie, T. A. (1962). *Mental health in the metropolis: The midtown Manhattan study.* New York: McGraw Hill.

Stack, C. (1974). *All our kin: Strategies for survival in a black community.* New York: Harper and Row.

Steele, R. E. (1978). Relationship of race, sex, social class, and social mobility to depression in normal adults. *Journal of Social Psychology, 104,* 37–47.

Steer, R., et al. (1977). Structure of depression in black alcoholic men. *Psychological Reports, 41* (pt. 2), 1235–1241.

Taylor, R. L. (1981). Psychological modes of adaptation. In L. Gary (Ed.), *Black men.* Beverly Hills, CA: Sage.

Thoits, P. A. (1982). Conceptual, methodological and theoretical problems in studying social support as a buffer against life stress. *Journal of Health and Social Behavior, 23,* 145–159.

U.S. Public Health Service, U.S. Department of Health and Human Services. (1979). *Healthy People: The surgeon general's report on health promotion and disease prevention.* Washington, DC: U.S. Government Printing Office.

Warheit, G. J., Holzer, C. E., & Schwab, J. J. (1973). An analysis of social class and racial differences in depressive symptomatology. *Journal of Health and Social Behavior, 14,* 291–299.

Weissman, M., & Klerman, G. (1977). Sex differences in the epidemiology of depression. *Archives of General Psychiatry, 34,* 98–111.

5

SUICIDE TRENDS OF BLACKS AND WHITES BY SEX AND AGE

Jacquelyne J. Jackson

INTRODUCTION

Almost a century ago, Émile Durkheim observed that suicide rates and educational levels in all countries were higher among males than among females. His generalization included the entire United States, but not her blacks: "Negro women, it seems, are equally or more highly educated than their husbands. Several observers report that they are also very strongly predisposed to suicide, at times even surpassing white women" (Durkheim, as quoted in Simpson, 1951, p. 167). The statistical observations of Durkheim's "several observers" are decidedly unreliable.

Existing data show no nineteenth-century educational superiority of black wives over their spouses (Jackson, 1973). Reported suicide rates during the last century of American blacks and whites are highly suspect. Recent suicide rates as social facts are certainly not absolutely reliable, but when they are compared to earlier rates, their approximation of reality is much better.

Purposes

This chapter first describes and compares trends between 1967 and 1986 in five-year annual averages of suicide rates of American blacks and whites, at age 15 or more years, by age and sex. The comparisons between the reported rates for suicide and all causes of death are especially useful in determining trends in the contribution of suicide to all deaths. Comparing the reported suicide and homicide rates is also important because suicide and homicide are often viewed as sharing narrow borders (see Hendin, 1969, p. 136).

The focus then shifts to standardized mortality ratios by marital status and sex of American blacks and whites at 25 or more years of age. These ratios (based on four-year annual averages of deaths in 1979–1982 and 1983–1986 for all causes of death, suicide, and homicide) permit comparisons of actual and expected deaths by marital status among black women, black men, white women, and white men.

It must be noted that explaining—as opposed to hypothesizing about—black suicides is not a major purpose of this chapter. Although the theory of suicidal behavior being influenced by interactive psychological and social factors applies equally as well to blacks as to whites, too little is yet known beyond this point about the greatly different and highly complex etiologies of black suicides. This major gap among blacks includes their different individual and subcultural attitudes about situationally based suicides, bungled attempts of suicide (i.e., where the intent was clearly death), and attempted suicides (i.e., where the intent was clearly not death).

Mary Monk has indicted that "[v]ery often the goal in public health is to prevent or control . . . suicide" (Monk, 1975, p. 186), but a crucially important notion—set forth now for later discussion—is that prevention or control of all black suicides is ill-advised. That is, under certain circumstances, black suicides represent positive views of mental health.

Sources and Statistical Treatment of Data

The sources for the five-year annual averages of reported death rates per one hundred thousand for all causes of death, suicide, and homicides are unpublished and published data of the National Center for Health Statistics (1970–1989). In some instances in the earlier years, the rates were calculated from raw data of the number of deaths provided by the National Center for Health Statistics and estimated population data obtained from the U.S. Bureau of the Census. The slight variations that may exist between the rates reported herein and those since modified by the National Center for Health Statistics are slight and do not change the trends or patterns presented below.

The Pearson product-moment correlation coefficient (r) was used to determine the strength and direction of relationships between such variables as suicide rates and ages. The level of confidence set for determining the significances of these relationships was .05. At this level, the probability is that in 95 times out of every 100, the statistically significant result is not due to chance alone. In many instances, the statistically significant results reported herein far exceeded a level of confidence of .001.

The standardized mortality ratio, a form of age adjustment of death rates, expresses "the observed number . . . [of deaths] as a percentage of the expected" number of deaths (Lilienfeld, 1976, p. 64). The standards that are used represent the four-year average annual death rates for all causes of death, suicide, and homicide, for all persons within the same race-sex-population (e.g., black women, 1979–1982).

It should also be noted that different age distributions used in calculating the standardized mortality ratios prohibit direct comparisons between and among the race-sex groups, including direct comparisons of the same race-sex group across time. But direct comparisons by marital status can be made of the standardized mortality rates within each race-sex group for each cause of death in each time period.

Two different sources of data were used to obtain the raw data requisite to calculating standardized mortality ratios per one million. The number of reported deaths between 1979 and 1986 by cause of death, marital status, race, sex, and age were obtained from the National Center for Health Statistics (1982–1989). The four available levels of marital status were never-married, married, widowed, and divorced. Separate data were not available for married persons who were living with and separated from their spouses. The ten-year age intervals began at 25–34 years and ended at 75 or more years of age. Population data from the U.S. Bureau of the Census (1980–1986) were used to determine for each applicable year the number of persons by marital status, race, sex, and age.

The customary caveats about the accuracy of the data being influenced by such factors as undercounting of specified populations and of actual suicides (see Stockwell, 1976; U.S. Department of Health and Human Services, 1988) also apply to the data presented in this chapter.

DEMOGRAPHIC TRENDS

Reported Suicide Rates

The race-sex-age specific suicide rates presented in table 5.1 are five-year annual averages for the years of 1967–1971, 1972–1976, 1977–1981, and 1982–1986.

There is only one exception to the consistently lower suicide rates among black females than among their counterparts in any other race-sex-age group: the 1967–1971 black female rate at age 15–19 years is 16 percent higher than the comparable white female rate. In all other instances, the black female rates are consistently lower than the comparable rates of black males, white females, and white males.

As expected, the changing suicide rates between the first and fourth time periods are inconsistent within and between each race-sex-age group. The increasing suicide rates at all ages among black males were most pronounced among the youngest (15–19 years) and the two oldest age groups. This trend of generally rising suicide rates among black males, and particularly so in their later years, was already apparent by 1978 (Jackson, 1981).

Unlike black males, the white male suicide rates increased only at ages 15–39 and 70 or more years of age. Increased black female rates occurred at ages 50–64 and 75 or more years of age. The least number of increased suicide rates within any age group occurred among white females at ages 15–24 and at 80 or more years of age.

Table 5.1

Five-Year Annual Averages of Suicide Rates per 100,000 of Blacks and Whites, 15 or More Years of Age, by Age and Sex, United States, 1967–1986

Race-Sex and Years	Age in Years														
	15-19	20-24	25-29	30-34	35-39	40-44	45-49	50-54	55-59	60-64	65-69	70-74	75-79	80-84	85+
BLACK WOMEN															
1967-71	2.9	5.1	5.2	5.0	4.4	3.9	3.7	3.1	2.4	2.2	2.3	3.0	1.8	1.2	1.6
1972-76	2.3	5.3	5.6	5.0	4.0	4.1	4.0	3.5	3.0	3.2	2.0	2.5	1.1	0.7	0.8
1977-81	2.4	4.1	5.2	5.2	4.4	4.5	3.4	3.2	3.2	3.0	2.1	2.5	2.0	1.6	1.0
1982-86	1.7	2.9	3.2	3.6	3.5	3.3	3.2	3.2	2.5	2.9	2.0	2.4	2.3	2.1	1.1
BLACK MEN															
1967-71	4.2	15.2	16.9	16.8	14.4	13.1	12.3	10.8	11.8	8.7	10.7	12.1	10.4	9.9	6.1
1972-76	6.4	21.5	24.6	20.4	17.4	13.4	14.0	12.1	11.3	11.1	11.2	13.6	12.5	8.0	11.2
1977-81	5.9	20.9	25.1	22.2	17.8	14.5	12.3	11.9	12.0	11.9	11.3	11.4	11.8	13.3	14.2
1982-86	6.8	16.8	20.5	19.8	17.4	13.4	12.7	11.9	12.1	11.2	13.4	15.6	12.6	19.6	13.1
WHITE WOMEN															
1967-71	2.5	5.3	7.6	9.0	11.6	13.0	13.3	13.9	12.7	11.3	9.9	8.8	7.5	6.5	4.7
1972-76	3.1	6.4	8.2	9.5	11.2	13.0	14.2	13.3	12.9	10.7	9.4	8.5	7.7	6.9	5.0
1977-81	3.5	6.5	7.9	8.5	9.5	11.0	11.6	11.7	10.7	9.0	8.4	7.5	6.9	5.8	4.9
1982-86	3.8	5.4	6.5	7.1	7.9	9.0	9.8	9.9	9.6	8.4	7.7	7.6	7.3	7.3	5.0
WHITE MEN															
1967-1971	8.9	17.1	18.2	18.5	21.5	24.7	27.6	30.6	34.9	35.7	35.8	37.7	43.0	51.8	53.7
1972-1976	11.9	24.6	23.2	22.3	22.2	24.4	28.3	29.2	31.9	32.6	34.9	38.7	43.0	48.1	52.1
1977-1981	14.7	28.1	27.8	23.9	23.7	23.2	24.0	25.7	26.9	28.5	31.1	37.5	44.9	49.0	52.4
1982-1986	16.4	27.0	26.7	25.2	23.6	23.7	24.7	26.4	28.4	28.2	30.6	40.7	50.7	59.4	58.6

Relationships between Suicide Rates and Age

As is now well established, the finding of a significantly positive relationship between age and suicide rate in the entire American population is not characteristic of most subgroups within that population. Herbert Hendin (1969, p. 5) reported much higher rates among younger than older blacks in New York City. This pattern was also apparent nationally between 1964 and 1978 (Jackson, 1982).

Positive correlations (r) between the suicide rates and age groups of white males within each of the four time periods (i.e., 1967–1971, 1972–1976, 1977–1981, and 1982–1986) were significant for beyond the .001-level of confidence. The significantly inverse relationships presented among black females exceeded the .001-level of confidence for the first three time periods, and the .05-level of confidence for the last time period.

There were no significant relationships at all between suicide rates and age among black males or white females. While these latter relationships were not significant, their directions among black males were all negative. In contrast, the white female relationships were positive between 1967 and 1971 and 1982 and 1986.

Thus, the general associations between increasing suicide rates with age found among white males are not found among black females, black males, and white females. What is more important within the present context, however, is the distinct difference by sex and age in black suicidal patterns.

Comparisons between Rates for Suicide and All Causes of Death

Table 5.2 contains five-year annual averages between 1967 and 1986 of race-sex-age specific rates for all causes of deaths among American blacks and whites at age 15 or more years. As may be readily apparent across the years, these death rates are highest for black males, followed in descending order by white males, black females, and white females. Not surprisingly, the positive correlations between the rates for all causes of death and age were quite strong within each of the four race-sex groups.

A question of great interest in this comparison of death rates from all causes of death and from suicide only is that of any change in the contribution of suicide to the overall death rate. The proportionate contribution of suicide rates to the rates for all causes of death generally decreased with increasing age.

Among black females, the significant correlations (r) between the rates for suicide and all causes of death in each time period are all negative. That is, their suicide rates decrease with increasing rates for all causes of death. The comparable pattern among white males is highly significant in the opposite direction. Similar data for black males and white females show insignificant relationships. The direction and strength of these relationships for each race-sex group could

Table 5.2
Five-Year Annual Average Rates per 100,000 for All Causes of Death of Blacks and Whites, 15 or More Years of Age, by Age and Sex, United States, 1967–1986

Race-Sex and Years	15-19	20-24	25-29	30-34	35-39	40-44	45-49	50-54	55-59	60-64	65-69	70-74	75-79	80-84	85+
BLACK WOMEN															
1967-71	87.1	114.5	194.2	287.5	441.6	638.8	901.2	1,225.6	1,707.8	2,436.8	3,393.5	4,570.0	5,936.1	7,661.0	12,128.1
1972-76	70.3	125.7	166.7	226.3	335.9	529.3	772.3	1,065.4	1,482.0	2,060.8	2,728.3	4,952.4	5,055.4	6,584.8	11,941.7
1977-81	53.6	94.7	134.0	140.1	260.1	405.3	618.2	925.6	1,293.1	1,864.6	2,432.7	3,832.9	4,996.0	7,103.3	11,655.5
1982-86	46.7	78.4	112.6	131.4	227.8	351.8	815.0	815.0	1,216.1	1,813.1	2,386.9	3,555.5	4,930.7	8,127.5	11,818.7
BLACK MEN															
1967-71	219.6	418.6	494.1	597.5	791.2	1,097.0	1,503.1	2,039.9	2,817.8	3,844.0	5,084.5	6,890.6	8,618.5	10,332.6	14,572.7
1972-76	180.3	378.9	476.2	555.3	712.3	970.4	1,403.6	1,945.3	2,682.5	3,548.1	4,644.2	7,156.0	7,807.9	9,194.7	14,980.5
1977-81	134.6	281.2	384.1	451.9	588.4	826.6	1,200.6	1,786.3	2,429.0	3,392.4	4,330.6	6,153.4	7,518.2	10,221.1	15,038.2
1982-86	120.4	229.0	303.8	410.7	536.9	738.6	1,060.7	1,542.4	2,195.1	3,196.6	4,153.4	5,943.6	7,727.7	11,682.2	14,890.1
WHITE WOMEN															
1967-71	57.3	64.5	71.4	96.3	156.3	235.8	371.2	556.5	819.9	1,226.6	1,937.8	3,155.0	5,389.4	9,028.5	17,650.3
1972-76	55.0	60.5	66.2	87.6	131.4	213.9	340.8	508.7	778.7	1,159.1	1,734.3	2,905.0	4,834.5	7,995.5	15,895.6
1977-81	53.8	58.3	60.6	74.3	109.5	180.2	293.9	463.1	697.3	1,085.5	1,612.6	2,577.8	4,147.8	7,167.4	14,466.4
1982-86	47.1	51.1	54.0	66.5	96.4	157.1	259.9	428.5	671.5	1,057.4	1,613.7	2,519.2	4,019.3	6,833.6	14,360.8
WHITE MEN															
1967-71	147.4	194.2	167.3	182.6	261.9	417.3	685.3	1,110.9	1,765.2	2,723.7	4,032.1	4,729.3	8,671.2	12,714.9	21,007.7
1972-76	148.1	190.6	167.0	174.1	237.0	376.2	516.3	998.8	1,605.5	3,558.2	3,713.6	5,627.8	8,249.3	11,962.4	19,663.3
1977-81	143.0	188.5	171.4	165.5	211.6	321.6	538.0	887.0	1,381.4	2,199.4	5,774.1	5,077.7	7,424.8	11,185.7	18,496.8
1982-86	119.1	164.0	153.4	164.4	199.2	289.8	466.7	784.5	1,276.4	1,990.3	3,041.1	4,699.7	7,152.5	10,848.0	18,496.8

have been anticipated from the previously reported relationships between suicide rates and age.

Comparisons between Suicide and Homicide Rates

Presented in table 5.3 are five-year annual averages between 1967 and 1986 of race-sex-age specific rates for homicide among American blacks and whites at age 15 or more years. The general pattern of substantially higher homicide rates among black males than among black females, white females, and white males is, of course, a long-established one.

The relationships between homicide and age among the race-sex groups differ somewhat from those found between suicide rates and age. Strongly inverse relationships appeared within each time period among black females, black males, and white males. While only insignificant relationships were found among white females, the direction of the relationship was positive in 1977–1981, and negative within the other three time periods.

Perhaps the most interesting findings pertaining to the relationships between the suicide and homicide rates of each race-sex group in each time period are shown in table 5.4. There is considerable variability among the race-sex groups. The positive relationships among black females are quite strong in the first three, but not the most recent time period. The positive relationships among black males are strong in each time period, but less so in the most recent than in the earlier years. In contrast, the negative relationships are significant among white males, but not among white females.

Marital Status and Mortality Experience

Table 5.5 contains standardized mortality ratios per million by marital status for all causes of death, suicide, and homicide at two adjacent time periods for each race-sex group. A given ratio represents the percentage of observed deaths to expected deaths. A ratio of 100 means an equivalent number of observed and expected deaths. Ratios below 100 show a greater number of expected than observed deaths. The reverse is true of ratios exceeding 100. To illustrate, the 1979–1982 mortality experience of never-married black women was 129.9 percent of the total black female population rate from all causes of death. In contrast, the mortality experience of comparable married women was only 76.4 percent.

As may be readily apparent, table 5.5 shows consistently lower ratios among the marrieds than among the unmarrieds in each race-sex group for each specified cause of death in each time period. Particularly striking are the variations between and among the race-sex groups in rank order by marital status of the standardized mortality ratios for suicide. Among black women, white women, and white men, the 1979–1982 ratio is highest for the divorced. The comparable black male ratio in both time periods is most disadvantageous for widowers. The 1983–1986

Table 5.3

Five-Year Annual Averages of Homicide Rates per 100,000 of Blacks and Whites, 15 or More Years of Age, by Age and Sex, United States, 1967–1986

Race-Sex and Years	Age in Years														
	15-19	20-24	25-29	30-34	35-39	40-44	45-49	50-54	55-59	60-64	65-69	70-74	75-79	80-84	85+
BLACK WOMEN															
1967-71	11.2	25.7	28.2	27.1	27.2	24.5	19.4	13.1	10.1	8.8	8.3	5.8	3.4	3.8	5.7
1972-76	13.7	28.8	30.5	28.2	25.4	23.2	19.2	14.2	11.6	9.8	7.1	10.1	8.2	4.8	7.1
1977-81	11.7	24.6	25.8	22.5	20.3	15.2	14.0	10.4	9.5	10.2	8.5	7.6	7.2	9.0	6.8
1982-86	10.8	19.5	21.9	18.7	16.1	13.5	10.2	8.2	7.1	6.6	7.6	7.5	9.1	9.5	10.6
BLACK MEN															
1967-71	59.0	143.7	161.0	151.2	136.4	121.8	102.9	80.3	60.7	48.0	37.7	27.4	19.2	15.1	17.4
1972-76	54.5	143.4	175.2	156.0	140.3	129.3	111.5	92.5	73.4	58.3	41.0	41.8	24.9	16.7	16.6
1977-81	54.3	113.0	144.6	131.0	115.9	99.8	87.0	76.3	59.9	48.3	37.9	30.0	27.6	22.6	21.2
1982-86	45.4	93.6	106.9	102.8	88.8	72.1	63.9	54.3	44.1	39.4	32.2	28.3	26.5	28.0	23.5
WHITE WOMEN															
1967-71	1.9	3.0	3.2	3.1	3.1	3.0	2.5	2.0	1.9	1.9	1.6	1.7	2.0	2.4	2.6
1972-76	3.1	4.3	4.5	3.8	3.8	3.6	3.0	2.6	2.3	2.1	2.0	2.4	3.0	3.5	3.0
1977-81	3.5	5.0	4.4	3.7	3.7	3.8	3.3	2.6	2.2	2.1	2.0	2.7	2.9	3.6	3.6
1982-86	3.1	4.9	4.6	3.7	3.6	3.7	3.1	2.6	2.2	2.1	2.1	2.1	2.7	3.5	3.4
WHITE MEN															
1967-71	5.0	10.5	12.2	11.7	11.0	9.9	8.4	7.5	7.2	6.5	5.9	4.9	4.4	4.7	4.7
1972-76	7.4	14.3	15.4	14.5	14.6	12.6	11.2	9.3	8.6	7.6	6.2	6.0	5.9	5.7	6.1
1977-81	9.7	17.6	17.5	15.7	15.2	13.7	12.1	10.2	8.0	7.3	6.1	5.6	5.2	5.8	7.5
1982-86	8.0	15.3	15.6	13.8	12.4	11.9	10.0	8.6	7.1	5.7	4.6	4.4	4.4	4.9	5.5

Table 5.4
Correlations (r) between Five-Year Annual Averages of Suicide and Homicide Rates of Blacks and Whites, United States, 1967–1986

Years	Black Females	Black Males	White Females	White Males
1967–1971	0.9489*	0.7737*	−0.0438	−0.6723*
1972–1976	0.9296*	0.8343*	−0.2387	−0.663*
1977–1981	0.8774*	0.9690*	−0.3103	−0.5867*
1982–1986	0.4803	0.5319*	−0.4303	−0.5864*

*Significant at or beyond 0.05.

suicide ratios are still highest for divorced black women and white men, but not for white women, where the highest rate is found among the never-marrieds.

Comparisons of the suicide and homicide ratios within each race-sex cohort also reveal variations. For instance, indirect comparisons between the apparent gaps in the suicide and homicide ratios of married black women seem to widen considerably between 1979 and 1982 and 1983 and 1986. This apparent pattern is decidedly more visible among never-married black men.

But what seems to be even more important is that the statistically significant correlations between the standardized mortality ratios for suicide and homicide among black women, black men, white women, and white men in 1979–1982 were found only among white men in 1983–1986.

DISCUSSION AND INTERPRETATION OF FINDINGS

Perhaps the most obvious beginning here is a return to the very beginning of this chapter. Some question was raised there about the reliability of Durkheim's ''several observers'' who claimed that the predisposition to suicide was quite high among American black women and often higher than that of comparable white women. That claim is still highly doubtful. The cause of death of many murdered black women was returned as suicide to protect their murderers.

Insufficient Explanations of Black Suicides

In any case, the five-year average of annual suicide rates between 1967 and 1986 show consistently lower rates among black women than among black men, white women, and white men. Why? This enigma has not yet been explained adequately by suicidologists garbed in the robes of anthropologists, psychiatrists, psychologists, sociologists, or those of similar ilk. In my judgment, a number

Table 5.5

Standardized Mortality Ratios per Million Expressed in Percentages for All Causes of Death, Suicide, and Homicide by Marital Status and Sex of Blacks and Whites 25+ Years Old, United States, 1979–1982 and 1983–1986 and Component Changes

Marital Status, Race and Sex	All Causes of Death			Suicide			Homicide		
	1979–1982	1983–1986	% Change	1979–1982	1983–1986	% Change	1979–1982	1983–1986	% Change
BLACK WOMEN									
Never married	129.9	131.3	1.1	122.3	124.8	2.0	130.4	122.6	-6.0
Married	76.4	72.6	-5.0	74.8	86.4	15.5	76.5	97.7	27.7
Widowed	113.5	108.1	-4.8	114.0	120.9	6.0	135.8	139.2	2.5
Divorced	103.8	96.0	-7.5	154.9	149.1	-3.7	143.6	121.3	-15.5
BLACK MEN									
Never married	163.1	159.2	-2.4	130.2	121.0	-7.1	158.4	270.4	-31.8
Married	79.7	78.2	-1.9	71.9	72.7	1.1	67.8	66.2	-2.4
Widowed	158.0	140.8	-10.9	151.9	192.3	26.6	149.0	171.8	15.3
Divorced	130.1	141.4	8.7	142.3	173.7	22.1	151.0	161.9	7.2
WHITE WOMEN									
Never married	128.2	127.9	-0.2	149.8	132.7	-11.4	138.9	115.5	-16.8
Married	73.5	71.9	-2.2	73.3	64.5	-12.0	67.4	84.4	25.2
Widowed	112.2	115.6	3.0	127.4	125.6	-1.4	142.8	100.3	-29.8
Divorced	159.0	136.7	-14.0	247.4	96.9	-60.8	269.0	212.6	-21.0
WHITE MEN									
Never married	154.6	149.4	-3.3	172.3	155.4	-9.8	177.4	161.7	-8.8
Married	80.6	83.5	2.9	64.2	69.3	7.9	63.9	60.1	6.0
Widowed	150.6	152.4	1.2	214.6	216.5	0.9	219.0	213.9	-2.3
Divorced	185.9	190.0	2.2	308.4	278.3	-9.8	340.9	292.0	-14.3

of important and different reasons are useful in understanding this explanatory failure.

In no particular order, one reason is the undue emphasis placed on a global definition of racism and attendant consequences, such as the failures of black motherhood. The literature of earlier years typically blamed all or almost all black mothers. The current trend of blaming black mothers who single-parent represents no substantial improvement over the earlier theories blaming black motherhood.

A second and highly compelling reason is the reliance upon data generated by "psychological autopsies" and "matched" comparisons of blacks who have actually committed suicide and blacks who have only attempted suicide. Co-joined with this reason are the abysmally small and unrepresentative samples whose findings are used to theorize about black suicide (see Breed, 1970; Kirk, 1976).

A third, and another compelling reason, is that, as in this chapter, comparisons of suicide rates of American black women, black men, white women, and white men are not controlled by such critically important variables as their socioeconomic status, their psychological state at the time of their suicides, and their access to and use of informal and formal social supports.

Consequently, while it is crystal-clear that suicide occurs much more often among black men, white women, and white men than among black women, the cause of these differential suicide rates is not yet known. Until sufficient evidence is amassed, explanations that are based on greater social integration within their families among black women than among black men, white women, and white men (as well as less exposure to racism than black men) are sophomoric and sophistic. Similar arguments can be adduced about black male suicides.

Suicide and Homicide

Unlike suicide rates, comparisons of rates for all causes of death and homicide show consistently lower rates among black women than among black men and white men, but not among white women. Reasonable explanations for this repeated finding through the past few decades include especially a combination of biological and sociocultural factors.

But, as noted earlier, some suicidologists view suicide and homicide among blacks as obverse sides of the same coin. Having read much of this literature, I interpret this notion to mean that blacks who are overwhelmed by racism, frustrated childhoods, dominance by their mothers, and the like (see, e.g., Kardiner and Ovesey, 1951; Hendin, 1969) become enraged and experience a need to "strike out." Presumably if blacks are inner-directed, their rage leads to suicide; if outer-directed, to homicide.

This theory of black suicide and homicide may be an intriguing notion, particularly among white psychoanalysts who rarely know more than a handful or so of blacks. What is obviously overlooked is the indisputable fact that the vast majority of blacks so overwhelmed do not commit suicide or homicide. The reality is that the annual number of blacks who commit suicide or who are killed is quite small.

The reported number of homicides and suicides among black men at age 25 or more years in 1986—not an unusual year—were only 5,069 and 1,174, respectively, out of an estimated population in that year of 6,237,000 black males at age 25 or more years. The percentage of black men in that population who committed suicide or were killed was only about 0.1 percent. Comparable data for black women show that their 281 suicides and 1,199 homicides represented only 0.01 percent of their estimated population. To reiterate the point, extremely few blacks kill themselves or are killed by others in any given year. Moreover, psychoanalytic explanations alone of black suicide are far too primitive and generally useless.

The public image of massive homicides among blacks is distorted by those who are more concerned with comparing black and white homicide rates than with the actual occurrences of homicide among blacks. The notion that black suicide is a grave problem is one that is typically promoted by black and white mental health professionals who believe that suicide is not a human right, but a dire sin.

Although it is still true that most black murderers murder blacks, often in "passion" murders, there also appears to be a trend of increased murders by blacks of strangers and enemies, as in drug-related killings and gang warfare. The increase in these "business killings" may help explain what appears to be a weakening relationship between suicide and homicide among black men.

Marital Status and Suicide

The standardized mortality rates by marital status for all causes of death, suicide, and homicide showed that the observed deaths among married persons are generally considerably lower than their expected deaths. This is not surprising. Bryce Christensen's (1988) recent review of relationships between health status and marital status stresses anew the health advantages of being and staying married. However, recent data from the prospective U.S. National Longitudinal Mortality Study tend to suggest that the mortality experiences by sex of black marrieds are not always better than those of black unmarrieds (Jackson and Perry, 1989).

The relationships between marital status and suicide among blacks suggest gender differences. It appears that staying married (and not necessarily happily married) may be more protective against suicide among men than among women. The substantial increase during the past several decades in black women who are not living with spouses does not appear to have generated a strong rise in the suicide rates of never-married, separated, widowed, or divorced black women. This is clearly an area for sociological investigation.

Extremely Aged Black Men

While still quite small in number, the trend between 1967 and 1986 of increasing suicide rates among extremely aged black men raises new questions about their motivations for suicide and, at the same time, underscores the complexity of the variability of suicidal motivations and resources among blacks. How well do existing theories explain suicide among extremely aged black men?

Consider Maurice Farber's view—still a contemporary one—that the expectedly high rates of American black suicide based on "the low level for them of hope in the future time-perspective of the society and the low level of the availability of succorance" are reduced because "demands for the exercising of competence [by them] are probably low, [thereby] exerting an influence toward a low rate" (Farber, 1968, p. 89). Consider Warren Breed's (1970) prediction of a positive relationship between upward social mobility and suicide rates among blacks. G. Franklin Edwards, a noted black sociologist, supported Breed's prediction. Or, consider Alton Kirk's (1976) proposition of a negative relationship between black suicide and black consciousness and his rejection of Hendin's (1969) explanation of self-hatred as the key to black suicide.

None of the above theories appears to be useful in explaining the still small, but growing suicide rates of extremely aged black men. How are these suicide rates explained by low demands for competence, upward social mobility, low level of black consciousness, or self-hatred? None of these theories has considered the influence of terminal illness upon suicide among the extremely aged.

"Living Suicides" and "Socially Useful Suicides"

For the sake of argument, a grain of truth helpful in understanding certain black suicides may be nesting in each of the above theories, but none of them provides a satisfactory explanation of the range of successful black suicides. In addition, except for Farber's (1968) psychological notion that the lack of hope may prompt suicide, these theories ignore entirely what I have termed "living suicides" and "socially useful suicides." Farber's (1968) theory of hope, I should note, is not linked in any way to terminal illnesses.

"Living suicides" refer to individuals whose personal behaviors and life-styles knowingly contribute to their earlier deaths. Think of a black man whose perennial unemployment and homelessness lead to protracted use of alcohol and poor nutritional intake, and, in turn, to his premature death. Then add to this concept the social conditions that prompt black male unemployment and homelessness. In other words, it is necessary to balance or weight appropriately the extent to which both individual and social factors affect the individual's personal behaviors and life-style.

"Socially useful suicides" are suicides committed by individuals experiencing terminal illnesses (including AIDS), or who, among the aged, prefer death to mere vegetation. These types of suicide are socially useful because they reduce the drain on the public coffers and remind us that life under any cost is not always preferable to death. This definition of socially useful suicides could be extended to include individuals who commit suicide in preference to being tried for first-degree murder when they know that they are guilty and that the evidence against them is preponderous. Committing suicide under these circumstances benefits society by saving monies that would otherwise be spent in legal fees and institutionalization.

In conclusion, mental health professionals and other persons hell-bent on preventing suicides of American blacks might also reflect upon the individual and social desirability of drinking hemlock.

REFERENCES

Breed, Warren. (1970). The Negro and fatalistic suicide. *Pacific Sociological Review, 13,* 156–162.

Christensen, Bryce, J. (1988, Spring). The costly retreat from marriage. *The Public Interest, 91,* 59–66.

Farber, Maurice L. (1968). *Theory of suicide.* New York: Funk & Wagnalls.

Hendin, Herbert. (1969). *Black suicide.* New York: Basic Books, Inc.

Jackson, Jacquelyne Johnson. (1973). Black women in a racist society. In Charles Willie, Bernard Kramer, & Bertram Brown (Eds.), *Racism and mental health* (pp. 185–268). Pittsburgh: University of Pittsburgh Press.

Jackson, Jacquelyne Johnson. (1981). *Suicide and homicide trends of blacks, United States, 1964–1978.* Paper presented at a seminar on Violence among Blacks, Washington, DC, Howard University.

Jackson, Jacquelyne Johnson. (1982). Death rate trends of black females, United States, 1964–1978. In Estelle Ramey & Phyliss Bergman (Eds.), *The health of women.* Bethesda, MD: National Institutes of Health.

Jackson, Jacquelyne Johnson, and Perry, Charlotte. (1989). Physical health conditions of middle-aged and aged blacks. In Kyriakos Markides (Ed.), *Health conditions of middle-aged and aged persons* (pp. 111–176). Newbury Park, CA: Sage Publications.

Kardiner, Abram, and Ovesey, Lionel. (1951). *The mark of oppression.* New York: Norton.

Kirk, Alton R. (1976). *Socio-psychological factors in attempted suicide among urban black males.* Unpublished doctoral dissertation, Michigan State University, East Lansing.

Lilienfeld, Abraham M. (1976). *Foundations of epidemiology.* New York: Oxford University Press.

Monk, Mary. (1975). Epidemiology. In Seymour Perlin (Ed.), *A Handbook for the study of suicide* (pp. 185–211). New York: Oxford University Press.

National Center for Health Statistics. (1970–1989). *Vital statistics of the United States,* vol. II, *Mortality, Part A. Public Health Service.* Washington DC: U.S. Government Printing Office.

Simpson, George (Ed. and trans.), & Spaulding, John A. (Trans.). (1951). *Suicide by Emile Durkheim, A study in sociology.* New York: The Free Press.

Stockwell, Edward G. (1976). *The methods and materials of demography* (cond. ed.). New York: Academic Press.

U.S. Bureau of the Census. (1980–1986). Current Population Reports, Series P–20. *Marital status and living arrangements: March 1980, March 1981, March 1982, March 1983, March 1984, March 1985, and March 1986*. Washington, DC: U.S. Government Printing Office.

U.S. Department of Health and Human Services. (1988). *First data book, A mortality study of one million persons by demographic, social, and economic factors: 1979–1981 follow-up, U.S. National Longitudinal Mortality Study* (NIH Publication No. 88–2896). Bethesda, MD: National Institutes of Health.

PART III

RACISM AND MENTAL HEALTH

6

BLACK MENTAL HEALTH AND RACIAL OPPRESSION

Joycelyn Landrum-Brown

INTRODUCTION

This chapter reviews the various ways in which racial oppression has impacted the mental health functioning of black Americans. In addition, practical strategies for coping with these impacts are presented. It is well documented that American society is a sexist, racist, classist, and ageist society (Bennett, 1966; Jordan, 1968; Kovel, 1970; Jones, 1972; Kerner Commission, 1968; Schwartz and Disch, 1970; Terry, 1970; Knowles and Prewitt, 1969; McConahay, Hardee & Batts, 1981; McConahay & Hough, 1976). Furthermore, many scholars view racism as a primary mental health problem in American society (Wright, 1975; Akbar, 1981; Willie, Kramer, & Brown, 1973). "Racism is an infection of the belief system, a mental illness with the following symptoms: 1) perceptual distortion, 2) denial of reality, 3) delusions of grandeur, 4) projections of blame (to the victim), 5) phobic reactions to differences" (Hilliard, 1978, p. 2).

Much has been written about the impacts of racial oppression on the psychological well-being of black people. Differing perspectives on the problem have produced a variety of theories regarding what the impacts of racial oppression are and what black mental health entails. Nevertheless, it appears that racism negatively affects the mental health functioning of both blacks and whites in American society (Fanon, 1968; Kovel, 1970; Freire, 1981; Terry, 1970; Jones, 1972; Akbar, 1984; Comer, 1980; Welsing, 1974).

In many ways, Western psychology, having evolved in a racist cultural system, has failed to provide a full and accurate understanding of black mental health. As a result, traditional Western mental health models have also failed to set standards that would validate the experiences of black Americans and provide effective coping strategies for adapting to a racist environment. When imposed on racially and culturally different groups, the standards of normality and mental health developed in Euro-American societies typically result in those groups being perceived as deviant or mentally ill (Kardiner & Ovesey, 1951, 1968; Karon, 1975; Wilcox, 1971). Blacks who think, feel, and act like Europeans are defined as normal and healthy and are subsequently rewarded with more educational and professional opportunities. The more a black person thinks, feels, and acts differently from a European, the more likely it is that he or she will be considered a troublemaker, a deviant, a sociopath, or a schizophrenic; such persons are typically punished for such behaviors. As a result, there has been a concerted effort to rehabilitate, correct, modify, break, and resocialize many of the so-called deviant behaviors which have been and still are critical to the survival of black Americans (Akbar, 1981). These "rehabilitation" practices, which started in the days of slavery, are maintained today through various forms of psychological conditioning, for example, the media, educational institutions, and incarceration.

In terms of mental health, it becomes clear that black people will never be able to develop optimal psychological functioning and affirm their cultural heritage and identity, as long as they are relating to the world through an anti-African, anti-self cultural perspective. American society, which is European in perspective, is anti-African in that it devalues African cultural heritage and perspectives and regards them as inferior to American cultural perspectives. It is anti-self for black Americans because it devalues them to the degree that they deviate from Euro-American standards and norms culturally and physically.

RACIAL OPPRESSION

While there are other forms of systemic oppression operating in American society that may also impact the mental health functioning of black Americans, the focus of this chapter is on racial oppression.

Racial oppression involves the mistreatment of a group of people because of their racial differentness or "perceived" racial inferiority. It may be overt or covert, intentional or unintentional. In general, racial oppression takes the form of mistreatment or abuse directed at those who are racially different: (1) physical abuse, (2) mental abuse, (3) emotional abuse, and (4) spiritual abuse. Any of these kinds of abuse might result in psychological damage that could impact the mental health functioning of a people. More specifically, abusive behaviors can include beating, torture, sexual assault, degradation, manipulation, deception, belittlement, intimidation, patronization, threats, infliction of fear, withholding of resources, refusal to take one seriously, discrediting, devaluation, misleading, making light of or minimizing feelings and needs, responding inconsistently or arbitrarily, making vague demands, stifling growth, and giving messages that one "should not feel angry."

Although some of these behaviors are overtly abusive and others are covertly abusive, all can be psychologically damaging. Even though racial oppression can be very damaging psychologically it is important to remember that it is only one of many interacting influences within the environment that can impact the mental health functioning of black Americans. It seems more realistic to consider that black psychological and mental health functioning is the result of the interaction of at least four main factors: (1) the influence of traditional African culture and heritage, (2) the influence of African-American culture and heritage, (3) the influence of European-American culture and heritage (including racism, sexism, and classism), and (4) the individual's personal attributes, capabilities, and limitations and his or her life experiences, relationships, and available resources within the family, group, and community systems.

In many instances the impacts of racial oppression are buffered by positive and supportive influences. Therefore, racial oppression tends to impact different individuals in different ways to different degrees.

IMPACTS OF RACIAL OPPRESSION

The impacts of racial oppression manifest themselves in various ways in regard to the mental health functioning of black Americans, including internalized racial oppression, conceptual imposition and incarceration, split-self syndrome, and inability to identify and utilize internal or external resources and support systems.

Internalized Racial Oppression

When blacks attempt to adapt to a racially oppressive environment, many frustrations must be constructively managed. Adaptation to racial oppression takes many forms; some are adaptive, others are dysfunctional. The responses are dysfunctional when there are more effective alternative strategies available or when they are used as an excuse to avoid taking reponsibility for one's own growth and concerns. These dysfunctional responses are similar to defense mechanisms in that they represent ways of sabotaging oneself or avoiding dealing effectively with problems.

Internalized racial oppression (Landrum & Batts, 1985) is a psychological response exhibited by racially different individuals to the negative messages inherent in racism. It involves the internalization or acceptance of racially oppressive messages transmitted by those who are racially different. A person may or may not be consciously aware of these reponses. At some level, however, the person accepts the message enough to have to defend against it psychologically.

Landrum and Batts (1985) outlined several forms of internalized racial oppression responses: (1) system beating, which involves getting over on or acting out against the system; (2) blaming the system, which involves not taking any responsibility for one's actions; (3) total avoidance and rejection of whites and the Euro-American system, evidenced as anti-white separatism; (4) denial of blackness and African heritage, including distrusting blacks, devaluing African culture, and overvaluing and accepting whites as superior; and (5) denial of the political significance of race and racism, including attempts to buy and earn acceptance, such as conspicuous consumption of material goods, and using status and educational degrees to elevate one's self-worth; self- and group sabotage, involving passivity, misdirected anger, in-group fighting, learned helplessness, and escape through drugs, food, sex, and sleep; and cultural alienation and identity conflict.

All of these forms are reactions to the racial oppression experienced in various situations. By reacting instead of acting proactively, the individual is ultimately controlled by the racism he or she experiences. Individuals may believe that they have made healthy choices in their responses to racial oppression; however, very often, a closer examination reveals that although the choices may have been good ones, they were made for the wrong reasons (e.g., "I'll prove I'm somebody; I'll get a Ph.D"). On the other hand, a choice might have been made out of an inappropriate anger response (e.g., "If I can't get a legitimate job, then I'll sell drugs"). In knowing one's self, one is less likely to allow negative societal messages to become internalized. By identifying and eliminating one's internalized racial oppression responses one is less likely to cooperate with the racially oppressive forces that they believe they are struggling against.

Conceptual Imposition and Incarceration

Conceptual imposition involves the forced imposition of one group's or individual's conceptual framework or worldview on another group or individual. When one is conceptually incarcerated (Nobles, 1978), one is able to see reality only through an imposed and culturally different perspective or worldview. The concept of worldview is defined as the way in which an individual or group perceives reality. A worldview sets up a framework by which one perceives and relates to the world and reality. It includes perceptions regarding nature, the self, other people, institutions, objects, the cosmos, and the creator. One's worldview is influenced by memories, expectations, assumptions, beliefs, attitudes, values, interests, past experiences, strong feelings, and prejudices. An example of conceptual imposition and incarceration in black Americans can be seen in the imposition and internalization of white, Anglo-Saxon, Protestant standards for viewing reality, using language, and making life-style choices. Black Americans are oftentimes punished in various ways for deviating from these standards. They are conceptually incarcerated because they are forced to respond to the world through a perspective that is alien and anti-self, and they are punished for perceiving and responding to the world differently. In addition, they may be conceptually incarcerated because they are unable to see the world in different ways that would be more psychologically self-affirming. In these ways, conceptual imposition and incarceration become forms of racial and cultural oppression. This concept is broader than internalized racial oppression because it encompasses a wider range of cultural variables other than race.

There are many ways to conceptualize the same basic reality. One way of perceiving is not necessarily better or worse than another way. While one way of viewing reality may be better for one person or group at a particular time for a particular situation, it may not necessarily be globally better for all people in all situations. The important point is that there are alternative ways of viewing reality which may be equally effective, functional, and adaptive.

Split-self Syndrome

The split-self syndrome is a result of accepting a polarized, hierarchical manner of thinking and accepting negative racial messages. It is a symptom that may result from internalized racial oppression or conceptual incarceration. Polarized thinking, characterized by "either/or" or "all or none" thinking, leads to a psychological ego defense referred to as "splitting" in object relations theory (Kernberg, 1976; Blanck & Blanck, 1974; Wilber, 1979). The "splitting off" or drawing of boundary lines within the self is accomplished by alienating the undesirable parts, repressing them, or projecting them, until the self-image is narrowed down to the acceptable and desirable parts. Hierarchical thinking leads to a continual comparison of aspects of self which are perceived as being better or worse than others. For blacks exhibiting this response, the evaluation and comparison of self are made against white standards.

In terms of psychological and mental health functioning, either/or thinking leaves out a whole spectrum of alternative perspectives. In either/or or "better than/less than" thinking, the world is seen as a multitude of incompatible dichotomies, and it may result in limiting one's coping responses to various situations. As a result, people, personal attributes, and events are seen as being either good or bad, rather than as having both good and bad aspects. This kind of dichotomized thinking may result in distorted self-perceptions that occur when certain devalued parts of one's self are alienated or split off from conscious awareness. This alienated or split-off self often represents the "bad me." For black Americans living in a society which devalues blackness and Africanness, the alienated or split-off self may represent their black identity (the "black me") or their African cultural heritage (the "African me"). The splitting appears to be the result of having internalized negative messages about their racial differences and the result of a desire to disown those differences in order to feel accepted and valued.

Disuse of Resources and Support Systems

Many mental health concerns arise when there are insufficient internal and external resources to cope with them. This insufficiency may result from a lack of awareness, non-use, or misuse of available resources. It is important that individuals learn to avail themselves of internal and external resources in order to manage their life-styles more effectively and to cope with racist and stressful environments. Internal resources involve personal strengths, coping skills, and strategies. External resources include family, friends, and organizational, institutional, and community support systems.

All environments and situations make certain demands on individuals, and to cope effectively with these demands an individual needs a variety of resources. For black Americans, racial oppression brings a special demand characteristic into most of their situational and environmental encounters. This demand characteristic involves having to discrimate whether or not racial oppression is a salient factor in those encounters and knowing how to cope constructively. Therefore, it is essential that black Americans have the internal and external resources that will help them cope with the demands and stresses inherent in racial oppression. The development of internal and external resources may serve to buffer the impact of racially oppressive situations.

Effective coping skills and strategies provide individuals with the ability to withstand difficult and frustrating situations, with minimal damage to self-esteem and sense of worth. Some adaptive coping skills include assertiveness, problem-solving and decision-making strategies, stress management, and anger management. As far as external resources are concerned, social support systems are a powerful mechanism for assuring that basic needs are met and for giving individual members a sense of validation and belonging as well as an open information network that could provide a potential direction for self-determination and psychological growth. Community, social, political, and religious organizations provide very effective support systems for black Americans. In addition, the black extended family system has been one of the institutions most significant to the survival of black Americans as a people. These support systems have also often provided the essential networks that have been helpful in continuing the dissemination of information regarding African cultural traditions and customs, historical perspectives, and philosophies that have provided an alternative world-view and mental health perspective.

THEORETICAL MODELS OF MENTAL HEALTH FUNCTIONING

Western Assumptions and Mental Health Models

Traditional Western conceptualizations of mental health have been a reflection of the Western philosophical paradigms that form the basis of Western psychology (Clark, McGee, Nobles, & Weems, 1975). The predominant paradigms of Western psychology in the twentieth century have been based on materialistic, mechanistic, hierarchical, reductionistic, and dualistic philosophical assumptions (Leahey, 1980). Hierarchical thinking operates in order to establish and maintain power imbalances derived from comparisons based on better than or less than judgments. Mechanistic philosophies assume that humankind and the universe operate in a linear, single cause–single effect manner. Materialistic philosophies propose that what is real is only that which can be perceived by the senses or by physical instruments. A reductionistic paradigm makes the assumption that all aspects of phenomena can be understood by reducing them to their smallest parts. Cartesian dualism results in a mental act of separating complementary aspects of a unified whole.

It appears that many mental health practitioners have been trapped by the conceptual limitations of their training in Western scientific thought (Nobles, 1972; Smith, 1974; Nichols, 1974). The result is a practitioner who is inflexible and unable to view reality from a perspective that is different from that prescribed by his or her profession. In addition, it results in a scientist/practitioner who is unable to view the world from a holistic, interrelated perspective, who ultimately sees only part of the picture.

Charles Tart (1975) suggested some examples of orthodox Western psychology assumptions: (1) humans are their body and nothing more; (2) humans are essentially independent from their surrounding environments; (3) each human is isolated from all others, locked within his or her own nervous system; (4) psychological energy is completely derived from physical energy, as expressed in physiological processes in the body; (5) humans have no function in a purposeless universe; (6) a healthy personality is one which allows the individual to be well-adjusted in terms of his or her culture; (7) since emotions interfere with logical reasoning and make individuals irrational, they should generally be suppressed or eliminated; (8) developing the logical mind, one's reasoning ability, is the highest accomplishment a person can aim for; (9) there is no reason or purpose for the existence of the universe; (10) what is real is what can be perceived by the senses or by a physical instrument; and (11) Western civilization is the greatest civilization that ever existed on this planet.

It is apparent from looking at these examples that these assumptions, inherent in orthodox Western psychology, are in conflict with holistic, spiritual, synthesis-forming philosophical perspectives. Therefore, any mental health system or model formulated on the basis of these assumptions would be in conflict with a holistic, spiritual model for mental health functioning.

M. Jahoda (1958) considered the criteria for mental health to involve (1) positive attitudes of the individual toward himself, (2) the degree to which the person realizes his or her potential through action, (3) the unification of functioning of the individual's personality, (4) the individual's degree of independence from social influences, (5) how the individual sees the world, and (6) the ability to take life as it comes and master it. A. H. Maslow (1954) viewed mental health as the tendency to actualize one's potentials; E. H. Erikson (1968) considered the psychodynamic notions of identity and ego strength to be crucial to any definition of mental health functioning. These definitions do not seem faulty in themselves; they are limited only in that they focus on individual psychological concerns and do not focus on a holistic perspective of well-being that considers healthy social, spiritual relationships or harmonious environmental relationships.

On the other hand, J. C. Coleman (1972) suggested that there was no "ideal model'' or even a ''normal model'' of humankind that could be used as a basis for comparing people. Coleman further indicated that the concepts of normal and abnormal are meaningful only with reference to a given culture. In other words, individuals are normal if they conform to societal expectations. With this definition there is some question whether ''normal behavior'' could be considered to be mentally healthy. For example, although racist and sexist attitudes prevail and appear to be the norm in American society, it is questionable whether these attitudes and beliefs foster growing relationships and mentally healthy worldviews.

Models of Black Psychological Functioning

Several models have been developed concerning the psychological functioning and mental health status of black Americans. Within the last four decades, an extensive literature has emerged that has proposed a social pathology model of black behavior and psychological functioning (Dreger & Miller, 1960, 1968; Kardiner & Ovesey, 1951, 1968; Pettigrew, 1964; Wilcox, 1971; Grier & Cobbs, 1968). In general, the social pathology model literature reflects an assessment of the degree to which blacks have deviated from the beliefs, attitudes, and behavioral styles that Euro-American culture has defined as normal and mentally healthy. This model tends to regard all black behavior in terms relative to Euro-American life-styles. Black behavior is seen as a reaction to racial oppression, rather than in a more holistic context which considers other factors as being influential. This model of black behavior and psychological functioning has been challenged by black researchers (Baratz & Baratz, 1969; Clark, 1972; Clark et al., 1975; Weems, 1974; Nobles, 1972; Akbar, 1981).

Black Mental Health Models

It is apparent that effective mental health functioning involves more than the absence of dysfunctional adaptations. R. Wilcox (1971) proposed a definition of positive mental health from a black perspective: (1) a conscious awareness that this society is hostile to one's existence; (2) an awareness of the stress of racial oppression; (3) the ability to deal with superordinates; (4) the lack of desire to oppress or to be oppressed; (5) a need to be involved in shaping and controlling one's own destiny; (6) a steady involvement in self-confrontation; (7) being steeped in an identity of one's own culture, history, and values; (8) a basic knowledge of the society's destructive characteristics (i.e., racism, sexism, classism, materialism); (9) an ability to perceive the humanity of oppressed people; and (10) the desire to think, feel, and act in a single motion—not to fragment oneself into emotion, intelligence, and action.

Another alternative criterion for optimal mental health in black populations has been developed by Na'im Akbar (1981). This conceptualization views normality as a oneness of the self and others and the consequent display of humanistic or natural behaviors. Mental health is considered to be the affirmative identification and commitment of one's African (natural) identity.

With the development of this conceptualization there appears to be a return to a more holistic kind of mental health system that was inherent within the philosophical traditions of the Africans in ancient Egypt. Within this system, psychological functioning not only involves the mental and emotional processes but also considers the spiritual aspect of human beings to be an essential part of mental health (James, 1976; Hilliard, 1983). "Reality for the ancient Africans was always conceived as the synthesis of the visible and the invisible, the material and immaterial, the cognitive and emotive, the inner and outer" (Nobles, 1986, p. 36).

Another model for optimal mental health functioning for black people appears to be represented in the African worldview and Afrocentric personality models (Nobles, 1980). The African worldview incorporates a framework for reality that involves a spiritual perspective and sees the interrelationship of all things through the oneness of the spirit, striving for harmony with nature, and stresses a group or collective perspective. In contrast, a Eurocentric worldview incorporates a more material perspective, categorizes and separates objects, strives for mastery over nature, and stresses an individual perspective.

Wade Nobles (1986) proposes that normal or natural psychological functioning for black people is represented by (1) a sense of self which is collective or extended, (2) an attitude wherein one understands and respects the sameness in one's self and others, (3) a clear sense of one's spiritual connection to the universe, (4) a sense of mutual responsibility, and (5) a conscious understanding that human abnormality or deviancy is any act that is in opposition to one's self, one's kind, or the creator's divine will.

One common factor in all these models is the holistic approach to perceiving and dealing with reality. This holistic approach seems tied to visualizing the interrelationships and spiritual connectedness of all things.

There appears to be a need for therapeutic models that would assist blacks in coping with racial oppression and its consequences. Several practical strategies and psychotherapeutic techniques that already exist could be adapted and incorporated into a holistic model. The following section presents some specific considerations and strategies that could be applied toward the development of optimal mental health functioning for black Americans living in a racially and culturally oppressive environment.

PRACTICAL STRATEGIES FOR COPING WITH THE IMPACTS OF RACIAL OPPRESSION

Importance of Self-knowledge in Mental Health Functioning

"Self-knowledge is the basis of all true knowledge" (James, 1976, p. 88). Self-knowledge is very important in mental health functioning because once individuals are aware of the truth about themselves, they will be able to understand why they are the way they are, to learn to love and accept themselves, and to develop strategies for changing those aspects of the self that are dysfunctional and hurtful. The degree to which an individual comes to know the self will be in direct proportion to the amount of truth that he or she can accept about who he or she is and how he or she relates to others. Individuals can learn a great deal about themselves by paying attention to the kinds of verbal and nonverbal interactions made within their relationships. In this way, one's relationships can teach one about the parts of oneself that one would like to deny or disown. Individuals can also learn much about themselves by watching and listening to themselves in their day-to-day interactions. This is not an easy process because many people do not really want to know the truth about themselves, especially the negative things.

There is much resistance to coming to terms with the negative aspects of one's self because most people do not want to feel insecure or uncomfortable. Taking an honest look at one's self puts one in the position of having to come to terms with some of one's more undesirable, unacceptable, and unlovable parts. However, by avoiding uncomfortable feelings, one also avoids opportunities for change and growth. Growth comes out of taking risks to be different and to change, and that rarely feels safe or comfortable at first.

Growth through self-exploration can be an unsettling process. It takes a real willingness to make a commitment to take the risk to look at one's self and to deal with the truth, no matter what one finds.

One of the biggest obstacles to growth is fear of the unknown, or what the change will mean in terms of expanded responsibilities. In some cases, people develop an attachment to suffering, to being oppressed, to hurting, to being victimized, to being abused, and to self-pity. This attachment to oppression is often based on an avoidance of taking responsibility for one's own healing and liberation. This may be related to a need to be taken care of by others and a desire to see others (or make others) solely responsible for one's oppression and problems. At a deeper level, attachment to oppression may be derived from a sense of inadequacy, a lack of confidence, a low self-esteem, and feelings of little worth. In many cases, the individual does not believe that he or she really deserves to feel better, to be liberated, to be happy, or to be successful. In general, it is important to look at how one's negative attitudes or internalized negative racial messages may be contributing to one's attachment to oppression. This is where the awareness and knowledge of self plays a crucial role.

Awareness is defined as the clarity with which one consciously and unconsciously perceives and understands the elements and events in one's life (Anthony, 1986). In many cases, one's level of awareness determines one's concept of reality. Awareness may limit or expand an individual's perceptions. By expanding awareness of oneself, the individual removes the distorted, biased, and faulty perceptions that would limit one's growth as a totally integrated, whole being.

If an individual has been programmed or socialized to believe false, distorted beliefs, then he or she will develop a belief system and life-style to justify and support those beliefs. When a person believes that something is true, whether or not it is, that individual will act as though it is true. The individual then collects facts and looks for cues in himself or herself, in others, and in the environment to support the beliefs no matter how false or irrational. In order to correct the distortion and false perceptions and beliefs, an individual must take a critical and honest look at himself or herself.

A critical look at one's self involves two components: a worldview analysis and a self-analysis. A worldview analysis helps individuals to examine their own personal reality schemes. This helps individuals to gain awareness of their assumptions, values, beliefs, and biases. A self-analysis helps individuals to examine their self-concepts, strengths, and weaknesses and their responses to situations and interactions with others.

One of the first steps in the self-analysis process is for one to give one's self permission to find out the truth about the self. It is important to observe the feelings that arise but not to condemn one's self. In this way, the individual will be empowered with the most accurate information about the self. It is also important to remember that the negative or positive descriptive connotations within the language may bias one's perceptions. As a result, it may be necessary to watch for value-laden connotations in one's self-descriptions.

One easy way to begin the self-analysis process is by developing a personal strengths and weaknesses list. The strengths and weaknesses should incorporate factors such as one's physical attributes and characteristics, personality, relationship styles and patterns, intellectual capabilities, and goal achievement capabilities, to give a few examples. This could be done by the individual and the significant others in his or her life. The two lists (strengths and weaknesses) should be as specific as possible. The next step is to make comparisons between the lists drawn up by the significant others and the individuals themselves and to look for similarities and differences. In making this comparison, the individual will want to add any items he or she may have overlooked and to make special note of those things that appeared on both lists.

An assessment is then made of the two lists, and the individual should consider his or her reasons for changing or not changing the things on the lists that have caused problems. It is important to note that strengths may also cause problems; for example, being a "nice person" can be a problem if being nice means allowing others to continue to oppress and abuse you. Some important questions to ask are (1) what am I getting out of staying the same?; (2) how am I being held back by not changing?; (3) what is my greatest fear about changing?; (4) which of these traits do I value and why?; (5) which traits do I have difficulty accepting and why?; (6) how do I handle the things about myself that I do not like? (do I forget them, deny them, admit them but do nothing, fight against them, try to change them?); (7) do I hold any false, distorted, or irrational beliefs about myself?; and (8) where did I learn them, and why do I hold on to them?

A variation of this self-exploratory exercise would involve the individual's making a list of all the positive and negative things that he or she has been told about himself or herself from various sources such as family, friends, teachers, significant others, the media, and enemies. The next step is to look at the messages that he or she has come to believe to be true (i.e., I have nappy hair; I'm ugly; I'm too dark; my nose is too big). These exercises provide additional information about the negative and positive messages about one's self that the individual has internalized.

From these exercises and the assessment questions, the individual can gain awareness of his or her available internal resources. Internal resources are the assets and skills that help one adapt, function effectively, identify external resources, and give a sense of well-being. In addition, the individual can determine what kinds of resources he or she needs to develop. Hopefully, the individual will gain some insight into why he or she believes what he or she does and how and from whom it was learned.

Healing Process

The healing process for black Americans living in a racially oppressive society requires letting go of any distorted and false, anti-self, anti-African messages that they have internalized. One strategy involves assisting individuals in the process of accepting and embracing the alienated parts of themselves. This is done by owning the alienated parts when they become apparent. Another strategy helps individuals to restructure their thoughts and perceptions in order to reduce the amount of distorted information that they have internalized. This is accomplished by checking one's thoughts and perceptions against all possible alternative perspectives.

One of the first concerns in helping blacks accept and embrace their alienated African/black selves is to identify the parts of themselves that they have split off utilizing polarized and hierarchical thinking. The task of therapy in these cases is to help individuals understand and work through their resistance to accepting the unwanted parts of themselves.

For black Americans, this therapeutic process would involve helping them understand why they have rejected or dislike various parts (e.g., hair texture, physical features, cultural heritage) and helping them learn to embrace and see the value in those various things. For some blacks, the splitting off takes place at a different level. In these cases, individuals may see themselves as separate, different from, and better than other black people. A similar therapeutic process would take place to help them understand why they have rejected other blacks and help them learn to accept and value the cultural and racial differences that they have rejected. The healing process helps foster learning that most things in life are not all or none, either/or, but both/and.

The healing process involves learning to embrace all parts of one's self.

Through the healing process, the self becomes more integrated. This is accomplished by using therapeutic techniques that allow one to restructure one's way of thinking about one's self, others, and reality in a way that is holistic and incorporates all aspects in an interrelated, integrated fashion. To rediscover and heal one's whole self is an ongoing process involving (1) identifying one's core spiritual self and one's psychological, emotional, and physical selves by prayer, meditation, objective self-observation, and self-monitoring); (2) understanding and working through the causes of the splitting by grieving the losses, hurt, and trauma and by venting the rage and anger; (3) identifying, accepting, and reclaiming the alienated parts of one's self and one's way of being in the world; (4) discovering and practicing being one's whole self, first with those who support and validate the individual's whole self, then later with those who might be oppositional; and (5) continuing the process of increasing awareness of the physical, mental, emotional, and spiritual aspects of one's whole self, in addition to increasing awareness of one's social, spiritual, and environmental relationships.

Becoming aware of one's feelings and dealing with them honestly and constructively are crucial to the healing process. Feelings can be used as cues to what one is saying to one's self about one's self, others, and the world around one. To utilize feelings in the healing process, first one has to give one's self permission to experience one's feelings. Next, one must believe that it is all right to have and experience them. Finally, one must trust one's self enough to believe that one will not lose self-control. In many cases, black Americans have been given messages that it is not all right to have certain feelings and to express them. Messages are given that it is not acceptable to feel and express that racism is part of a problem that one is experiencing. If a feeling is expressed, it may be invalidated, ignored, or criticized.

Feelings are a part of one's whole self, and they must be acknowledged, accepted, and expressed in constructive and appropriate ways. When one denies one's feelings, one denies a part of one's whole self. Denial of feelings contributes to and maintains self-alienation. When one denies, distorts, represses, or suppresses one's feelings, one does not get rid of them; one just blocks their natural outlet. Eventually, feelings find their way out through other inappropriate ways, such as illness, hurting others, or hurting one's self. It is important to remember that feelings are emotional responses; an individual is not his or her feelings. One does not have to be controlled by one's feelings; one can observe them and make choices about what to share, how much, when, and with whom.

An effective way to facilitate identifying and experiencing feelings is to begin to express them to those who will support and encourage their expression. It might be necessary to start by expressing less threatening feelings at first, with the eventual goal of being able to express appropriately both threatening and non-threatening feelings. An individual should remember that it is not always appropriate or constructive to share feelings with everyone. However, it is helpful to know what one is feeling whether one chooses to express it or not. It is important to be able to identify the times when it is appropriate and constructive to express one's feelings.

When looking at the impacts of racial oppression, it is important to understand how to express, constructively and appropriately, the feeling of anger. Anger is a natural, frequently occurring response to racial oppression. When one has not learned to express anger appropriately, it is often misdirected. Anger has maladaptive and adaptive functions. It can energize coping activity or disrupt information processing and problem-solving efforts. It can serve as a cue that something is wrong, or it can instigate aggressive behavior. Anger can be effectively managed by learning to identify things that provoke anger responses and by preparing to handle them constructively or to avoid them. Anger can also be managed effectively by learning to express it assertively when the provoking situation occurs. If the situation is not conducive to the appropriate and constructive expression of an anger response, then the individual must find a constructive way to express the anger, for example, exercise or some other physical activity, talking about it, or writing it out. The important thing is not to let it build up and fester until it is inappropriately directed or causes illness.

When one has learned how to choose constructively and appropriately which feelings to express, when to express them, how to express them, and to whom to express them, the individual becomes emotionally liberated. When one can transform one's way of being in the world to be more in harmony with others and nature and to be more in line with the creator's divine plan, then one will be spiritually liberated. When one comes to accept and love those aspects of one's physical self that one cannot change and to feel good about one's self whether or not one changes the aspects that one does not like but could change, then one will be physically liberated. When one learns how to monitor and reconstruct one's worldview and way of being in the world into an approach that is more psychologically self-affirming, then one will become conceptually liberated. All of these forms of liberation are necessary for one to be truly free in a holistic sense.

Conceptual Liberation

When persons become conceptually liberated they free themselves from the conceptual restraints that bind their capacities for becoming self-determining and self-affirming. Conceptual liberation involves restructuring personal perceptions and thoughts in ways that will counter distorted and false beliefs, assumptions, and messages that lead to negative self-perceptions, anti-self perspectives, and a fragmented worldview. The restructuring process helps individuals to construct buffers against the negative psychological messages that are inherent in racism. Many of these internalized negative messages contribute to assertiveness problems, depression, stress, and destructive expressions of anger.

In order to restructure perceptions and thoughts, persons must first become aware of what they are. This process involves listening to what one says to one's self about self, others, situations, and the experiences in one's life. When one becomes clear about the ways in which self and others are perceived, and the ways in which situations and experiences are interpreted, then one is in a better position to evaluate whether those perceptions are valid, distorted, or faulty. If it is determined that the perceptions are invalid, distorted, or faulty, these perceptions should be restructured to fit the truth more accurately. This process involves questioning one's perceptions and checking to determine whether there are other possible ways to perceive situations. One literally talks one's self out of believing that one's hair is "bad hair," and one talks one's self into perceiving both the positive and negative attributes of one's hair texture, being careful not to compare one's hair against an imposed standard for what "good hair" is like. In addition, one must work through the emotionally charged messages and memories that have come to be associated with having "bad hair."

It should be considered that learning to manage one's thoughts and perceptions in order to minimize the negative impacts of racial oppression involves changing long-standing patterns of thinking that may have become habitual. The process is an ongoing one that takes time, practice, and effort to be effective. Negative and anti-self thinking often becomes an unconscious habit which can be broken.

Perceptual restructuring and conceptual liberation within a holistic framework would allow individuals to see the good and bad aspects in themselves, others, events, and situations. These perceptions would not be evaluated in terms of a better than/worse than perspective, but in ways that would allow individuals to make more objective responses that would incorporate both aspects. By seeing all aspects individuals would perceive obstacles, frustrations, and problems as opportunities for growth toward self-development rather than as barriers. A key question for individuals to ask themselves is "Is there another way to look at this situation, person, event?"

Coping with Internalized Racial Oppression

As stated before, becoming aware of negative internalized messages and one's responses to them are the first steps toward coping with internalized racial oppression. Coping with internalized racial oppression involves making constructive, growthful, and proactive choices regarding responses to threatening situations, rather than reactionary responses. It involves choosing not to cooperate with one's oppression by (1) finding and utilizing opportunities to empower oneself and one's people; (2) taking responsibility for one's problems when it is warranted; (3) learning not to sabotage oneself and one's group; (4) not buying into negative racial messages (e.g., antiwhite or antiblack); (5) not basing one's self-worth on performance, degrees, status, prestige, or the amount of money or material goods that one has acquired; (6) learning to love one's self and the black people enough to be self-affirming and supportive; (7) being able to take a positive, assertive, and constructive stand against anti-self and negative messages; (8) spending money wisely; (9) learning to deal with anger constructively and appropriately; and (10) exploring African and black American philosophies, history, and cultural heritage.

Identifying and Utilizing Resources

Becoming aware of and overcoming conceptual imposition and incarceration, the split-self syndrome, and internalized racial oppression are initial steps to coping with the impacts of racial oppression. These steps are individual ones and form the foundation upon which additional internal resources such as coping skills can be established. Coping skills include (1) assertiveness training, (2) stress management strategies, (3) communication and interpersonal skills, (4) anger management strategies, (5) spiritual growth and development approaches, (6) physical well-being and health maintenance strategies, and (7) problem-solving and decision-making skills.

In addition to these skills, perception and thought-restructuring techniques are useful coping strategies that allow individuals to monitor and control their perception of threatening and stressful events in order to remain calm enough to make good decisions, to engage in effective problem-solving strategies, and to overcome various obstacles or barriers that might be presented. Perception restructuring is a key factor in reducing the negative thoughts that are associated with and contribute to states of depression. In many cases, just changing the way in which one perceives a situation can influence how one feels. If one focuses on the negative aspects of a situation and discounts the positive aspects, and continues to do this in a habitual way, he or she will feel hopeless and depressed.

Perception and thought restructuring is also critical in stress management strategies where distorted thinking can influence one's perceptions of how threatening the stressor actually is. Racial oppression is a stressor in the lives of black Americans because it is stressful to live under the threat that one's opportunities might be unjustifiably blocked or one's life ended because one is black. In learning to deal with the stress of racial oppression, blacks need to be able to assess objectively when the threat is real, how much of a threat is involved, and whether factors other than race (e.g., class, age, sex) are involved. If it is determined that the individual is in effect stressed out when it is not justified, then other measures may be taken, for example, perceptual restructuring, relaxation strategies, exercise, and other tension-releasing activities or the support and validation of others.

In addition, an individual's perceptions, beliefs, and thoughts can play a major role in whether an individual is assertive. Donald Cheek (1976) has suggested that assertive behavior for black people must be adjusted to meet the demands of the situation, especially when blacks deal with whites who are not familiar with black communication styles. Cheek suggests that, for blacks, the best definition of assertiveness is an honest, open, and direct, verbal or nonverbal expression which does not have the intent of putting someone down. Within this model of assertiveness, it is important that blacks make conscious efforts to choose the most appropriate assertive message, one that would take into account cultural communication style differences.

It is crucially important that black Americans also identify, develop, and utilize their available external resources such as community, friendship, familial, and organizational support systems and networks. Identifying and utilizing both internal and external resources and support systems will provide additional coping strategies for self and group empowerment which will lead toward overcoming the impacts of racial oppression and improving the mental health functioning of black Americans.

SUMMARY

It has been shown that black people are racially oppressed in many ways in American society. As a result, there appear to be some important impacts of racial oppression that need to be considered when looking at the mental health functioning of black Americans. This is not to say that racial oppression is the only or even the most important factor to consider when looking at the psychological functioning of black Americans, but it is one factor. Although there are mediating factors which might limit and reduce the impact of racial oppression, the mental health functioning of many black Americans has been affected in at least one of four ways. The first way involves the amount of racially oppressive messages that has been internalized. The second way involves the extent to which the worldview and conceptualizations of black Americans have been defined, imposed, and limited by the philosophical assumptions and language structure and connotations in American society. The third way considers the negative impacts of anti-self, antiblack, anti-African cultural messages on the self-perceptions of black Americans. The final way involves the extent to which blacks have been limited in the awareness of and the development of the internal and external resources and support systems necessary to combat the racially oppressive forces in American society.

It is important to be aware of the ways in which dysfunctional responses to racial oppression get in the way of black people being able to organize, collaborate, network, mentor, and support one another. Black mental health workers, educators, and students need to learn to identify, understand, and overcome the dysfunctional impacts of racial oppression.

In general, some key factors in developing optimal black mental health should involve (1) liberation from dysfunctional internalized racial oppression responses and conceptual incarceration; (2) self-transformation through self-awareness, self-acceptance, self-determination, self-mastery (involving the control and discipline over the dysfunctional aspects of self), and self-actualization (through physical, mental, emotional, and spiritual growth); and (3) the development of internal and external resources for self and group empowerment through the use of coping skills and strategies; community, family, friend, and organizational support systems; and the development of positive relationships, socially, spiritually, and environmentally.

Overall, optimally functioning black persons are not driven by dysfunctional responses to internalized racial oppression. They are not limited by the conceptual restraints of an imposed, anti-self worldview. They are not alienated from parts of themselves or from their African heritage and culture. They are not limited in their awareness of available internal and external resources; and they can use these resources for adaptive, healthy, and growthful psychological functioning.

Greater awareness of the various negative impacts of racial oppression and their consequences, combined with a commitment to be liberated, will enable black Americans to empower themselves in ways that will truly allow for the development of optimal mental health.

REFERENCES

Akbar, Na'im. (1981) Mental disorder among African-Americans. *Black Books Bulletin*, 7(2).

Akbar, Na'im. (1984). *Chains and images of psychological slavery*. Jersey City, NJ: New Mind Productions.

Anthony, Robert. (1986). *Total self-confidence*. New York: Berkley Books.

Baratz, J. C., & Baratz, S. S. (1969). *The social pathology model: Historical basis for psychology's denial of the existence of Negro culture*. Washington, DC: American Psychological Association Paper.

Bennett, L. (1966). *Before the Mayflower: History of the Negro in America, 1619–1964*. New York: Macmillan.

Blanck, G. & Blanck, R. (1974). *Ego psychology: Theory and practice*. New York: Columbia University Press.

Cheek, Donald K. (1976). *Assertive black . . . puzzled white: A black perspective on assertive behavior*. San Luis Obispo, CA: Impact Publishers, Inc.

Clark, C. X. (1972). Black studies or the study of black people? In R. L. Jones (Ed.), *Black psychology*. New York: Harper and Row.

Clark, C. X., McGee, D. P., Nobles, W. W., & Weems, L. X. (1975). Voodoo or I.Q.: An introduction to African psychology. *Journal of Black Psychology*, 1(2), 9–29.

Coleman, J. C. (1972). *Abnormal psychology and modern life* (5th ed.). Glenview, IL: Scott, Foresman and Co.

Comer, J. P. (1980). White racism: Its root, form and function. In R. L. Jones (Ed.), *Black psychology* (2d ed.). New York: Harper and Row Publishers.

Dreger, R. M., & Miller, K. S. (1960). Comparative psychological studies of Negroes and whites in the United States. *Psychological Bulletin, 57*, 361–402.

Dreger, R. M., & Miller, K. S. (1968). Comparative psychological studies of Negroes and whites in the United States: 1959–1965. *Psychological Bulletin Monograph*, Vol. 70.

Erikson, E. H. (1968). *Identity, youth, and crisis*. New York: W. W. Norton.

Fanon, F. (1968). *The wretched of the earth*. New York: Grove.

Freire, Paulo. (1981). *Pedagogy of the oppressed*. New York: The Continuum Publishing Corporation.

Grier, W. H., & Cobbs, P. M. (1968). *Black rage*. New York: Basic Books.

Hilliard, A. (1978). *Return to the source: African origins of western civilization*. Unpublished resource bibliography.

Hilliard, A. (1983). *Return to the source: African origins of western civilization*. Presentation at Ohio State University.

Jahoda, M. (1958). *Current concepts of positive mental health*. New York: Basic Books.

James, G. G. M. (1954, 1976). *Stolen legacy*. San Francisco: Julian Richardson Associates.

Jones, J. (1972). *Prejudice and racism*. Reading, MA: Addison-Wesley.

Jordan, W. (1968). *White over black: American attitudes toward the Negro: 1550–1812*. Baltimore, MD: Penguin Books.

Kardiner, A., & Ovesey, L. (1951). *The mark of oppression*. New York: Norton.

Kardiner, A., & Ovesey, L. (1968). On the psychodynamics of the Negro Personality. In G. Gordon & K. Gergen (Eds.), *The self in social interaction*. New York: Wiley.

Karon, Bertram P. (1975). *Black scars: A rigorous investigation of the effects of discrimination*. New York: Springer Publishing Co.

Kernberg, O. F. (1976). *Object-relations theory and clinical psychoanalysis*. New York: Jason Aronson.

Kerner Commission. (1968). *National advisory commission on civil rights*. New York: Bantom.

Knowles, L., & Prewit, K. (Eds.). (1969). *Institutional racism in America*. Englewood Cliffs, NJ: Prentice-Hall.

Kovel, J. (1970). *White racism: A psychohistory*. New York: Vintage Books.

Landrum, J. & Batts, V. (1985). *Helping blacks cope with and overcome the personal effects of racism*. Paper presented at the annual meeting of the American Psychological Association Convention, Los Angeles, CA.

Landrum, J. & Batts, V. A. (1985). *Internalized racial oppression*. Unpublished working paper, Virginia Commonwealth University, Richmond.

Leahey, Thomas H. (1980). *A history of psychology*. Englewood Cliffs, NJ: Prentice-Hall.

Maslow, A. H. (1954). *Motivation and personality*. New York: Harper and Row.

McConahay, J. B., Hardee, B. B., & Batts, V. A. (1981). Has racism declined in America? *Journal of Conflict Resolution, 25*(4), 563–579.

McConahay, J. B., & Hough, J. C. (1976). Symbolic racism. *Journal of Social Issues, 32*(2), 23–45.

Nicholas, E. (1974, February 22). Culture affects thought process. *Guidepost*, p. 7.

Nobles, W. W. (1972). African philosophy: Foundations for black psychology. In R. L. Jones (Ed.), *Black psychology*. New York: Harper & Row.

Nobles, W. W. (1973). Psychological research and the black self-concept: A critical review. *Journal of Social Issues, 29*, 11–31.

Nobles, W. W. (1978, February). *African consciousness and liberation struggles: Implications for the development and construction of scientific paradigms*. Unpublished paper presented to the Fanon Research and Development Conference on "The Theory and Practice of the Social Scientist in the Context of Human Development: Developing People and Institutions for Creative Struggle,'' Port of Spain, Trinidad.

Nobles, Wade W. (1980). Extended self: Rethinking the so-called Negro self-concept. In R. L. Jones (Ed.), *Black psychology* (2d ed.). New York: Harper & Row.

Nobles, Wade W. (1986). *African psychology: Toward its reclamation, reascension, and revitalization.* Oakland, CA: Institute for the Advanced Study of Black Family Life and Culture, Inc.

Pettigrew, T. F. (1964). *A profile of the Negro American.* Princeton, NJ: D. Van Nostrand.

Schwartz, G., & Disch, R. (1970). *White racism: Its history, pathology, and practice.* New York: Dell.

Smith, N. (1974). The ancient background to Greek psychology and some implications for today. *The Psychological Record, 24*, 309–324.

Tart, Charles T. (1975). *States of consciousness.* New York: E. P. Dutton.

Terry, R. (1970). *For whites only.* Grand Rapids, MI: Eeordmans.

Weems, L. X. (1974). Awareness: The key to black mental health. *Journal of Black Psychology, 1*(1), 30–37.

Welsing, F. (1974). The Cress theory of color-confrontation. *Black Scholar, 5*, 32–40.

Wilber, K. (1979). *No boundary: Eastern and western approaches to personal growth.* Boulder, CO: Shambhala.

Wilcox, R. (Ed.). (1971). *The psychological consequences of being a black American.* New York: Wiley.

Williams, C. (1976). *The destruction of black civilization.* Chicago: Third World Press.

Willie, Charles V., Kramer, Bernard M., & Brown, Bertram S. (Eds.). (1973). *Racism and mental health.* Pittsburgh: University of Pittsburgh Press.

Wright, B. (1975). *The psychopathic racial personality.* IL: Institute of Positive Education.

7

Stress, Coping, and Social Support: Their Effects on Black Women

Patricia J. Dunston

Excessive stress has historically impacted black women from the beginning of slavery to the present day. Writers such as Paula Giddings (1984), Sharon Harley (1978), and Rosalyn Terborg-Penn (1978) have described the inordinate life event stresses which have impacted black women from the seventeenth to the twentieth century. These authors depict black women who, against unsurmountable odds, have managed to cope with an array of life events over which they had no control. They described naturally evolving support systems which served as buffers against these uncontrollable stressors. Giddings (1984) recaptures the racism and sexual exploitation of black women to caste them in the roles of whores and chattel property. For example, black women were skillful at poisoning their masters and burning their homes when faced with cruel treatment under slavery. When faced with the pressures of breeding, black slave women used various contraceptives and abortives to fight the system. Freed from slavery, black women were allowed no historical change. Needless to say, the years of freedom brought the zealousness of continued racism and discrimination.

As noted by Harley (1978), from 1815 to 1848, black women were barred entrance into factory work despite the growing number of women permitted such work. Black women were often subjugated to work as domestic servants, work that had become the basis of their existence during slavery, work that most American white women during the 1800s considered degrading. By 1847, black women in Philadelphia were mainly employed as washerwomen and domestic servants. Small numbers of black women found employment as needlewomen, dressmakers, and hairdressers; however, the majority of black women continued to perform the same duties they had performed under slavery. In spite of the plight of the majority, a few black women became professionals and held positions of teachers, writers, and activists. Despite their underemployment and the newly found status of a few, black women always found it necessary to work. Black couples relied on both the man's and the woman's employment for survival along with extended family support. Single black women depended heavily on extended family for support. Both couples and single black women struggled for a meager existence.

Discrimination against black women continued to be the rule rather than the exception. Terborg-Penn (1978) highlights the barriers black women faced from white women during the women's movement. Black women were barred access into abolitionist groups and women's rights organizations. In some instances, black men were more readily accepted into such groups. For example, Frederick Douglass, William C. Nell, and Charles Lenox Remond are noted for the support they got from white abolitionist women. Sojourner Truth, who was at the forefront of the women's movement, on the other hand, was perceived as someone who was disruptive to the cause. Her blackness was not questioned, but her womanhood was. Black women overcame these barriers, too, by forming their own black organizations and clubs.

With this brief historical backdrop in mind, it can be stated that historical change continues to be a slowly evolving process. Black women continue to be plagued by many of the similar racial, cultural, and structural factors that impinged upon them hundreds of years ago.

The Census Bureau data for 1984 reveal that 49.5 percent of black families are female-headed in comparison to 16.8 percent of white families. Among the black female-headed families, 9.2 percent are husband absent, 8.4 percent are separated, 9.2 percent are widowed, 10.7 percent are divorced, and 14.6 percent are single (never married). All have an average of 1.59 children, 1.16 earners, and a 2.01 ratio of earners to nonearners. The white female-headed families are 2 percent husband absent, 1.8 percent separated, 3.6 percent widowed, 5.6 percent divorced, and 1.5 percent single (never married). White female-headed families have an average of 1.0 children, 1.39 earners, and a ratio of 1.09 earners to nonearners. Their mean income was $22,515 compared with $13,182 for black female-headed families (U.S. Department of Commerce, Bureau of the Census, 1986).

There exists, then, a significantly greater number of black female-headed families than white female-headed families and a significantly greater number of black female-headed families who have less income earning power. Within married-couple families, 29 percent of white families have wives in the labor force full time and 12 percent have wives in the labor force part time with mean incomes of $41,367 and $36,404, respectively. For black married couples, 25 percent of wives work full time and 5 percent part time with mean incomes of $34,579 and $23,973, respectively (U.S. Department of Commerce, Bureau of the Census, 1986). Obviously, it is more from necessity that black wives enter the labor force. There are significant differences between the incomes of black and white couples; white couples earn considerably more than black couples.

Occupationally, black women have approximately equivalent rates of participation in the labor force as do white women. However, black women have a 39 percent greater chance of contracting job-related illnesses and serious work-related injuries than do white women. They are also more likely to be employed as laborers, technicians, and in the service occupations than in professional or managerial jobs (U.S. Department of Health and Human Services, 1985). Specifically, 59 percent more white women hold white-collar jobs than black women, while 85 percent more black women hold blue-collar jobs. Similarly, 49 percent more black women hold service-oriented jobs than white women (U.S. Department of Commerce, Bureau of the Census, 1983). The data thus far presented provide a snapshot of the structural and racial differences between black and white women in the 1980s.

These data also lend support to the statement that black women are exposed to excessive and probably more frequent stressors that are not experienced by their white counterparts. Black women's stresses are an outgrowth of cultural, structural, and most likely discrimination experiences. Their exposure to stress raises issues with regard to their mental health. The social status and economic trends that have been reported for black women are of tremendous and discernible significance particularly in societies where social status and economic achievements are highly valued. As documented above, an increasing number of black women, irrespective of social class, face financially straining life circumstances and are among the group of women who are most likely to have to care for children. Research has shown that financial strain leads to mentally debilitating conditions such as depression (e.g., Goldman & Ravid, 1980).

Stress, then, is a process worthy of understanding because it serves to explain how psychologically relevant events become translated into impairing mental illnesses. What can be found in the stress literature are the efforts to refocus research which was once devoted to illuminating the differences in the stress experiences of different racial and socioeconomic groups. Investigators are now focusing on the possibility that race, sex, and class differences in subsequent mental illness may be indicative of differences in vulnerability to stress (e.g., Kessler, 1979). The major contributing body of knowledge directed toward this refocus is gleamed from research in three interwoven areas: life stress, social supports, and coping. The focus of this chapter then becomes the examination of the existing literature in these three areas for the purpose of providing an understanding of their importance to black women. It discerns gaps in knowledge relative to the impact of stress, coping, and social support on the mental health of black women. Illustrative excerpts from case study data are utilized throughout to provide a context for grasping the impact of stress, coping, and social support in the lives of black women. This chapter considers race, sex, and class as critical variables in understanding the stress experiences of black women in relation to their mental health. It considers these variables to be structural, cultural, and racial variables which undoubtedly greatly impact on black women's lives.

THEORETICAL EXPLANATIONS OF STRESS

Stress has taken on many definitions in the literature, some of which are vague as well as imprecise (Kasl, 1984). An early definition of stress was that of a flight response (Cannon, 1929). Hans Selye (1976) defined stress as a physiological response to noxious agents. R. S. Lazarus (1966) defined stress, in a psychological sense, in reference to an internal state of the individual who perceives threats to physical or psychic well-being. Stress is further conceptualized in terms of stressors that are an outgrowth of major life events, such as death of a spouse (Dohrenwend & Dohrenwend, 1981); persistent difficulties or strains over time, such as one's job or marital relationship (Pearlin & Schooler, 1978); and everyday stresses or small hassles, such as being late for work (De Longis, Coyne, Dakof, Folkman, & Lazarus, 1982). Yet another definition of stress places particular emphasis on the relationship between the person and the environment—a relationship that is bidirectional with each factor acting on the other. This definition assumes that beliefs and appraisals of one's personal control enter into the person-environment interaction and serve to determine the outcome of a stressful experience (Folkman, 1984). Therefore, personal control refers to both the person's belief about controlling the outcome and to the person's appraisal of the situation to be controlled.

The definitions of stress that have been presented here all vary in their emphasis. The early definitions placed emphasis on physiological change in response to an environmental situation (e.g., Cannon). Later definitions emphasized the cognitive appraisal of stress (e.g., Lazarus), the type and intensity of the stressor (e.g., Pearlin & Schooler), and the belief and appraisal of control in relation to the stressor (e.g., Folkman). Research suggests that individuals may differ in their response to stress. At a physiological level, there may be differences in reactivity. At a cognitive level, the problem may be appraised differently. An individual's reaction to the type and intensity of a stressor may also vary in relation to physiological change and cognitive appraisal. At the control level, belief and appraisal would differ with each individual. While individual differences cannot be negated, it can be argued that the void in the literature with respect to identifying the stressful experiences of women, and the stressful experiences of black women in particular, makes the issue of individual differences nonconsequential. Most important, the life situations of black women as a group remain to be systematically investigated in relation to stress.

During a review of the literature for some 20 years, very little empirical evidence was derived relative to gaining a perspective on the stress experiences of black women. In her review of the literature on the stress of caring, D. Belle (1982) notes that the literature paints an almost genderless picture with regard to pinpointing the stress experiences of women; for example, the "contagion of stress" from husband to wife has not been empirically investigated. Theories on the psychology of women emphasize women's orientation to the experiences, wishes, and needs of others which, in an extreme form, can lead to a loss of self in response to overwhelming responsibility. Similarly, marriage has been found to expose women to an increased risk of stress (Bernard, 1971; Radloff, 1975). Men, on the other hand, do not share in such experiences. Caring for children also brings everyday stresses. In addition, occupational roles, family, and community responsibilities bring other stressors into the lives of women.

Research suggests that women's work may be stressful and detrimental to their health. M. Colligan, M. Smith, and J. Hurrell (1977) found that those persons who were employed in health care professions were overrepresented in the population who sought treatment for mental health problems. Most of the health care professionals found to be at risk were women. S. Haynes and M. Feinleib (1980) found women clerical workers to be at a higher risk of coronary heart disease than other women workers or housewives. Working women with several children were found at risk for heart disease. Women, whether employed or not, who rear young children and have low incomes are at risk for depression (Brown, Bhrolchain, & Harris, 1975; Radloff, 1975). M. Weissman and E. Paykel (1974) found depressed mothers to be less involved with and less affectionate toward their children than women who did not suffer from depression. Socioeconomic stress also leads to child abuse among mothers (Garbarino, 1976). In a study conducted by D. Belle, M. Guttentag, and S. Salasin (1980), findings from 43 low-income mothers indicated that the living environment, problems with the law, and parenting correlated with mental health measures.

Theoretically and empirically there exist gaps in the literature with respect to the stress experiences of women. Research on stress has focused on stress resulting from changes such as death or illness. As noted by V. P. Makosky (1982), volume of change is important; for example, numerous changes in a short period of time. The focus on daily hassles and strains (e.g., De Longis et al., 1982; Pearlin & Schooler, 1978) is a move toward pinpointing the volume of stressors; however, relatively few studies conducted include women and none report findings from studies with black women. Similarly, although perception of personal control is theoretically relevant (Folkman, 1984), it remains to be empirically tested. Research suggests that stressful experiences and discrete events are contributors to mental health problems. Studies have reported group differences in depression which are not accounted for by life scores. Women, people of low socioeconomic status, and minorities all exhibit elevated symptom scores which are not explained by differences in event scores (e.g., Radloff, 1975). It is acknowledged that measurement problems still exist within stress measures. However, group differences must continue to be examined. Most important of all, the stress experiences of black women—a racial, cultural, and structurally vulnerable group—remain empirically unvalidated. Research on the relationship between stress and mental health among black women is sorely needed.

E. J. Smith (1981) noted that, because of their racial, historical, structural, and cultural position in American society, black women have encountered mental health–related problems. Factors such as migration, frustration, selected urban stresses (e.g., unemployment, poverty, racism) have been attributed to mental health problems among black women (Smith, 1981; Howze, 1977; Belle, 1980). Although these factors are probable stressors for black women, their realm of stressful experiences remain virtually unknown.

In a pilot study conducted by Dunston, Reaves, and Willis (1984), 14 black women described a total of 59 experiences, some of which created stress in their lives; for example, having children and rearing children can create varying degrees of stress. As one respondent reported:

I wanted a child but didn't expect it to be the way it happened, i.e., having a family is not the same when you're living apart; she calls someone daddy that's not, it hurts sometimes.

Although the above description characterizes the lives of many women, an increasingly and disproportionate number of black women share the same or similar experience. As stated earlier, 49.5 percent of black families are female headed in comparison to 16.8 percent of white families. The inordinate stress of child rearing and work is further expressed by the same respondent:

My child comes first, when I get paid I make sure she has everything first. . . . It is hard though raising her by myself. As long as I have a job it won't be too hard.

This same black woman can be structurally equated with many black women. At the time of the interview, she was employed as a billing clerk, placing her among the 85 percent of black women who hold similar blue-collar positions. To be black and female has other stressors as well which stem from the racial experience. As a second respondent recalled:

My sister and I were in a grocery store and a little white boy told his brother not to drink out of the water fountain because a "nigger" had drank from it.

Clearly this woman encountered an experience that has its roots in the racial experience. Only a few black women may have had an identical experience; however, many black women experience racism and discrimination in blatant and in subtle forms. Such experiences must be identified and evaluated in terms of stress and in relation to the mental health of black women. The experiences cited above in all probability were accompanied by feelings of alienation, frustration, and a sense of powerlessness. These feelings have been identified in past research as precursors to mental health disorders (Olmedo & Parron, 1981). It is clear that the stressful experiences of black women have received little investigation, but their buffers against stress have received more empirical attention.

THE ROLE OF SOCIAL SUPPORT

The concept of social support has taken on a variety of definitions and meanings throughout the literature. Most definitions of social support assume that relationships with others have the resulting benefit of providing a reduction in the stress that is associated with stressful life experiences. Social support, therefore, is acknowledged as a mediator or buffer of stress (Cobb, 1976). Researchers have found that social support provides protection for the physical and mental health of men who lose their jobs and that the quality of the mother-child relationship is related to social support (Gore, 1978; Hetherington, Cox, & Cox, 1978). Therefore, most of the investigations examining social support have assessed the buffering utility of the construct (Caplan, 1979; House, 1980; Lowenthal & Haven, 1968; Miller & Ingham, 1976; Pinneau, 1976). Theoretically, social support has been hypothesized as having both direct and indirect effects on stress (e.g., Antonovsky, 1974; Caplan, 1979). With all the evidence that supports the utility of social supports in buffering stress, there still remains uncertainty whether social supports always serve as a buffer or are in effect a stressor (Kessler & McLeod, 1984; Tolsdorf, 1976; Tucker, 1982; Straus, 1980).

Social supports have been recognized as a historical and contemporary source of strength in black families and as a mechanism for reducing stress in black single-parent families (Malson, 1983; McAdoo, 1982, 1984; Nobles, 1976; Stack, 1974). Social supports for black families are usually kin. Black families rely on kin more so than on neighbors or friends. Black women's social supports are often found to be mothers and sisters (Stack, 1974; McAdoo, 1980). M. Malson (1983a) found that coworkers are often named as part of the social supports of black working women. Social supports provide help with finances, child rearing, and child care. Friends serve as confidants and often provide mental health services as was illustrated by a respondent from the pilot study:

Something about her, influenced me, I guess because she was sincere, genuine, not perfect, was just sincere and a true friend. Made me feel I could trust her regardless of the extent of the problem I could talk to her about it. We didn't see or talk to each other everyday. Things I would feel uncomfortable saying to someone else I could tell her, and I didn't feel any shame about it. At that time, I was really going through more than I'm going through now. (Dunston et al., 1984)

Another respondent reported:

My best friend was always very open and willing to listen. I used to have deep periods of depression and would cry a lot. Whenever I called my friend, she would always come over and listen; not necessarily offer suggestions or be overly sympathetic, she would just listen. It made me feel very good that someone cared about me as a person and they were interested in my well-being and my welfare. (Dunston et al., 1984)

M. B. Tucker (1982) has found evidence of the deleterious effects of lack of social support. In her sample of black, female drug abusers, she found that nonsocial coping strategies (e.g., substance use) were related to lack of social support. These black women tended to engage in behaviors which did not resolve problems but possibly created other stresses. Women drank when relations with mates were not optimal. The greatest use of drugs to cope was associated with less support and the desire for more friends. Social supports mediated drug use as well but not in the expected direction. Talking to male relatives when angry or depressed was related to drug use among these women.

Malson (1983b) reports on the social supports of ten black, single-parent females. These women identified supports which ranged from 30 to 104 persons. Besides immediate kin, extended kin, friends, coworkers, men, and older children formed their networks for support. Again, social supports provided financial, child care, domestic, and emotional support. Malson's findings support earlier studies on the role of social supports for black women. Needless to say, much more empirical knowledge remains to be gleaned on the relationship between stress and social support.

It appears that family and friends serve as the primary social support networks for black women. The frequent interaction with kin by black women and families appears to have a different pattern than that found in white families (Hays and Mindel, 1973). Yet, it remains unknown how much the social supports of black women contribute to stress reduction or serve as stressors. A high percentage of black women from both the lower and middle classes live in urban areas. They are faced with and are exposed to a greater number of environmental hazards, substandard and overcrowded housing, violence, and crime. Black women's occupational risks are greater than those of their non-minority counterparts. Black women between the ages of 45 and 64 have a prevalence rate for hypertension 85 percent higher than white women; furthermore, black women between the ages of 25 and 44 have a prevalence rate for hypertension that is 2.6 times greater than white women of the same age (U.S. Department of Health and Human Services, 1985). As the research suggests, social supports may help black women cope with social, economic, and psychological stress; however, social supports cannot be a black woman's only recourse for mental health.

Belle (1982) notes that economic strain can exact a toll on a woman's support system in the same manner in which she is subjected to stress. L. Pearlin and J. Johnson (1977) found that the intimacy of the marital bond provides a good source of social support. A significant number of low-income black women are without such support. The economic strains felt by an increasing number of married, middle-class black couples would raise the question whether black women who are married frequently find social support from their partners. D. Brown and L. Gary (1985) report that among 91 married black women, 19.6 percent felt spouse support was their most important resource. Irrespective of social class, black women rely on relatives and friends for social support. The bidirectional stress created by such a reliance remains uninvestigated. Similarly it is assumed that the quality of social support would vary over time and may even differ within and among certain classes of black women. Similarly, the role of social supports in providing negative consequences for stress experiences and as key stressors remains uninvestigated. There are but a few investigative inquiries which attempt to provide answers to the role of social supports in the stress experiences of black women. Left unanswered are "What are the relationships among stress, social support, and mental health for black women?" and "How do social supports foster adequate coping or negative coping?"

Theoretically, there remains a great need for conceptual building on the relationship of stress and social support. As currently conceptualized, social support can provide both direct and buffering effects for stress. Social supports may help to interpret the perception of stress and help alleviate the stress once experienced. It is conceivable that during different experiences social supports may serve different roles. For example, social support may be the stressor and social support may interpret the perception of stress with much more intensity that if the person had gone through the experience alone. These hypotheses would further serve to delineate the role of social support in stress.

STRESS, COPING, AND SOCIAL SUPPORT

Any discussion of stress and social support would not be complete without a focus on coping. Research on coping has been explored in one or two ways. Respondents are asked to respond to lists of events and then indicate how they coped in general or to a specific event which occurred during the recent past. Other investigators have required respondents to identify the most stressful event of the recent past and describe the coping strategies they used (e.g., Folkman & Lazarus, 1980; Billings & Moos, 1984; Stone & Neale, 1985). Social support is often classified as a type of coping strategy (e.g., Billings & Moos, 1984). There is a gap in knowledge relative to coping with multiple events or stressors as well as coping with positive events. One noted exception has been the work of L. I. Pearlin and C. Schooler (1978). Still, the relationships among coping, social supports, and mental health remain an area about which knowledge must be gleaned.

A. Billings and R. Moos (1984) examined stress, coping, and social resources among mental health center outpatients diagnosed with unipolar depression; coping responses differed between depressed patients and nondepressed controls. Depressed patients used information seeking and emotional discharge most often as coping strategies. They either talked with someone about the problem, or they let their feelings out. The nondepressed group used problem solving as a strategy for coping with problems. They made a plan of action or worked harder to resolve the problem. Problem solving and regulating affect were related to fewer symptoms of depression. The number and supportiveness of social resources were found to be inversely related to depression and physical symptoms. The quality of social resources was much more related to the sample's functioning than was the quantity of their resources. Women made more emotional-discharge types of coping responses than men. Family environment and family strains affected women more strongly than men.

A. J. Stewart and P. Salt (1981) examined stress, life-styles, depression, and illness among graduates of an elite women's college. Single career women reported more symptoms of depression and illness than housewives and married working mothers. Across the groups of women, work stress was more highly correlated with illness and family stress with depression. Thus, these two studies have noted gender and life stress differences in relation to symptoms. In the Stewart and Salt (1981) study, working wives were found not to be as vulnerable to stress as would be expected by their assumption of dual roles. On the other hand, women graduates of elite colleges who are married and work may not work out of necessity. Their motivation level could foreseeably be lower. They may experience less stress than single career women. Billings and Moos (1984) did not find sex differences in exposure and susceptibility to stressors as reported in other community samples (e.g., Amenson & Lewinsohn, 1981).

The type of coping strategy appears to effect stress responses but in a situation-specific fashion (Mullin & Suls, 1982). Coping has been generally defined as both the cognitive and behavioral effort to master, tolerate, or reduce demands that tax or exceed a person's resources (Pearlin & Schooler, 1978; Cohen & Lazarus, 1979). It has been conceptualized as a dispositional trait or habitual preference to approach problems in a certain manner. However, considerable controversy remains about both the measurement and the conceptualization of coping. Some researchers question the assumption of consistency of coping behavior across situations, viewing coping strategies as efforts to deal with specific situations (e.g., Pearlin & Schooler, 1978). Since few studies have examined this issue, cross-situational consistency has been difficult to affirm. Concerns have also been elevated around the accuracy of respondents' reports of coping strategies they use, questions have been raised about the generally used techniques of self-report (see Stone & Neale, 1985; Horowitz & Wilner, 1980), and calls have come for more indirect assessment of coping. Still, little empirical evidence exists in support of such a position. With conceptual and measurement issues abounding, there is a gap in knowledge relative to understanding the relationship between coping and responsiveness to life events (Kessler, Price, & Wortman, 1985).

The coping of black women has been examined in relation to self-esteem and in relation to discrimination (Myers, 1980; Lykes, 1983). L. Meyers (1980) asked, ''Do Black women cope better?'' She found that black women rely on family and friends to provide support during times of trouble. She further found that black women rely on other black women to cope with experiences of racism and sexism. The women coped with stereotypes and perceptions of being single, black parents. They were able to feel good about themselves. M. B. Lykes (1983) conducted a secondary analysis of oral history transcripts of successful black women. She found that women whose life problems included racial and sexual discrimination used more than one strategy to cope with the problem and took direct action to handle the problem. Perceptions of control determined the type of coping strategy. The more control women perceived they had over the situation, the more likely they were to take direct action.

Indirectly, coping has been examined in research which has focused on black women's sex role ideology, interrole conflicts, and utilization of social supports (e.g., Malson, 1983a; Harrison & Minor, 1978; Neighbors, Jackson, Bowman, & Gurin, 1983). These studies have found that multiple roles pose no internal conflicts for black women, that the type of conflict influences the choice of coping strategy, and that religion and social supports serve as buffers for stress. Historical and sociological works (e.g., Hull, Scott, & Smith, 1982) describe the manner in which black women have coped from the days of slavery to the present day. In total, the contributing body of literature on black women's coping in response to life stresses is meager.

Taken together, the stress, coping, and social support literature is void with respect to providing knowledge about black women's functioning. It was once believed that black women were the principal targets of racism and sexism (e.g., Beale, 1970; Jackson, 1972). The racial and structural positions of black women as reflected by U.S. Census data would lead most blacks to believe that black women remain the targets of racism and sexism. Despite their status, black women tend to exhibit behaviors which reflect an adaptation to their environment. There is a need for research that systematically examines the stress-coping social support paradigm in relation to the mental health of black women.

There is evidence that a relationship exists among stress, coping, social support, and mental health. The direction of this relationship must be empirically clarified. Measurement must take into account gender and race when seeking to identify stressful life events. The role of social support as a stressor or buffer of stress must be examined within the context of its occurrence. Coping needs continued examination with respect to consistency and situation specificity. Most important is the need for research that focuses on the stress–coping–social support paradigm as it examines the mental health of black women. The implications of the investigation of the stress–coping–social support paradigm for mental health cannot be overstated.

IMPLICATIONS FOR MENTAL HEALTH

The cry for public attention to be drawn to the mental health needs of minority women has been consistently highlighted and documented (e.g., President's Commission on Mental Health, 1978; Olmedo & Parron, 1981). However, attention to this need fails to be so accordingly documented. This is stated in light of the fact that a review of the literature on stress has attested to the lack of a concerted effort to investigate its link to mental health among minority women and black women in particular. Such a lack of attention continues to exacerbate the mental health needs of black women. Economically, black women are barred from access to a variety of mental health treatment options. The increasing costs of private mental health treatment and restrictions on public mental health treatment place both middle- and lower-class black women in jeopardy for access. They become forced out of the system, and their needs for treatment are left unmet. The black woman's cry for help may be heard only when she becomes a statistic of child abuse or when depression has taken its toll with increased symptomatology.

A sense of personal control over situations and one's own life becomes difficult at best for black women. They experience discrimination and racism in both blatant and subtle forms. The support received by kin, friends, and coworkers can eventually be given less willingly. The support system can begin to feel overwhelmed by constant requests for assistance. The black woman begins to feel increased isolation, and stress becomes more direct when buffering has reached diminished returns. The perceived resiliency of black women as a group to adapt can eventually succumb sizeable numbers of black women to experience the debilitating effects of stress. Much has been written about strong black women and their ability to adapt. Black women have tended to accept their stressful situations; however, they are not as unpenetrable as we have been led to believe. The high rate of hypertension among black women is but one indicator of their stress. The high rates of depression among women are suggestive of sex differences in the susceptibility to mental health symptoms. Black women have become most susceptible because of the quantity of life changes believed to take place in their lives. It is foreseeable that black women will suffer in the decades to come because their mental health needs will continue to be unmet.

REFERENCES

Amenson, C. S., & Lewinsohn, P. M. (1981). An investigation into the observed sex differences in prevalence of unipolar depression. *Journal of Abnormal Psychology, 90*, 1–3.

Antonovsky, A. (1974). Conceptual and methodological problems in the study of resistance resources and stressful life events. In B. S. Dohrenwend & B. P. Dohrenwend (Eds.), *Stressful life events: Their nature and effects*. New York: Wiley.

Beale, F. (1970). Doubleday jeopardy: To be black and female. In T. Cade (Ed.), *The black woman*. New York: New American Library.

Belle, D. (1980). Who uses mental health facilities? In M. Guttentag, S. Salasin, & D. Belle, (Eds.), *The mental health of women*. New York: Academic Press.

Belle, D. (1982). The stress of caring: Women as providers of social support. In L. Goldberger and S. Breznitz (Eds.), *Handbook of stress: Theoretical and clinical aspects*. New York: Free Press.

Belle, D. (1983). The impact of poverty on social networks and supports. In L. Lein & M. Sussman (Eds.), *The ties that bind: Men's and women's social networks*. New York: Haworth Press.

Bernard, J. (1971). The paradox of the happy marriage. In V. Gornick & B. Moran (Eds.), *Woman in sexist society; Studies in power and powerlessness*. New York: Basic Books.

Billings, A., & Moos, R. (1984). Coping, stress, and social resources among adults with unipolar depression. *Journal of Personality and Social Psychology 46*(4), 877–891.

Brown, D., & Gary, L. (1985). Social support network differentials among married and unmarried black females. *Psychology of Women Quarterly, 9,* 229–241.

Brown, G., Bhrolchain, M., & Harris, T. (1975). Social class and psychiatric disturbance among women in an urban population. *Sociology, 9,* 225–254.

Cannon, W. B. (1929). *Bodily changes in pain, hunger, fear, and rage.* New York: Appleton-Century-Crofts.

Caplan, R. D. (1979). Social support person-environment fit, and coping. In L. A. Ferman & J. P. Gordus (Eds.), *Mental health and the economy.* Kalamazoo, MI: W. E. Upjohn Institute for Employment Research.

Cobb, S. (1976). Social support as a moderator of life stress. *Psychosomatic Medicine, 38*(5), 300–314.

Cohen, F., and Lazarus, R. (1979). Coping with the stresses of illness. In G. C. Stone, F. Cohen, & N. E. Adler (Eds.), *Health psychology* (pp. 217–254). San Francisco: Jossey-Bass.

Colligan, M., Smith, M., & Hurrell, J. (1977). Occupational incidence rates of mental health disorders. *Journal of Human Stress, 3,* 34–39.

De Longis, A., Coyne, J. C., Dakof, G., Folkman, S., & Lazarus, R. S. (1982). Relationship of daily hassles, uplifts, and major life events to health status. *Health Psychology, 1,* 119–136.

Dohrenwend, B. S., & Dohrenwend, B. P. (Eds.). (1981). *Stressful life events and their contexts.* New York: Prodist.

Dunston, P., Reaves, J., & Willis, K. (1984). Significant life experiences, interviews. Unpublished raw data.

Folkman, S. (1984). Personal control and stress and coping processes: A theoretical analysis. *Journal of Personality and Social Psychology, 46*(4), 839–852.

Folkman, S., & Lazarus, R. (1980). An analysis of coping in a middle aged community sample. *Journal of Health and Social Behavior, 21,* 219–239.

Garbarino, J. (1976). A preliminary study of some ecological corelates of child abuse: The impact of socioeconomic stress on mothers. *Child Development, 47,* 178–185.

Giddings, P. (1984). *When and where I enter: The impact of black women on race and sex in America.* New York: Bantam Books.

Goldman, N., & Ravid, R. (1980). Community surveys, sex differences in mental illness. In M. Guttentag, S. Salasin, and D. Belle (Eds.), *The mental health of women.* New York: Academic Press.

Gore, S. (1978). The effect of social support in moderating the health consequences of unemployment. *Journal of Health and Social Behavior, 19,* 157–165.

Harley, S. (1978). Northern black female workers: Jacksonian era. In S. Harley & R. Terborg-Penn (Eds.), *The Afro-American woman: Struggles and images.* New York: Kennikat Press.

Harrison, A., & Minor, J. (1978). Interrole conflict, coping strategies, and satisfaction among black working wives. *Journal of Marriage and the Family, 40,*(4), 799–805.

Haynes, S., & Feinleib, M. (1980). Women, work, and coronary heart disease. Prospective findings from the Framingham Heart Study. *American Journal of Public Health, 70,* 133–141.

Hays, W. C., & Mindel, C. H. (1973). Extended kinship relations in black and white families. *Journal of Marriage and the Family, 35,* 51–56.

Hetherington, E., Cox, J., & Cox, R. (1978). The aftermath of divorce. In J. H. Stevens,

Jr., and M. Matthews (Eds.), *Mother-child father-child relationships.* Washington, DC: National Association for the Education of Young Children.

Horowitz, M., & Wilner, N. (1980). Life events, stress, and coping. In L. W. Poon (Ed.), *Aging in the 1980's: Psychological issue.* Washington, DC: American Psychological Association.

House, J. S. (1980). *Work stress and social support.* Reading, MA: Addison-Wesley.

Howze, B. (1977). Suicide: Special references to black women. *Journal of Non-white Concerns in Personnel and Guidance, 5*(2), 65–72.

Hull, G. T., Scott, P. B., and Smith, B. (Eds.). (1982). *But some of us are brave: Black women's studies.* Old Westbury, NY: The Feminist Press.

Jackson, J. (1972). Black aged: In quest of the Phoenix. In J. Jackson (Ed.), *Triple jeopardy: Myth or reality.* Washington, DC: National Council on Aging.

Kasl, S. V. (1984). Stress and health. *Annual Review of Public Health, 5,* 319–342.

Kessler, R. (1979). Stress, social status, and psychological distress. *Journal of Health and Social Behavior, 20,* 259–272.

Kessler, R., & McLeod, J. (1984). Social support and psychological distress in community surveys. In S. Cohen and L. Syme (Eds.), *Social support and health.* New York: Academic Press.

Kessler, R., Price, R., & Wortman, C. (1985). Social factors in psychopathology: Stress, social support and coping processes. *Annual Review of Psychology, 36,* 531–572.

Lazarus, R. S. (1966). *Psychological stress and the coping process.* New York: McGraw-Hill.

Lowenthal, M., & Haven, C. (1968). Interaction and adaptation: Intimacy as a critical variable. *American Sociological Review, 33,* 20–30.

Lykes, M. B. (1983). Discrimination and coping in the lives of black women: Analyses of oral history data. *Journal of Social Issues, 39*(3), 79–100.

Makosky, V. P. (1982). Source of stress: Events or conditions. In D. Belle (Ed.), *Lives in stress: Women and depression.* Beverly Hills, CA: Sage Publications.

Malson, M. (1983a). Black women's sex roles: The social context for a new ideology. *Journal of Social Issues, 39*(3), 101–114.

Malson, M. (1983b). The social-support systems of black families. In L. Lein & M. Sussman (Eds.), *The ties that bind: Men's and women's social networks.* New York: Haworth Press.

McAdoo, H. (1980). Black mothers and extended family support network. In L. Rogers Rose (Ed.), *The black woman* (pp. 125–144). Beverly Hills, CA: Sage Publications.

McAdoo, H. (1982). Levels of stress and family support in black families. In H. I. McCubbin, A. E. Cauble, & J. M. Patterson (Eds.), *Family stress, coping and social support.* Springfield, IL: Charles Thomas.

McAdoo, H. (1984). *Single mothers alone.* New York: Routledge, Kagan, & Paul.

Miller, P. M., & Ingham, J. (1976). Friends, confidants, and symptoms. *Social Psychiatry, 34,* 481–503.

Mullin, B., & Suls, J. (1982). The effectiveness of attention and rejection as coping styles. *Journal of Psychosomatic Research, 26,* 43–49.

Myers, L. (1980). *Black women: Do they cope better?* Englewood Cliffs, NJ: Prentice-Hall.

Neighbors, H., Jackson, J., Bowman, P., & Gurin, G. (1983). Stress, coping, and black mental health: Preliminary findings from a national study. *Prevention in Human Services, 2*(3), 5–30.

Nobles, W. (1976). *A formulative and empirical study of black families* (Contract 90-C–

255). Washington, DC: Department of Health, Education and Welfare, Office of Child Development.

Olmedo, E., & Parron, D. (1981). Mental health of minority women: Some special issues. *Professional Psychology, 12*(1), 103–111.

Pearlin, L., and Johnson, J. (1977). Marital status, life-strains and depression. *American Sociological Review, 42,* 704–715.

Pearlin, L. I., and Schooler, C. (1978). The structure of coping. *Journal of Health and Social Behavior, 19,* 2–21.

Pinneau, S. R. (1976). Effects of social support on psychological and physiological strain (Doctoral dissertation, University of Michigan, 1975). *Dissertation Abstracts International,* 5359B–5360B.

President's Commission on Mental Health. (1978). Report of the Task Panel on Special Populations: Minorities, Women, Physically Handicapped. *Task Panel Reports,* vol. III. Washington, DC: U.S. Government Printing Office.

Radloff, L. (1975). Sex differences in depression: The effects of occupation and marital status. *Sex Roles, 1,* 249–266.

Selye, H. (1976). *The stress of life* (2d ed.). New York: McGraw-Hill.

Smith, E. J. (1981). Mental health and service delivery systems for black women. *Journal of Black Studies, 12*(2), 126–141.

Stack, C. (1974). *All our kin.* New York: Harper and Row.

Stewart, A. J., & Salt, P. (1981). Life stress, life-styles, depression, and illness in adult women. *Personality and Social Psychology, 40*(6), 1063–1069.

Stone, A., & Neale, J. (1985). New measure of daily coping: Development and preliminary results. *Journal of Personality and Social Psychology, 46*(4), 892–906.

Straus, M. (1980). Social stress and marital violence in a national sample of American families. *Annals of the New York Academy of Sciences, 347,* 229–250.

Terborg-Penn, R. (1978). Discrimination against Afro-American women in the woman's movement, 1830–1920. In S. Harley & R. Terborg-Penn (Eds.), *The Afro-American woman: Struggles and images.* New York: Kennikat Press.

Tolsdorf, C. (1976). Social networks, support and coping: An exploratory study. *Family Process, 15*(2), 407–417.

Tucker, M.B. (1982). Social support and coping: Applications for the study of female drug abuse. *Journal of Social Issues, 38*(2), 117–138.

U.S. Department of Commerce, Bureau of the Census. (1983). *A statistical analysis: Women in the United States.* (Current Population Report Series, P–23, No. 100). Washington, DC: Author.

U.S. Department of Commerce, Bureau of the Census. (1986). *Money income of households, families and persons in the United States: 1984.* (Current Population Report Series P–60, No. 151). Washington, DC: Author.

U.S. Department of Health and Human Services. (1985). *Report of the Secretary's Task Force on Black and Minority Health.* Washington, DC: Author.

Weissman, M., & Paykel, E. (1974). *The depressed woman.* Chicago: University of Chicago Press.

PART IV

Psychiatric Diagnosis and Treatment

8

ETHNIC AND CULTURAL FACTORS IN PSYCHIATRIC DIAGNOSIS AND TREATMENT

James L. Collins, Eliot Sorel, Joseph Brent, and Clyde B. Mathura

BACKGROUND

Blacks have been diagnosed as having mental illness more frequently than whites for over 100 years (Pasamanick, 1963; Rosenstein & Millazzo-Sayre, 1975). The studies that reported these results have been criticized for poor research methodology, cultural bias, and pseudo-scientific racial theories. These investigations continue, however, and L. N. Robins, J. E. Helzer, and M. N. Weissman (1984) found in a series of studies funded by the National Institute of Mental Health that, with few exceptions, nonwhites were more frequently diagnosed as having certain mental disorders than whites. These studies, which utilized the Third Edition of the Diagnostic and Statistical Manual (DSM-III) of the American Psychiatric Association to make less subjective and more reliable diagnoses, were conducted in New Haven, Connecticut; Baltimore, Maryland; St. Louis, Missouri; and Los Angeles, California. Statistically significant differences were found between whites and nonwhites in the diagnosis of simple phobias, manic episodes, agoraphobias, and cognitive impairment.

J. I. Escobar et al. (1986) criticized the methodology of the Los Angeles study, and he found that the performance of a community sample of mixed ethnicity on the mini-mental status examination (MMSE), a brief examination which measures cognitive functioning, was influenced by age, educational level, ethnicity, and the language of the interviewer. He felt that several items were culturally biased and that when they were excluded from the MMSE ethnic differences in the rates of severe cognitive impairment between whites and nonwhites disappeared. He concluded that the MMSE should be revised and that certain items be eliminated or reweighed to diminish the influence of social and educational factors. Escobar concluded that the MMSE in its current form was culturally biased against Spanish-speaking patients.

J. Collins, J. Wells, and D. Pearson (1975) found in a 1975 study that race may have been a factor in the diagnosis of latent and undifferentiated schizophrenia in black and white populations at a large government hospital. Approximately 3,000 inpatient psychiatric records were reviewed. Blacks constituted 28 percent and whites 70 percent of the total sample of 3,000. Significantly, paranoid schizophrenia was more often diagnosed in the black patients (58.1 percent) than in the white patients (41.8 percent). Whites were more frequently found to have latent schizophrenia (7.1 percent) than blacks (1.9 percent). Undifferentiated schizophrenia was more frequently diagnosed in whites (18.4 percent) than in blacks (10.6 percent). The authors concluded that, even assuming the diagnosis of schizophrenia was accurate in all the patients, the diagnostician has the opportunity to place the patient subjectively in various categories of severity based upon his clinical assessment. The subjectivity of the diagnostician can never be completely eliminated, even with the DSM-III diagnostic criteria which have been utilized in more recent studies of this type.

J. Collins, L. Rickman, and C. Mathura (1980), who conducted a similar study at Howard University Hospital in Washington, D.C., reviewed approximately 1,600 patient records of patients who were admitted over a five-year period. These patients were predominately black; only 32.5 percent were diagnosed as having paranoid schizophrenia. Although the population did not demographically match the population at the federal hospital, the authors believe that the significantly lower rate of paranoid schizophrenia diagnosed at Howard by predominately black psychiatrists may have been due to a greater cultural rapport between the patient and diagnostician.

L. Hendrix, J. Collins, L. Rickman, C. Mathura, and J. Bayton (1983) found that, in attempting to verify the validity of the Diagnostic Interview Schedule (DIS) used by Robins in the nationwide epidemiological survey, greater diagnostic agreement was observed for alcoholism and depression than schizophrenia. The DIS interview results were compared to psychiatric interviews performed by staff psychiatrists, and the concordance between the psychiatric interview and the diagnostic interview schedule was lower for schizophrenia than it was for alcoholism or depressive symptoms. The authors felt that several shortcomings were inherent in the diagnostic interview schedule, and the DIS interviewers considered the questionnaires too wordy, complicated, and anxiety provoking for much of the study population. Questionnaire items pertaining to sexual experiences, antisocial behaviors, and thoughts of death were found to be especially troublesome for some patients. Hendrix concluded that the DIS may not have content validity for low-income black patients. Like Escobar, Hendrix concluded that race, education, ethnicity, and socioeconomic status must be considered in conducting any psychiatric epidemiological interviews.

Mental health professionals as well as the general public continue to ask whether blacks and other nonwhites are more susceptible to mental disorders than whites. Race has been shown to be a risk factor for cardiovascular disease. (Blacks are fifty percent more likely to develop hypertension than whites.) Hypertension has been correlated with emotional stress and anxiety. Many wonder whether race is also a risk factor in developing a psychiatric illness such as schizophrenia. There is currently no conclusive evidence to support this speculation. Future research may clarify the epidemiology of mental disorders and better define the environmental, physiological, psychological, and cultural factors that contribute to the development of psychiatric illness.

H. S. Gross (1969) and V. R. Adebimpe (1981) reported that, although blacks are diagnosed as suffering from mental disorders more frequently than whites, blacks do not receive outpatient psychotherapy as frequently as white patients do and they are more likely to be treated in group therapy or to receive only medication with periodic medical follow-up and no psychotherapy at all. This observation is reported even when the availability of a therapist and financial constraints are not a problem for the black patient.

The national shortage of psychiatrists and the relatively high cost of individual psychotherapy have resulted in most black patients receiving their psychotherapy from white nonpsychiatric therapists in public and community mental health facilities. The dropout rate is high, and many black patients are not considered good candidates for individual psychotherapy by white therapists. If the black and other minority patients are to receive comprehensive psychiatric treatment in public and community mental health facilities, white psychotherapists must appreciate the effects of race, socioeconomic status, and culture on the psychotherapeutic process. They must not attempt to treat the black patient as if he were white, nor should they overemphasize the patient's color to the point that patient and therapist are overly anxious and uneasy with each other.

C. Pinderhughes (1973) reported that black patients tend to present certain resistances to therapy with greater frequency than other racial and ethnic groups. He observed that, in his experience, blacks feel a price must be paid for any assertive action with whites, and they reflect a sense of victimization, pessimism, distrust, and fear which make the denial of problems or the passive surrender to them seem safer than an assertive attempt at problem solving. He feels that most black patients will perceive and anticipate racial prejudice and discrimination by the white therapist.

Both the therapist and patient may enter the therapeutic relationship with preconceived attitudes and feelings about each other which are based on both unconscious and conscious perceptions. These conscious and undistorted feelings are referred to as the "real relationship." Research has shown that race and ethnic differences are factors which may influence this real relationship and frequently impair the establishment of an effective therapeutic alliance.

No matter what form of psychotherapy is utilized, it is essential that the therapist and patient agree to work as a team to enhance constructive changes in the patient's problematic patterns of cognitive behavioral and emotional functioning. The inability to develop an adequate therapeutic alliance is felt to be one of the most significant reasons for the failure of many black patients to return for treatment after the initial diagnostic interview. S. P. Sue (1977) demonstrated that over 50 percent of 1,000 blacks seeking counseling did not return after the first interview.

E. Jones (1974) reported that the first eight interview sessions are critical in the development of the therapeutic alliance. If a patient returns for at least eight sessions, the probability of continuing in psychotherapy is high. This is especially true for black patients. If the white therapist focuses on helping the patient through this transition period, the patient may overcome much of his resistance to starting psychotherapy. Mutual fear and mistrust between therapist and patients from different racial, ethnic, and cultural backgrounds make this transition period difficult. This distrust makes many black patients reluctant to confide in their white therapist, and many white therapists are intimidated by their black patients.

The following two cases illustrate the racial issue presented by two black patients to a white psychiatrist.

CASE I. The patient is a middle-aged black professional woman who is separated and has one child. She presented herself for psychiatric consultation following an outburst of anger on her job with paranoid ideations about her coworkers. After a few sessions, the therapist reported this dialogue with her:

Race is irrelevant in the doctor patient relationship if the doctor is like you, is not prejudiced, has no assumptions about the nature of a person of another race; accepts people as they are; is flexible enough to learn other languages; is unthreatened by a person of another gender or another race.

From our first meeting, it is clear to me you impose no group stereotype of how mid-forties, black females should think. I was alternately verbally aggressive, humorous and demanding, and you made it clear you both saw me and heard me. You did not raise an eyebrow at my love of classical music or having lived outside the United States.

This acceptance of me as a person allowed me to accept you as a person, including your being a white male. You have offered no views which would "type" me as a black, mid-forties female. I could talk about the future or my past without reference to race, or without you saying "and how does it feel as a black woman?" We discussed race the same as we discussed the nature of my work. You have no difficulty with my lower working class past or my striving to be upper middle class in taste (and hopefully, income). I tell you about the deprivations of my working class family and its slow transition into the middle class. I slid between these groups in my attitudes and behavior, and you understood. I speak standard English and "Patois" and you understand me. I curse a lot (the influence of a man who attended college with me). You don't bat an eye when I say "nigger" or "mother f—." We concentrate on what is being said, not the language it's said in. Never have you asked me to translate. We teach each other, you show me the ways I am a bigot, I try to teach you the ways in which race is insignificant except when white women take away a black man and the ways that class identity is more important. It helps that you are a white man. You represent the unobtainable yet the societal goal: an educated, handsome, successful white male. If I can gain your acceptance, then I can be accepted by this culture.

CASE II. This is a 28-year-old, single, black male, government worker who was referred for paranoid ideations, insomnia, poor self-image, and violent thoughts. He was clinically depressed and dysfunctional at work.

During the initial interview, he showed a knife to the psychiatrist and asked him if he was afraid to be alone with him in his office. He did not attempt to harm the therapist, but at a later session he wrote him a letter describing the incident.

The first time I met you, I was thinking here is another white mother f— trying to make a dollar off of some poor black man by telling him how my reality has nothing to do with the real world, and that for some thirty-odd years I have been living the life of a caveman.

I wanted to *kill him* because he was going to make me a non-person by taking away the things I believed in, stood for, and most of all to try and sum up my big life, hate, confusion, compassion, depression, love, rejections, violence, etc., etc. All this in 30 minutes, how in the f— could any one human being do this to another? The thought of going back in time and remembering and upheaving all that senseless worthless bull made me hot all over. Dr. ———— seemed small and helpless in his office; it seemed very big at the time I noticed also that it was far away from everything else like another planet, almost dream-like. As I sat there thinking how I would get rid of this little man with all the questions, that in time would provoke this thing in me, the Mad Man, the Angel of Death. I wanted to push him out the window but I could not get up from the sofa—it was like my A— had this big weight tied to it, and if I did move the distance between us seemed forever, he in one world and I in another. For me to make and take such a move the mad man needed to be fueled just a little more. I thought just a few more questions should do it mother f—, and you're dead. The heat that once covered my body and controlled my mind began to cool, that I did not like at all, because this was the day, my day to kill, to answer the call to close the book, to end the legacy and why not? I was the last one, and my father had been calling me for a long time and he was not going to let me be different. I had to do something to feel the heat again, so I pulled out the knife hoping this would make him lose control and I would have him where I want him—dead like me. But when I pulled the knife, he disappeared. He reduced himself to nothing—it was like I was in the room by myself except for his voice, that was calm and warm. The heat I once felt turned to ice. I believed that he helped me that day by not letting me intimidate him. He simply turned all I was feeling in to some kind of picture and made me look at myself. I clearly remember him saying, "Now, Charles (pseudonym), look at you, man. You don't want to hurt me. Now slow down, be cool, man get yourself together." And then he smiled and somehow touched something in me that wanted to live. From that day to this one, Dr. ———— has been a real friend. I feel that he knows my pain and shares in it.

In both of these cases, the patients expressed their fear and suspicion of the therapist because he was white and they initially perceived him as judgmental and superior. They attempted to overcome their fear by categorizing the therapist as a different type of white person, one who could accept them for who and what they were. This acceptance and understanding seems particularly essential for black patients before they can trust the white therapist, at least enough to establish a therapeutic alliance.

J. Brent (1985) believes that the mutual fear and mistrust between blacks and whites in the United States are embedded in a shared multicultural history lasting over 350 years. This mistrust created stereotypic behavior of whites and blacks consisting of white dominance and black submission. This behavior has become habitual and automatic by most persons on both sides of the color line. Brent calls this pattern of behavior "the game." He theorizes that it was developed during slavery in the south by whites and blacks who feared and at times hated each other, but appreciated their mutual interdependence for survival. Each acted as if there were an insurmountable barrier between them when, in fact, many were related by blood as a result of interbreeding. They perceived a categorical distinction between each other based on racial differences which justified white dominance.

This dominance could only be enforced with white civil and military power, but this power was never absolute and it often required the collusion of slaves. Blacks engaged in constant resistance and periodic rebellion, and in many southern communities they often outnumbered the whites. The perception of absolute white power was maintained by mutual deception and complicity. Both groups acted as if they would be destroyed if this power relationship were reversed, or if they treated each other as equals. This deception became almost universal. Each culture could understand the other only if they temporarily suppressed their own cultural orientation and viewed the other's world as if they were a member of the opposite group. This periodic glimpse of each other's world seemed to permit occasional meaningful relationships, and an exchange of honest feelings between them.

An example of Brent's game is eloquently described in Alex Haley's (1978) *Roots* in the dialogue between Master Lee and Chicken George, who are sharing a long, monotonous, dusty wagon ride on the way to a cock fight. Master Lee says, suddenly:

"What you thinkin' about so hard boy?"

"Nothin' " he replied. "Wasn't thinkin' about nothin', Massa."

"Somethin' I ain't never understood about you niggers!" There was an edge in Massa Lee's voice. "Man try to talk to y'all decent, you right away start acting stupid. Makes me madder'n hell, especially a nigger like you that talks his head off if he wants to. Don't you reckon white people would respect you more if you acted like you had some sense?"

"Well, suh, I means like it depen' on what white folks you talkin' to, Massa, leas' ways dat's what I gits de impression."

Massa Lee spat disgustedly over the side of the wagon. "Feed and clothe a nigger, put a roof over his head, give him everything else he needs in the world, and that nigger'll never give you one straight answer!"

In order to stop irritating Massa Lee, he tested the water by saying, "you wants de straight up-an' down truth, Massa, I b'lieves mos' niggers figger dey's bein' smart to act maybe dumer'n dey really is, 'cause mos' niggers, is scairt o' white folks.''

"Scared!" exclaimed Massa Lee. "Niggers slick as eels, that's what! I guess it's scared niggers plottin' uprisings to kill us every time we turn around! Poisonin' white people's food, even killin' babies! Anything you can name against white people, niggers doin' it all the time and then white people act to protect themselves, niggers hollerin' they so scared!''

Chicken George thought it would be wise to stop fiddlin' with the Massa's hair-trigger temper. "Don't b'lieve none on yo' place ever do nothin' like dat, Massa,'' he said quietly.

"You niggers know I'd kill you if you did." (Haley, 1978, pp. 418–425)

Before the ride was over, Chicken George was able to convince Master Lee to permit him to marry, and later Master Lee even tossed in a wedding gift of a bottle of whiskey and a new hat. The game of ignorance, subordination, and complicity played by George was successful in helping him achieve his goal of marriage and his continued survival in the barbed and hostile environment of slavery.

J. Blassingame (1972) wrote in *The Slave Community* that "the plantation was a battlefield where slaves fought masters for physical and psychological power." Although the society which enforced slavery was powerful and subjugated the slaves initially by coercion, slavery could be maintained only in the absence of an aggressive master or overseer by attempting to influence the minds of the slaves. They attempted to make the slaves believe that they were inferior to whites, that they deserved to be slaves because of their inferiority, and that they must adjust to their low status and not revolt. The slaves adjusted to this psychological coercion in several ways. Some incorporated their masters' disdain for them and became docile and passive; others fought back; some feigned ignorance and passivity to keep the master and overseers from observing them too closely; others physically confronted the plantation overseers and never hid their anger and rage at their bondage; a few ran away; and many of the women sexually submitted to their masters and overseers and demonstrated mastery over their oppressors by their sexual dominance. Most developed the survival skill of submitting their bodies to the fields, the lash, and the rope, but they never let the whites understand them or control their minds. Feigning submission was a closely guarded secret and an essential survival skill.

The mutual fear and mistrust between blacks and whites in the era of slavery was based on the perception that each group suspected the other of desiring to destroy them. Both groups feared that they could not survive on the American continent without the knowledge and assistance of the other.

Many blacks perceived that their survival depended on the perception by whites that they were ignorant, submissive, and compliant. Many whites felt they needed to make blacks believe that they were more knowledgeable, omnipotent, fearless, and ruthless toward any indication of disobedience. White dominance and black subordination seemed to be a necessary pattern of mutual deception during the era of slavery, and Brent believes that this game is still played in contemporary society by the majority of blacks and whites when they interact with each other.

Since psychotherapy can be an extremely intense and intimate relationship, Brent's game can be expected to be present when the therapist and patient are of different races. The following excerpt describes the black patients' conscious attempt to keep the white therapist from understanding their most intimate thoughts and secrets.

In 1914, Mary O'Malley (1972) of St. Elizabeth's Hospital in Washington, D.C., published an article entitled, "Psychosis in the Colored Race: A Study in Comparative Psychiatry," in which she stated:

There is little known of the psychology of these people. The colored are secretive by nature as well as by cultivation . . . it requires a great amount of painstaking effort and hours of toil to obtain any conception of the mechanisms of the Negro mind (Thomas & Sillen, 1972, p. 12)

Were Dr. O'Malley's black patients playing the game of ignorance and submission like Chicken George and not permitting her to share their secrets and intimate thoughts and feelings? We believe that the white therapists of today must exert the effort and toil described by Dr. O'Malley to overcome the black patient's conditioned mistrust of them and their mutual fear and mistrust of blacks.

After a few years of relative calm in U.S. race relations, the country has experienced a resurgence of racial unrest in the late 1980s, and many blacks believe that race relations have become worse over the past decade. Basic trust in others begins to emerge from early relationships in infancy. If these relationships are generally positive and continuously reinforced during childhood and adolescence, the adult will usually achieve the ability to establish and maintain appropriate and lasting close interpersonal relationships. Many blacks and whites in the U.S. have never developed this basic trust in each other.

Both Pinderhughes and Brent observed that the majority of poor black children living in urban ghettos have had little direct contact with whites during their early developmental years, and that their familiarity with whites and the mainstream white culture is extremely limited. If they receive the traditional harsh, negative indoctrination describing the deceit and treachery of the white world, it may be almost impossible for them to ever establish basic trust with whites. Many whites receive a similar negative indoctrination about blacks, and a positive relationship is achieved only if they "transform" each other into "exceptional" members of the opposite race. This transformation may involve either perceiving each other as colorless, or more often acting as if they were of the same race. Whenever the issue of color can no longer be suppressed, however, the fears and anxieties of both parties return, and the relationship may disintegrate.

The suppression of fearful thoughts about members of the opposite race consumes considerable emotional energy. If the therapist is unwilling to invest this energy, he may abandon the patient or facilitate the patient's withdrawal.

A. J. Rush (1985) describes three principal factors which affect the therapeutic alliance in brief supportive psychotherapy: (1) the patient, (2) the therapist, and (3) the psychiatric illness or disorder.

Both the psychiatrist (therapist) and patient must actually participate in a "working relationship" if the therapeutic goal is to be achieved. This principle, derived from Sigmund Freud, remains viable today. When Freud began to develop his techniques of psychoanalysis in the late nineteenth century, he was firm in his belief that the patient must become an active collaborator in his psychotherapy. In 1910, Freud delivered his fifth lecture on psychoanalysis entitled "Transference and Resistance." He stated at that time that

The patient, that is to say, directs towards the physician a degree of affectionate feeling (mingled, often enough, with hostility) which is based on no real relation between them and which—as is shown by every detail of its emergence—can only be traced back to old wishful phantasies of the patient's which have become unconscious. . . . Our patients' resistance to recovery is no simple one, but compounded of several motives. . . . The flight from unsatisfactory reality into what, on account of the biological damage involved, we call illness (though it is never without an immediate yield of pleasure to the patient) takes place along the path of involution, of regression, of a return to earlier phases of sexual life. (Strachey, 1957, p. 51)

The therapist then must help the patient overcome these resistances to recovery. The patient may not start therapy or may prematurely stop it if these resistances are not alleviated. According to this concept, patients may have both positive and negative feelings toward the therapist, which are not based on the actual relationship between them but are unconscious issues which they bring to the therapy from their past. Patients also have strong feelings and attitudes toward the therapist based on their undistorted interactions and perceptions which are of conscious origins like racial stereotypes. The authors believe that conscious and unconscious factors contribute to racial prejudice in both groups.

Racial stereotypes are used to form group boundaries. Pinderhughes (1973) believes that "members of any group form paranoid aggressive bonds towards common outside targets." He suggests that group members must repress their disruptive body processes and behavior. "Sexual arousal, hostile discharges, excretory behavior and sudden loud noises are disruptive and are repressed in all societies." He believes that these behaviors are given negative value, and group members must try to rid themselves of these undesired behaviors. This process begins in childhood and is facilitated by finding a convenient person or group of people outside the reference group to project these negative feelings and attitudes onto. Blacks as a group have often been conveniently scapegoated by whites to serve this purpose. If this process works effectively, group members can continue to admire and respect each other by learning to hate and project their own unacceptable behaviors onto others. These group behaviors are felt to be universal and are not limited to blacks and whites.

Racial hatreds and animosities were common throughout Europe and West Africa for centuries. When diverse nationalities begin to colonize North America, some historians speculate that the necessity to minimize their centuries-old animosities was facilitated by their ability to create simply two races—one black, one white. Neither of these races are homogeneous, but, even at the present time when we speak of blacks and whites, we tend to forget that this reference is purely a creation of convenience.

If slaves had been permitted to maintain their ethnic and cultural distinctions from West Africa, their ancient rivalries and hatreds would probably have destroyed countless slaves in Colonial America. If French, German, Italian, Irish, Spanish, and other European-Americans had continued to act out their centuries-old national rivalries and hatreds, the country would probably not have survived.

Could racism and racial stereotypes have been created and continue in the service of creating group bonds across various nationalities and cultures to foster mutual survival? This hypothesis is purely speculative, but empirically we are all aware that racial stereotypes and animosities continue with intense feeling even to the present time.

For a member of one group to embrace a member of the other group is often seen as heretical or even treasonous by members of one's own group. The only way to cross this impenetrable barrier is to create an illusion that the outsider is a member of one's own group. This can be done by accepting a new group member as an "honorary" member, as long as he is able successfully to pass the initiation rights of the reference group and, at least superficially, deny his previous identity. This process is more clearly seen when we look at the treatment of expatriots from other countries. Communist Russian defectors and immigrants are regularly accepted as American citizens if they reject their previous citizenship, denounce their "false" ideology (communism), embrace our ideology (democracy), learn to mimic our behaviors, speech, and dress, and at least superficially accept our predominant cultural norms.

Blacks regularly bestow honorary membership on whites if they are perceived as unprejudiced, understanding, and appreciative of black culture and heritage. Whites regularly bestow honorary membership on blacks if they are perceived as intelligent, hardworking, and nonthreatening. Achieving honorary status into a different ethnic or racial group has definite responsibilities and obligations. One must by and large relinquish one's former group membership. Speaking Russian or displaying the Russian flag from one's house is not acceptable behavior in a midwest suburban community in the United States. Speaking "black dialect" or not wearing a suit and tie to a corporate boardroom is also considered in poor taste by the white corporate board members. Displaying a confederate flag from a white-owned grocery store in a black inner-city neighborhood is another example of poor taste in violating the privileges and responsibilities of honorary group membership in a different race or ethnic community. If one violates the prescribed group norms, one will be summarily banished from the group.

The white therapist who is sincerely interested in achieving group acceptance or honorary membership from his black patients must work much harder than the foreign immigrant has to work in achieving full U.S. citizenship. The therapist must learn the cultural values and group norms, the language, the attitudes, the goals, and the values of the black patients with whom he or she is dealing. If the black patient is middle class, the norms may be different from those in the lower socioeconomic classes. If the patients are from an urban community, their values and norms may be different from those from a rural community. Each community is different from the next in subtle but significant ways. In order to be given honorary status into the black culture, the therapist must have a knowledge and appreciation of the culture of his patients.

TREATMENT TECHNIQUES

The previous portions of this chapter have reviewed some of the historical problems associated with the psychiatric diagnosis and treatment of black and other nonwhite patients. The authors believe that many of these difficulties can be overcome if the therapist is diligent and dedicated to the principle that psychotherapy in its many varieties is a beneficial treatment modality and can be utilized with patients who are racially and culturally different from the therapist.

We have found the following techniques beneficial in our clinical work and believe that they may be of some help to the therapist who recognizes that he or she has problems working with black patients.

Establishment of a Therapeutic Alliance

The therapist must establish a positive therapeutic alliance and proceed with a complete evaluation. The initial focus should be on getting the patient to return for at least one more session at a time. If the therapist feels that he or she did not receive a positive rapport in the first session and the patient may not return, it is sometimes helpful to call and remind the patient of the second session and to call to reschedule if the patient has missed a session.

In R. Ursano & R. Hale's (1986) review of brief individual psychotherapies, it was mentioned that the first few sessions that a therapist has with the patient are really diagnostic interviews and should not be thought of as actual psychotherapeutic sessions. If patients fail to return, they are not necessarily dropping out of therapy, but they may be leaving because they did not find what they were looking for—an empathetic therapist.

Interventions and technical procedures are different during the initial therapeutic sessions than in ongoing psychotherapy. For instance, most therapists do not try to alleviate all the patient's anxieties and answer all of their questions during the psychotherapeutic process, but anxiety relief in answering appropriate questions completely and honestly should be attempted during the initial diagnostic interviews. Although this courtesy should be routine for veteran therapists, it must be pointed out that black and other lower-socioeconomic class patients are generally treated by the least experienced therapists, medical students, social work students and psychology graduate students, and postgraduate physicians training in psychiatry. These novice therapists may be too anxious themselves to place the patient adequately at ease during the initial interview, and their own anxiety may facilitate the patient's failure to return.

During the evaluation phase, the therapist must consider the interaction of the patient's diagnosis, ego strength, and physical health and the specific selection criteria for the type of therapy to be utilized, and then he or she must finally choose the most appropriate treatment for each patient. According to T. Karasu (1986), at least 400 different types of psychotherapy exist, and practitioners of each specific method claim that they are all different and that each is effective because of its unique qualities. Different diagnostic conditions require different types of psychotherapy.

Dealing with Fears and Anxieties

The therapist should focus on his own fears and anxieties concerning developing a therapeutic alliance with the black patient. He or she must learn to treat the patient, not the stereotype. Most white Americans have learned the negative stereotypes about black patients, and, in order to overcome the negative and at times frightening stereotypes, the therapist may have to suppress these fears skillfully and see the patient for who he or she really is and not simply as a characterization of the racial stereotype. This process may require the therapist initially to examine his or her earlier experiences with blacks and be introspective about his or her own comments and behaviors during the sessions. Additional supervision or consultation may be necessary to help overcome the white therapist's negative countertransference or conscious ambivalent feelings toward blacks.

Similarities and Differences

The therapist must emphasize similarities but not deny racial, cultural, and socioeconomic differences. The white therapist may focus on those qualities in the patient that are similar to his own or may even make the patient an "honorary white" and treat the patient as if there were no racial differences at all. This technique may be effective at first, but this alliance is only superficial.

The black patient may likewise reciprocate and make the white therapist an "honorary black." In our experience when the realities of the racial differences become an issue later on in the treatment, conflict usually occurs, and the patient or therapist may then find good reasons to stop the treatment. This "superficial" therapeutic alliance which denies racial differences requires significant emotional energy by both the patient and the therapist. This constant expenditure of emotional energy significantly detracts from the goal of psychotherapy.

Facilitating Affective Experiencing

A more difficult technique is to use the emotions that the racial differences generate and facilitate unfreezing and releasing previously withheld feelings. In many black patients the opportunity to verbally attack or intimidate the white therapist like "Charles" did to his therapist in the second case study may provide the patient an opportunity to release tightly controlled rage and ultimately experience a wider range of beneficial positive as well as negative emotions toward the therapist and other important people in his life. Karasu (1986) found in his review of the most popular currently practiced psychotherapy techniques that three change agents were prevalent in most techniques of psychotherapy:

1. Affective experiencing, defined as arousing excitement and responsiveness to suggestion by the unfreezing and releasing of feelings. This example was previously demonstrated in Case II when Charles threatened his therapist but later accepted the therapist as a real friend.

2. Cognitive mastery defined as "those techniques of treatment which use insight and reasoning in an attempt to effect changes in the patient by the acquisition and integration of new perceptions, thinking patterns, and self-awareness." Case II: "Now, Charles, look at you, man. You don't want to hurt me." This dialogue given in a reassuring and supportive tone was able to help the patient perceive the therapist as a nonthreatening white.

3. Behavioral regulation defined as "learning to modify one's behavioral responses by better managing and controlling one's actions and habitual responses through reinforcing new learning with repetition and practice of the positive therapeutic changes." Case II: "And then he smiled and somehow touched something within me that wanted to live. I feel that he knows my pain and shares in it." The patient was able to constrain his hostile urges to destroy the therapist and not perform an act of criminal behavior.

Karasu concluded that some form of affective experiencing is essential in psychotherapy but that change is more lasting when affective experiencing is utilized in combination with the other two techniques as accomplished by the therapist in Case II.

We believe that there are few interpersonal situations which generate stronger emotions than the experience generated when blacks and whites are able to give up their learned racial prejudices and stereotypes and to develop a trusting relationship with a member of the opposite race. The opportunity presents itself for the skillful therapist to channel these emotions into a positive therapeutic experience with the skillful use of Karasu's affective experiencing, cognitive mastery, and behavioral regulation. If the black patient can learn to develop a working alliance with the white therapist, we submit that the patient will be able to take on the more difficult challenge of resolving his unconscious conflicts which have caused him to seek psychotherapy. Although the task is formidable, we feel it is possible. We encourage other colleagues to proceed to refine their clinical and professional skills to overcome one of our society's more difficult challenges: understanding and eliminating racial prejudices and discrimination.

REFERENCES

Adebimpe, V. R. (1981). Overview: White norms and psychiatric diagnosis of black patients. *American Journal of Psychiatry*, *138*(3), 279–285.

Blassingame, J. (1972). *The slave community—Plantation life in the ante bellum south.* New York: Oxford Press.

Brent, J. (1985). *Black face.* Unpublished manuscript.

Collins, J., Rickman, L., & Mathura, C. (1980). Frequency of schizophrenia and depression in a black inpatient population. *Journal of the National Medical Association, 729*, 851–858.

Collins, J., Well, J., & Pearson, D. (1976). *A description of Walter Reed Army Medical Centers in-patient psychiatric service population, 1973–1975.*

Escobar, J. I. et al. (1986, October). Use of the mini-mental state examination (MMSE) in a community population of mixed ethnicity. *Journal of Nervous and Mental Disease, 174*(10), 607–614.

Gross, H. S. (1969). The effect of race and sex on the variation of diagnosis and disposition in a psychiatric emergency room. *Journal of Nervous and Mental Disorders, 148*, 638–642.

Haley, A. (1978). *Roots.* Garden City, NY: Doubleday, 1978, pp. 418–425.

Hendrix, L., Collins, J., Rickman, L., Mathura, C., & Bayton, J. (1983). The N.I.M.H. Diagnostic Interview Schedule: A test of its validity in a population of black adults. *Journal of the National Medical Association, 75*(7), 667–671.

Jones, E. (1974). Social class and psychotherapy: A critical review of research. *Psychiatry. 31*, 307–320.

Karasu, T. (1986, June 6). The specificity vs. non-specificity dilemma: Identifying therapeutic change agents. *American Journal of Psychiatry, 143*, 687–695.

Pasamanick, B. (1963). Misconceptions concerning differences in the racial prevalence of mental diseases. *American Journal of Orthopsychiatry, 33*, 72–86.

Pinderhughes, C. (1973). Racism and psychotherapy. In Willie, C. V., Kramer, B. M., & Brown, B. S., (Eds.), *Racism and mental health* (pp. 61–121). Pittsburgh: University of Pittsburgh Press.

Robins, L. N., Helzer, J. E., & Weissman, M. N. (1984). Lifetime prevalence of specific psychiatric disorders in three sites. *Archives of General Psychiatry 41*, 949–958.

Rosenstein, M. J., & Millazzo-Sayre, J. (1975). Characteristics of admission to selected mental health facilities (DHHS, Adm. 81–1005). Superintendent of Documents. Washington, DC: U.S. Government Printing Office.

Rush, A. J. (1985). Short term directive therapies. *American Psychiatric Association Annual Review, 4*, 562–572.

Strachey, J. (1957). *Complete psychological works of Sigmund Freud.* Standard Edition, vol. XI, pp. 49, 51. London: Hogarth Press.

Sue, S. P. (1977). Community mental health service to minority groups. *American Psychologist, 32*, 616–624.

Thomas, A., & Sillen, S. (1972). *Racism and Psychiatry*. New York: Brunner/Mazel, p. 12.

Ursano, R., & Hales, R. (1986, December 12). A review of brief individual psychotherapy. *American Journal of Psychiatry, 143*, 1507–1517.

9

SOCIAL FACTORS IN DIAGNOSIS AND TREATMENT

Clyde B. Mathura and Melanie A. Baer

The many changing tentacles of oppression and discrimination in the United States have not been kept out of the therapy session. The black patient, the victim of such oppression and discrimination, has been made to face special hurdles in his or her desire to seek treatment for mental disorders.

The reality is that with the overwhelming shortage of black therapists in all facets of the mental health profession the black patient will be interacting one on one with a nonblack, most likely white therapist. Furthermore, the overrepresentation of black patients in the hospital psychiatric wards, clinics, and community agencies can only add to the present state of mixed race patient-therapist alliances.

As a starting point, the mere minority status of blacks along the realm of economic, professional, and educational criteria tends to put them at a disadvantage in the therapy treatment condition. This "we"/"they" categorization along these highly valued criteria in U.S. society is not conducive to healthy, open communication in mixed race, mixed values alliances. In addition, various idiosyncratic characteristics of the black subculture which differentiate it from idiosyncrasies of white culture—language and slang nuances, differing career tracks, family structures, and dress and hairstyles—only widen the therapeutic gap.

This chapter analyzes the multiple social factors that are among the most conclusive to emerge from the phenomenology of the black patient in a mental health arena. Special emphasis is placed on research reports of race, social class, gender, and age factors within the alliance.

RACE

A number of concerns have been discussed in the literature regarding the mental health diagnosis and treatment of black clients. Some have suggested that black patients run a high risk of psychiatric misdiagnosis (Adebimpe, 1981). B. E. Jones and B. A. Gray (1986) state that blacks are more often misdiagnosed as schizophrenic and that affective disorders are consistently underdiagnosed in black patients. Even when age, sex, and social class were controlled for, similar results were found (Raskin, Crook, & Herman, 1975). Included among factors that these authors cite as causes for these misdiagnoses are cultural differences in language and mannerisms, difficulties in relating between black patients and white therapists, and the myth that blacks rarely suffer from affective disorders.

Problems in the mental health treatment of black patients have received much consideration in the literature. Differences in treatment modalities have been noted. For instance, black patients have been found to be referred less frequently for individual, outpatient treatment than white patients. Furthermore, blacks are more likely to receive pharmacotherapy than are white patients. The most common question that has been raised, however, is whether a white therapist can effectively help a black client. It has been noted that black clients are far more likely to be in treatment with white therapists than with therapists of their own race, which makes this question highly relevant.

Several studies have found that blacks indicate preference for black therapists over white therapists (Stranges & Riccio, 1970; Riccio & Barnes, 1973; Pinchot, Riccio, & Peters, 1975; Wolkon, Moriwaki, & Williams, 1973; Jackson, 1975; Thompson & Cimbolic, 1978). In these studies, black subjects indicated that they preferred a black therapist or counselor over a racially different helper. This stated preference may result from a number of factors. Blacks may feel that white therapists represent the majority culture which has contributed to the serious racial oppression they have experienced, and that white therapists cannot fully empathize with their feelings because of racist attitudes. They may perceive black therapists, who share the same racial and cultural heritage, as preferable because of this commonality. Several factors that have not been adequately addressed in many of these studies may also account for the findings. For instance, the responses of subjects to questions regarding preference for therapist ethnicity may depend upon the subject's perception of the purpose for which the response will be used (e.g., solely for research purposes or to determine actual counselor selection). The racial climate at the time and place of the studies is also an important consideration in the subject's interpretation. The findings of the preference studies conducted with black subjects during the civil rights movement, which found blacks to state preference for a black therapist, are likely to reflect the prevailing attitude of that time. The setting of the studies is an important consideration as well. For instance, black students who attend a predominantly black university may be more identified with the black culture and therefore more likely to indicate preference for a black therapist than students who choose to attend a more ethnically mixed or a predominantly white university. All of these factors should be considered for an adequate interpretation of the studies on preference for therapist ethnicity.

While a client's preference for therapist is not directly related to the outcome of psychotherapy, it is a factor related to a client's initiation of and involvement in treatment. In clinical settings, if a client's feelings against seeing a racially different therapist are so strong that the client would refuse to become involved in therapy if assigned to such a therapist, this concern should be appropriately considered and arrangements should be made accordingly. On the other hand, a client may request a racially similar therapist in order to defensively avoid dealing with feelings or issues that have to do with race in therapy. For such clients, a racially different therapist may be extremely helpful in facing and working through these feelings that may otherwise be avoided.

A number of studies have investigated outcome variables in the mental health treatment of black clients. These variables seem to be the most appropriate measure of therapy effectiveness because of their relevance to the end product of actual therapy and will therefore be examined closely. In these studies there seemed to be a trend suggesting that the outcome of one session may be less favorable for racially different therapist-client pairs than the outcome of longer term psychotherapy.

Most of the studies that have investigated the outcome of therapy with black subjects have looked at only a single interview (Banks, Berenson, & Carkhuff, 1967; Grantham, 1973; Ewing, 1974). These studies tended to find that black clients were more satisfied with the treatment when the counselor was black than when the counselor was white. However, a study by E. K. Proctor and A. Rosen (1981) which measured the subject's satisfaction with treatment after the second session did not find black subjects' satisfaction with treatment to be related to the racial makeup of treatment dyads.

A few studies have looked at more than a single session of psychotherapy with black clients. E. E. Jones (1978) measured both process and outcome variables of short-term, insight-oriented therapy. Black and white female, neurotic clients were assigned to a black or white male therapist. No differences were found on either client or therapist outcome ratings based on racial matching. Differences were found, however, on process measures. Similarly, in a 15-hour group therapy modality (Cimbolic, 1973), black students were as willing to see at least one of the two white counselors in the study as one of the two black counselors for individual counseling afterwards.

In several outcome studies the duration of therapy was not fixed, but varied. Most of these studies measured the duration of therapy itself to determine client dropout rate. Dropout and early termination from therapy have been considered a significant problem in minority mental health. D. W. Sue et al. (1982) have found that American minorities terminate therapeutic services after one contact at a rate greater than 50 percent, in contrast to a 30-percent termination rate for Anglo clients. However, only two of six studies that measured dropout rate in therapy under conditions of ethnic similarity and ethnic dissimilarity found a higher dropout rate when the therapist and client were racially different. In the one study, A. R. Heffernon and D. Bruehl (1971) trained four black and four white college men in Rogerian counseling techniques, then assigned them to two groups. Each group consisted of three eighth-grade black boys. In this study, the counselors met with their groups once a week for eight weeks. Although there were no differences in reactions to counseling between the groups based on paper-and-pencil instruments, all of the counselees of black counselors chose to attend counseling rather than go to the library, whereas only 11 of 23 counselees having white counselors did not choose the library. One particularly interesting finding of this study is that all the counselees of one white counselor preferred counseling to the library, and this counselor was the only white counselor who had substantial previous contact with ghetto blacks. A study by J. T. Gibbs (1975) also used dropout rate as a therapy outcome variable. Using case records of all black students enrolled in a university to determine the duration of treatment for black students using the university mental health clinic, Gibbs found that students averaged 5.32 sessions with black therapists as opposed to 4.14 sessions with white therapists.

The majority of studies measuring dropout rate in therapy did not find any differences based on racial matching between therapist and client. A. Vail (1978) studied early termination from individual therapy in a community mental health clinic with lower-class black patients assigned to therapists who were either black or white. There was no significant difference in dropout rate based on therapist race. No significant correlations were found between remaining in treatment and black patients' attitudes toward whites. In the Proctor and Rosen study (1981), dropout rate was assessed and was not found to be related to racial composition of therapist-client pairs. Similarly, in another condition of the Jones (1978) study, the dropout rate of the black and white clients was assessed and no differences between the groups were found. Finally, G. J. Neimeyer and M. Gonzales (1983) did not find the duration of counseling to be related to racial similarity between treatment dyads with their white and nonwhite subjects.

Two studies employing black subjects in which the duration of therapy varied looked at factors other than dropout rate. M. S. Griffith (1975) determined the length of therapy for black and white clients who had initiated outpatient treatment at a community mental health clinic. A subsample of 64 clients was then selected for follow-up interviews. Racially similar dyads had a longer length of treatment; however, racial matching was not related to client perceptions of satisfaction. Furthermore, clients did not identify racial factors as important to their decisions to discontinue treatment. In an extensive study by E. E. Jones (1982), black and white patients, evenly divided by race, were seen in individual psychotherapy for a mean of more than 31 treatment hours. Half the patients in each group were in racially similar therapist-client matches, and half were in racially dissimilar pairings. There were no differences in therapist measures of psychotherapy outcome as a function of therapist-client racial match. It is important to note that patients were excluded from this study who did not continue in treatment for more than eight therapy sessions. It seems that racial matching is most likely to have its greatest impact in that early stage of treatment. This assertion is supported by the research that yielded less favorable findings for white therapist–black client pairs undergoing a single interview (Banks et al., 1967; Grantham, 1973). Jones (1982) suggests that, if a white therapist can establish an effective therapeutic alliance relatively rapidly, successful outcomes can be achieved.

The findings of the outcome studies strongly suggest that racially different therapists can be as effective as black therapists with black clients. This appears to be true particularly in psychotherapy relationships of a duration longer than one session. It is likely that either therapist or client variables that contribute to more effective outcomes cause treatment to continue beyond one session. A number of factors may hinder cross-cultural therapy effectiveness. Mental health professionals would do well to be aware of racist feelings in themselves and to work through them when they arise. Furthermore, they must be open to perceiving and understanding the influences of racist forces on the problems of their black clients. Another factor that can affect the success of cross-racial psychotherapy is a lack of cultural awareness or understanding on the part of the therapist. Therapists who are unfamiliar with the culture of their client would probably find it difficult to empathetically understand the client. In addition, therapists must become aware of their own ethnicity and cultural heritage and to come to value and respect racial differences.

Reviewers of this literature have arrived at various conclusions. While J. M. Sattler (1977) concluded that the therapist's race is, for the most part, not a significant variable in these studies, M. S. Griffith (1977) concluded that the research literature suggests that racial differences have a somewhat negative effect upon psychotherapy. S. L. Garfield and A. E. Bergin (1978) conclude, "The fact that almost no studies have been reported by 'real' therapy comparing black and white therapists seriously limits the inferences to be drawn from this literature" (p. 257).

There are also potentially confounding factors that have not been assessed in many of these studies yet may account for the findings. For instance, most of these studies did not consider the influence of social class on the findings. Other factors that were seldom accounted for included those previously mentioned, such as the political climate at the time or place of the study, the racial identity of the subjects, and the subjects' perception of how the findings of the study may affect them. The impact of these and other factors must be assessed before definitive conclusions about cross-racial therapy effectiveness can be drawn.

SOCIAL CLASS

There has been evidence that lower-class patients in mental health treatment receive more serious diagnoses than higher-class patients. It is likely that examiner bias has contributed to misdiagnosis in lower-class populations. One study investigated the effect of social class factors on diagnostic evaluations. The Rorschach Inkblot Test was employed in a study designed to examine the role of socioeconomic class factors on examiner bias (Haase, 1964). The findings of this study demonstrated a bias against the lower-class patients in prediagnostic impressions, diagnostic scores, and prognostic scores. There was also a statistically significant tendency for psychologists to diagnose lower-class patients as character disordered or psychotic as opposed to normal or neurotic for the middle-class patients. It has been argued, on one hand, that these findings are a result of prejudice against lower-class patients. However, it might also be argued that social class in itself is an index of less pathology and better prognosis. E. Jones (1974) suggests that, because lower-class patients are diagnosed less hopefully, are less likely to be accepted into treatment, and are more likely to be victims of negative bias on the part of therapists, that a self-fulfilling prophesy may explain these findings.

While the studies investigating the effects of social class on diagnosis are sparse, a number of studies have considered the impact of class factors on mental health treatment. Jones (1974), in a comprehensive review of the literature on social class and psychotherapy, found that lower-class patients are less likely than higher-class patients to be accepted into treatment. Even when the cost of treatment was ruled out as a contributing variable, lower-class patients were found to receive significantly less treatment than higher-status patients (Schaffer & Myers, 1954; Brill & Storrow, 1960). The Schaffer and Myers study also found that there was a relationship between the rank of the therapist and the social class of the patient; senior clinic staff tended to treat patients from high social classes, and residents tended to treat patients from the lower social classes.

This research suggests a strong relationship between social class and acceptance into treatment. Higher-class patients are more often treated with psychotherapy, and lower-class patients are more often treated with electroshock, tranquilizers, and confinement (Hollingshead & Redlich, 1958). This does not appear to be related exclusively to the lower-class patient's preference for treatment modality, however, because one study conducted at a psychiatric clinic found that 52 percent of lower-class patients indicated that they wanted insight therapy, 48 percent wanted advice, and only 14 percent wanted medication (Goin et al., 1965). Furthermore, there is no clear evidence that lower-class patients do not possess the characteristics necessary for successful involvement in psychotherapy.

Some research has also looked at dropout rate and social class. The findings suggest a relationship between social class and tendency for early dropout from treatment as well as a relationship between social class and length of treatment. Some research has shown that minority clients tend to drop out of treatment after fewer sessions than white clients (Sue & Sue, 1977), and these differences may be accounted for in part by social class differences. Jones (1974), in his review of the literature on social class and psychotherapy, found that only two studies failed to find a strong association between social class and continuation in psychotherapy and that the weight of the data indicates that there is a correlation between social class and continuation in psychotherapy.

The specific problems that may come from living in poverty often demand immediate solutions. Lower-income clients may be overwhelmed with reality concerns such as inadequate housing or unemployment. Such concerns may cause these clients to be focused on mere survival on a day-to-day basis. Until these concerns are appropriately addressed, it is unlikely that such individuals will be able to do what is typically required of them in psychotherapy. The therapist must focus on situational problems which may need to stabilize before deeper personal problems can be dealt with.

The lower-class client is most likely to enter psychotherapy with little or no knowledge about or understanding of the therapy process. In the first few sessions of therapy, the client is at high risk for premature termination. Lower-class patients will probably have expectations about treatment that are different from the expectations of the therapist. Each patient, therefore, must be educated about his or her role as a client and the psychotherapy process, including the expected time frame of the therapy, the specific goals of the therapy, and the manner in which the client's concerns will be addressed. It is important that parameters such as fees and payment schedules be agreed upon initially and reflect the client's ability to pay. Specifically educating lower-class clients about psychotherapy may help reduce anxiety about this unfamiliar endeavor. Vague or incomplete descriptions of the goals, process, and parameters of psychotherapy by the therapist may increase the patient's anxiety and increase the likelihood that the patient will terminate therapy prematurely.

It has been suggested that some mental health practitioners may be more effective with lower-class patients, although the research is not conclusive in this area. Since psychotherapists are not typically classified in the lower social classes by reason of their educational and professional status, some writers have suggested that many psychotherapists may not be able to empathize or work effectively with their lower-class clients.

However, it has also been suggested that the present social class of the therapist is less relevant than the therapist's social class of origin. In this view, therapists who had lower-class backgrounds may be more able to understand lower-class patients than therapists of middle- and upper-class backgrounds. D. B. Kandel (1966) looked at the social class of origin of psychiatric residents and the social class of patients in a hospital setting. In this study, each patient was assigned to a psychiatric resident who chose whether or not to include psychotherapy in the treatment plan. The residents from a lower social class of origin (III and IV) saw approximately equal proportions of each class of patients in therapy. However, the residents from higher social class origins (I and II) chose to become involved in psychotherapy with 100 percent of their Class I patients and only 65 percent of their Class V patients. Although this evidence suggests that therapists from lower social classes of origin are more likely to undertake psychotherapy with lower-class patients, there is no suggestion that psychotherapy is more or less successful when the therapist and client are from similar social class backgrounds.

There has been some suggestion that therapists who deal with racial issues in the first few sessions seem to be more successful at keeping lower-class black patients in treatment (Krebs, 1971). There is also evidence that therapists who have more clinical experience have lower dropout rates with lower-class patients (Baum, Felzer, D'Zmura, & Schumaker, 1966). It appears that a multitude of factors may be involved in the successful treatment of lower-class patients in mental health settings and that these factors merit further investigation to improve the quality of mental health treatment in economically and socially deprived populations.

In conclusion, the research suggests that lower-class patients in mental health treatment are more often diagnosed as severely impaired, are less frequently accepted for treatment, are more likely to drop out of therapy prematurely, and are more likely to have a shorter duration of therapy than higher-class patients.

GENDER

The effects of client gender on mental health diagnosis and treatment have been the subject of much debate over the years. The Diagnostic and Statistician Manual of Mental Disorders, Third Edition (DSM-III) is the primary diagnostic tool of mental health professionals. This manual refers to gender differences in many of the psychiatric diagnoses. It is suggested that certain disorders occur more frequently in men, and other disorders occur more frequently in women. However, some investigators have suggested that the criteria for some of these disorders are restrictive and reflect sex bias. DSM-III has been criticized for failing to represent female patients, in particular, adequately (Rudden, Sweeney, Frances, & Gilmore, 1983). A revision of this manual, currently under way, will attempt to improve upon some of the gender-related problems.

The question of whether there are differential effects of therapist or client gender on the therapy process or outcome has been addressed in the research. E. E. Jones and C. L. Zoppel (1982) found that clients remain in treatment significantly longer with a therapist of the same gender. In addition, clients seen by women therapists in this study perceived their therapist as more accepting, attentive, and comprehensible than clients seen by male therapists. The clients did not appear to identify or perceive directly any sort of sex bias; they simply judged women therapists as forming superior therapeutic alliances. In regard to the therapists' ratings of outcome, women therapists rated their women patients as significantly more improved than their male patients. Regardless of client gender, women therapists rated their clients as having greater overall success in therapy, as having undergone a greater degree of change in basic personality structure, and as experiencing greater satisfaction with treatment.

Garfield and Bergin (1978), however, in their extensive review of research on gender differences in psychotherapy, conclude that there is very little evidence to support any conclusions about the effects of same-sex versus opposite-sex pairs on therapy outcome. They found that the great majority of studies that investigated the relationship between therapist sex and outcome of therapy did not find any differences attributable to therapist sex.

A few studies have looked specifically at gender differences in therapy with black patients. Grantham (1973), in a study using black college students as subjects, found a relationship between counselor sex and client depth of self-exploration. Black female subjects seen by female counselors, regardless of race, explored themselves more deeply than did subjects seen by male counselors. However, client satisfaction with counseling was not found to relate significantly to the sex of the counselor. A study by C. E. Briley (1977) found that black male students preferred a male counselor for far more problems than they preferred a female counselor. However, Vail (1978) found that male therapists, regardless of race, were less effective with black male patients than with black female patients and that black and white female therapists were also less effective with black patients of their own sex, although this finding was not as pronounced as the finding for male therapists.

The varied findings of these studies offer little help in clarifying the effects of gender on the mental health treatment of black clients. Gender considerations, however, can be of great importance in counseling and psychotherapy. Many clients may have great difficulty working with a therapist of a certain gender because of dynamic issues related to problems with persons of that particular gender. Some of these clients may actually be unable to work with therapists of a certain gender. Of those who do not fall into that category and of those who could work with a therapist of either gender, many may choose a therapist of the gender with which they feel most comfortable to avoid dealing with the feelings that arise when in a relationship with someone of the gender with which they have difficulty relating.

AGE

The effects of the client's or mental health practitioner's age on mental health treatment has been an important topic of consideration. There has been much debate concerning the treatability of older patients. Many mental health professionals perceive older patients as more rigid, more characterologically fixed, and more resistant to change than younger patients. They are therefore perceived as poorer candidates for insight-oriented psychotherapy. In fact, one study found that patients over 39 years of age were overrepresented in the psychiatric inpatient service and underrepresented in individual psychotherapy (Lubin, Hornstra, Lewis, & Bechtel, 1973). There is no clear evidence, however, that a relationship exists between age and either continuation in psychotherapy or psychotherapy outcome (Garfield and Bergin, 1978).

It has been our observation that black, geriatric, psychiatric populations have as much a need for individual psychotherapy as other psychiatric populations.

Furthermore, the assumption that such patients are unable to use insight in psychotherapy seems only to have limited further the effectiveness of the mental health care of elderly black patients. Adequate consideration must be given to psychological factors in the treatment of these patients. Many elderly patients can be effectively treated on an outpatient basis with appropriate supports.

In the mental health treatment of elderly black patients, intervention must address many social problems that contribute to their difficulties as well. The many physical as well as societal changes that come about with aging can contribute to changes in the emotional well-being of the elderly. There is a great need for mental health professionals to incorporate into geriatric treatment programs a knowledge of these factors. In addition, referral sources must be built up to direct the elderly toward assistance in such areas as transportation, legal assistance, attainment of social security benefits, general home care and housing maintenance, and attainment of adequate medical care. In addition, providing opportunities for involvement in leisure and exercise activities that facilitate increased social contact can help treat the loneliness and isolation that are significant mental health problems in the black geriatric community. Mental health treatment programs must address these problems in the treatment planning of geriatric patients. In our perspective, the mutual treatment of intrapsychic difficulties and social psychological problems is the most effective strategy for the mental health treatment of black geriatric patients. There seems to be a great need for day hospitals and outpatient treatment programs involving multidisciplinary treatment of geriatric patients. Such programs can help treat the medical, psychological, and social problems of elderly black patients and therefore provide the comprehensive treatment that is so greatly needed in this population.

On the other end of the age spectrum, there has been an emphasis on the mental health needs of black children. S. M. Stehno (1982) stated that differential treatment of black children exists in mental health service systems; black children are underserved. In addition, black children are more likely to be treated by the public sector than the private sector.

CONCLUSION

Idiosyncrasies aside, there is overwhelming evidence to suggest that the major hurdles which confront the black patient in a mixed race therapy situation can be reduced to differences in socioeconomic status. Implicit between the lines of the research findings reported here are the difficulties in reporting on a representative ''black'' patient. The reader need only be transported across the socioeconomic classes of lower, lower middle, middle, upper middle, lower upper, and upper for both blacks and whites with all their attendant accessories to understand the complexity of drawing unequivocal conclusions. Yet the pervasive nature of racism serves to enhance the differences in socioeconomic status and the other social factors reported here.

It is our belief that as further work is built upon the data summarized in this chapter and with dissemination in the mental health discipline, differences in therapy can only be diminished. Additional progress will follow with further reporting on the roles of religion, dress, language, deductive thought patterns, sex roles, and other factors in the black population. Perhaps only then can the nonblack therapist be equipped with the intangibles needed for successful treatment outcome—Who is this person sitting across from me? What are his or her needs and wants? What environment will he or she return to after this session? Can I truly understand the urgency, the trauma as expressed? Can I respond in kind?

REFERENCES

Adebimpe, V. R. (1981). Overview: White norms in psychiatric diagnosis of black patients. *American Journal of Psychiatry, 138*(3), 279–285.

Banks, G., Berenson, G. G., & Carkhuff, R. R. (1967). The effects of counselor race and training upon counseling process with Negro clients in initial interviews. *Journal of Clinical Psychology, 23*, 70–72.

Baum, O. E., Felzer, S. B., D'Zmura, T. L., & Schumaker, E. (1966). Psychotherapy, dropouts, and lower socioeconomic patients. *American Journal of Orthopsychiatry, 36*, 629–635.

Briley, C. E. (1977). The relationship between race, sex, type of problem and interpersonal trust in determining ethnic-racial preference for counselor. (Doctoral dissertation, Eastern Texas State University, 1977). *Dissertation Abstracts International, 38*, 3282-A.

Brill, N. Q., & Storrow, H. A. (1960). Social class and psychiatric treatment. *Archives of General Psychiatry, 3*, 340–344.

Cimbolic, P. T. (1973). Counselor race and experience effects on black clients. *Journal of Consulting and Clinical Psychology, 39*, 328–332.

Ewing, T. M. (1974). Racial similarity of client and counselor and client satisfaction with counseling. *Journal of Counseling Psychology, 21*, 446–449.

Garfield, S. L., & Bergin, A. E. (1978). *Handbook of psychotherapy and behavior change: An empirical analysis* (2d ed.). New York: Wiley.

Gibbs, J. T. (1975). Use of mental health services by black students at a predominantly white university: A three year study. *American Journal of Orthopsychiatry, 45*, 430–445.

Goin, M. K. et al. (1965). Therapy congruent with class-linked expectations. *Archives of General Psychiatry, 13*, 133–137.

Grantham, R. J. (1973). Effects of counselor sex, race, and language style on black students in initial interviews. *Journal of Counseling Psychology, 20*, 553–559.

Griffith, M. S. (1975). Effects of race and sex of client and therapist on the duration of outpatient psychotherapy (Doctoral dissertation, University of Colorado, 1975). *Dissertation Abstracts International, 36*, 4157B.

Griffith, M. S. (1977). The influences of race on the therapeutic relationship. *Psychiatry, 40*, 27–40.

Haase, W. (1964). The role of socioeconomic class in examiner bias. In F. Reissmen et al. (Eds.), *Mental health of the poor*. New York: Free Press.

Heffernon, A. R., & Bruehl, D. (1971). Some effects of race of inexperienced lay counselors on black junior high school students. *Journal of School Psychology*, *9*, 35–37.

Hollingshead, A. B., & Redlich, F. C. (1958). *Social class and mental illness*. New York: Wiley.

Jackson, J. (1975). Black college students' preferences of black and white counselors in a white university (Doctoral dissertation, 1975). *Dissertation Abstracts International*, *36*, 5824A.

Jones, B. E., & Gray, B. A. (1986). Problems in diagnosing schizophrenia and affective disorders among blacks. *Hospital Community Psychiatry*, *37*(1), 61–65.

Jones, E. (1974). Social class and psychotherapy: A critical review of research. *Psychiatry*, *37*, 307–320.

Jones, E. E. (1978). Effects of race on psychotherapy process and outcome: An exploratory investigation. *Psychotherapy: Theory, Research and Practice*, *15*, 226–236.

Jones, E. E. (1982). Psychotherapists' impressions of treatment outcome as a function of race. *Journal of Clinical Psychology*, *38*(4), 722–731.

Jones, E. E., & Zoppel, C. L. (1982). Impact of client and therapist gender on psychotherapy process and outcome. *Journal of Consulting and Clinical Psychology*, *50*(2), 259–272.

Kandel, D. B. (1966). Status homophily, social context, and participation in psychotherapy. *American Journal of Sociology*, *71*, 640–650.

Karasu, T. B., Stein, S. P., & Charles, M. A. (1979). Age factors in patient-therapist relationship. *The Journal of Nervous and Mental Disease*, *16*(167), 100–104.

Krebs, R. L. (1971). Some effects of a white institution on black psychiatric outpatients. *American Journal of Orthopsychiatry*, *41*, 589–596.

Lubin, B., Hornstra, R. K., Lewis, R. V., & Bechtel, B. S. (1973). Correlates of initial treatment assignment in a community mental health center. *Archives of General Psychiatry*, *29*, 497–504.

Neimeyer, G. J., & Gonzales, M. (1983). Duration, satisfaction, and perceived effectiveness of cross-cultural counseling. *Journal of Counseling Psychology*, *30*(1), 91–95.

Pinchot, N., Riccio, A. C., & Peters, H. J. (1975). Elementary school students' and their parents' preferences for counselors. *Counselor Education and Supervision*, *15*, 28–33.

Proctor, E. K., & Rosen, A. (1981). Expectations and preferences for counselor race and their relation to intermediate treatment outcomes. *Journal of Counseling Psychology*, *28*, 40–46.

Raskin, A., Crook, T. H., & Herman, K. D. (1975). Psychiatric history and symptom differences in black and white depressed inpatients. *Journal of Consulting and Clinical Psychology*, *43*, 73–80.

Riccio, A. C., & Barnes, K. D. (1973). Counselor preferences of senior high school students. *Counselor Education and Supervision*, *13*, 36–40.

Rudden, M., Sweeney, J., Frances, A., & Gilmore, M. (1983). A comparison of delusional disorders in women and men. *American Journal of Psychiatry*, *140*(12), 1575–1578.

Sattler, J. M. (1977). The effects of therapist-client racial similarity. In A. S. Burman & A. M. Razin (Eds.), *Effective Psychotherapy*. New York: Pergamon.

Schaffer, L., & Myers, J. K. (1954). Psychotherapy and social stratification: An empirical study of practice in a psychiatric outpatient clinic. *Psychiatry*, *17*, 83–93.

Stehno, S. M. (1982). Differential treatment of minority children in service systems. *Social Work, 27*, 39–45.

Stranges, R., & Riccio, A. (1970). Counselee preference for counselors: Some implications for counselor education. *Counselor Education and Supervision, 10*, 39–46.

Sue, D. W., Bernier, J. E., Durran, A., Feinberg, L., Pedersen, P., Smith, E. J., & Vasquez-Nuttall, E. (1982). Position paper: Cross-cultural counseling competencies. *The Counseling Psychologist, 10*(2), 45–52.

Sue, D. W., & Sue, D. (1977). Barriers to effective cross-cultural counseling. *Journal of Counseling Psychology, 24*(5), 420–429.

Thompson, R. A., & Cimbolic, P. (1978). Black students' counselor preference and attitudes toward counseling center use. *Journal of Counseling Psychology, 24*(5), 420–429.

Vail, A. (1978). Factors influencing lower-class black patients remaining in treatment. *Journal of Consulting and Clinical Psychology, 46*(2), 341.

Wolkon, G. H., Moriwaki, S., & Williams, K. J. (1973). Race and social class as factors in the orientation toward psychotherapy. *Journal of Counseling Psychology, 20*, 312–316.

PART V

FAMILY AND COMMUNITY VIOLENCE

10

Understanding Family Violence: An Afrocentric Analysis Based on Optimal Theory

Linda James Myers

The phrase family violence would seem a contradiction in terms in an orderly, healthy society. Why are those whose union is assumed sacred (common law or not) being moved to the point of violence toward one another and their offspring? What is at the root of the anger and hostility? A society in which three out of five married women will experience violence from their partners within the duration of their marriage is at risk of disintegrating from within. As the bonds of the family, the basic unit of social organization, are weakened internally, the very fabric of civilization is weakened, and moral corruption and confusion are manifest. What happens to the Afro-American family in such a society, and what are the implications for black mental health and illness? This chapter pursues these ideas and questions more fully, paying particular attention to the logical conclusions of the analysis based on the optimal psychological theory of an Afrocentric worldview. This task is accomplished in three phases: (1) the framework of optimal theory is briefly outlined; (2) the roots of family violence and its meaning at the personal-individual, familial-community, and cultural-social levels are explored; and (3) the methods that must be employed to ameliorate the situation are discussed for each level.

OPTIMAL THEORY

Family violence in black families cannot be fully understood without some consideration being given to racist and sexist oppression and the impact of that oppression on the culture and socialization of Afro-Americans. To provide greater clarity and breadth to the discussion, a nonracist/nonsexist (optimal) analysis of the problem is presented. The basic premise is that movement from an optimal to a suboptimal conceptual system accounts for most family violence. L. J. Myers (1988) identifies the roots of optimal psychology to be grounded in the cultural and historical beginnings of humankind and human civilization (Eisler, 1987). As the philosophical assumptions and principles of the ancient traditional African worldview (Nichols, 1976) are identified and examined, the parameters of consciousness (thought/feeling) structured to yield maximal positivity in experience can be articulated. Based on the assumption that a man or woman could elevate his or her consciousness (awareness) to be in union with the infinite (deification), the ancients laid the foundation for optimal thought. The reasoning, based on the union of opposites, or diunital logic, yields both/and conclusions. As such we seek to reason with the unity that contains and transforms (transcends) all opposites. For example, the law of opposites informs us that, in order to know one most fully, we must first know too, its opposite; otherwise, the one simply becomes "isness" or "suchness." In order to fully comprehend good, the positive, one must know its opposite or not good, evil or negativity. The interaction of the two becomes the basis of life or existence itself (i.e., male and female, magnetism, natural forces). In terms of human experience, the necessity and purpose of so-called negativity is to bring us back to the realization of our oneness, our true identity as the expression of infinite spirit (that which is known in extrasensory fashion, as is consciousness, energy, God) when we see ourselves as separate from it. Given that the purpose or function of negativity is edification, moving us toward increased knowledge of self as one with the source of all good, we can reason that nothing from which good comes can be truly bad. The opposites have subsequently been transformed, unified, contained, and transcended.

Within this reality construction (Myers, 1984) self-knowledge becomes the basis of all knowledge, as self-love is the basis of all love. The purpose of life is to come to realize who one is as the individual and unique expression of infinite spirit. The method by which this goal is accomplished is the use of human and spiritual networks (ntuology). As such, an implicit order can be identified, moving from the most inward to the most outward. To the extent I love and respect myself, I will love and respect those closest to me. If I fail to realize self-love, love for others will be difficult to manifest, and disorder will creep into my relationships and into those of my future generations. This outcome is the natural consequence of the true nature of my being, which is one with the ancestors, the yet unborn, nature, and my entire community. The same energy is infinitely and uniquely manifest through a recycling process of reincarnation.

As this energy spectrum is perpetuated in humankind through the family system, we see the means of transmission and influence brought to bear on the nature and manifestation of that energy. Culture and socialization become very important in this regard, for they provide the basic structure for perception, thought, feeling, experience, and ultimately history. At the level of cultural deep structure, a conceptual system has shaped the way of life of a people and given form to its reality (Myers, 1987). Through the socialization of the young, this reality is passed on to generation after generation, since the philosophical assumptions and principles structuring one's view of the world (conceptual system) deep structure, seldom change without conscious effort.

Optimal theory suggests that to the extent that interrelatedness and interdependence of all things is comprehended, a supremely good order can be discerned, which must place the highest value on positive interpersonal relationships, the mechanism affording the greatest order and longevity of the overall system. Afro-Americans, indeed all of humankind, have as a part of their ancestral past this reality. It must be rediscovered if we are to attain health as a world community.

ROOTS OF FAMILY VIOLENCE

Within a culture that socializes its adherents to believe not only in their own individualism and autonomy, but also in the discrete and segmented nature of all aspects of reality, the basis for cohesion and order will in time be found lacking. The conceptual system of dominant socialization in such a society is at best suboptimal, in that it emphasizes the material aspects of reality to the point of using such to define human worth, values, and ultimately experience. In other words, worth comes to be based on how one looks, what one owns, where one lives; acquisition of objects becomes the highest value; and material gain and domination can be the justification for the enslavement of a race of people (Africans), the annihilation of another (Native Americans), and the subjugation of over half of its own (women).

For the individual, the consequences from our optimal perspective of such a socialization will be an alienation from self (Akbar, 1981). The individual, lacking the basis for a sense of intrinsic worth, peace, and well-being, will look outside himself or herself to find it (often turning to alcohol and drugs). Such an external orientation, continually reinforced by the society, distorts the notion and nature of love to the degree that it is internalized. Without the wherewithal for a more than temporary, illusory love of self, things fall apart. When one lacks a solid foundation of self-love, one is not fully capable of loving others; consequently love/hate relationships emerge between and among family members. Since the child learns much about social relations and interaction through modeling, a vicious cycle can be set in play, if the child has not learned to love constructively. Of course, racism compounds the negative impact of suboptimal socialization, as does sexism.

The insecurity, anger, and frustration often felt at unconscious levels are projected toward others (most often those closest to us) in abusive behavior. For a black male who has internalized the suboptimal conceptual system, unemployment not only can have a devastating effect on his self-image and morale, but also result in family disruption and violence. R. J. Sampson (1987) presents data which identify the structural linkages among unemployment, economic disruption, and family disruption in urban black communities. He goes further, in supporting our thesis, by showing that the scarcity of employed black men increases the prevalence of families headed by females, and, in turn, black family disruption substantially increases the rates of black murder and robbery, especially by juveniles. Those effects were found to be independent of income, region, race, age composition, density, city size, and welfare benefits, and they are similar to the effects of white family disruption on white violence. The interdependence and interrelatedness of these phenomena must be explored more fully.

C. F. Johnson and J. Showers (1985) found, after analyzing child abuse reporting records of 616 children in a metropolitan children's hospital, that boys were referred for abuse more often than girls. Black children were reported disproportionately more often than were white children. Mothers were the most frequent perpetrators of abuse, although males constituted more than half of the abusers. The abused child/adult abuser cycle will be impossible to break given what we have learned, until the depth and pervasiveness of the problem are addressed on a community and societal level.

We now have a fragmented social structure that reinforces family disruption in an institutionalized (though possibly unintentionally so) way. That is, the fragmentation occurs at all levels and is inculcated in the individual through the conceptual system of dominant socialization and in the family through the system of social, political, and economic organization. In society the reinforcement of fragmentation is self-perpetuating.

J. Daniel, R. L. Hampton, and E. H. Newberger (1983) report findings that indicate that black families who abuse their children suffer from poverty, social isolation, and stressful relationships with and among kin. Maternal depression and poor mobility were noted more frequently in black families where children's injuries were seen as accidental. Yet, these families were seen as having many strengths in comparison to the families whose children were diagnosed as abused. Although a family's ability to protect a child from an environmental hazard may be enhanced by the association of the mother's sense of well-being and connection to kin and community, family parental competency is eroded qualitatively and quantitatively by the burdens associated with child abuse. For black families, the contexts of child abuse appear to be those of severe economic adversity (material constraints), the absence of someone to turn to for help (social alienation and isolation), a death in the family (segmented sense of life), a history of having suffered serious personal violence (generational cycles), and the presence of a child who may be delayed in social and cognitive development.

Thus the roots of family violence run to the very core of the social construction of reality propagated in this culture. The disorderly, uneven allocation of material resources, social alienation and isolation, and segmented sense of life become part of a self-perpetuating cycle that can be broken only by major intervention strategies that dare to examine the role of our own worldview (structured by our suboptimal conceptual system) in the generation and maintenance of the problem.

METHODS OF AMELIORATION

Family violence must be addressed holistically. As we argued in the previous section, although the potential to be violent is universal, the suboptimal conceptual system of dominant socialization in this culture serves to predispose and reinforce such an outcome. Therefore any intervention that is to be effective must take into consideration attacking those roots. An internally consistent alternative construction of reality that is rational, immersed in the dispensation of love, and geared toward the good of all has been presented in the theoretical frame of reference of our analysis, optimal theory. This perspective has been described as Afrocentric (centered in Africa as the historical point of generation); it is also based on feminine principles (Myers, 1986). However, the racism and sexism that are so pervasive in our society share with family violence their roots in the suboptimal conceptual system of dominant socialization in the West. Being so, the alternative presented here may be difficult for some to appreciate, as it reflects a black and female orientation, similar to that which existed in the beginnings of human culture and civilization (Sjoo and Mor, 1987). The reality reflected in family violence in this society is very much influenced by sexism and racism; they are intertwined for they come from the same core, a faulty, socially reinforced mentality. This is not to say that all, or even the majority in the society, accept family violence, racism, or sexism. What is suggested is that the predisposition to and the reinforcement for each are part of the very fabric of our construction of reality in this society, institutionalized as the lens through which we perceive, think, feel, act, and experience.

Let us try out a new lens, so that our perspective can be enlarged. An individual who feels intrinsically worthy, as in optimal thought, has within an inherent love of self and the basis of love for others. Even the frustrations of material deprivation get a fresh and clearer reading from a stance which sees self as one with the source of all. Because self is viewed differently, so must one's mate come to be appreciated for more than the external can inform. One's children, the extension and reflection of self, become valued and appreciated differently. One's relationship to one's community changes as it too becomes an extension of self. Moving back to that characteristic of black culture, the extended family becomes a prized necessity.

The entire nuclear family structure and system of organization will need to be reevaluated. Two parents encounter great difficulty in raising conscious, confident, competent children in this culture. Single-parent families, much less those comprising children having children, bespeak a significant breakdown and disruption of the family constellation. Sex roles are called into question, with a bent toward greater fluidity of roles for functionality. Dating and mating practices must be reexamined, so must human sexuality in general.

The role of the media in fostering or diminishing family violence must be considered as well as the role of every social institution from formal education to government. Clearly, a massive educational intervention is called for, not because conceptual systems can change overnight, but so that people can understand more fully the impact of their current socialization and make more conscious informed decisions about their worldview choices.

SUMMARY

The health and strength of a society and civilization can be measured by its basic unit of organization and socialization, the family. All kinds of data would indicate our need to examine and reassess the family structure and functioning in this society. An optimal Afrocentric perspective has been taken to address the issue of family violence, particularly as it pertains to the black family. Such a perspective offers greater understanding of the roots of family violence, as well as direction for its amelioration.

Although it is beyond the purview of this chapter to delineate all of the measures to be taken to ameliorate the problem of family violence in this society, education has been identified as a major method of intervention. Whether in small self-help groups organized by individuals, through churches and social organizations, or in more formal settings staffed by professionals, massive exploration and self-examination must be undertaken not just for the victims of family violence or the victimizers, but for the health, safety, and well-being of us all.

REFERENCES

Akbar, N. (1981). Mental disorder among African-Americans. *Black Books Bulletin*, *7*(2), 19–24.

Daniel, J., Hampton, R. L., & Newberger, E. H. (1983). Child abuse and accidents in black families: A controlled comparative study. *American Journal of Orthopsychiatry*, *53*(4), 645–653.

Eisler, R. (1987). *The chalice and the blade: Our history and our future*. San Francisco: Harper and Row.

Johnson, C. F., & Showers, J. (1985). Injury variables in child abuse. *Child Abuse and Neglect*, *9*(20), 207–215.

Myers, L. J. (1984). The psychology of knowledge: The importance of world view. *New England Journal of Black Studies*, *4*, 1–12.

Myers, L. J. (1986). Transcending oppression: A black feminist perspective. *Woman and Therapy*, *5*(4), 39–49.

Myers, L. J. (1987). The deep structure of culture: Relevance of traditional culture in contemporary life. *Journal of Black Studies*, *18*(1), 72–75.

Myers, L. J. (1988). *Understanding an Afrocentric world view: Introduction to an optimal psychology*. Dubuque, IA: Kendall/Hunt.

Nichols, E. (1976, November). The philosophical aspects of cultural difference. Paper presented at the meeting of the World Psychiatric Association, Ibadan, Nigeria.

Sampson, R. J. (1987). Urban black violence: The effect of male joblessness and family disruption. *American Journal of Sociology*, *93*(2), 348–382.

Sjoo, M., & Mor, B. (1987). *The great cosmic mother: Rediscovering the religion of the earth*. San Francisco: Harper and Row.

11

BLACK-ON-BLACK HOMICIDE: THE IMPLICATIONS FOR BLACK COMMUNITY MENTAL HEALTH

Carl C. Bell

In 1986 blacks accounted for 44 percent of the murder victims in the United States, and, as in previous years, more than 90 percent of those black victims were slain by black offenders; yet blacks constituted only about 12 percent of the population (Federal Bureau of Investigation, 1987). Black men have a 1 in 21 chance of becoming a homicide victim, and black women have a 1 in 104 chance; white men have a 1 in 131 chance of being a homicide victim, and white women have a 1 in 369 chance. Black-on-black murder is the leading cause of death in black males from 15 to 44 years of age and the leading cause of death in black females from 15 to 34 years of age. It has also been reported that from 1979 to 1981 there were more than 60,000 excess deaths among America's minority citizens. These excess deaths were defined as fatalities that would not have occurred if the mortality rates for minorities had been as low as they were for white Americans. Homicide was among the health problems that accounted for this disparity and accounted for 38 percent of the excess deaths in black men under the age of 45 (Secretary's Task Force on Black and Minority Health, 1985). Nationally, depending on the year examined, homicide rates in blacks have been from five to ten times higher than the rates in whites. Furthermore, since fewer than 6,000 black men were killed during the entire Vietnam war, there have been several single years during which more black men were killed in this country than were killed during that war.

Not only are most of these homicides intraracial, i.e., black-on-black, but they most frequently occur between people who know one another. From 1976 to 1983, black homicide victims knew their assailant in 59.8 percent of the homicides which occurred during those years. Among black males, homicide victims knew their assailant in 58.3 percent of the cases and over 75 percent of those men who knew their assailant knew him as a friend or an acquaintance.

Black female victims knew their assailant in 65.8 percent of the cases, and in 43.8 percent of those homicides the assailant was a family member (Centers for Disease Control, 1986). Related to the fact that most victims and offenders knew each other is the fact that most often the homicide was classified as a primary homicide (64.8 percent), i.e., a homicide not related to any other felony, but one which usually occurred during a nonfelony circumstance such as an argument.

Clearly, from these statistics, it is easy to see why homicide has been considered a major public health problem in this country (Koop, 1985). The problem takes on even greater significance when one considers that homicide frequently removes a life earlier than other major causes of death, such as cerebrovascular disease, and, as a result, is a greater cause of years of potential life lost. Furthermore, when one considers that homicide is the end point of interpersonal violence, and how many aggravated assaults (also known as "incomplete homicides") occur, the toll of interpersonal violence in the black community becomes even more staggering. It has been estimated that for every one homicide there are 100 assaults (Rosenberg & Mercy, 1986). In 1984 there were over 1.6 million aggravated assaults in this country (Bureau of Justice Statistics, 1986), and the rate of aggravated assault victimization is higher among blacks, which results in physical injury being more common in black victims of assault (Dietz, 1987). The cost of treatment for these individuals; the cost of days lost from work, school, or other meaningful activities; and the cost of the disabilities resulting from these assaults are likely to be in the millions of dollars. In addition, when one considers the impact of high rates of victimization on the quality of life in the black community, one realizes the damage cannot begin to be estimated in terms of money. The devastating impact of a homicide on the family of the victim and perpetrator of the homicide cannot be measured economically. The emotional impact of being the victim of a nonlethal assault and the damage such an assault does to countless thousands of black individuals is not quantifiable in terms of dollars and cents. The full effects of children witnessing such violence is unknown, but many of the children who witness violence suffer from post-traumatic stress disorder and have many other behavioral disturbances in childhood and adult life. Battered women suffer more frequently from general medical problems and psychological symptoms of stress such as suicide attempts, alcoholism, drug abuse, and depression (Stark & Flitcraft, 1982). Furthermore, family violence is often a reason cited for divorce and, as a result, can be thought of as one of the destructive forces trying to eat away at the black family. Finally, living in a milieu with high rates of murder and violence takes a particularly high toll on the psyche of the black male who is frequently the target of this aggression (Bell, 1980).

Thus, it should be apparent that black-on-black homicide and the antecedents which lead to the commission of a homicide cause a great deal of damage to the black community. Why then has this problem gone unaddressed since as early as 1932 when H. C. Brearley noted the homicide rates for blacks was seven times that of whites (Brearley, 1932)? This question must be answered because the answers are relevant to the reasons why so little is being done about the problem currently. Until the reasons for such inaction against this serious problem are addressed, the problem will continue to receive less than adequate attention.

OBSTACLES TO SOLVING THE PROBLEM

A number of myths about the problem of homicide cause the community to disown the problem as a community problem. One such myth is that a leading contributor to the black homicide rate are the homicides that are committed by whites against blacks and that these homicides are the result of police shootings or other racially motivated situations. This false belief causes the community to get into a great uproar when a white policeman shoots and kills a black victim, but to do very little about the more common family, friend, or acquaintance homicide. Although it is agreed that any use of lethal force by police officers should be investigated to assure the claim that the action was justified, the expenditure of great amounts of energy on a small problem while the greater problem goes unattended is an error. For the past ten years, about 20,000 people have been killed each year by homicide, and about 9,000 of these have been black. In contrast, about 365 police shootings per year have resulted in a death, and about half of the people shot are black. Clearly, the causes of approximately 9,000 deaths deserve more attention than the cause of 183. Another myth about homicide, which puts the problem in the lap of the criminal justice system rather than in the community, is that criminals are responsible for the high homicide rates among blacks. The reality is that the majority of homicides which occur between blacks are primary homicides, i.e., homicides which are not committed during another felony, such as robbery, but rather are crimes of passion which contain elements of expressive aggression and impulsivity; and as such would seem to be the type of homicide that would be better suited to community interventions. On the other hand, the prevention of homicides by strangers, which are often secondary homicides (i.e., homicides committed during a felony, such as robbery, and which seem to have a more instrumental aggressive motive rather than an expressive aggressive motive) would seem to continue to belong in the purview of the criminal justice system. After all, whereas most people who commit felonies such as robbery would not do so if they were sure to get caught, this does not hold true for the majority of murders which are not planned before they are committed. This is not to say that the criminal justice system is completely devoid of responsibility in preventing murders which are crimes of passion nor that the community is likewise devoid of responsibility in preventing felony murders, but only that efforts by different elements of society should be exerted where they will have the most impact. Taking a public health philosophy toward violence or placing some responsibility for the black-on-black homicide problem in the community is especially crucial since, according to the FBI, "the fact that three out of every five murder victims in 1986 were related to (16 percent) or acquainted with (42 percent) their assailants'' supports the ''philosophy that murder is primarily a societal problem over which law enforcement has little or no control'' (Federal Bureau of Investigation, 1987). The myth of criminals being responsible for large numbers of black homicide victims also causes black apartment dwellers and home owners to keep readily available loaded guns in order to protect themselves from criminals such as burglars. Unfortunately, that gun is more likely to be used against a family member or friend during a heated argument than against a burglar. Another myth is that gang-related homicides are common causes of homicides in major cities, but an examination of the facts reveals that approximately 1 percent of the nation's homicides are gang related, and in cities like Los Angeles, California, and Chicago, Illinois, gang-related murders represent about 3 and 5 percent of the homicides, respectively (University of California at Los Angeles, and Centers for Disease Control, 1985; Block, 1985). Such a myth causes the community to misdirect available resources toward causes of homicide which, although important, are less prevalent. One last myth that diverts community ownership of the homicide problem is the myth that out-of-control drug fiends are killing people. A closer examination of drug-related homicides reveals that it is not a drug-induced frenzy that causes one person to murder another, but rather the disputes over the business of selling illegal drugs. Many of these misleading myths come from the manner in which the media focus on the problem of homicide in the community. By giving significant media attention to the less prevalent but more sensational aspects of the homicide problem, the community is misled into believing that these less prevalent causes of homicide are the most common and, as a result, frequently either do not take any responsibility for correcting the homicide problem or misdirect their resources toward less prevalent, although important, causes of homicide. Until the community learns the facts about the major causes of black-on-black homicide, it will continue to be deluded by the media.

Another obstacle to solving the problem is the lack of a clear understanding of the epidemiologic variables of sex, age, race, circumstance, and victim/ offender relationship, all of which influence the dynamics of homicide, and how these variables assume different importance in different communities and how they change over time. As a result, one often sees a lack of community specificity in homicide intervention strategies. Blacks are more likely to be killed in a home with a handgun during a verbal argument, and if the victim is male the offender tends to be a friend or acquaintance, but if the victim is female the offender tends to be the victim's husband. Hispanic males are more likely to be killed in the street with a handgun or knife during verbal arguments, physical fights, criminal activities, or gang warfare; and offenders are usually friends, acquaintances, or strangers, but not family members or intimates. Violence that results in the homicide of women, young children, and the elderly and violence that results in a homicide occurring in the home are rare among Hispanics. Whites are more likely to be killed in a home with a handgun during criminal activities with offenders usually being friends or acquaintances, but strangers constitute a close second category (University of California at Los Angeles & Centers for Disease Control, 1985; Block, 1985). Thus, homicide prevention strategies designed to reduce homicide in blacks should emphasize reducing the potential for lethal violence in the home during a verbal argument. Unfortunately, many blacks view black-on-black crime prevention activities as efforts that will reduce a significant proportion of black-on-black murder. Such black-on-black crime prevention activities are geared toward preventing such crimes as robbery and burglary, but in Chicago, for example, if all of the robberies, rapes, and burglaries from 1965 to 1981 had been prevented, over 70 percent of the homicides which occurred during that period would have still occurred. Similarly, homicide prevention efforts to reduce gang-related homicides in Chicago would have reduced the 12,892 homicides which occurred in Chicago from 1965 to 1981 by 670 or 5.2 percent. On the other hand, such a prevention effort would have reduced all teenage murders by 25 percent and would have reduced the Latin teenage murders by 50 percent (Block, 1985). From these examples, it should be clear how a consideration of the variables of sex, age, race, circumstance, and victim/offender relationships should influence homicide prevention strategies. Another example of how age considerations should influence homicide prevention strategies is the finding that most murders of young children began as child abuse. An example of how circumstances of homicide should influence the framing of homicide interventions comes from the observation that the rates of drug-related homicides vary greatly from city to city with some cities having a significant proportion of their homicides stemming from this problem while others do not. However, even cities where drug-related homicides constitute a significant proportion of the homicides, such as New York, the rates of the homicides caused by interpersonal disputes are still greater than drug-related homicides; therefore, it would be an error to focus on the prevention of drug-related homicides alone (Tardiff & Gross, 1986). From the above discussion, it should be clear that homicide is a multifaceted, multidimensional problem which takes on different characteristics in different communities and that this complexity is responsible for some of the difficulty in addressing the problem of black-on-black homicide. H. M. Rose (1981) and C. R. Block (1985) have clearly demonstrated that homicide dynamics change over time, and this aspect of homicide makes it all the more difficult to address it effectively. Thus, a given circumstance, e.g., gang-related murders or drug-related murders, may not significantly contribute to the homicide toll in a community during one year, but might the next. These changing dynamics, influenced by social forces such as changing availability of job opportunities for youth or the influx of a new drug to be distributed, make the problem of homicide intervention all the more complex. All of these considerations make homicide patterns appear to be very convoluted and baffling. As a result, some communities adopt homicide prevention strategies which do not fit their particular circumstance. This is another obstacle that prevents the community from adequately addressing the problem of black-on-black murder.

The lack of basic empirical research designed to provide the community with the epidemiologic understanding of black-on-black homicide so that the community can be armed with accurate knowledge to combat the problem is also an obstacle. In addition, research and outcome studies on prevention strategies designed to reduce black-on-black murder have been lacking. For example, a recent review of the literature notes the relationship between acquired central nervous system damage and violence (Bell, 1986a; Bell, 1987a), and how epidemiologic studies indicate that such acquired central nervous system damage (such as head injury) is more common in blacks (Bell & Kelly, 1987). However, little research has been done on blacks to shore up the connections between head injury and the potential for future violence. Although this etiologic factor may be partly responsible for the higher rates of homicide in blacks, most of the studies conducted have been done on whites. Similarly, it has been suggested that physicians directly treat those acquired biologic conditions leading to violence by using various medications that seem to have promise in reducing violence that stems from such contributing causes as head injury (Bell, Prothrow-Smith, Smallwood-Murchison, 1986). Propranolol is one such medication which has been shown to be useful in this regard, but the bulk of the subjects used in the research on propranolol were white, and, since propranolol has been reported to be less effective in black hypertensives, questions have been raised about propranolol's efficacy in blacks who are explosive. Unfortunately, as C. E. Schorer noted, "[T]oo few black patients have been included in studies [on explosiveness] to reach any conclusions about the efficacy of propranolol, or whether race is a differentiating factor" (Schorer, 1987, p. 221).

Other obstacles which inhibit the community from mounting an effective strategy for reducing black-on-black homicide concern racial/ethnic attitudes, fears, and blame placing. Some blacks lack a sense of racial/ethnic identity, and they have mistaken desegregation for integration (Bell, 1986b; Powell, 1982). As a result, those unfortunate blacks may be less willing to take ownership of the problem of black-on-black murder and less willing to take action to change the problem. Other blacks who are firmly rooted in their racial/ethnic identity have concerns about how whites will respond to the issue of black-on-black murders being made public; yet, in order to intervene effectively, the problem must be made public. They are very concerned about raising biologic variables associated with violence because these variables may be interpreted by whites as being innate characteristics of blacks rather than as being acquired characteristics (such as head injury) and because this misinterpretation may fuel white racism. Another inhibiting dynamic concerns who is blamed for the problem, and who is felt to be responsible for correcting the problem. One of the leading theories of why the black homicide rate is so high is the "subculture of violence" theory which proposes that blacks have a subculture (developed from the violence of slavery, racism, and the effects of discrimination, unemployment, and poverty) that not only tolerates violence but expects and promotes it (Meredith, 1984). This theory, which is focused in subcultural dynamics, is questionable, and it leads to inappropriate rationalizations for murder, thereby discouraging further research and hindering the development of intervention strategies short of major subcultural change. Contrary to the subculture of violence theory, the situational sociologic dynamic of poverty has been shown to be a major variable in determining homicide rates, and when the variable of socioeconomic status is held constant, the vast difference in homicide rates between racial/ethnic groups drops out (Flango & Sherbinou, 1976; Loftin & Hill, 1974; Williams, 1984). Thus, the racism that is responsible for the finding that three times as many blacks, Hispanics, and Native Americans are impoverished compared to whites is also blamed for the higher homicide rates in blacks. Furthermore, it is situational sociologic dynamics such as poverty which predisposes blacks to be at greater risk from acquired biologic factors that may contribute to impulsive violence (Bell, 1986c; Bell & Kelly, 1987). As a result, blacks blame whites for the problem of black-on-black murder, and they feel that, until the racism that generates the disproportionate numbers of impoverished blacks stops, there is nothing blacks can do about the problem of black homicide. Some blacks also feel that to place any of the responsibility for black homicide rates on blacks is to blame the victim and that blacks have enough negative responses from whites and should not have to endure a similar negative view from other blacks. Thus, the problem may be selectively unattended to in an effort to decrease the aspersions cast on blacks.

Similarly, some whites have not fully embraced the surgeon general's recommendations that violence against self and others is a major public health problem which should be addressed with public health interventions (Koop, 1985). Since 1984, when the issue of violence against self and others was placed on the public health agenda, a number of states and local areas have begun social and legislative initiatives aimed at reducing suicide but not homicide. For example, in Illinois suicide was over two times more frequent in whites than blacks, and homicide was over seven times more frequent in blacks than whites (State of Illinois, Department of Public Health, 1986); the state social and legislative initiatives designed to address suicide but not homicide may be interpreted as a form of institutional racism. Some whites feel that, since the problem is black-on-black in nature, they do not own any responsibility for the problem, and any efforts to respond to the problem should come from blacks. Furthermore, there is still considerable tension between the racial/ethnic groups, and some whites avoid raising a negative aspect about the black community for fear of being attacked as racists. Also, there are some whites who have not addressed the problem of black-on-black murder because of an underlying fear that, if blacks stop killing blacks, they will start killing whites. Finally, there are some whites who figure that, since blacks are doing such a good job of killing themselves, why should whites interfere.

Thus, there are many obstacles to developing and initiating strategies to reduce black-on-black murder. Fortunately, some individuals and communities have overcome these obstacles, and the problem has begun to be solved.

SOLUTIONS

Consciousness Raising

Since the problem of black-on-black homicide is such a large, complex one, many of the solutions will have to originate from well thought out policies that will be able to influence large numbers of blacks. In order to intervene on this level a number of the above obstacles will have to be overcome, and a great deal of community development will need to be accomplished to put such policies in place. Public awareness and education are mandatory to remove the obstacles inhibiting the problem solving and to begin community development. This awareness and education should focus on destroying the myths of homicide, creating an understanding of the dynamics of common homicide circumstances, developing a commitment for policy action, developing black community ownership of the problem, and stimulating self-help initiatives. For example, the black community must be told and retold that from two-thirds to three-fourths of the black-on-black homicides occur between family, friends, and acquaintances and that a loaded, readily available handgun in the home is 118 times more likely to shoot a family member or a friend than a burglar. Blacks who own guns need to be encouraged to unload their guns and store them properly. Black-targeted radio shows must begin to raise the issue and to correct the black community's misconceptions about homicide (Bell, 1987b). Large community efforts such as the Black-on-Black Love Campaign in Chicago, Illinois, the Blacks Mobilized against Crime in Richmond, Virginia, the Save Our Sons and Daughters in Detroit, Michigan, the March against Crime in Flint, Michigan, the Massachusetts Conference on Violence and Public Health in Boston, the Black Mental Health Alliance Conference on Black-on-Black Homicide: A Mental Health Crisis in Baltimore, Maryland, and the District of Columbia, the Public Health Commission Task Force on Victimization and Violence in Washington, D.C., the New Orleans Association of Black Social Workers Anti-Violence Program in New Orleans, Louisiana, and others must be started, refined, and continued. These community efforts must be clearly focused and targeted based on a thorough understanding of the dynamics of black-on-black violence; otherwise, some of the efforts will be misdirected and ineffective. All of these public awareness and consciousness-raising efforts enlighten the public to the problem of black-on-black murder as well as the problem of interpersonal violence in the black community. This enlightenment makes the work of community development to prevent black-on-black murder much easier because it enables the community to be receptive to the idea of intervening in the problem.

Primary Prevention Solutions

Homicide victims and perpetrators have a propensity for getting into physical altercations more than most people (Dennis, Kirk, Knuckles, et al., 1981; Rose,

1981).Understanding this fact demands that the educational curriculum in primary and secondary schools teach kids how to resolve conflict; for example, if one is verbally insulted, one can pretend that he or she did not hear the insult and ask the offender to repeat the remark; the repeated insult will be far less aggressive and venomous. Such techniques have been taught successfully, resulting in a reduction in the need for fighting behavior. One physician has developed a curriculum that appears to be effective in reducing peer violence in public schools (Prothrow-Stith, 1987). Another curriculum has been developed to increase knowledge and skills useful in reducing family violence, which is a frequent precursor to domestic homicide (Family Violence Curriculum Project, 1984). The community needs to advocate that these curricula become an integral aspect of primary and secondary school programs. Coloring-rhyming books, such as "A Gun IS NOT for Fun," should be distributed to more preschool children (Hylton & Puryear, 1985).

Vocational services for teenagers have been shown to offer young people a legitimate way of making money which satisfies their need to make money without engaging in illegal activities such as selling drugs which may lead to violence. Such vocational services steeped in culturally relevant social supports, such as occur in the House of Umoja in Philadelphia, Pennsylvania, often deter teenagers from becoming involved in gang-related activities which can also lead to violence (Sulton, 1987). Communities must begin to band together and offer such programs to teenagers if gang violence and gang-related homicides are ever to decrease.

Families under stress must get support from community-based services. It has been demonstrated that the establishment of social networks for such families reduces the isolation and tension and thus reduces the abusive, violent potentials in the family. For example, abuse of both children and elderly people can be prevented by the initiation of a day-care program or a volunteer elderly respite care program which are designed to reduce some of the stress engendered in caring for a helpless family member. Parenting classes, family orientation to supportive services in the community, family counseling and family therapy, and other nurturing services can prevent family violence which might otherwise lead to murder. There is evidence that rocking infants provides neuropsychiatric stimulation that is necessary for proper central nervous system development and that such development is necessary for future adequate impulse control (Prescott, 1975). Grandmothers have known for years that rocking infants soothes them so that they can grow up with a sense of internal security; such tips can be taught in parenting classes. The community must ensure that their hospitals and the physicians who care for pregnant teenagers use all of their influence to connect those teenage parents to an educational support system.

Furthermore, the number of interpersonal violent episodes whose etiologic base is implanted in an organic personality syndrome for which acquired central nervous system damage (for example, perinatal trauma, head trauma, or infection) is a significant predisposing factor is unknown (American Psychiatric Association, 1987). Clearly, epidemiologic studies show that lower socioeconomic groups are more predisposed to receiving head injuries (Jennett & Teasdale, 1981). More specifically, blacks have more such injuries than whites; for example, head trauma from free-falls (Ramos & Delany, 1986) and auto accidents (Clark, 1965). One study which outlined the biopsychosocial characteristics of children who later committed murder found that head injury caused by falls from roofs and car accidents was present in two-thirds of the sample (Lewis, Moy, & Jackson, 1985). Another study investigated the psychiatric, neurological, and psychoeducational characteristics of 15 death row inmates and found that all of them had extensive histories and evidence of head injury (Lewis, Pincus, & Feldman, 1986). These findings along with the high prevalence of coma in black subjects (Bell, Thompson, Shorter-Gooden et al., 1985), suggest that acquired biological causes (as opposed to genetic biological causes) may be partly responsible for the disproportionately high levels of black-on-black murder. Another acquired biological cause of violence has been linked to alcohol abuse, which has been shown to deplete serotonin levels in the brain (serotonin is an important neurotransmitter which plays a role in the regulation of aggression). Impulsive violent offenders with antisocial or intermittent explosive personality disorders and impulsive arsonists have been shown to have low levels of the major metabolite of serotonin in their cerebrospinal fluid (Linnolia, Virkkunen, Scheinin, et al., 1983). More research on high-risk populations should be undertaken to confirm these proposed etiologic factors. It would seem that, considering the already firmly established public health implications of central nervous system trauma and alcohol abuse, efforts to improve infant care, to prevent children from having free-falls from windows, and to reduce alcohol consumption in the black community are in order.

Finally, some blacks have identity problems and lack ethnic pride. This seems to add to the devaluation of blacks and, as a result, makes their lives less valuable so that homicide and other attacks are felt to be justified. These attitudes must be corrected. Black middle-class business people and business professionals must adopt strong ethnic values and look out for their less fortunate brothers and sisters. A good example to follow is the Black-on-Black Love Campaign in Chicago where a black hair-care company has adopted a building in a housing development. Funds were spent on a mural that exhibits black pride, a library, a computer lab, and a ceramics shop. For the past two years, as a result of this investment in poor blacks, there has been no graffiti on the walls, there are fewer fights, and gang activity in the building has decreased. Similar investments must be made in similar cities and on a larger scale. L. E. Gary and G. L. Berry (1985) have noted that a strong sense of their blackness may have prevented some blacks from being victims of drug abuse, and, since the National Institute of Alcohol Abuse and Alcoholism has estimated that about one-half of all homicides in the United States are related to the use of alcohol (Alcohol, Drug Abuse, and Mental Health Administration, 1985), a final primary prevention solution to be recommended here are efforts to improve ethnic identity in blacks.

Secondary Prevention Solutions

From 30 to 40 percent of the women murdered in this country are killed by their husbands or lovers usually after being beaten by those men for years. Unfortunately, wife beating is probably the most common but least reported crime in the United States (Illinois Coalition against Domestic Violence, 1986). M. A. Straus, S. K. Steinmetz, and R. J. Gelles (1980) have estimated that each year from 15 to 30 percent of U.S. couples experience marital violence and that each year about two million women are beaten by men. More recently, Straus (1986) has estimated that each year one and a half million women receive medical attention because of an assault by a male partner. E. Stark and A. Flitcraft (1982) estimate that from three to four million women are beaten each year and that battering accounts for one of every five visits to the emergency room by women and half of all injury episodes. Since nonlethal violence is a frequent antecedent to homicide (Straus, 1986) and since blacks have disproportionately higher rates of domestic murder (Block, 1985), one might expect that domestic violence would be disproportionately higher for blacks than for whites; however, the studies on domestic violence and woman abuse are in conflict on this point. For example, Straus, Steinmetz, and Gelles (1980) found that black husbands assaulted their wives four times more often than white husbands assaulted their wives, and that black wives were twice as likely as white wives to have assaulted their husbands. P. A. Klaus and M. R. Rand (1984), however, found no difference in the victimization rates of blacks and whites for violent crimes by spouses or ex-spouses. The reasons for these disparities are unclear, but they may have to do with other variables such as class, income, occupation, employment status, and education (Barnhill, 1980; Okun, 1986). Clearly, the extent of domestic violence is unknown in the black family. Only a few empirically based studies identify victims of family violence in the black community; as a result of this missing data base, no one clearly understands how or where to intervene. What is known, however, is that in Chicago, for example, domestic homicide is most common among blacks, and it accounted for nearly 20 percent of the assault homicides from 1965 to 1981 (Block, 1985). It is also known that the bulk of black-on-black murders results from crimes of passion and that the perpetrators are very remorseful. Several studies, which have been written on the treatment of the perpetrators of impulsive interpersonal violence, indicate that, when they are invited to participate in treatment aimed at reducing behavior that could lead to homicide, many individuals cooperate and benefit from such treatment (Lion, 1972; Lion & Bach-y-Rita, 1970; Okun, 1986). Of course, it helps to have such individuals mandated to receive such treatment (Attorney General's Task Force on Family Violence, 1984).

Taking all of the above into consideration, it becomes clear that a secondary prevention strategy to be enacted should be the identification and treatment of individuals who have already been victims or perpetrators of violence short of murder. This task can be performed in currently existing medical institutions such as emergency rooms, physician's offices, clinics, and health care facilities in correctional institutions. Early identification of tendencies toward domestic or peer violence permits interventions that may preclude a future homicide. Since the medical profession is responsible for treating the sublethal damage which stems from violence, it is incumbent for health professionals to develop skills and techniques to identify individuals at risk. Protocols for identifying, as well as treating, victims of interpersonal violence are available and have been shown to work in emergency rooms where such patients are frequently found (Surgeon General's Workshop on Violence and Public Health, 1986). Screening forms have been shown to be useful in identifying mentally ill patients who have been victimized, and such patients can be referred to a victimization service linked to a mental health agency (Bell, Taylor-Crawford, Jenkins, et al., 1988). The identification of the black mentally ill who are victimized is especially crucial as victimization is common in this population and has a significant impact on treatment. Furthermore, it has been reported that the rate of homicidal deaths among psychiatric emergency room patients was twice as high as that of the general population (Hillard, Zung, Ramm, et al., 1985). Screening in general medical clinic settings can also be useful (Bell, Hildreth, Jenkins, et al., 1988). For example, if all gynecologists asked their female patients whether they were experiencing domestic violence, there would be a case-finding vehicle for domestic violence, and once victims were identified handbooks for domestic violence victims could be distributed to them. Perpetrators of repetitive sublethal violence could also be identified and treated. A review of the literature reveals that several medications (e.g., propranolol, lithium, trazadone, and carbamazepine) have been useful in treating perpetrators of impulsive violence and that such medications, along with psychotherapy, can aid these offenders (Bell, 1986a; Bell, 1987a). Individuals who have already been perpetrators or victims of violence can also be identified and treated in correctional institutions by health care professionals providing there is support from institutional policies such as those recommended by the National Commission of Correctional Health Care (1987). (Incidentally, health professionals in correctional institutions can also ensure that inmates become educated about the facts of homicide and how they can avoid becoming victims or perpetrators of homicide.)

There are flaws in the ways in which the criminal justice system handles domestic violence. For example, the police method for intervening in domestic violence is ineffective if it consists of merely advising a spouse batterer to walk around the block to cool off. In a study on domestic violence conducted in Kansas City, Kansas, in 1977, it was found that in 85 percent of the cases the police had been called to the residence at least once prior to the murder and in 50 percent of the cases five times or more before the murder (Police Foundation, 1977). The community needs to lobby for changes in the policy regarding how the police respond to domestic violence since some policies seem to be more effective than others in reducing domestic violence. For example, having the police press charges in an apparent case of battering instead of the victim pressing charges is reported to be more effective in bringing the batterer to trial. Furthermore, detaining the batterer and giving him or her a choice of going to jail or undergoing counseling seems to encourage batterers to get and stick with treatment (Attorney General's Task Force on Family Violence, 1984; Lystad, 1986).

Finally, there is a lack of coordination among the professional groups about solving the problem of the black-on-black violence which often leads to black-on-black murder. Liaisons should be made among black community groups, black police associations, black physicians, black nurses, and so on, so that multidisciplinary coalitions can get together to do some basic empirical research and test interventions derived from this study. Such coalitions must also convince the black church to take a greater role in responding to the issue of black-on-black murder. Ministers should survey their congregations to determine whether there is a need for victim services among their flock. Services such as home-based "sofa bed" shelters can be begun using existing church resources. Black professional mental health groups can train black clergy in family therapy techniques designed to reduce family violence, and these services can be offered by the church.

Tertiary Prevention Solutions

Unfortunately, tertiary prevention occurs after a homicide has been committed. The morbidity experienced by the family and friends of homicide victims and perpetrators may be significant and demand that these co-victims be serviced by health professionals and social support systems. Family members and friends of a homicide victim who was murdered in a grisly fashion must cope with feelings of grief, stress, and depression which may lead to posttraumatic stress disorders and major depressions (Rynearson, 1986). In Los Angeles, California, it has been estimated that about 200 children per year witness the violent deaths of their parents and in Detroit, Michigan, it has been estimated that over 300 children witness a homicide. Clearly, victim services must be in place to treat the family members, friends, and children who are the co-victims to homicide. Support groups such as Save Our Sons and Daughters in Detroit must be developed to help the parents of murdered children.

Individuals who commit murder may be suffering from significant neuropsychiatric impairment (Lewis, Pincus, & Feldman, 1986), and an understanding of the neurology of rage and how this dynamic may predispose an individual to be murderous (Elliott, 1976) indicates that such individuals may need treatment. A number of such individuals, who have either served time in prison for murder or (more rarely) been released from sentencing as not guilty by reason of insanity, may live in the community. Often these individuals need help to cope with their impulsive act of homicide, to readjust to the community, and to manage a chronic mental illness; unfortunately, service provider and community feelings often preclude such persons from getting the treatment they need.

CONCLUSIONS

There is a meaningful role for the black community in preventing homicide. Certainly the problem is too pervasive to be relegated to only one segment of the black community such as the black police associations, the black physician associations, the black church, or any other. All of the segments of the black community must work together, and much of what has been suggested can be accomplished without grants or large sums of money. It takes the dedication and willingness of black professional and nonprofessional people who realize that every time a black-on-black murder occurs a little piece of them dies.

REFERENCES

Alcohol, Drug Abuse, and Mental Health Administration. (1985). Minority health ADAMHA concern. *Alcohol, Drug Abuse, and Mental Health Administration News, 11*, 6.

American Psychiatric Association. (1987). *Diagnostic and statistical manual of mental disorders* (3rd ed., rev.). Washington, DC: American Psychiatric Press.

Attorney General's Task Force on Family Violence. (1984). *Report of the Attorney General's Task Force on Family Violence.* Washington, DC: U.S. Department of Justice.

Barnhill, L. R. (1980). Clinical assessment of intrafamilial violence. *Hospital and Community Psychiatry, 31*, 543–547.

Bell, C. C. (1980). Racism: A symptom of the narcissistic personality disorder. *Journal of the National Medical Association, 72*, 661–665.

Bell, C. C. (1986a). Coma and the etiology of violence, part 1. *Journal of the National Medical Association, 12*, 1167–1176.

Bell, C. C. (1986b). Impaired black health professionals: Vulnerabilities and treatment approaches. *Journal of the National Medical Association, 78*, 1139–1141.

Bell, C. C. (1986c). Preventing violence. *The New Physician, 35*, 7–8.

Bell, C. C. (1987a). Coma and the etiology of violence, part 2. *Journal of the National Medical Association, 1*, 79–85.

Bell, C. C. (1987b). Preventive strategies for dealing with violence among blacks. *Community Mental Health Journal, 23*, 217–228.

Bell, C. C., Hildreth, C. J., Jenkins, E. J., et al. (1988). The need for victimization screening in a poor, outpatient medical population. *Journal of the National Medical Association.*

Bell, C. C., & Kelly, R. P. (1987). Head injury with subsequent intermittent nonschizophrenic, psychotic symptoms and violence. *Journal of the National Medical Association, 11*, 1139–1144.

Bell, C. C., Prothrow-Stith, D., & Smallwood-Murchison, C. (1986). Black-on-black homicide: The National Medical Association's responsibilities. *Journal of the National Medical Association, 78*, 1139–1141.

Bell, C. C., Taylor-Crawford, K., Jenkins, E. J., et al. (1988). Need for victimization screening in a black psychiatric population. *Journal of the National Medical Association.*

Bell, C. C., Thompson, B., Shorter-Gooden, K., et al. (1985). Prevalence of coma in black subjects. *Journal of the National Medical Association, 77*, 391–395.

Block, C. R. (1985). *Lethal violence in Chicago over seventeen years: Homicides known to the police, 1965–1981*. Chicago: Illinois Criminal Justice Information Authority.

Brearley, H. C. (1932). *Homicide in the United States*. Chapel Hill, NC: University of North Carolina Press.

Bureau of Justice Statistics. (1986). *Crime and justice facts, 1985*. Washington, DC: U.S. Department of Justice.

Centers for Disease Control. (1986). *Homicide surveillance: High-risk racial and ethnic groups—Blacks and Hispanics, 1970 to 1983*. Atlanta, GA: Centers for Disease Control.

Clark, K. (1965). *Dark ghetto*. New York: Harper & Row.

Dennis, R. E., Kirk, A., Knuckles, B. N., et al. (1981). *Black males at risk to low life expectancy: A study of homicide victims and perpetrators* (Project funded by NIMH Grant No. 1 R01 MH36720). Washington, DC: Center for Studies of Minority Group Mental Health.

Dietz, P. E. (1987). Patterns in human violence. In R. E. Hales & A. J. Frances (Eds.), *Psychiatric update: The American Psychiatric Association annual review* vol. 6, pp. 465–490. Washington, DC: American Psychiatric Press.

Elliott, F. A. (1976). The neurology of explosive rage. *Practitioner, 217*, 51–60.

Family Violence Curriculum Project. (1984). *Preventing family violence: A curriculum for adolescents*. Boston: Massachusetts Department of Public Health.

Federal Bureau of Investigation. (1987). *Crime in the United States: 1986*. Washington, DC: U.S. Department of Justice.

Flango, V. E., & Sherbinou, S. L. (1976). Poverty, urbanization, and crime. *Criminology, 14*, 331–346.

Gary, L. E., & Berry, G. L. (1985). Predicting attitudes toward substance abuse use in a black community: Implications for prevention. *Community Mental Health Journal, 21*, 42–51.

Hillard, J. R., Zung, W., Ramm, D., et al. (1985). Accidental and homicidal death in a psychiatric emergency room population. *Hospital and Community Psychiatry, 36*, 640–643.

Hylton, E., & Puryear, C. (1985). *A gun is not for fun*. Detroit: "Cee" Co.

Illinois Coalition against Domestic Violence. (1986). *Handbook for domestic violence victims*. Chicago: Illinois Criminal Justice Information Authority.

Jennett, B., & Teasdale, G. (1981). *Management of head injuries*. Philadelphia: F. A. Davis.

Klaus, P. A., & Rand, M. R. (1984). *Bureau of Justice Statistics Special Report: Family violence*. Washington, DC: U.S. Department of Justice.

Koop, C. E. (1985). *Surgeon General's Workshop on Violence and Public Health: Source book*. Washington, DC: National Center on Child Abuse and Neglect.

Lewis, D. O., Moy, E., & Jackson, L. D. (1985). Biopsychosocial characteristics of children who later murder: A prospective study. *American Journal of Psychiatry, 142*, 1161–1167.

Lewis, D. O., Pincus, J. H., & Feldman, M. (1986). Psychiatric, neurological, and psychoeducational characteristics of 15 death row inmates in the United States. *American Journal of Psychiatry, 143*, 838–845.

Linnolia, M., Virkkunen, M., Scheinin, M., et al. (1983). Low cerebrospinal fluid 5-

hydroxyindolacetic acid concentration differentiates impulsive from nonimpulsive violent behavior. *Life Sciences, 33,* 2609–2614.

Lion, J. R. (1972). The role of depression in the treatment of aggressive personality disorders. *American Journal of Psychiatry, 129,* 347–349.

Lion, J. R., & Bach-y-Rita, G. (1970). Group psychotherapy with violent outpatients. *International Journal of Group Psychotherapy, 20,* 185–191.

Loftin, C., & Hill, R. H. (1974). Regional subculture and homicide. *American Sociology Review, 39,* 714–724.

Lystad, M. (Ed.). (1986). *Violence in the home: Interdisciplinary perspectives.* New York: Brunner/Mazel.

Meredith, N. (1984). The murder epidemic. *Science, 5,* 42–47.

National Commission of Correctional Health Care. (1987). *Standards for health services in jails.* Chicago: National Commission of Correctional Health Care.

Okun, L. (1986). *Woman abuse: Facts replacing myths.* Albany, NY: State University of New York Press.

Police Foundation. (1977). *Domestic violence and the police: Studies in Detroit and Kansas City.* Washington, DC: Police Foundation.

Powell, G. J. (1982). A six-city study of school desegregation on self-concept among Afro-American junior high school students: A preliminary study with implications for mental health. In B. A. Bass, G. E. Wyatt, & G. J. Powell (Eds.), *The Afro-American family* (pp. 265–316). New York: Grune & Stratton.

Prescott, J. W. (1975, November). Body pleasure and the origins of violence. *Bulletin of Atomic Scientists,* pp. 10–20.

Prothrow-Stith, D. (1987). *Violence prevention curriculum for adolescents.* Newton, MA: Educational Development Center.

Ramos, S. M., & Delany, H. M. (1986). Freefalls from heights: A persistent urban problem. *Journal of the National Medical Association, 78,* 111–115.

Rose, H. M. (1981). *Black homicide and the urban environment.* U.S. Department of Health and Human Services, National Institute of Mental Health. Washington, DC: U.S. Government Printing Office.

Rosenberg, M. L., & Mercy, J. A. (1986). Homicide: Epidemiologic analysis at the national level. *Bulletin of the New York Academy of Medicine, 62,* 376–399.

Rynearson, E. K. (1986). Psychological effects of unnatural dying on bereavement. *Psychiatric Annals, 16,* 272–275.

Schorer, C. E. (1987). Behavioral efficacy of propranolol in black patients. *Journal of the National Medical Association, 79,* 221–22.

Secretary's Task Force on Black and Minority Health. (1985). Report of the Secretary's Task Force on Black and Minority Health, vol. 1: *Executive Summary* (DHHS Publication No. PHS 0–487–637). U.S. Department of Health and Human Services. Washington, DC: U.S. Government Printing Office.

Stark, E., & Flitcraft, A. (1982, Summer/Fall). Medical therapy as repression: The case of the battered woman. *Health and Medicine,* pp. 29–32.

State of Illinois, Department of Public Health. (1986). *Vital statistics—Illinois 1984.* Springfield: State of Illinois.

Straus, M. A. (1986). Domestic violence and homicide antecedents. *Bulletin of the New York Academy of Medicine, 62,* 446–465.

Straus, M. A., Steinmetz, S. K., & Gelles, R. J. (1980). *Behind closed doors: Violence in the American family.* Garden City, NY: Anchor Books.

Sulton, A. T. (1987). *National Symposium on Community Institutions and Inner-city Crime: Shaping the future agenda of urban crime control policy and research.* Washington, DC: Police Foundation.

Surgeon General's Workshop on Violence and Public Health. (1986). *Surgeon General's Workshop on Violence and Public Health Report* (DHHS Publication No. HRS-D-MC 86–1). Washington, DC: Health Resources and Services Administration, U.S. Public Health Service, U.S. Department of Health and Human Services.

Tardiff, K., & Gross, E. M. (1986). Homicide in New York City. *Bulletin of the New York Academy of Medicine, 62,* 413–426.

University of California at Los Angeles, Centers for Disease Control. (1985). *The epidemiology of homicide in the city of Los Angeles, 1970–79.* Atlanta, GA: Department of Health and Human Services, Public Health Service, Centers for Disease Control.

Williams, K. R. (1984). Economic sources of homicide: Reestimating the effects of poverty and inequality. *American Sociology Review, 49,* 283–289.

PART VI

LEGAL AND SOCIAL POLICY ISSUES

12

LEGAL ISSUES IN MENTAL HEALTH

Alice Gresham Bullock

It has been about 27 years since serious changes began in the focus of the law and mental health systems. More attention has been given to the legislation, major court decisions, administrative rulings, and related public policies that helped spawn the changes. Indeed, the many developments in this area created a specialty in law that did not exist 27 years ago: mental health law.

The mental health activism of the 1960s and 1970s has provided the mentally ill with a guarantee of substantive and procedural due process in the commitment and treatment of the mentally ill which includes a requirement that the patients be treated in the least restrictive environment. It seemed a natural progression that, with treatment in the least restrictive environment, a deinstitutionalization movement would follow. The development of deinstitutionalization and the community-based living approach for mental patients formed the basis for the development of zoning restrictions and related challenges.

Contemporary writings and court decisions now signal some tempering of the aggressive legal approach taken up through the late 1970s. There now appears to be a recognition of inherently competing interests in legal issues related to mental health care. Indeed, there has been far less judicial intervention in institutional affairs over the past 7 years than there was in the preceding 20 years.

This chapter reviews the salient developments in mental health law from the beginning of reform and traces its evolution through the transitional period of the 1980s. A detailed examination of all the issues that affect the mentally ill requires a book unto itself. Thus, there is no attempt to cover every issue likely to affect the mentally ill. Where possible, the impact of mental health law on the black mentally ill is discussed. Save for the criminal area, however, not much evidence demonstrates a differing impact of mental health laws on blacks as opposed to any other racial group.

CIVIL COMMITMENT

Civil commitment refers to state-imposed involuntary detention based on a determination that a person is mentally ill and dangerous to himself (or herself) or to others. Obviously, this definition focuses on dangerousness, but the basis for civil commitment has not always depended on a finding that a person is dangerous to himself or to others. From the inception of an organized system of mental health care, the commitment question centered around the patient's need for care. Even when procedures for commitment varied, this standard remained constant.[1] The last 20 years, however, have seen this traditional notion of commitment give way to an increased concern about the need for greater due process and related safeguards.

Thus, changes in how the rights of individuals versus the interest of the state are viewed are credited with providing the impetus for the dramatic activism of federal and state courts in this area. Beginning with *Lessard v. Schmidt*[2] in 1972, a three-judge panel of the Federal District Court in Wisconsin held that the standard for commitment was proof beyond a reasonable doubt that the individual was mentally ill and dangerous to himself or others.[3] In addition, the court determined that such dangerousness was to be measured by some recent overt act, an attempt or threat to harm oneself or others. At the same time, the court provided that the individual is entitled to the full panoply of procedural safeguards such as notice, a probable cause hearing, privilege against self-incrimination, and consideration of a least restrictive alternative to inpatient care.[4]

The year 1975 marked the first time in many years that the United States Supreme Court had heard a civil commitment case when it decided *O'Connor v. Donaldson*.[5] Kenneth Donaldson challenged the constitutionality of his continued confinement to a mental hospital under 42 U.S.C. 1983 (a civil rights statute) contending that he had a right to treatment or he should be released. In responding to Donaldson's challenge, the court held that the mentally ill had a right to liberty and that mental illness alone could not justify involuntary hospitalization if that person is not dangerous to himself or others.[6] This decision laid the groundwork for mental patients to challenge confinement and treatment on a constitutional basis.

As a result of the momentum gained with these decisions, all state legislatures moved to tighten civil commitment standards and replaced their treatment-oriented criteria with "dangerousness" criteria. While tightened standards, on the one hand, serve the very useful function of ensuring due process in recognition of individual rights, it has had the unintended result of denying treatment to many seriously mentally ill persons who cannot be involuntarily committed and who do not seek or accept treatment voluntarily (Shah, 1981; Peele, Gross, Arons, & Jafri, 1984). A task force report on the homeless mentally ill aptly makes the point when it states that

[w]orkable commitment laws are not easily drawn. If such laws are drafted in more general terms, to easily permit hospitalization of the mentally ill, they may become subject

to abuse. On the other hand, narrow commitment criteria emphasizing the autonomy of individuals make it impossible to commit persons who, according to many psychiatrists, should be committed. (Appelbaum, 1984; Munet, Kaufman, & Rich, 1980; Peele, et al., 1984)

Once due process safeguards were in place, concerns were raised about the standards to be used in applying those commitment criteria. The threshold question in this area is what should be the standard of proof to be met by the state to commit involuntarily a mentally ill person. The Supreme Court answered the question in *Addington v. Texas.*[7] The Court refused to apply the tougher criminal standard of "beyond a reasonable doubt." Distinguishing a civil commitment proceeding from a criminal prosecution, Chief Justice Burger writing for the majority stated that a "civil commitment proceeding can in no sense be equated to a criminal prosecution, . . . state power is not exercised in a punitive sense."[8] The Court recognized the near impossibility for the state to prove either mental illness or dangerousness against the stricter criminal standard which would result in the rejection of some persons who need institutionalized psychiatric care.[9] In attempting to strike a balance between the legitimate concerns of the state and the rights of the individual, the Court adopted an intermediate standard of proof. It said that proof by clear and convincing evidence is constitutionally adequate.[10]

Although the conservative commitment standards adopted over the last 20 years are still the accepted norm, *Addington* and its progeny have led some to conclude that the trend toward "criminalizing" the commitment process has run its course (Appelbaum, 1984). This view was reinforced by the decision of the Supreme Court in the case of *Parham v. J.R.*[11] in which the issue was whether rigid adversarial procedures should be applied for parents to consent to the involuntary commitment of their child. The Court noted that constitutional due process was not always synonymous with a formal judicial hearing.[12]

Recognizing the difficult position in which mental health care providers, mental health advocates, psychiatrists, mental health lawyers, and, not least of all, the mentally ill find themselves, attempts are being made to strike a balance between the rights of the mentally disabled and other important societal interests. The National Center for State Courts, through its Institute on Mental Disability and the Law, has issued *Guidelines for Involuntary Civil Commitment (Mental and Physical Disability Law Reporter [MPDLR],* 1986). The drafters indicate that the guidelines do not attempt to provide a model civil commitment statute but to provide a blueprint for "best utilizing the present civil commitment laws' strengths and overcoming their weaknesses." A member of the task force who participated in drafting the guidelines observes that the "participants judiciously balanced leading due process rights with legitimate concerns that mentally ill persons are not receiving the treatment and services they need in order to either get better or be stabilized in the community."[13]

CRIMINAL COMMITMENT

Competency to stand trial is a legal determination that an individual has sufficient present ability to consult with his or her lawyer with a reasonable degree of rational understanding of the facts and the proceedings against him or her.[14] This is the first point at which a person may be criminally committed. The basis for the doctrine lies in the belief that every litigant has a due process right to participate meaningfully in the conduct of his or her trial.[15]

The purposes served by requiring a person to have a minimal level of mental capacity to stand trial include safeguarding the accuracy of the adjudication and providing fundamental fairness in the proceeding. Only if a defendant understands the facts and nature of the charges against him or her can he or she effectively exercise the rights guaranteed to him or her.

Once found incompetent to stand trial (IST), generally, the person is confined to a hospital,[16] the trial is delayed, and bail is denied. However, *Jackson v. Indiana*,[17] the seminal case in this area, held that a person found incompetent to stand trial cannot be confined in excess of "a reasonable period of time necessary to determine whether competency may be regained." If the court concludes that competency will not be restored, then "the state must either institute the customary civil commitment procedures or release the defendant." Note that *Jackson* does not preclude automatic commitment upon a finding of incompetency to stand trial. The Supreme Court did, however, emphasize that "[a]t least, due process requires that the nature and duration of commitment bear some reasonable relation to the purpose for which the individual is committed."[18] The application of *Jackson* principles can leave the individual in limbo because he or she cannot stand trial due to incompetency and, on the other hand, he or she may not meet civil commitment standards; therefore, the individual must be released.[19]

Often confused with incompetency to stand trial is the insanity defense. In fact, the insanity defense is given disproportionately more attention even though incompetency to stand trial involves the greatest number of cases. Indeed, the defense is successfully used in very few cases. Since John Hinckley was found not guilty by reason of insanity in 1982, the insanity defense has been the most hotly debated issue in mental health. Reflecting public concern over the ability of defendants to "beat the rap and an enduring fear of the threat posed by insanity acquittees,"[20] legislatures acted quickly to reform insanity laws (Callahan, Mayer, & Steadman, 1987; Klofas and Weisheit, 1986). Reforms have taken many forms. Some states have abolished a specific plea of not guilty by reason of insanity. The standard of proof, the locus of the burden of proof, the tests used, the alternative defense of guilty but mentally ill (GBMI), and the commitment and release procedures have all undergone some change in the name of reform (Steadman, & Morrissey, 1984, 1986).

It is apparent that the real problem fueling the controversy is the disposition of defendants acquitted of violent acts by reason of insanity. Thus, public safety is the issue. Once acquitted, the defendant is technically free to go. In practice, however, most insanity acquittees are involuntarily committed through regular civil commitment proceedings.[21]

Moreover, the Supreme Court has held that a person found not guilty by reason of insanity (NGRI) is not entitled to automatic release after acquittal even if detained for a period equivalent to the maximum term he or she could have served had he or she actually been committed.[22] It has been said that this decision may reflect a public mood that the right of the public to feel safe from the criminally mentally ill should weigh heavier against the insanity acquittee than the acquittee's right to be left alone. That signal appears to have been received in at least one federal court which held that a presumption of continuing mental illness based on a not guilty verdict by reason of insanity is not unconstitutional.[23]

It has been observed that individuals found not guilty by reason of insanity have "had an easier route into and a more difficult route out of the institutions than have their civilly committed counterparts."[24] It appears that there is a trend toward either requiring or permitting court review of commitment periodically to ameliorate this problem. Such review means more court involvement in the disposition and supervision of persons acquitted by reason of insanity. In any case, such periodic review by the courts should, to some extent, satisfy the concerns of the public to be protected against premature release of a dangerous, mentally ill person and the need of the individual for due process.

It does not appear that blacks form a significant percentage of NGRI pleas. Charles Owens offers that social and cultural reasons may have the effect of hiding black offenders who need mental health services (Owens, 1979). In addition, he suggests that there is a negative inducement to plead NGRI because a person diverted to a mental institution may serve more time than if found guilty (Owens, 1979).

RIGHT TO TREATMENT

The notion of a right to treatment was conceived by Morton Birnbaum, a physician lawyer, in the 1960s. That concept was first acknowledged in *Rouse v. Cameron* in 1966 when the federal court for the District of Columbia Circuit held that a patient must be treated or released from a mental hospital. That decision led to the landmark decision in *Stickney v. Wyatt*,[25] an Alabama federal district court case which determined that civilly committed mental patients had a constitutional right to treatment.

Citing *Rouse v. Cameron* (1966), the court stated that when patients are involuntarily committed they have a constitutional right to treatment that will give them a realistic opportunity to be cured or to improve their mental condition. The court further stated that "absent such treatment, the hospital is transformed into a penitentiary where one could be held indefinitely for no convicted offense."[26] This is contrary to the purpose of civil commitment which is treatment. *Wyatt* established 35 standards that the court held necessary for the adequate

treatment of the mentally ill.[27] On appeal to the Fifth Circuit upholding the
decision the court cited its decision in *O'Connor v. Donaldson* (1975) where it
held there was a constitutional right to treatment.[28] It is important to note that
when *Donaldson* went to the Supreme Court, the Court refused to rule on the
right-to-treatment issue saying that the issue was not presented. Donaldson was
awarded attorneys' fees and damages from doctors who had violated his right
to liberty after being involuntarily confined for 15 years. It was the first time a
mental patient had ever obtained damages from doctors who had violated constitutional rights, and it paved the way for mental patients to seek redress for
violation of these constitutional rights. The Supreme Court decision not to rule
on the constitutionality of the right to treatment in *Donaldson* notwithstanding,
lower courts, relying on other lower court precedents, have held that a federal
right to treatment does exist.[29]

Wyatt and *Donaldson* were followed by a ground swell of cases which adopted
the constitutional right-to-treatment view.[30] State legislatures responded to the
ground swell by providing a statutory right to treatment (Lyon, Levin, & Zusman,
1982). Despite the judicial decisions mandating the existence of such a right,
whether it does in fact exist in practice is another question. The fact remains
that in none of the major right-to-treatment cases has the court order been fully
complied with. While progress has unquestionably been made, full compliance
has not been achieved and many question whether it ever will. Compliance has
not been achieved partly because of the failure of state legislatures to appropriate
much needed funds to accommodate the changes. Although Judge Johnson said
in *Wyatt* that failure to appropriate funds is no reason to deny the constitutional
right, the practical fact of the matter is that compliance cannot be achieved
without the funding.

When the Supreme Court granted certiorari to *Youngberg v. Romeo*[31] it was
widely hoped that the Court would settle the issue of the existence of a constitutional right to treatment since it had denied the existence of a statutory right
in *Pennhurst v. Halderman*.[32] Much to the disappointment of mental health
advocates, the Supreme Court again declined the opportunity to settle the issue.
In *Youngberg* the Supreme Court narrowly framed the issue so as to avoid ruling
on the general constitutional right to treatment. It held that civilly committed
retarded persons had a constitutional right to freedom of movement and personal
safety. It added that such a person is entitled to minimal habilitation (training)
necessary to secure his or her constitutional rights. While the Court did not
clearly reject the notion of a broader constitutional right, its narrow decision
indicated an unwillingness to adopt it. The court also held that the judgment of
health professionals is to be given presumptive correctness.

The fallout from *Youngberg* has been mixed. Although the Supreme Court
did provide leeway for what might be characterized as an expansive reading of
its decision, some commentators chose to read it narrowly.[33] Where *Youngberg*
provided for the right to safe conditions, mental patients have successfully sued
for damages. Courts have expanded that right in some instances to include

adequate food, shelter, medical and dental care, and protection from dangerous situations and harmful noise levels.[34]

The *Youngberg* right to be free of undue bodily restraints includes the right to make trips into the community, freedom from restraints that are not necessary for treatment or training, and freedom from restraints that limit or eliminate an ambulatory patient's mobility by wheelchair or properly equipped transportation vehicles.[35]

One of the most controversial areas relying on the *Youngberg* principles is the right to refuse treatment. Of particular concern was the right to refuse chemical treatment. It was *Rennie v. Klein*[36] that provided that dangerous, mentally ill, civilly committed mental patients retain a qualified constitutional right to refuse antipsychotic drugs. The Third Circuit was reaffirming its original determination, but it was based this time on the administrative review procedure provided by state law. Note that the *Rennie* court provided that the right to refuse ended where such refusal endangered the patient or others.

Citing *Rennie*, several other courts have found a limited right to refuse antipsychotic medication.[37] All of these decisions rested on a determination that the right to refuse chemical medication was satisfied by internal administrative review procedures. Other court decisions reinforcing the *Youngberg* approach involve the right to refuse treatment based on common law and state statute. The first important case was *Rogers v. Okin*[38] in which the First Circuit upheld the Massachusetts procedure permitting competent, involuntarily committed mental patients to make their own treatment decisions and allowed courts to make decisions for incompetent patients using substituted judgment. The Court of Appeals noted that the state procedure was more rigorous than *Youngberg* required.

Since *Youngberg* there has been no question that mental patients are entitled to sufficient training to exercise their constitutional rights, although some of the decisions signal reluctance to provide for a right to anything but training to maintain minimum or basic skills.[39] Deference to professional judgment is required by the *Youngberg* decision. As well, professional judgment enjoys presumptive correctness.[40] It is this deference and this presumption that potentially limit the right to treatment as well as the right to refuse treatment.

DEINSTITUTIONALIZATION

The doctrine of least restrictive environment significantly helped to foster the deinstitutionalization movement of the 1960s and 1970s. In part, it was the result of efforts to redress the inadequacy of large mental institutions and the sorely lacking treatment of institutionalized persons. Moreover, as mental patients housed in large institutions were provided treatment in the least restrictive environment, deinstitutionalization was inevitable. Indeed, litigation in this area has most often involved efforts to close large institutions and enjoin their construction.[41]

The movement was given momentum by *O'Connor v. Donaldson*[42] with its decision that a mental patient has a right to be released from an institution if that person poses no danger to himself or herself or to others. That principle was followed by *Youngberg v. Romeo*[43] which recognized a right to treatment in the least restrictive environment. However, *Youngberg*, coupled with the Supreme Court decision in *Pennhurst v. Halderman*,[44] has left the status of deinstitutionalization unclear. There have been, however, several decisions which might signal a trend toward limiting the doctrine of least restrictive environment which will in turn limit deinstitutionalization.[45]

ZONING

The community-based living approach underpinning the deinstitutionalization concept is based on the belief that the mentally disabled should have "the patterns of life and conditions of everyday living which are as close as possible to the regular circumstances and ways of life of society" (Nirje, 1976). However, such community-based living arrangements have been described as anathema for local governments, and they are commonly viewed as infringing upon local government control over land use (Steinman, 1986; Appelbaum, 1983).

Local governments have impeded development of group homes by a variety of methods. The most commonly used methods include zoning areas as single-family residential areas, imposing burdensome special exception uses, or classifying group homes as rooming houses or nursing homes permissible only in commercial zones. Many housing developments have imposed restrictive covenants limiting the definition of family, and others have expressly prohibited group homes.

Since zoning is a matter of local law, litigation has largely been concentrated in the state courts where the issue has centered on denial of due process and equal protection by exclusionary zoning in areas zoned single family. The issue has yet to be heard by the United States Supreme Court, although the Court does appear to approve by implication of per se exclusion of group homes from single-family residential areas.[46] In the *Village of Belle Terre v. Boraas*, the Supreme Court upheld the constitutionality of a local ordinance that restricted land use to single-family dwellings. It is important to note that the case did not involve mentally ill patients, but rather, unrelated college students.

The decision in *Village of Belle Terre* was followed a year later by *City of Cleburne, Texas v. Cleburne Living Center*[47] wherein the Court found discriminatory a local zoning restriction on group homes in multifamily residential zones. What the Supreme Court did not say may be more revealing than what it did say. The justices left open the question of whether the city's special use permit requirement was constitutional on its face as applied to mentally retarded persons and it did not speak to the definition of family. The Court decided that under the facts of that case there was a denial of equal protection.[48]

In 1977 when the issue of exclusionary zoning again came before the Supreme Court,[49] the Court invalidated an ordinance that defined family to include some but not all blood relatives. For these purposes, the ordinance did not include the occupant's grandson among blood relatives. The court found justification for the goal sought to be achieved by the ordinance. But the goals were "served marginally, if at all, by the ordinance."[50] In 1984 the Supreme Court denied certiorari to a Macon County, Georgia, case in which the state court had found valid an ordinance that limited occupancy of single-family dwellings to not more than four unrelated adults.[51] Certiorari was denied for lack of a federal question, which appears to reaffirm the *Belle Terre* decision since it was cited as precedent by the state court.

State litigation has focused primarily on (1) whether the residents of a group home constitute a family; (2) sovereign immunity, and (3) overriding state policy.[52] *City of White Plains v. Ferrioli*[53] was as early case that expanded the definition of family to permit a group home in a single-family residential area to include a married couple, two biological children, and ten foster children despite the ordinance requiring a biological relationship between all residents. These cases focus on whether a group home constitutes a single housekeeping unit. When deciding whether a group home is a rooming house or a nursing home restricted to commercial zones, the courts have relied on the single housekeeping unit analysis in *Ferrioli* to strike down the restriction.[54]

Restrictive covenants against selling or renting facilities to group homes in residential areas are not uncommon. Since such restrictions are generally valid, the courts have supported group homes on the basis of overriding public policy to provide care and treatment for the mentally handicapped or have construed covenants to limit only the structure of the building.[55] Where a governmental agency or one of its contractors operates a group home, the home has been upheld through governmental immunity. Because this involves one governmental unit overriding the authority of another governmental unit, a balancing of interests is imperative.[56]

At least one commentator has minimized the effect of state court decisions as a means of addressing local exclusionary zoning practices. Deborah Schmedemann believes that the successful state court suits are largely symbolic since the basis for these decisions in large measure has been to force local governments to expand the definition of family in cases where the "family" is composed of children, not adults.[57] "It is a substantial leap from ordering a community to admit a home for the mentally retarded or children, to ordering a community to allow a facility housing mentally ill."[58] Schmedemann also finds little to commend courts in overruling local ordinances on policy grounds since, she says, "there is no necessary reason for state courts to constrain local autonomy and engender political protest, when the state's policy goals might be achieved in some other manner."[59]

It is apparent that states have also been active in shaping the development of group homes. By statute, thirty-four states have approved the location of group homes in residential areas.[60] Although group homes appear to be receiving wider acceptance in the judiciary and the legislatures, in residential areas, community resistance remains high. It may be that to guarantee placement of mentally handicapped in the community will require that the state exempt group homes from local zoning requirements altogether.[61]

HOMELESS MENTALLY ILL

Over the last twenty years, federal and local policies along with legislative and judicial actions have directly impacted on the homeless mentally ill. The problems have been caused by a combination of factors which, when viewed separately, have served laudable purposes. For example, it has been the aggressive advocacy for the civil liberties of the mentally ill over the last twenty years that has caused a shift in focus for civil commitment and development of rights of mental patients inside and, to some extent, outside institutions. But it is a widely held belief, particularly within the mental health profession, that aggressive advocacy has not always necessarily resulted in serving the best interest of the mentally ill.

Indeed, a task force of the American Psychiatric Association (Peele, Gross, Arons, & Jaffri, 1984) recognizes that the judicial system plays an important role in serving the mentally ill, but the adversarial nature of the system itself often works at cross-purposes with the needs of the mentally ill. The development of the least restrictive environment with its emphasis on deinstitutionalization and the notion that a mental institution is the most restrictive alternative fueled an aggressive effort to move the mentally ill into the community into a more homelike environment.[62] Although the theory behind the movement was agreeable, it is generally accepted that, in practice, deinstitutionalization has failed for a number of reasons. All too many victims of that failure can be found wandering the streets (Peele et al., 1984).

Many believe that the development of the right to treatment has helped some patients get better treatment but has simultaneously decreased the accessibility of treatment for others. Such lack of accessibility seems to apply particularly to those released to community-based facilities. Similarly, the development of the right to refuse treatment has had some impact on the plight of the homeless mentally ill (Peele et al., 1984). As discussed previously, civil commitment laws have been tightened, permitting more mentally ill persons to go untreated. The homeless typically do not seek treatment voluntarily. The American Psychiatric Association task force report suggests that inflexible commitment laws contribute to the problem because no intermediate alternative is made available: a person is either involuntarily committed to an institution or is totally free. However, it should be noted that some states have enacted laws permitting court-ordered outpatient treatment.

Persons found incompetent to stand trial often find themselves in legal limbo and ultimately "on the street." They cannot stand trial because of their mental condition but they will not necessarily be placed for treatment. If, after a competency hearing as required by *Jackson v. Indiana* (1972), it is determined that such a person will never return to competency, he or she must be released, his or her mental state notwithstanding. Further hospitalization then depends on whether the person meets civil commitment standards. As there are no clear-cut solutions to the problem of the homeless mentally ill, the task force report of the American Psychiatric Institute (Peele et al., 1984) suggests several worthwhile options which involve changes to the civil commitment process as a starting point. In addition, since the early 1980s, advocates have been suing state and local governments to provide services and shelter to the homeless. These suits have met with some success on a state constitutional basis and on state statutory laws.[63]

Although it is clear that ethnic and racial minorities are overrepresented among the homeless and that a high percentage of homeless persons suffer from some form of mental illness, the data are insufficient to draw conclusions about the incidence of mental illness among the homeless ethnic and racial minorities.

LIABILITY OF HEALTH PROFESSIONALS AND FACILITIES

Of no little importance to the health profession has been the development of the psychiatrist's duty to warn as it relates to patients and third parties. Such liability arises generally in connection with decisions to treat, detain, release, or not to treat a patient. *O'Connor v. Donaldson* (1975) held that, even if mentally ill, without more, it is unconstitutional to confine one who is not dangerous and is capable of surviving with the help of family and friends. The hospital superintendent was held personally liable for money damages for violating the patient's right to liberty whether the superintendent knew or should have known that the action he took would violate the patient's rights. This case was discussed in some detail previously when it was pointed out that this decision laid the groundwork for mental patients to lodge a constitutional challenge to confinement and treatment.

As was made clear by the decision in *Tarasoff v. Board of Regents of the University of California*,[64] mental health professionals are placed squarely on the horns of a dilemma. The Supreme Court of California held a psychotherapist and the treating hospital liable for damages when the psychotherapist knew or should have known that the patient posed a serious danger of violence. Under the circumstances, the court held that there was a duty to warn an identifiable victim or to notify the police. Thus, while health professionals must release nondangerous persons or be held liable, they may also be held liable for releasing persons who later commit violent acts.

Subsequent to the *Tarasoff* decision, there appeared to be a trend toward expanding the liability of a psychiatrist for acts of a patient beyond a duty to protect identifiable victims. However, in a more recent case,[65] the court maintained the principle as established in *Tarasoff* to limit liability to narrowly defined situations in which there is a threat to an identifiable victim.

Currie v. United States[66] found that there was no duty of the therapists at the

Veterans Administration Hospital to civilly commit a patient determined by hospital officials to be dangerous but not mentally ill. The court determined that the professionals had exercised accepted professional judgment, practice, and standards in the examination, management, treatment supervision, and release congruous with the North Carolina statute. In fact, the hospital had repeatedly urged the patient to admit himself voluntarily for treatment by warning his employer and by notifying the police.

This case appears to be a recognition by the court that it is not the courts but, rather, the treating professionals who are in the best position to make the first-line judgment on commitment.[67]

NOTES

1. It should be borne in mind that the traditional system was, in part, based on a large state hospital system.

2. Lessard v. Schmidt, 349 F. Supp. 1078 (E.D. Wis. 1972), vacated and rem'd on other grounds, 414 U.S. 473 (1974), redecided, 379 F. Supp. 1376 (E.D. Wis. 1974), vacated and remanded on other grounds, 421 U.S. 957 (1975), redecided 413 F. Supp. 1318 (E.D. Wis. 1976). The issues were eventually declared moot because Wisconsin revised its statute to incorporate many of the Lessard principles.

3. Ibid. at 1095.

4. Prior to Lessard, the issue of whether due process was required in involuntary commitment cases was in juvenile cases. See, In re Gault, 387 U.S. 1 (1966).

5. O'Connor v. Donaldson, 422 U.S. 563 (1975).

6. Ibid. at 576. Note that the Court did not decide that dangerousness is a constitutional requirement or that there is a constitutional right to treatment.

7. Addington v. Texas, 441 U.S. 418 (1979).

8. Ibid. at 428.

9. Ibid.

10. Ibid. at 425.

11. Parham v. J.R., 442 U.S. 584 (1979).

12. Guidelines for involuntary civil commitment, 10 MPDLR, vol. 10, 1409, May 1986.

13. Parry, Civil commitment: Three proposals for change, 10 MPDLR 334 at 337, May 1986. The article offers a critique of the models for civil commitment introduced by the Mental Health Law Project (1977), the American Psychiatric Association (1982), and the National Center for State Courts Task Force (1986).

14. Dusky v. United States, 362 U.S. 402 (1960) at 402. Some state statutes provide a different test for incompetency to stand trial, but they are not inconsistent with Dusky.

15. Drope v. Missouri, 420 U.S. 162 (1975).

16. There are figures on the number of persons confined to mental institutions on the basis of IST, but it is unclear how many are black. It is reported, however, that blacks are admitted to mental institutions due to IST more often than are whites. See Owens, C. E. *Mental health and black offenders*, Lexington Books, 1979, p. 27.

17. Jackson v. Indiana, 406 U.S. 715 (1972).

18. See the discussion on homeless mentally ill later in this chapter.

19. Jackson v. Indiana at 908. Note that while the competency determination is made

by the court there is heavy reliance on the opinions of psychiatrists and other mental health professionals.

20. See *Bulletin of A. Aca. of Psychiatry and the Law*, vol. 13, 405–415 (1985) (data from a two-year study of NGRI patients).

21. Jones v. United States, 463 U.S. 354 (1983).

22. Benham v. Ledbetter, 609 F. Supp. 125 (D.C. Ga. 1985) (on remand from Benham v. Edwards, 678 F.2d 511 (5th Cir. 1982).

23. But see Wexler, *Mental health law*, Plenum Press, 1983.

24. Rouse v. Cameron, 373 F.2d 451 (1966). Note that this was a criminal case.

25. Wyatt v. Stickney, 325 F. Supp. 781 (M.D. Ala. 1971).

26. Wyatt v. Stickney at 784. See also, Covington v. Harris, 419 F.2d 617 (1968).

27. Wyatt v. Stickney, 344 F. Supp. 387 (M.D. Ala. 1972), aff'd sub. nom., Wyatt v. Aderholt, 503 F.2d 1305 (5th Cir. 1974).

28. Wyatt v. Aderholt, 503 F.2d 1305 (5th Cir. 1974).

29. O'Connor v. Donaldson, supra, note 5.

30. See Drake, J., Judicial interpretation of *Wyatt v. Stickney*, Ala. L. Rev. 299–312 (1981); Appelbaum, P. S. Legal Issues at 297, supra note 8.

31. See Mills, M. J. (1982), The right to treatment: Little law but much impact, *Psychiatry 1982: The American Psychiatric Association annual review* (361–370), American Psychiatry Press. See also, Welsch v. Likens, 550 F.2d 1122 (the Fourteenth Amendment requires that civilly committed retarded inpatients have a right to at least minimally adequate treatment). Eckerhart v. Hensley, 475 F. Supp. 908 does not say that there is a constitutional right to treatment, but it does say that due process requires that medical treatment decisions be made in a context designed to protect patients from arbitrary deprivation of personal liberty.

32. Youngberg v. Romeo, 457 U.S. 311 (1982). This case involved a civilly committed, mentally retarded person who sued under the Fourteenth Amendment claiming a right to freedom of movement and personal security within the institution. Although Youngberg involved a mentally retarded patient, it is clear that it applies equally to the mentally ill. See Gann v. Delaware State Hospital, 543 F. Supp. 268 (D. Dela. 1982).

33. Pennhurst State School and Hospital v. Halderman, 451 U.S. 1 (1981).

34. See Civil Rights of Institutionalized Persons Act, 7 MDLPR 5–8.

35. ARC of North Dakota v. Olson, 561 F. Supp. 473 (D.N.D. 1982), modified on other grounds, 713 F.2d 1384 (8th Cir. 1983). Society for Goodwill to Children, Inc., 737 F.2d 1239 (2d Cir. 1984).

36. Scott v. Plante, 691 F.2d 634 (3rd Cir. 1982); Society for Goodwill to Retarded Children, Inc.

37. Rennie v. Klein, 653 F.2d 836 (3rd Cir. 1981).

38. Project Release v. Prevost, 722 F.2d 9601 (2d Cir. 1983). United States v. Leatherman, 580 F. Supp. 977 (D.D.C. 1983); R.A.J. v. Miller, 590 F. Supp. 1319 (N.D. Tex. 1984).

39. Rogers v. Okin, 738 F.2d 1 (1st Cir. 1984). See also, Bee v. Greaves, 744 F.2d 1387 (10th Cir. 1984); Colorado v. Medina, 705 P.2d 961 (Colo. Sup. Ct. 1985).

40. ARC of North Dakota v. Olson, supra, note 35. (The Court provided that a constitutional right to training to maintain minimal self-care skills existed. It did not provide a right to treatment or habilitation.) Scott v. Plante, at note 36; Woe v. Cuomo, 729 F.2d 96 (2d Cir. 1984). But see Society for Goodwill to Retarded Children, Inc. v. Cuomo, 737 F.2d 1239 (2d Cir. 1984).

41. See Stensvad v. Reivitz, 601 F.Supp. 128 (W.D. Wis. 1985); Accord, Large v. Superior Court, 714 P.2d 399 at 408 (Ariz. 1986).

42. See Kentucky ARC v. Conn, 510 F. Supp. 1233 (W.D. Ky. 1980).

43. O'Connor v. Donaldson, supra, note 5.

44. Youngberg v. Romeo, supra, note 32.

45. Pennhurst State School and Hospital v. Halderman, supra, note 33.

46. Society for Goodwill to Retarded Children, Inc. v. Cuomo, supra, note 40; see also, New York ARC v. Carey, No. 82–7441 (2d Cir. Mar. 31, 1983).

47. Village of Belle Terre v. Boraas, 416 U.S. 1 (1974).

48. City of Cleburne, Texas v. Cleburne Living Center, 105 S.Ct. 3249 (1985).

49. Three justices agreed with the result but would have held that the designation of mentally retarded person is a quasi-suspect classification and would have struck down the ordinance on its face.

50. Moore v. City of East Cleveland, 431 U.S. 494 (1977).

51. Ibid. at 500.

52. Macon Ass'n for Retarded Citizens v. Macon-Bibb Cty. Planning & Zoning Comm'n, 314 S.E. 2d 218, dismissed for lack of substantial federal question, 105 S. Ct. 57 (1974).

53. See Steinman, L. D., The impact of zoning on group homes for the mentally disabled. Note 59. See generally 2A Rathkope, The law of zoning & planning, sec. 17A.05 (4th ed. 1982).

54. City of White Plains v. Ferrioli, 313 N.E. 2d 756 (1974).

55. Oliver v. Zoning Comm'n of Chester, 326 A.2d 841 (1974); Douglas City Resources, Inc. v. Daniel, 280 S.E. 2d 734 (1981); Magony v. Bevilacqua, 432 A.2d 661 (R.I. 1981); Contra, City of Guntersville v. Shull, 355 So. 2d 361 (Ala. 1978); Region 10 Client Management, Inc. v. Town of Hampstead, 424 A.2d 207 (1980); Culp v. City of Seattle, 590 P.2d 1288 (1979).

56. City of Livonia v. Dept. of Social Services, 378 N.W. 2d 402 (1985); Costley v. Caromin House, Inc., 313 N.W. 2d 21 (Minn. 1981); Berger v. State, 364 A.2d 993 (1976).

57. For discussion generally, see Steinman, L.D., The impact of zoning on group homes for the mentally disabled at 16 and 17.

58. Schmedemann, Note: Zoning for the mentally ill: A legislative mandate, 16 *Harv. Jour. on Legislation*, 877 (Summer 1979).

59. Ibid.

60. Ibid. She also notes that courts are inefficient because they can rule only on the case before it.

61. Ibid. at 18–25 for comprehensive discussion of the statutory approaches to limiting zoning discretion.

62. See, generally, Schmedemann, D. A., supra, note 58.

63. It was feared that, in an effort to comply with the court order in Wyatt v. Stickney to reduce the patient staff ratio, hospitals reduced the number of people being treated. It became clear that the result of Wyatt and similar cases could be the premature release of the mentally ill into the community without adequate services for them. Note that Dixon v. Weinberger, 405 F. Supp. 974 (D.C.D.C. 1975) attempted to answer the problem by requiring that when mentally ill patients are released from an institution there be provided community-based services.

64. See Callahan v. Carey, S. Ct. N.Y. County, Index No. 42582/79 (suit brought

to establish that under state constitution and state law the city must provide adequate shelter); Accord, Hodge v. Ginsberg, 303 S.E. 2d 245 (W. Va. 1983).

65. Tarasoff v. Board of Regents of the University of California, 529 P.2d 553 (1974); reargued 551 P.2d 334 (1976).

66. Thompson v. County of Alameda, 614 P.2d 728 (1980).

67. Currie v. United States, No. C–85–0629-D (M.D.N.C. Oct. 3, 1986); See, generally, Miller, R. *Currie v. United States: Tarasoff* comes south, MPDLR (Nov.–Dec. 1986).

REFERENCES

Addington v. Texas, 441 U.S. 418 (1979).

Appelbaum, P. S. (1983). Zoning out the mentally disabled. *Hospital Community Psychiatry*, 399–400.

Appelbaum, P. S. (1984). Legal issues. *The Chronic Mental Patient at 295.*

ARC of North Dakota v. Olson, No. A1–80–141 (D.N.D. 1982).

Bee v. Greaves, 744 F. 2d 1387 (10th Cir. 1984).

Benham v. Ledbetter, 609 F. Supp. 125 (D.C. Ga. 1985).

Berger v. State, 364 A. 2d 993 (1976).

Bulletin of A. Aca. of Psychiatry and the Law (1985). Vol. 13, 405–415.

Callahan v. Carey, S. Ct. N.Y. County, Index No. 42582/79.

Callahan, L., Mayer, C., & Steadman, H. (1987). Insanity defense reform in the United States—Post Hinckley. 11 MPDLR 54–59 at 54.

City of White Plains v. Ferrioli. 313 N.E. 2d 756 (1974).

City of Celburne, Texas v. Cleburne Living Center, 105 S. Ct. 3249. (1985).

City of Livonia v. Dept. of Social Services, 378 N.W. 2d 402.

City of Guntersville v. Shull, 355 So. 2d 361 (Ala. 1978).

Civil Rights of Institutionalized Persons Act, 7 MDLPR 5–8.

Colorado v. Medina, 705 p.2d 961 (Colo. Sup. Ct. 1985).

Costley v. Caromin House, Inc., 313 N.W. 2d 21 (Minn. 1981).

Covington v. Harris, 419 F. 2d 617 (1969).

Culp v. City of Seattle, 590 P. 2d 1288 (1979).

Currie v. United States, No. C–85–0629-D (M.D.N.C. Oct. 3, 1986).

Dixon v. Weinberger, 405 F. Supp. 974 (D.C.D.C. 1975).

Douglas City Resources, Inc. v. Daniel, 280 S.E. 2d 734 (1981).

Drake, J. (1981). Judicial interpretation of *Wyatt v. Stickney*. Ala. L. Rev., 299–312.

Drope v. Missouri, 420 U.S. 162 (1975).

Dusky v. United States, 362 U.S. 402 (1960).

Fulton, J. P. (1984). *The Insanity Defense and its Alternatives: A Guideline for Policymakers* at 33.

Gault, In re, 387 U.S. 1 (1966).

Guidelines for involuntary civil commitment. (1986, May). 10 MPDLP Vol. 10, 1409.

Jackson v. Indiana, 406 U.S. 715 (1972).

Jones v. United States, 103 S. Ct. 3043 (1983).

Kentucky ARC v. Conn, 510 F. Supp. 1233 (W.D. Ky. 1980).

Klofas, J., & Weisheit, R. (June 18, 1986). Pleading guilty but mentally ill: Adversarial justice and mental health. Presented at the XII International Congress on Law and Psychiatry.

Large v. Superior Court, 714 P. 2d 399 at 408 (Ariz. 1986).

Lessard v. Schmidt, 349 F. Supp. 1078 (E.D. Wis. 1972).

Lyon, M. A., Levin, M. L., & Zusman, J. (1982). Patient bill of rights: A survey of state statutes. Mental Disability Law Reporter 178–201, Vol. 6.

Macon Ass'n for Retarded Citizens v. Macon-Bibb Cty. Planning & Zoning Comm'n, 314 S.E. 2d 218 (1974).

Magony v. Bevilacqua, 432 A 2d 661 (R.I. 1981).

Miller, R. (1976, November-December). *Currie v. United States: Tarasoff* comes south. MPDLR.

Mills, M. J. (1982). The right to treatment: Little law but much impact. *Psychiatry*: The American Psychiatric Association annual review. American Psychiatry Press, 361–370.

Moore v. City of East Cleveland, 431 U.S. 494 (1977).

Munet, M. R., Kaufman, K. R., & Rich, C. L. (1980). Modernization of mental health act: Commitment patterns. *Bull. A. Acad. Psychiatry Law*, 8, 83–93.

New York v. Carey, No. 82–7441 (2nd Cir. Mar. 31, 1983).

Nirje, Bengt. (1976). The normalization principle. In *Changing patterns in residential services for the mental retarded* 231 (Krugel & Shearer rev ed.).

O'Connor v. Donaldson, 422 U.S. 563 (1975).

Oliver v. Zoning Comm'n of Chester, 326 A. 2d 841 (1974).

Owens, C. E. (1979). *Mental health and black offenders*. Lexington, MA: Lexington Books, p. 27.

Parham v. J.R., 442 U.S. 584 (1979).

Parry, R. J. (1986, May). Civil commitment: Three proposals for change. 10 MPDLR 334 at 337.

Peele, R., Gross, B., Arons, B., & Jafri, M. (1984). The legal system and the homeless. The Homeless Mentally Ill; A Task Force Report of the American Psychiatric Association at 265.

Pennhurst State School and Hospital v. Halderman, 451 U.S. 1 (1981).

Project Release v. Prevost, 722 F. 2d 9601 (2nd Cir. 1983).

R.A.J. v. Miller, 590 F. Supp. 1319 (N.D. Tex. 1984).

Rathkop, A. H. (1982). *The law of zoning & planning* 2A Section 17A.05 (4th ed.).

Region 10 Client Management, Inc. v. Town of Hampstead, 424 A2d 207 (1980).

Rennie v. Klein, 653 F. 2d 836 (3rd Cir. 1981).

Rogers v. Okin, 738 F. 2d 1 (1st Cir. 1984).

Rouse v. Cameron, 373 F. 2d 451 (1966).

Schmedemann, D. A. (Summer 1979). Zoning for the mentally ill: A legislative mandate. *Harvard Journal on Legislation*. Vol. 16.

Scott v. Plante, 691 F. 2d 634 (3rd Cir. 1982).

Shah, S. A. (1981). Legal and mental health system interactions; major developments and research needs. *International Journal of Law and Psychiatry*. Vol. 4, 219 at 226–227.

Society for Goodwill to Retarded Children, Inc. v. Cuomo, 737 F. 2d 1239 (2nd Cir. 1984).

Steadman, H. J., & Morrissey, J. P. (1984). Assessing the impact of insanity defense reforms. Albany, NY: N.Y. State Office of Mental Health.

Steadman, H. J., & Morrissey, J. P. (1986). The insanity defense: Problems and prospects for studying the impact of legal reforms. 484 Annals 115.

Steinman, L. D. (1986). The impact of zoning on group homes for the mentally disabled: A national survey. 2.

Stensvad v. Reivitz, 601 F. Supp. 128 (W.D. Wisc. 1985).

Tarasoff v. Board of Regents of the University of California, 529 P. 2d 553 (1974).

Thompson v. County of Alameda, 614 P. 2d 728 (1980).

United States v. Leatherman, 580 F. Supp. 977 (D.D.C. 1983).

Village of Belle Terre v. Boraas, 416 U.S. 1 (1974).

Welsch v. Likens, 550 F. 2d 1122.

Wexler, D. B. (1983). *Mental Health Law*. New York: Plenum Press.

Woe v. Cuomo, 729 F. 2d 96 (2nd Cir. 1984).

Wyatt v. Stickney, 344 F. Supp. 387 (M.D. Ala. 1972).

Wyatt v. Stickney, 325 F. Supp. 781 (M.D. Ala. 1971).

Wyatt v. Aderholt, 503 F. 2d 1305 (5th Cir. 1974).

Youngberg v. Romeo, 457 U.S. 311 (1982).

13

MENTAL HEALTH AND SOCIAL POLICY

Mary S. Harper

It has been customary to say that an individual's adaptation at any given point in time is determined by an interplay among the biological, social, cultural, environmental, genetic vulnerability, and psychological factors impinging on him or her at that moment and in his or her recent and distant past.

Good physical and mental health; intelligence; membership and role in the family and integrated communities; adequate food, shelter, and clothing; a good education; a successful career; and a positive self-image and social class can be counted on the positive side of mental health. Extreme poverty, a psychologically broken family, a poorly integrated community, membership in a culturally deprived minority group, poor education and school achievement, poor job performance, and no access to health care amount to what P. L. Berkman (1967) has called "cumulative deprivation," which might contribute to poor mental health and inadequacy of adaptation (Hollingshead & Redlick, 1958; Leighton et al., 1963; Wilensky, 1961).

Residents of poor, transient, and nonfamily residential areas are expected to have higher rates of psychiatric problems than residents of stable, high-status, husband-wife family areas (Goldsmith, Jackson, Rosen, & Babigian, 1982; Holzer, Goldsmith, Jackson, & Swanson, 1985). Health may be conceptualized as the ability to live and function effectively in society and to exercise maximum self-reliance and autonomy; it is not necessarily the total absence of disease.

F. J. Menolascino (1986) has defined mental illness as occurring at that time when a cluster of behavioral signs and symptoms come together and become overly disruptive of the person's ability to function effectively in the mainstream of his or her family and community.

The approach to diagnosing mental disorders in racial and ethnic persons should be multiaxial, probably including as axes the syndrome; personality disorder; physical disability; possible precipitating, predisposing, and contributory events; culture; and level of social function (American Psychiatric Association, 1968).

In viewing diseases narrowly, social factors—poverty, for example—might be seen in an unspecified way as decreasing the individual's resistance to the disease. In a multiaxial system, poverty might be seen as increasing a genetically established vulnerability to cognitive disorganization in several ways: by increased life stress, by reduced available resource (such as money to pay medical bills or to obtain transportation to a health care facility for an appointment), and by an association with social relations dysfunction by limiting the individual's flexibility in learning such functioning (Strauss, 1979). If sociocultural factors are to be understood in relationship to psychopathology in the individual patient or person, this impact on the various axes defined above must be established.

To understand the impact of central cultural and social influences on psychopathology, we must understand the factorial "loading" of three key words: social, cultural, and psychopathology.

Social summarizes a multiplicity of events in the human environmental sphere and usually includes social status, socioeconomic status, institutional affiliation, age, sex, race, class, nature of ecological stress. Social also implies the prevailing social structure and the degree of autonomy, mobility, and legitimate power in it (King, 1978; Gerson, 1976).

Culture summarizes a multivariate entity from child-rearing practices to kinship systems. I see culture as history. It is the total way of life of a group of human beings, primarily the shared patterns of values, beliefs, and feelings which are characterized by a distinct worldview, codes of conduct, and a definition of reality to satisfy biological and psychological needs. Culture guides values which serve as the major premise and foundation.

A central concern with regard to culture and psychopathology is how behavior is structured, organized, and influenced by underlying cultural rules or the extent to which culture reality creates conditions of vulnerability making the advent of mental illness more likely for individuals or groups of the culture as a whole (King, 1978; Levine, 1976).

Psychopathology. In the literature, there is no consensus as to what constitutes psychopathology. Generally what is covered in the literature are the behaviors that are disturbing to others and the inability to function in various psychosocial areas. L. M. King (1978) reports that the most critical problem with the focus on psychopathology has been the failure to develop some baseline data on what is mental health as opposed to what is mental illness; therefore, we must continue to raise the question and concern about the problems inherent in arriving at a definition of what constitutes psychopathology and to what extent the diagnosis of "labeling" is influenced by the given sociopsychological and sociocultural context and perceptions. There are great variations within the black race in regard to social and cultural phenomena. It is sometimes these variations that give rise to misdiagnosis.

PREVALENCE OF MENTAL DISORDERS

In any given six-month period, approximately 29.4 million adult Americans (18.7 percent of the population) suffer from one or more mental disorders covered by the Diagnostic Interview Schedule (DIS) developed by L. N. Robins and his colleagues, which allows lay interviewers to assess the presence, duration, and severity of symptoms necessary for the diagnostic criteria in the Diagnostic and Statistical Manual (DSM-III) (Robins, Helzer, Croughan, & Ratcliff, 1981). The DIS includes the following diagnoses and conditions:

* Substance abuse (alcohol and drugs)
* Affective disorders (depression, dysthymia, etc.)
* Antisocial personality
* Anxiety/somatoform disorders (phobic disorders, obsessive-compulsive disorders, and somatization disorders)
* Schizophrenic/schizophreniform disorders
* Cognitive impairment (severe) (based on Mini Mental State Examination Score of 0–17).

The DSM-III permits a clinician to evaluate a patient on each of five dimensions (referred to as axes) as follows:

Axis I: Clinical psychiatric syndrome(s) and other conditions

Axis II: Personality disorders

Axis III: Physical disorders

Axis IV: Severity of psychosocial stressors

Axis V: Highest level of adaptive functioning in the past year.

The diagnosis should include as many of the five axes as are appropriate. The first three axes constitute the official diagnostic assessment. Axes IV and V are generally intended for special clinical and research settings, but they can also be used to provide information to supplement the official diagnosis when appropriate (DSM-III, 1980).

The American Psychiatric Association's (APA) decision regarding what behaviors constitute mental illness has a considerable impact on the complex political and social policy questions. One has to constantly be reminded of the stigma and social consequences of a diagnosis of mental illness in our society in terms of driving licenses, employment, and selected civil rights. For example, homosexuality was considered a mental disorder until 1973 when it was deleted from the DSM-III by a vote of the membership of the APA. Similarly, after the controversy was raised by women's groups over the proposed inclusion of premenstrual dysphoric disorder in the DSM-IIIR, it was voted to change the name to perilateral dysphoric disorder and include the diagnosis in an appendix rather than in the central text. Mental health and social science disciplines must be concerned about labeling a person as mentally ill or as having a mental disorder. Incidentally, the nomenclature in the DSM-III is mental disorder, not mental illness. For further information pertaining to protection and advocacy for people who are labeled mentally ill, see the literature from the Mental Health Law Project (1987). The most frequent DIS disorders are alcohol abuse/dependence, phobia, drug abuse/dependence, and dysthymia. The most frequent DIS disorders for females are phobia, major depressive episodes without grief, dysthymia, and obsessive-compulsive disorders (Taube & Barrett, 1985).

Fewer than one-fifth of the individuals identified with any mental disorder in a six-month period consulted any mental health specialist or general medical physician. The refusal to get mental health services is caused mostly by stigma, lack of acceptance of the disorder, lack of accurate diagnosis, lack of access to mental health services, lack of referral to mental health services, lack of transportation in the rural areas, and lack of money.

The number of organizations providing mental health services rose from 3,005 to 4,302 between 1970 and 1982, an increase of 43 percent, but 53 percent fewer psychiatric beds were available in 1982 than had been in 1970. State and county mental hospitals accounted for about 57 percent of all psychiatric beds in 1982, compared with 79 percent in 1970. For the same period, outpatient services (except in private practice) decreased partly because of the change in policy for lack of reimbursement of such services.

After day treatment centers tripled between 1969 and 1979, there was a decrease in 1981. Most admissions to inpatient services are voluntary except for those to state and county mental hospitals, where the largest percentage was involuntary—noncriminal commitment and minorities (blacks and Hispanics).

Commercial insurance was the most frequently reported principal payment source for inpatient psychiatric admissions under the age of 65 to private hospitals and nonfederal general hospitals. For each type of inpatient psychiatric service, more than 70 percent of the admissions were readmissions to inpatient psychiatric care. This is truly a revolving door phenomenon which results partly from the lack of public policy and social policy for after-discharge care for persons leaving the mental institutions. Lack of employment, lack of role in the family and community, and lack of a continuum of care and treatment in the community, as well as stigma, give rise to readmissions. It is a public policy and social policy responsibility to have adequate community-based mental health programs and a continuity of care. Such readmissions constitute personal loss for the patient as well as a waste of the taxpayers' money.

Schizophrenia was the most frequent primary diagnosis for admission to state and county mental hospitals and to public and multiservice nonfederal general hospitals. Affective disorder was the most frequent primary diagnosis for admission to private psychiatric hospitals and nonpublic, nonfederal general hospitals. Alcohol-related disorders were the most common for admission to the Veterans Administration (VA) medical centers (Taube & Barrett, 1985). The median days of stay for admissions to state and county hospitals, VA medical centers, and private psychiatric hospitals were similar and considerably longer than the median days in multiservice, nonfederal general hospitals.

Epidemiological research is needed to study the differential diagnoses as well as the median days of stay. Blacks are frequently diagnosed as schizophrenic, and they are generally housed in state and county psychiatric facilities.

In 1982, more than 290,000 full-time equivalent (FTE) staff were employed in U.S. mental organizations (this number does not include nurses aides, licensed practical nurses, and orderlies). There has been an increase in FTE psychologists, registered nurses, and social workers but a decrease in psychiatrists and other physicians.

EXPENDITURES

According to Carl Taube and S. A. Barrett (1985), in 1980, the total expenditure for mental health care in the United States was between $19.4 billion and $24.1 billion. These expenditures represent approximately 7.7 percent of the total expenditures for general health and approximately 0.7 percent of the nation's gross national product. In 1986, the direct care cost for mental illness was $36 billion annually (*Science*, May, 1986). Nursing home costs were between 7.5 and 9.0 percent of the total direct mental health care cost.

On an average, state mental health agencies spent 66.5 percent of their budgets in state mental hospitals and 29.7 percent in community-based programs, but there was great variability across states. In 1984, state and county mental hospitals accounted for half of the psychiatric beds and were the predominant type of psychiatric beds available in all but nine states (Redlick, Witkin, Atay, Fell, & Manderscheid, 1987).

Some of the psychosocial stressors experienced in the black population include

- Conjugal (marital and nonmarital)
- Parenting (particularly, the single-parent family)
- Other interpersonal relationships (racism, low self-esteem, and feelings of hopelessness)
- Living circumstances and arrangements, geographic location
- Financial (low pay, unemployment, underemployment)
- Legal (particularly the high incarceration rate for black males 24–26)
- Development
- Physical illness or injury
- Other psychosocial stressors such as prejudice, discrimination, lack of access to adequate quality of care, low self-esteem
- Family functioning, structure, and role.

In the highest level of adaptive functioning, the diagnosis is to be made in terms of the following relationships:

- Social relations
- Personal relations
- Interpersonal relations
- Intrapersonal relations
- Occupational functions
- Use of leisure time.

MENTAL HEALTH SERVICES AND CARE

Historically, the community provided homes or detention for the poor and their families until about 1800. The homes gradually became places for the insane. In 1860, the states began to assume responsibility for the mentally ill and built state asylums or mental hospitals.

In 1860, state hospitals existed in 28 of the 33 states (Rothman, 1971). By the turn of the century, a series of alternatives to these public facilities began to appear: psychopathic, private, VA, public health services, and general hospitals (Talbott, 1983).

Beginning in the twentieth century, outpatient clinics became commonplace, but hospitals remained the primary locus for care and treatment for those suffering from chronic illness.

In 1955, state hospitals achieved their highest census, and primacy in the delivery of mental health services began to decline after that (Kramer, 1985). Several forces, occurring then and now, have resulted in a massive shift from public hospitals to community auspices:

- The philosophy of community mental health
- Pharmacological and social therapeutic innovations
- Pressures from civil libertarians and patient rights and advocacy groups
- Federal assumption of funding for the chronically ill in communities through Medicaid, Medicare, and Social Security income.

The net result of this historic shift in locus of care and treatment of the chronically ill was twofold:

- The mental hospital's role was altered as the primary source of care. It must be noted that 56 percent of the psychiatric beds are still in these facilities, and 30 percent of their patients are elderly (over 60 years of age).
- The system moved from providing custodial care in most asylums to active treatment and rehabilitation in most of the community-based mental health programs, centers and services.

There have been other recent shifts in the delivery of mental health services; namely, the nursing home has become the major provider of mental health services to the elderly:

- From 50 to 70 percent of the nursing home residents have either a primary or secondary diagnosis of a mental illness.

- Approximately, 668,000 patients with chronic mental illness reside in nursing homes.

- Of the 668,000 patients, 72,000 have chronic mental illness without physical disorders; 35,000 have both mental and physical disorders; and 561,000 are senile, almost 75 percent of whom also have physical disorders.

- Approximately 75 percent of the residents with mental illness receive at least one medication for a mental disorder, almost half receive a tranquilizer, and about one-third receive some kind of psychological therapy.

- About 90 percent of the residents with mental illness were identified as presenting behavior problems compared with about half of physically ill residents (Garrison, 1986).

From a social policy perspective, some of the shift of mental health services to the nursing home resulted from reimbursement from the federal government and the private insurance payors. Persons in state hospitals were not eligible for Medicaid and Medicare reimbursement. From the start (20 years ago), Medicare put severe restrictions on mental health care. Medicare has a 190-day lifetime limit on inpatient psychiatric care, 150 days for any one benefit period (Koran, 1981). For this reason, much of the mental health care for the aged is delivered in general hospitals, for which there is no such limitation on psychiatric care; the benefits are the same as for medical care (Stotsky, B. A., & Stotsky, E. S., 1983; Koran, 1981).

Medicare also restricts psychiatric services to $250 per patient per year with a 50-percent coinsurance rate (U.S. Department of Health and Human Services, 1980), which makes mental health care costly or unavailable to many and discourages participation by psychiatrists in the treatment of patients in nursing homes or in clinics (Stotsky and Stotsky, 1983). Medicare requirements that mental health services be given under medical supervision excludes some types of providers. Freestanding community mental health centers (CMHCs) cannot receive direct Medicare reimbursement (Flemming, Buchanan, Santos, & Rickards, 1984).

Medicare's Diagnostic Related Groups (DRGs) are less suited to mental health than physical health care (Goldman, Pencus, Taube, & Regier, 1984; Gattozzi, 1986) although they are appropriate for some psychiatric care services in general hospitals. Psychiatric services and long-term care are temporarily exempted. Of the 467 DRGs, 19 are Medicare DRGs for mental disorders (Gattozzi, 1986).

Outpatient mental health treatment under Part B of Medicare is restricted by a dollar cap and requires a 50-percent copayment by the beneficiary (Select Committee on Aging, 1988). Coverage for care in intermediate-care nursing facilities (ICFs), which is appropriate for patients with chronic disorders like Alzheimer's disease, is not available at all under Medicare (Select Committee on Aging, 1988).

Medicare legislation, enacted in 1965, provided coverage for mental health and remained substantially the same until approximately 1987. The Omnibus Budget Reconciliation Act of 1987 (OBRA–87) made a number of significant changes aimed at increasing the coverage for these services. The first change was an increase in the annual payment cap for outpatient physician's services for the treatment of mental illness. The 1965 cap amount of $312.60 a year was increased to $1,375, and an exception of the cap was provided for brief office visits to regulate medication. Thus, Medicare programs now provide more access to physician services for mentally ill patients.

In addition, Congress wrote into the law a program instruction explicitly recognizing outpatient hospital coverage in partial hospital services. Medicare's recognition should promote greater use of these services. Other provisions of the law provide coverage of clinical psychologists in hospitals and rural health clinics (Judd, 1988).

Since its start in 1965, Medicaid has been more generous than has Medicare with regard to mental health services. From a social policy concern, there are a number of problems for the mental health system. First, Medicaid reimbursement encourages institutionalization. Medicaid is generally for individuals with low incomes; therefore, a person must become impoverished to become entitled to Medicaid. Medicaid pays for about one-half of all nursing home care in the United States; its policies shape the industry (U.S. General Accounting Office, 1982). Since Medicaid is a combined federal and state program, there may be very large variations in coverage, access, and entitlements. For example CMHCs are covered by Medicaid in some states but not in others (U.S. General Accounting Office, 1982). Medicaid money is not earmarked for psychiatric care. Medicaid coverage has been cut in recent years, especially by placing new limits on the length of stay (LOS) and by limiting the reimbursement rates for inpatient psychiatric care (Sharfstein, Eist, Sack, Kaiser, & Shadoan, 1984). Thus, both programs throw the burden for care for the indigent mentally ill back on the state and county governments and limit the access of the poor and blacks to mental health care.

The nursing home reform provisions of OBRA–87 provide for preadmission screening of mentally ill persons to ensure proper placement. They also require that nursing homes accurately assess and meet the psychosocial needs of their patients. The Health Care Financing Administration (HCFA) is developing regulations to implement these changes, and it will monitor their impact, when they become effective in 1990, on the utilization and quality of services provided to people with mental or behavioral disorders who reside in nursing homes and other settings (Judd, 1988).

SUPPLEMENTAL SECURITY INCOME

Supplemental Security Income (SSI) is basically a welfare program; over half of the disabled have behavioral, social, and mental disorders (U.S. Department of Health and Human Services, 1980; Robins et al., 1981). Thus SSI funds many of the mentally ill. Many of the mentally ill in board and care homes are funded by SSI.

In general, mental health care, treatment, and projects are funded by private insurance, out-of-pocket, Medicaid, Medicare, SSI, and other third-party payers such as corporations, organized labor unions, selected pension plans, and state and county funds.

Another social policy conflict is the care of the elderly with mental and behavioral problems in nursing homes. Most nursing homes are not staffed with qualified individuals to provide mental health services (Liptzin, 1986). The state mental hospitals have a legislative mandate to provide active treatment and rehabilitation for mentally ill patients, but the nursing homes do not have that mandate at this time. Therefore, the major treatment for many of the residents with mental disorders is psychotropic drugs. In a recent survey, it was found that 62 percent of the nursing home residents were on psychotropic drugs even though some of them did not have a primary psychiatric diagnosis/disorder (Burns, Lawson, & Goldstrom, 1985).

At the present time, there is not one full-time board-certified psychiatrist in any of the 26,817 nursing homes and related care homes in the United States; however, about twenty-five psychogeriatric nurse specialists were recently hired in some of the proprietary and VA nursing homes. A part of the lack of training and appropriate mental health services for the mentally ill in the nursing home is due to an institution for mental disease (IMD) classification by the HCFA.

By statute, Medicare and Medicaid deny reimbursement for nonelderly patients of IMDs, which Medicaid regulates. In effect, IMDs are defined as facilities that engage primarily in providing care for mental diseases to more than 50 percent of their residents regardless of age. The threat of being classified an IMD, and thereby losing Medicaid reimbursement for nonelderly patients, provides a strong incentive for nursing homes to avoid providing any mental health services to any of their patients. As a result, almost no mental health assessment or treatment is provided in nursing homes even though research indicates a significant proportion of elderly nursing home residents suffer from mental health problems (Taff & Scallet, 1986).

In many instances, the nursing home will not accept patients with behavioral problems or a mental disorder. The HCFA publishes guidelines which are intended to assist in IMD identification and an instruction series (FSIIS) FY 76–44, FY 76–97, and FY 76–150, section 4390, Services to Individuals Age 65 or Older in Institutions for Mental Diseases (IMDs), dated December 1982, transmittal no. 3.

USE OF SHORT-TERM GENERAL HOSPITALS BY PATIENTS WITH PSYCHIATRIC DIAGNOSIS

One of the most important changes in the delivery of psychiatric inpatient care in the past several decades has been an expansion of the role played by short-term general hospitals. Short-term general hospitals, rather than psychiatric hospitals, are now the most likely place for hospitalization for a mental disorder to occur (Kiesler & Silbulkin, 1983). In 1983, an estimated 1,347 nonfederal general hospitals (NFGHs) provided any combination of separate inpatient, out-patient, and partial care services. The 1,347 nonfederal general hospitals with separate psychiatric services reported that the 1984 inventory represented 23 percent of the 5,783 NFGHs operating in the United States during 1983, as reported in the annual survey of the American Hospital Association (AHA) in 1984 (National Center for Health Services Research, 1985). Although the total number of NFGHs with separate psychiatric units decreased over the period from 1981 to 1983, the number of additions have substantially increased to almost 30 percent from just over 1 million persons during 1981 to about 1.3 million persons (Redlick et al., 1987; Liptzin, 1987). The tremendous increase in mental health services in NFGHs has social policy implications in terms of less stigma for the mentally ill and better access for minorities and the elderly. In addition, the NFGH care must be reimbursed by Medicare and Medicaid for mental health serviced rendered in NFGHs. There have been few studies on the quality of mental health care provided by the general hospitals, the cost effectiveness of such services, and the outcomes of these services.

The next major change in the noninstitutional delivery of mental health services is involvement of the primary care physician, the general practitioner, and the family physician, all referred to here as the primary care practitioner (PCP). The major provider of mental health services in noninstitutional settings is the PCP since five out of six office visits for mental health services are provided by nonpsychiatric physicians (NPP). Minorities and the elderly are notably under-represented in psychiatrists' office visits. In one study, it was found that 71 percent of the NPP-prescribed psychotropic drugs were prescribed for patients who did not have a psychiatric diagnosis (Schurman & Mitchell, 1985).

Another major social policy concern in mental health is deinstitutionalization. In practice, the term deinstitutionalization is used in the literature to refer to a broad scope of patient-connected events, ranging from carefully planned local efforts to achieving the ideal. The ideal and essential components of deinstitutionalization as conceptualized by B. S. Brown (1975) included

- The prevention of inappropriate hospital admission through the provision of community alternatives to treatment
- The release to the community of all institutional patients who have been given adequate preparation for such a change
- The establishment and maintenance of community support systems for noninstitution-alized persons receiving mental health services in the community (Brown, 1975).

R. V. Weclew (1975) contends that community-based services tend to be irrelevant to the needs of Latino patients and that this results in the underutilization of such services. J. A. Mayo (1974) points out similar problems in the community treatment of blacks. Other studies deal with difficulties in providing relevant treatment to rural patients and to elderly patients (Becker & Schulberg, 1976).

Although the first half of the 1970s saw little expression of concern about the plight of mental patients discharged or transferred to nursing homes, boarding homes, and so on, the most visible "marker" from a social policy concern was the 1977 General Accounting Office's report to Congress entitled, *Returning the Mentally Disabled to the Community: Government Needs to Do More.* This report supported the disability and feasibility of the community approach, and it also identified several problems and issues.

The report identified the following social policy issues:

* Issues related to the selection of patients for community care (a very high percentage of patients released were disadvantaged persons and minority members)
* Issues related to the treatment of patients in the community
* Issues related to the greater community (community resistance and opposition effects on the patient's family)
* Financial and fiscal issues
* Legal and quasi-legal issues
* Informational issues and accountability
* Difficulties in locating and following or monitoring patients in the community
* Inadequacy of existing evaluation and follow-up studies to establish liaison with the community support systems.

Major social policy recommendations by the GAO to Congress:

* All federal deinstitutionalization efforts should be overseen by a congressional committee.
* Presidential objectives on deinstitutionalization should be established.
* Federal interdepartmental objectives on deinstitutionalization should be generated.
* The responsibilities of related agencies should be clarified by the secretary of the Department of Health, Education, and Welfare.

The mental health movement in the United States in some ways parallels other activities and social policies concerned with the rights of mental patients. During the late 1800s and early 1900s, in the face of economic depressions, the state legislators were unable to appropriate sufficient funds to provide decent care and to hire qualified staff. Economy and patient custody were the watchwords of the time, and the asylums became overcrowded and prison-like, and the combination of security custody and economy made the mental institutions frightening and depressing places in which the rights of the patients were all but forgotten. In many instances, patients were stripped of all privacy and dignity; all their personal possessions were taken away, and they were herded into large dining rooms, dormitories, shower baths, and toilets without privacy or partitions.

Patients' rights are privileges and entitlements of patients in a mental health system. Some of the major categories of patients' rights include civil rights—the basic rights of any citizen in our society, whether a mental patient or not:

1. The right to vote
2. The right to buy and sell property
3. The right to marry.

Until recent years, most mental patients were declared incompetent and were deprived of their civil rights as part of the basic commitment process. This is seldom the case today since competence and commitment proceedings are now separated in virtually all of the states. As a part of social policy, procedures and standards are needed to ensure that patients are aware of their civil rights, and a system is needed to monitor the assurance of civil rights.

Patients also have legal rights—the special rights of patients in mental health institutions and programs:

1. The right to contact and be represented by an attorney
2. The right to seek a writ of habeas corpus
3. The right to file complaints with responsible authorities.

The special legal rights are often spelled out in the state's mental health statutes. These statutes are frequently not known by the patient, by his or her family, and even by the staff.

Human rights granted to patients ensure the right to a safe environment, including the following conditions:

1. Clean facility and treatments,
2. Physical care and medical services for persons in facilities classified as total institutions,
3. Assurance of protection from any threat or assault from staff or other patients, and
4. A balanced diet of food in a clean and safe environment;

The right to an aesthetic and humane environment; and the right to privacy and personal freedom, including

1. Freedom from unnecessary seclusion or restraints,
2. Privacy while bathing, showering, and toileting,
3. The right to review one's own clinical records, and
4. The right to make calls and write letters.

Patients have a right to treatment—the entitlement of a person in the mental health system to an early and adequate diagnosis and course of treatments, including

1. The right to an early diagnostic evaluation
2. The right to a physical as well as mental diagnosis
3. The right to evaluation in the least restrictive environment
4. The right to expeditious transfer upon a decision to take such action
5. The development and maintenance of an individualized treatment plan and progress reviews
6. The right to informed consent
7. The right to know what disciplinary procedures will be meted out for antisocial behaviors
8. The right to professional review of treatment and a second opinion.

The right to treatment also encompasses special attention and safeguards regarding certain treatment procedures, especially those that are intrusive:

1. Electroconvulsive therapy
2. Behavior modification therapy (especially aversive procedures)
3. Intramuscular injections of psychotropic medications
4. Psychosurgery
5. Reality therapy.

Other unique rights pertaining to mental patients are rights which apply because of the unique risks to patients in mental health programs. These rights include

1. The right to adequate payment for labor performed
2. The right to refuse treatment and prescribed medications
3. The right to be informed and to review experimental or research procedures and the right to withhold consent thereto without punishment (McPheeters, 1977).

Many states have developed standards for implementing these rights. It is the responsibility of the administrator to ensure that the patient's rights are not violated. The accountability and responsibilities must be included in the statutes, public policies, and social policies.

ISSUES OF SPECIAL CONCERN TO CHRONICALLY MENTALLY ILL WOMEN

Despite the recent attention given to the chronically mentally ill (CMI) as a disadvantaged group, individual persons suffering from chronically disabling mental health problems still remain "faceless" and are seldom mentioned in clinical research. In many instances, the CMI is regarded as almost genderless by both researchers and clinicians.

From their research on CMI women, Mary Test and S. B. Berlin (1981) found that

- Women are more likely than men to be diagnosed as neurotic, and men are more likely than women to be diagnosed as having alcohol disorders.

- The data are ambiguous about whether men or women are at greater risk for mental illness. Men show higher rates of admission to state and county mental hospitals; women show higher rates of admission to community mental health centers. Before any comparisons can be made, the type of mental illness must be explicitly defined.

- Although the data are sparse and subject to different interpretations, available information suggests that people from lower social classes have a higher risk of mental illness than people from higher social classes.

- People who are separated or divorced show higher rates of mental illness than people in other marital categories. Furthermore, the data imply that rates of mental illness are much higher among single men than among single women.

- Regarding age, the highest rates of mental illness for women occur in the 25–44 age group; the second highest, in the 15–24 age group. For men, these two groups also have the highest rates, but the order is reversed. In addition, men in the youngest group, 18 and under, have a much higher rate of admission to mental health facilities than females in that age group.

RESEARCH

Mental illnesses, in comparison with other medical disorders, have always received disproportionately low shares of research and treatment resources. The main reason for this has often been the public stigma attached to mental illness. However, direct costs for mental illness top $36 billion annually, and schizophrenics occupy 40 percent of all long-term hospital beds, according to the National Institute of Mental Health (NIMH). The fiscal year 1987 research budget for NIMH, however, is slated to be less than $200 million. The federal research dollar per patient is $14 for schizophrenia and $10 for depression. The equivalent for heart disease is $130; for muscular dystrophy, $10,000. Depression results in 16,000 suicides a year among adolescents alone. The government pays for 85 percent of the research on mental illness; the rest is paid for with private funds (*Science*, 1986).

MENTAL HEALTH RESEARCH FROM A SOCIAL POLICY PERSPECTIVE FOR BLACKS

A heuristic model should be used. In such a model, the primary relationship is (1) the person, family, community; (2) the setting for the care; (3) access, quality cost/pricing; and (4) redistribution and equity of social, economic, and social welfare resources.

Mental health research is required, including (1) study of family policy (Zimmerman, 1979); (2) study of family process; (3) study of functioning and structure for the prevention of mental disorders, behavioral problems, and deviance; and (4) study of social impact, social policies, and public policies pertaining to mental health in general and specifically to blacks, the elderly, and other minority groups.

Social impact assessment should be made of existing treatment/care modalities, length of stay in care programs, care settings, care by paraprofessional/professional/family care giver, public facility versus private facility, diagnostic and care procedures, access to rehabilitation versus custodial care and warehousing, and risk factors involved in care and treatment modalities.

Selected research on patterns of utilization of mental health services should include the following:

- Epidemiologic studies: prevalence and incidence estimation
- Longitudinal studies on risk factors in precipitating, predisposing, and contributing to mental disorders
- Exploration of the use of risk factor indicators for treatment planning
- Development of models to improve interagency and interfacility, family/provider, cooperation and coordination, and the impact of such models on service utilization and treatment outcomes
- Design and test of holistic models to treatment planning and therapeutic interventions involving family and health providers
- Design of a comprehensive and uniform record-keeping system which includes cost estimates and varied types of helping activities
- Studies on the early stages of the help-seeking process including conception, definition and labeling of distress, and their influence on coping strategies and help-seeking behavior
- Studies to identify effective black therapists and agencies
- Studies on nonusers of professional help and the alternative helping sources
- Studies on the impact of the race or ethnicity of the health provider on the treatment/ rehabilitation outcomes in the care of racial/ethnic patients
- Studies of the impact of race on selected conditions such as Alzheimer's disease, schizophrenia, depression, alcoholism, suicide, and cognitive decline.

POLICY

Alfred J. Kahn (1969) defines policy as the general guide to action, the cluster of overall decisions relevant to the achievement of the goal, the guiding principles, the standing plan, the basic emphasis of the policy approach to the problems, and the interactions of the individual in relation to society.

Policy spans the entire range of public and social activities, including safety of the environment, access to health care (mental health and physical health), transportation, safe housing, education, social service, law enforcement, patients' rights, income security, human rights, civil rights, religious freedom, privacy and freedom of information, informed consent, fair commitment laws, unlawful detention, right to active treatment, and the right to refuse medications, electroconvulsive therapy, and psychosurgery.

Three policy models—the rational policy model, the organization policy model, and the bureaucratic policy model all have their roots in organizational theory (Allison, 1969). Thomas Dye (1975) has identified others: elite theory, group theory, incrementalism, and institutionalism. Thus, depending on the objectives of the group, the content of the policy as well as the anticipated outcomes, or the model policy may be viewed as rational choice, political outcome, system output, preference of the governing elite, an equilibrium reached among contending interest groups, institutional outcome, or incremental modification of past policies.

SOCIAL POLICY

In viewing the existing definitions of social policy, Kahn interprets social policy to be "the care of principles or guiding ideology behind the series of separate, social welfare measures" (1969, p. 32). Such measures include income maintenance, housing, health (mental and physical), education, recreation, manpower and employment, and licensure and certification procedures and processes for mental health and long-term care workers and the personal social services.

Both policy, in general, and social policy appear to be equally concerned with issues of redistribution, equity, quality, and access.

It is essential that all special-interest advocate groups and individuals be able to perform policy analysis and social impact assessment. All too often we criticize a policy from an emotional or judgmental level. Often, without having made an analysis of the policy or an assessment of its social impact, we describe the policy as racist, unfair, or discriminatory.

One analytical framework for the study of social policy offered by Titmuss (1974) and modified by S. L. Zimmerman (1979) includes

- The nature of the benefit
- The nature of the entitlement to the benefit (i.e., whether it is legal, contractual, contributory, financial, discretionary, or professionally determined)
- The target of the entitlement (individuals, families, groups, or territories)
- The target's socioeconomic, biological, racial, ethnic characteristics or profile
- The methods or procedures employed to determine access to and the allocation and utilization of benefits.

SOCIAL IMPACT ASSESSMENT

Social impact assessment is a procedure for anticipating "the unanticipated consequences of purposive social action" in order to forestall or offset their adverse effects (Wolf, 1976, p. 58). Social impacts are defined as those changes in social structures and behaviors that are forecasted to occur as a direct or indirect result of the implementation of a policy, plan, regulation, rule, or law.

C. P. Wolf (1976) outlines the following steps for conducting social impact assessment:

• Develop a profile or set of baseline data as a before measure of a policy event.

• Make a projection by generating a time series for detecting trends so that the deviation from baseline conditions established in the profiling step can be forecast.

• Identify significant impacts, primarily through mental rather than real-life experiments because, though the problem may be predictable, social impact assessment cannot establish the experimental controls or conditions needed for predictive studies.

• Display and describe impacts so that others may view them. Assess the impact of various effects, whether or not they are quantifiable.

• Evaluate impacts with the public, that is, attach values and assign weights to the assessed impacts in term of their beneficial or adverse social effects.

Social impact assessment is not the same as program evaluation, which is concerned with social performance. Social policy is concerned with individuals, social relationships, and social purpose, equity, and redistribution.

Family policy (Zimmerman, 1976) concerns family functioning as it affects the well-being of individual family members and society at large.

In mental health, social policy and family policy must be used, analyzed, assessed, monitored, and fairly implemented.

Social policy analysis and social impact assessment may be applied to deinstitutionalization of the mental patient or the mentally retarded, income maintenance, foster care, adult day care, educational programs, mental health programs, hypertension programs (treatment and prevention), communities, acquired immune deficiency syndrome (AIDS) programs for various racial and ethnic groups; teenage pregnancy programs, excessive disabilities among blacks, and the impact of sites for mental health service delivery. Research methods identified as appropriate for policy analysis include content analysis of articles in the mass media, announcements in the Federal Register, articles in the journals of mental health and the law, testimonies delivered at public hearings, mail surveys and findings from questionnaires, and the Congressional Record. It is especially important to monitor announcements of the policy changes that solicit individual and group responses published in the Federal Register.

Policy study research (Anderson, 1984; Dye, 1975) in social policy and mental health may involve a description of the content of public policy, an assessment of the impact of environmental forces on the content of public policy, an analysis of the effects of various institutional arrangements and political processes on public policy, an inquiry into the consequences of various public and social policies for the political system, and an evaluation of the impact of public policy on society, both in terms of expected and unexpected outcomes.

Social policy study of mental health services education and delivery is especially needed in rural areas and the inner city and for special populations such as the elderly and blacks. To a large extent, social policy and public policy determine health care (mental and physical)—the quality, access, cost, and entitlements.

By and large, sociologists and psychologists have not played a strong role in research in mental health policy, according to C. A. Kiesler (1983), who has defined mental health policy as

The de facto or de jure aggregate of laws, practice, social structures, or actions occurring within our society the intent of which is improved. Mental health of individuals and groups, the study of such policy includes, the descriptive parameters of the aggregate, the comparative assessment of particular techniques evaluation of a system and its parts, i.e., human resources available and needed cost benefit, analysis of practices or actions and the cause and effect relationship of one set of policies, on another policy such as mental health policies on welfare and health as well as the study of institutions or groups seeking to affect policy. (Kiesler, 1980, p. 18).

Kiesler advocates a top-down approach to mental health policy analysis.

Policy research can be descriptive, evaluative, or theoretical in nature.

Social policy research must be interdisciplinary; it must combine aspects of psychology, medicine, sociology, and nursing, and it must involve political scientists, health care administrators, health care practioners and providers, the families of the patients, psychiatric statisticians, epidemiologists, educators, academicians, research institutes and centers, individuals, and governments (federal, state, county, and local), advocacy groups, special interest groups, ombudsmen, and international scholars.

Some preliminary readings on mental health policy might include:

- *Mental health and social policy*, David Mechanic (1980)
- *Financing psychotherapy*, Thomas McGure (1980)
- *Mental illness in the United States*, Dohrenwend, B. P., et al. (1980)
- *Economics, mental health and the law*, Jeffrey Rubin (1978)
- *The President's Commission on Mental Health*, vols. 2, 3, and 4 (1978)
- *Experimental methods for social policy research*, Fairweather, G. W. and Tornatzskey, L. G. (1977)
- *Linking health and mental health*, Braskowski, Marks, and Badman (1981)
- *Public policy and long term care: Domestic and international*, Mary S. Harper, in H. J. Altman, ed., *Alzheimer's Disease* (1987)

- *Policy analysis*, Marvin R. Burt (1974)
- *Public policy making*, James E. Anderson (1984)
- *The agency: A guide to public policy*, Bennett M. Rich and Martha Baum (1984)
- *Mental illness in nursing, nursing homes: Agenda for research*, Mary S. Harper and Barry Lebowitz (1986).

In mental health and social policy, special concerns must be focused on the following:

- The impact of deinstitutionalization of the mentally ill and the mentally retarded
- The delivery of mental health services (sites, quality, cost, and access)
- Commitment laws, processes, and rules
- The impact of advocacy by the family and special groups
- Inner cities and rural areas
- Funding formulas
- Access to affordable care
- The stigma of mental illness
- Increased coordination among agencies, clinics, and treatment units
- Research in the prevention of mental illness and excessive disabilities
- Qualification, licensure, certification, and supervision of mental health workers
- Rights of the patient
- Rights of the family
- Rights of the health care providers
- Privacy afforded the patient and family
- Ombudsman (presence, role, and freedom of observations and reporting)
- Involvement of the family, business coalitions and the community, politicians, legislators, academicians, and clinical practitioners at all levels (paraprofessional and professional)
- Medical and clinical ethics, including the issues of resuscitation and the use (or not) of life-sustaining mechanisms
- The rationing of health care (for example, no rural dialysis for welfare patients, no organ transplants for people age 65 and above, the cap on medicine)
- Mental illness and the competency of many individuals who are severely mentally ill and are legally competent to conduct their business and make decisions about their lives, including a study of the impact of competence status and hearing on treatment outcomes and biases toward elders and racial/ethnic groups, and whether decisions as to competency are judicial ones, not medical ones
- Diagnoses and predictions of dangerousness (the diagnosis and definition of dangerousness varies with each state and sometimes by virtue stereotypes such as race and ethnicity. Most mental patients are not violent or dangerous. A psychiatrist or mental health worker may predict dangerousness under two circumstances: (1) immediate

danger of violence within the next few hours and (2) under good clinical conditions, a psychiatrist may be able to make a reasonable prediction about a person's potential for violent behavior (not dangerousness). It is much easier to predict whether a person will be harmful to himself than to others (Brooks, 1984).

REFERENCES

Allison, G. (1969, September). Conceptual models and the Cuban missile crisis. *The American Political Science Review, 63*, 689–711.

American Psychiatric Association Task Force on Nomenclature and Statistics (draft). (1968). Diagnostic and Statistical Manual of Mental Disorders III. Washington, D.C.: American Psychiatric Association Press.

Anderson, James E. (1984). *Public policy making (3rd ed.)*. New York: Holt, Rinehart, and Winston, p. 5.

Becker, A., & Schulberg, H. D. (1976, January 29). Phasing out state hospitals—A psychiatric dilemma. *New England Journal of Medicine, 294*, 255–261.

Berkman, P. L. (1967). Cumulative deprivation and mental illness. In M. F. Lowenthal, P. L. Beckman, et al., (Eds.), *Aging and mental disorders in San Francisco* (pp. 52–80). San Francisco: Jossey-Bass.

Brooks, A. D. (1984). Defining the dangerousness of the mentally ill: Involuntary civil commitment. In M. Craft & A. Craft (Eds.), *Mentally abnormal offenders* (pp. 280–307). London: Balliere Tindal.

Brown, B. S. (1975, November 4). Deinstitutionalization and community support systems." Statement by the Director, National Institute of Mental Health (mimeograph).

Burns, B. J., Lawson, David, & Goldstrom, I. D. (1985, September 23–26). *Mental disorders among nursing home patients: Preliminary findings from the National Nursing Home Survey pretest*. Paper presented at the meeting of the World Psychiatric Association, Edinburg, Scotland.

Dawson, Deborah A., Cynamon, Marcie, & Fitti, Joseph E. (1988, January 18). *AIDS knowledge and attitudes for September 1987*, No. 148. Hyattsville, MD: National Center for Health Statistics.

Diagnostic and Statistical Manual III. (1980). Washington, DC: American Psychiatric Association Press, p. 23.

Dohrenwend, B. P., Dohrenwend, B. S., Gould, M. S., Link, B., Neugebaur, R., & Wunsch-Hitzig, R. (1980). Mental illness in the United States: Epidemiological estimates. New York: Praeger.

Dye, Thomas. (1975). *Understanding public policy*. Englewood Cliffs, NJ: Prentice Hall.

Flemming, A. S., Buchanan, J. G., Santos, J. F., & Rickards, L. D. (1984). *Mental health services for the elderly: Report of a survey of community mental health centers*, vol. 1. Washington, DC: Action Committee to Implement the Mental Health Recommendations of the 1981 White House Conference on Aging.

Garrison, P. J. (1986, August/September). Quality of care for people with mental illnesses in nursing homes of growing concern. *Focus, 7*(7), 2.

Gattozzi, A. A. (1986). *Prospective payment of mental health care*. Rockville, MD: National Institute of Mental Health Public Inquiries.

Gerson, E. M. (1976). The social characteristics of illness: Deviance or politics? *Social Science Medicine, 10*, 29–24.

Goldman, H. H., Pencus, H. A., Taube, C. A., & Regier, D. A. (1984). Perspective payment for psychiatric hospitalization: Questions and issues. *Hospital and Community Psychiatry, 35*, 460–464.

Goldsmith, H. F., Jackson, D. J., Rosen, B. M., & Babigian, H. M. (1982). Utilization of mental health services in a middle size metropolitan area: A typological approach to understanding the relationship between social rank and utilization of mental health services. In R. A. Bell, H. F. Goldsmith, R. K. Len, & S. Sobel (Eds.), *Social indicators for human services systems.* Louisville, KY: University of Louisville, Department of Psychiatry and Behavioral Science.

Helzer, J. E. III, Goldsmith, H. F., Jackson, D. J., & Swanson, J. W. (1985, February 25). *Indirect indicators of need for mental health services.* Paper presented at the NIMH Workshop on Needs Assessment, Rockville, MD.

Hollingshead, A. B., & Redlick, F. C. (1958). *Social class and mental illness: A community study.* New York: Wiley.

Judd, L. L. (1988, March 2). Testimony before Select Committee on Aging, House of Representatives, Washington, DC.

Kahn, Alfred J. (1969). *Theory and practice in social planning.* New York: Russell Sage Foundation.

Kiesler, C. A. (1980). Mental health policy as a field of inquiry for psychology. *American Psychologist, 35*, 1066–1080.

Kiesler, C. A. (1981). Barriers to effective knowledge use in national mental health policy. *Health Policy Quarterly, 1*, 201–215.

Kiesler, C. A. (1983). Psychology and mental health policy. In M. Hersen, A. E. Kazdin, & A. S. Bellak (Eds.), *The Clinical Psychology Handbook.* New York: Pergamon Press.

Kiesler, C. A., & Silbulkin, A. E. (1983). Proportion of inpatient days for mental disorders: 1969–1978. *Hospital & Community Psychiatry, 34*(7), 606–610.

King, L. M. (1978). Social and cultural influences on psychopathology. *Annual Review of Psychology, 29*, 405–433.

King, L., Dixon, V., & Noble, W. (1976). *African philosophy: Assumptions and paradigms of research in black persons.* Los Angeles: Fanon Center Publication.

Koran, L. M. (1981). Mental health services. In M. I. Roemer (Ed.), *Health care delivery in the United States* (pp. 235–237). New York: Springer.

Kramer, M. (1985). *Psychiatric services and the changing institutional scene.* Rockville, MD: National Institute of Mental Health.

Leighton, D., et al., (1963). *The character of danger: Psychiatric symptoms in selected communities: Vol. 3. The Sterling County's study of psychiatric disorders and socio-cultural environment.* New York: Basic Books.

Levine, E. M. (1976). Psycho-cultural determinants in personality development. *Volta Review, 78*, 258–267.

Liptzin, B. (1986). Major mental disorders and problems in nursing homes: Implications for research and public policy. In Mary S. Harper, & B. Lebowitz (Eds.), *Mental illness in nursing homes: An agenda for research* (DHHS Publication No. GDM 86–1459). Washington, DC: U.S. Government Printing Office, pp. 41–55.

Liptzin, B. (1986). The geriatric patient and general hospital psychiatry. *General Hospital Psychiatry, 9*, 198–202.

Mayo, J. A. (1974, November-December). "The significance of socio-cultural variables in psychiatric treatment of black outpatients." *Comprehensive Psychiatry, 15*, 41–48.

McPheeters, H. L. (1977, June 1–3). Implementing standards to assure the rights of mental patients. Proceedings of a symposium held in Atlanta, GA.

Menolascino, F. J. (1986). The nature and types of mental illness in the mentally retarded. *Psychopharmacological Bulletin*, *22*(4), 1060–1071.

National Center for Health Services Research. (1985, October). *Use of short term general hospitals by patients with psychiatric diagnosis* (Research Note No. 8). Rockville, MD: National Center for Health Services Research.

National Institute of Mental Health. (1979). *Deinstitutionalization: An analytical review and sociological perspective*, series D, No. 4 (DHEW Publication No. ADM 79–351). Superintendent of Documents. Washington, DC: U.S. Government Printing Office.

National Institute of Mental Health. (1987, August). *Minority mental health services research*. Conference proceedings held in Rockville, MD.

Protection and advocacy for people who are labeled mentally ill. (1987, January). Washington, DC: Mental Health Law Project for the National Association of Protection and Advocacy System.

Redlick, R. W., Witkin, M. D., Atay, J. E., Fell, A. S., & Manderscheid, R. W. (1987, October). *Separate psychiatric services in non-federal general hospitals, United States 1983*. Statistical Note No. 186. Rockville, MD: National Institute of Mental Health.

Redlick, R. M., Witkins, J., Atay, J. E., Fell, A. S., & Manderscheid, R. W. (eds.). (1988, January). *Distribution of psychiatric beds, United States and each state, 1984*. Statistical Note No. 186. Rockville, MD: National Institute of Mental Health.

Robins, L. N., Helzer, J. E., Croughan, J., & Ratcliff, K. S. (1981). National Institute of Mental Health Diagnostic Interview Schedule. *Archives of General Psychiatry*, *38*, 381–389.

Rothman, D. J. (1971). The discovery of the asylum: Social order and disorder in the New Republic. Boston: Little, Brown.

Schurman, R. A., & Mitchell, J. B. (1985, June 30). *Non-psychiatrist physician's mental health care for the aged, Final Report* (Grant No. 1-Rol-MH, 39605–01).

Science. (1986, May). Giving mental illness its research due, Editorial, Vol. 232, p. 1084.

Select Committee on Aging, House of Representatives, U.S. Congress. (1988, March). *Mental health and aging: The need for an expended federal response*.

Sharfstein, S. S., Eist, H., Sack, L., Kaiser, H., & Shadoan, R. A. (1984). The impact of third party cutbacks on the private practice of psychiatry: Three surveys. *Hospital and Community Psychiatry*, *33*, 478–481.

Stotsky, B. A., & Stotsky, E. S. (1983). Nursing homes improving a flawed community facility. *Hospital and Community Psychiatry*, *34*, 238–242.

Strauss, John S. (1979). Social and cultural influences on psychopathology. *Annual Review of Psychology*, *30*, 397–415.

Taff, G. E., & Scallet, L. J. (1986). *Intergovernmental health policy on mental health alcoholism, and drug abuse report on issues of policy: The mentally ill in nursing homes*. Washington, DC: George Washington University.

Talbott, J. A. (1983). Twentieth century developments in American community psychiatry. *Psychiatric Quarterly*, *54*, 207–219.

Talbott, J. A., & Glick, I. D. (1986). The inpatient care of the chronically mentally ill. *Schizophrenia Bulletin*, *12*(1), 111–121.

Taube, Carl A., & Barrett, S. A. (1985). *Mental health United States* (DHHS Publication No. ADM 85–1378). Rockville, MD: National Institute of Mental Health, Division of Biometry and Epidemiology.

Test, Mary A., & Berlin, S. B. (1981). Issues of special concern to chronically mentally ill women. *Professional Psychology, 12*(7), 825–847.

Titmuss, R. M. (1974). *Social policy.* New York: Pantheon.

United States Department of Health and Human Services. (1981). *Toward a national plan for the chronically mentally ill.* DHHS Pub. No. (ADM) 81–1077. Washington, DC: U.S. Government Printing Office.

United States General Accounting Office. (1977). *The elderly remain in need of mental health services* (GAO/HRD–82–112). Washington, DC: General Accounting Office.

Weclew, R. V. (1975). The nature, prevalence and level of awareness of "curanderismo" and some of its implications for community mental health. *Community Mental Health Journal, 11*, 145–154.

Wilensky, H. L. (1961). Orderly careers and social participation: The impact of work history on social integration in the middle mass. *American Sociological Review, 26*, 521–539.

Wolf, C. P. (1976, Spring). The state of the art: Social impact assessment. *Sociological Practice I*, pp. 56–69.

Zimmerman, S. L. (1976, November). The family and its relevance for social policy. *Social Casework, 57*, 547–554.

Zimmerman, S. L. (1979, August). Policy, social policy, family policy: Concepts, concerns, and analytic tools. *Journal of Marriage and Family*, pp. 487–492.

PART VII

Positive Mental Health

14

PSYCHOSOCIAL COMPETENCE: TOWARD A THEORY OF UNDERSTANDING POSITIVE MENTAL HEALTH AMONG BLACK AMERICANS

Louis P. Anderson, Chuck L. Eaddy, and Ernestine A. Williams

The purpose of this chapter is to discuss certain topics relating to internal, familial, and sociocultural factors that are relevant to positive health among black Americans. In particular, as a central theme, it examines the concept of psychosocial competence. Our belief is that the traditional conceptualizations of mental health of black Americans have been so narrowly defined that their usefulness has been limited in explaining how black Americans develop and successfully cope, adapt, and problem solve under relatively stressful life circumstances. In order to understand effective functioning, it is necessary to have an appreciation of the concept of competence. Thus, in the first section we examine the principles inherent in the concept of competence. Following this discussion are reviewed, in order, specific internal, familial, and sociocultural factors which contribute to positive mental health.

COMPETENCE

The seminal work of Robert White (1974) has contributed greatly to our redefining mental health concepts so as to place more emphasis on understanding what it means to interact competently with one's environment. Among others, White (1974) and J. F. Rychlak (1981) provided us with guiding principles to define competence operationally. Broadly, competence refers to effective functioning within one's environment.

At first glance, the concept of competence may appear to be very basic and simplistic. However, in order to appreciate competency-based models of human functioning, one must take into account three very important principles: a transactional perspective, adaptation, and cultural relativity.

A *transactional* model of human behavior is implicit in most definitions of competence. Within this perspective, the individual is seen as being in a constant struggle to manage his or her environment. It is a basic premise of this view that man has a genetic predisposition to survive (Sameroff & Chandler, 1975). The primary mechanism of survival, *adaptation*, is so highly developed in man that it is thought to be one of the major marks of the species. It is the adaptability of black Americans that has allowed us to survive the brutality of slavery and centuries of racism. It was the slaves' adjustment in diet, emotions, family life, and religious practices that guaranteed the survival of the race (Jenkins, 1982).

The competency model attempts to bridge sociocultural and psychological dimensions of human existence. Humans are seen as being involved in a reciprocal system with the environment. Both the individual and the environment make demands on the other. Moreover, both are malleable. This plasticity (Sameroff & Chandler, 1975) is present at birth and allows humans to make adjustments to the environment. To understand this point, let us look at transactions at two levels: the interpersonal and societal.

It is believed that a major characteristic of a resilient infant is his or her ability to influence the caretaker's responsiveness and feelings of efficacy. For example, an infant whose crying abates when fed, exacts change on the environment and vice versa. Competence implies that a child should be judged to be competent when he or she is instrumental in obtaining appropriate care from the environment (Goldberg, 1977). Thus, as far back as infancy, we *actively* structure and organize our interpersonal environment in order to get our needs met.

Although the social environment is malleable, its degree of malleability is highly dependent on racial, cultural, and social class factors. For example, because of their power base and degree of influence, the energy that white middle-class Americans expend to impact changes on the psychosocial environment is markedly less than that of the average black individual. For some members of black society, effective interactions involve compromising and adapting to the realities set forth by the environment. Thus, the individual may have to yield and accept conditions that are beyond his or her power to change. Effective functioning does not mean necessarily a blissful existence. In some cases, frustration, anxiety, vigilance, and depression may be seen as normal or the only methods of coping with a stressful environment.

We now have evidence to support the view that black Americans are under high degrees of stress. Research is suggesting that the basal stress levels and physiological reactivity for black men (Myers, 1982), women (Anderson, in press), and children (Myers & King, 1985) are significantly higher than for whites. In general, these findings suggest that, for the average black individual, major coping resources are required in order to meet effectively the challenges of the environment. However, despite stressful environmental conditions, the vast majority of black Americans function effectively. Competence for the infant as well as for adults in specific life situations is determined, in part, by how well the problematic situation can be altered so that it is no longer problematic. Therefore, in order to assess competence, the assessor has to take into consideration (1) the process by which an individual solves the problematic life situation, (2) the options available to the individual in dealing with the situation, (3) the context (e.g., the plasticity of the environment), and (4) the consequences of the response.

The point of view just presented is in sharp contrast to former approaches of explaining human behavior. Traditionally, a static linear perspective, which leads to deficit interpretations of human behavior, has been used. The elaboration of competency-based models moves to the foreground of our interest a greater appreciation for adaptation and a willingness to understand behavior within a sociocultural context. Wider economic, political, and social factors, in which the individual is embedded, are understood as being contributors to how individuals respond to life situations.

Traditionally, conceptualizations of human behavior have tended to emphasize behavioral outcomes based on white middle-class norms as opposed to appreciating the process that the individual undertakes in order to come to grips with the environment. For example, although assertiveness is valued in this society, such behavior may pose certain problems for black males. Mindful of this fact, some black males purposefully choose to limit their own assertive tendencies. Such behavioral strategies are typical for black Americans.

To judge the functioning of an individual in isolation without taking into consideration the particular assumptions, values, and adaptive strategies of that cultural group would lead to faulty conclusions. Although humans are subject to certain universal determinants, it is our culture which provides the medium within which we satisfy our needs.

In the remainder of this chapter, we discuss those factors that appear to contribute to resiliency and positive mental health among black Americans. We have divided our discussion into two broad areas, the first of which is an examination of the internal factors that contribute to effective functioning.

INTERNAL FACTORS

Perception

Arguably a factor that is fundamental to effective interaction with the environment is perception. Perception is seen and understood as the selective and organizing gateway to the mind (Rice, 1987). Perception is the way in which information from the senses is given meaning and a value judgment. Perceptual biases are the result of inherited emotional sets as well as the experience of the individual. These sets lead to people seeing things in either a negative or a positive way. Evidence points to the existence of perceptual biases related to inherited emotional sets so that, even at birth, the positive and negative evaluations of events are not random (Janis, 1982). One basic judgment made during perceiving is whether or not an event is pleasant and valuable to the person. If an event is perceived to be negative, it may be organized in the memory as stressful (Janis, 1982). Such organization depends on the threat value of the event and the coping resources available to the individual.

We know that individuals actively process information from the environment. As we attend and perceive, certain aspects of how the world operates become a part of our memory. With regard to black Americans, G. G. Jackson (1982) suggests that black Americans are right hemispherically dominated. This represents a cognitive style that is (1) intuitive and abstractive, (2) nonverbal and creative, and (3) less accessible to scientific investigation. He hypothesizes that brain hemispheric dominance is related to the physical environment and that the adaptation to it is made in the form of child-rearing practices, social structure, and values. This cognitive style helps to form the schema (Piaget, 1955) of the black American, and it represents what he or she has learned about the world and how to relate to it. Certain schemata are universal, for example, gravity. There is a universal understanding of the law of gravity and how one relates to it. However, other schemata show a high degree of individual and cultural uniqueness. For example, the schema for interpersonal relationships may vary from one individual to another. For some, the world is a safe environment in which they are encouraged to be open and honest and to feel appreciated. On the other hand, the environment is realistically seen as hostile and threatening. It appears as though the healthy black American processes new information about the environment and allows an elaboration of his or her schema. This process is similar to the Piagetian notion of accommodation. Accommodation prevents fixation of rigid ways of seeing things. In other words, healthy black Americans process information about the environments that they are in and become aware of the nuances. Thus, they have a wider range of coping resources and experiences. They incorporate new information into their already existing view of the world and act accordingly. When one interacts with one's environment, one adds meaning to the way in which the world is seen. This creates a greater adaptability to different situations in different environments.

Individuals in insular social networks have been found to have higher degrees of stress (Williams & Anderson, in press) and to engage in destructive interactions with their children (Wahler, 1980). The general feeling is that a homogeneous and closed network of friends can be problematic because it limits one's social contact and connectiveness with the environment. For black Americans, it is very important to be flexible and open to the elaboration of ways in which to see the world. The schemata for situations contain the rules for what behavior is most effective in what situation. Therefore, by elaborating the ways in which they view the world, black Americans are allowing themselves the freedom to interact more effectively and efficiently.

The Relationship between Language and Effective Problem Solving

Cognitive development is seen as the mode of operations developed out of human experience that forms the individual's capacity to take in information, evaluate it, hypothesize various solutions, and select one as being the most effective (Rice, 1987). Thus those black Americans who examine situations and take into consideration many relationships, possibilities, and implications before making a decision, may be better problem solvers because they have more options and alternatives.

Research supporting the relationship between problem solving and effective functioning has focused on the importance of language. D. G. Norton (1969) conducted a study that compared black and white children in regard to their family interaction and cognitive development. One of the most important overall findings was the correlation between good language models in the child's home and the ability to choose the most effective solution from a number of alternatives. In this study, "good" language referred to any language with rules which allows evaluating solutions and coming to the most appropriate conclusion. The association between good language and cognitive development is that effective use of language permits manipulation of ideas on an abstract rather than concrete level (Powell, 1973). Contrary to common opinion, careful analysis revealed that black children from lower socioeconomic families have "good" effective language models. These children communicated with their families and peers with the linguistic rules specific to their environments.

Coping

It is important to note that black Americans, in general, are competent and self-developing. However, there are many sources of stress, discomfort, anxiety, and frustration that the average black American experiences. These stressors have led to the development of a variety of coping strategies. Coping is broadly defined as mental and behavioral acts that are taken to control, manage, and reduce internal strategies and external demands (Rice, 1987). These internal and external demands are commonly referred to as stress. Generally, stress leads to symptoms of emotional and physical distress. Consequently, how a person copes with stressful encounters determines his or her emotional response. Coping is the one variable that influences our adaptational outcomes and consequently our mental health. By definition, coping is not static. Instead, it should be regarded as a process. According to R. S. Lazarus and S. Folkman (1984), there are three main features of the coping process: (1) what a person thinks and what he or she actually does, (2) the context, and (3) the outcome relative to change in behaviors, thoughts, and emotions.

Coping efforts can be divided conveniently into active, albeit direct, and indirect strategies. Active coping involves efforts made to change the source of stress or discomfort. Among others, such strategies include changing one's behavior, evaluating environmental hassles and barriers, and learning new skills. Active coping involves an active problem-solving activity which ultimately changes the source of the stress or discomfort. As implied in the discussion of competency, coping effectiveness would vary by situation and the range of possible response options available. Often, only powerful people are able to change directly the source of the stress. For example, a graduate student who experiences conflicts with her advisor may attempt to change her behavior or learn new skills (active coping) in an effort to reduce the conflict (e.g., hopefully the advisor's behavior would be modified based on the student's behavioral changes.) If these attempts fail, another strategy, and the most direct, would be to eliminate the source of stress completely by being instrumental in getting the advisor fired. Unfortunately, most people like the graduate student find themselves not being in a position to change actively the source of their stress. They are thus faced with using indirect strategies.

Indirect strategies are those modes of coping (e.g., denial, selective attention, avoidance, forgetting, rationalization) that lead to either changing the way the stressor is perceived or reducing the distress associated with the stressor without changing the objective situation (Lazarus & DeLongis, 1983). Examples of indirect strategies are statements such as: "It was not as bad as I thought"; "The end will come soon and I won't have to deal with him anymore"; "I don't have to get upset over his remarks, he is just a jerk." The goal of indirect coping methods is to reduce the stress by regulating the emotions and changing the threat value of the encounter. In a study, recently completed by Louis Anderson, the use of a coping desensitization procedure, which allowed children suffering from sickle-cell anemia to assess stressful situations and then to relax and rehearse controlling catastrophizing thoughts, was successful in producing reductions of from 28 to 46 percent in anxiety and pain.

By and large, indirect coping strategies may present problems in the long run because they do not completely resolve the problematic situation. Moreover, the extreme of indirect strategies involve the distortion of reality and self-medication. If a person fails to resolve the difficulty or rigidly copes in the same manner, the stressful encounter will reoccur (Haan, 1977). Well-functioning blacks use a variety of coping strategies. We now turn our attention to one of the most misunderstood strategies used by blacks—vigilance.

Vigilance

I. L. Janis (1982) defines vigilance as a system of interrelated processes in which an individual (1) uses rational problem-solving skills, (2) engages in systematic information searches, (3) considers alternative hypotheses about sources of difficulty, and (4) evaluates alternative solutions in a relatively flexible and unbiased fashion. In addition, vigilance represents what V. Harding (1975) terms the "aware cognitive flexibility style." This style is one in which the black individual becomes aware of the ambiguities and complexities of race in American society. This person is aware of alternatives and recognizes that there is a struggle. However, the individual stands poised and ready to evaluate the environment in order to have effective interactions. This style embodies relative open-mindedness, nondefensiveness, and a willingness and readiness to generate creative coping strategies for dealing with the experience of being a black American. An important aspect of these coping strategies is that they can be seen on a continuum, having both negative and positive possibilities for personal and social adjustment. If carried to an extreme, vigilance can result in panic and frantic searches for solutions. Other internal resources that are used for coping include the personal traits that buffer the person. The most important of these appear to be self-esteem and perception of control.

Self-Esteem

Self-esteem is frequently used to refer to a sense of positive self-regard, of having a good feeling about oneself. When people feel good about themselves, they are less likely to respond to or interpret an event as emotionally draining or stressful (Rice, 1987). In addition, these persons can cope better in the event of a stressful situation (Horowitz, 1979; Janis, 1982). Historically, there has been disagreement about the adequacy of self-esteem in blacks. Some researchers have proposed that black Americans developed low self-esteem and negative self-concepts (Clark & Clark, 1947). The argument was that, by internalizing negative evaluations from white Americans, blacks developed a relatively unfavorable self-appraisal. Another hypothesis was that black Americans showed preference for whites and had more positive attitudes toward whites than toward their own race and, consequently, manifested feelings of self-hatred (Asher & Allen, 1969). Much of the past writing on the self-esteem of blacks is based on unrepresentative small samples, poorly controlled studies, anecdotal evidence that is less than adequate to explain the complex behavior of black Americans.

There has been considerable criticism of these views on black self-esteem. More contemporary psychologists and recent research show that the majority of blacks do not have lower self-esteem or more negative self-concepts than do white Americans (Demo & Parker, 1986; Harris & Stokes, 1978; Bewley, 1977).

Previous researchers who investigated self-esteem among blacks have advanced two major hypotheses: the social comparisons and reflected appraisals theories (Rosenberg, 1979). The social comparison principle states that those from underprivileged groups (i.e., blacks) compare themselves to those with more advantaged backgrounds (i.e., whites) and internalize the unfavorable result in the form of negative self-evaluation. The principle of reflected appraisal states that self-definition and evaluation are determined by comparison with others. Here, however, the frame of reference or comparison group for blacks is other blacks. The fact that blacks use other blacks for reflected appraisal has been researched and well documented (Pettigrew, 1971; Rosenberg, 1979).

It would appear, then, that those individuals who use reflected appraisals for self-evaluation would develop and maintain relatively positive self-esteem. Thus, those blacks who compare themselves with their own reference group avoid experiencing the potentially damaging consequences of failing to compare favorably to relatively objective standards of social success as defined by the dominant group (Pettigrew, 1971). In support of this view, J. W. Hoelter (1982) found that blacks maximize appraisals. In other words, it was those significant others who were perceived to have the most positive evaluations that had a greater impact on the self-esteem among blacks as compared to whites. It appears, then, that black Americans can develop and maintain a good sense of self. Instead of comparing themselves to the larger society, they can selectively reflect on appraisals from those blacks in their immediate environments. It is likely that more favorable appraisals are made in their common environment.

Locus of Control

A number of researchers have linked self-esteem with the perception of control that we feel that we have over our lives. Locus of control refers to the expectancy that personal actions will be effective to control or master the environment (Rotter, 1966). In this model, people vary on a continuum between external and internal locus of control. Individuals with an internal locus of control orientation attribute responsibility to themselves and, thus, will act to shape or influence the environment. Conversely, an external locus of control is said to be characteristic of one who is likely to view others as responsible for the events or outcomes in life. Black Americans have been found to be more externally oriented (Battle & Rotter, 1963; Valecha & Ostrum, 1974). Although positive attributes have been assigned to the internally motivated person and negative attributes to the externally motivated person, an external orientation may be a positive attribute in black Americans. P. Gurin, J. Veroff, and S. Feld (1960) suggest that an external orientation may represent a reality of life and lead to more positive self-concepts among blacks. For example, B. L. Hendrix (1980) found a positive correlation between self-esteem and external locus of control for black high school seniors. It appears that an external orientation for blacks represents the recognition of the existence of factors such as discrimination and racism that can influence their success or failure. However, this recognition of external factors by blacks has not been consistently found to relate to actual performance. So, although there is a realization that potent external environmental factors exist, this realization does not necessarily adversely affect an individual's effective interaction with the environment.

FAMILIAL AND SOCIOCULTURAL FACTORS

Numerous factors beyond the internal functioning of the individual impact upon the mental health of black people. A detailed review of related literature is too broad for the scope of this section; instead, general themes and some relatively recent research related to familial and social issues are presented.

Black Family Literature

Interest in black family life has been far from lacking. R. Staples and A. Mirande (1980) pointed out that, in the decade of the 1970s alone, over 50 books and 500 articles concerning black family functioning were published. However, this discussion has been, to say the very least, less than unified in terms of the conclusions reached. A. Mathis (1978) grouped the study of black families under two competing perspectives: The "American-dilemma" perspective views black families in terms of the dominant American culture as normative, and his second perspective views black families in relation to African culture as normative. Authors taking the former perspective have tended to view the black family as dysfunctional (e.g., Frazier, 1939; Moynihan, 1965; Rainwater, 1965); the latter have tended to point out the strengths of the black family as a coping mechanism for existing in a racist society (e.g., Young, 1974; Hill, 1972; Nobles, 1974b).

A number of recent authors have pointed out the weakness in much of the previous work done concerning black families owing to theoretical biases, poor methodology, weak research design, and inadequate samples (e.g., Milburn, 1986). In light of these problems, some have attempted to conduct empirically based research designed to offer insights into the actual internal and external dynamics of black families (Gary, Beatty, Berry, & Price, 1983; Gary, Brown, Milburn, Thomas, & Lockley, 1984; Lewis & Looney, 1983).

The Nuclear Black Family

W. R. Allen and S. Stukes (1982) pointed out that the life-styles of black families are heterogeneous, that they vary in kinship structure, geographic location, values, and social class status. Therefore, rather than discuss all black families as a homogeneous group, it would be more accurate to delineate those factors in well-functioning black families that appear to be related to their good mental health.

J. M. Lewis and J. G. Looney (1983) discuss the relative health or pathology in black families in terms of their level of competence. They describe family competence as "the quality of possessing attributes necessary or helpful to achieve or accomplish given tasks" (Lewis & Looney, 1983, p. 4). They asked what a psychologically healthy family, as a small social system, does for its members. To answer this question, they began with T. Parsons and R. Bales' (1955) concept of two cardinal tasks: (1) to raise children who become autonomous and (2) to provide sufficient emotional support for stabilizing the parents' personalities and continuing their emotional maturation. To these, they added that a family should function in such a way as to establish for its members a balance between attachment and separateness, consistent with the greatest likelihood for the adaptive success of individual members at different phases of life.

In discussing the interactional structure of the family system for those black families who fall on the healthy or "optimal" end of the continuum of family competence, Lewis and Looney (1983) pointed out a number of positive factors including:

1. In the marriage relationship, power is shared and intimacy is achieved.
2. The parents are authoritative but not authoritarian.
3. Intimacy is not primarily concerned with physical sexuality, but rather with an environment of communication wherein deeply held feelings, thoughts, and vulnerabilities can be shared.
4. There is no evidence of competing coalitions existing within the family.
5. Both high levels of individual autonomy and closeness coexist.
6. Problems are solved primarily through negotiating.
7. A wide range of feelings are expressed, and empathic responses to affective messages are not uncommon.
8. Members appreciate and feel fortunate to be part of the family.
9. Other factors include high levels of initiative, a tolerance for mistakes, and viewing human motivation as complex and sexuality as a natural expression.
10. Values ranked highly include personal and family security, health, and happiness.

L. E. Gary et al. (1983) found that, as a result of their research, stable (competent) families are those who encounter problems and resolve them successfully using internal resources. They noted that these families genuinely cared for each other, were enthusiastic about life, were able to maintain orderliness in their lives, and were highly religious.

Both of these studies found that income was positively correlated with the level of health functioning; however, they were unsure whether healthy functioning individuals are more likely to attain greater financial success, or whether financial stability leads to improved mental health.

Extended Family/Friend Network

Empirical studies whose focus goes beyond the nuclear family are also scarce in the literature concerning healthy psychological functioning among blacks (Milburn, 1986; Gary et al., 1984).

In his discussion of "family networking," W. Nobles (1976) describes how the extended family plays a crucial role in providing such services as child care, financial aid, and counseling.

In related work, H. P. McAdoo (1978, 1982), in studies of middle-class suburban and urban black families, found that those experiencing the most stress are more likely to have increased interactions with relatives. Support from these extended family networks was primarily of two types: instrumental (i.e., money, clothing, and child care) and emotional (i.e., counseling and advice).

After studying 285 subjects from a southern black community, W. W. Dressler (1985) also found that the provision of instrumental and emotional support was related to healthy mental functioning. However, findings indicated that the effects of this support were not the same for both sexes. Males within the family system who perceived themselves as receiving familial assistance had significantly fewer depressive symptoms than women. Although for women over the age of 35 the positive effects were evident, they were not as powerful; women under 35 were not found to benefit greatly from familial support in this study. Dressler attributed this apparent lack of positive effects from the support offered to younger women to their being, at the same time, expected to adhere more closely to family advice. In short, the cultural expectation that younger women be more obedient than their autonomous male counterparts led to stress that offset the positive effects of support.

The importance of friends in providing support was pointed out by C. Stack (1974). She discussed how this system involved the trading and exchange of such things as clothing, food, and money as well as emotional support (see also Martineau, 1977; Warren, 1975).

N. G. Milburn stated that "social networks of family and friends that are less dense with multidimensional relationships provide support that may not be readily available in networks composed of all-family or all-friend members" (1986, p. 36). Related to this, Gary et al. (1984) found, as a result of research, that the type of problem experienced is more indicative of where people go for help than are any demographic or sociocultural factors. For instance, for financial assistance, respondents were more likely to turn to informal sources (i.e., family and friends); with health-related problems, they were more likely to seek formal resources (i.e., medical professionals).

The Black Church and Social Institutions

The significance of the church in the lives of black people has often been cited (Frazier, 1964; Hill, 1972; Franklin, 1974; Staples, 1976; McQueen, 1977; Allen & Stukes, 1982). Perhaps one of the most complete descriptions was provided by Robert Staples (1976).

Staples discussed a number of characteristics of the black church related to its functioning as a source of support. The church serves in the maintenance of family solidarity as a conserver of moral values having to do with right or wrong behavior. It confers status to those who very often derive little respect or recognition from the dominant culture. He pointed out that the black church is a source for leadership development and historically has been the center for black protest. In addition, it allows for the release of tension through spiritual expressiveness, and it is a source for social interactions and entertainment.

A number of recent authors have asserted that the black church does not play as crucial a role in providing for emotional support as do family and friends (Gary et al., 1984; Milburn, Thomas, & Gary, 1984; Linbald-Goldberg & Dukes, 1985). It is understandable that, as other avenues have opened up for black people in terms of social, political, and career opportunities, the all-inclusive function of the church might become somewhat less significant. However, as the needs of the community have changed, so has the role of the church. A very recent example of this is the action that black churches have taken in responding to the need for child care by establishing in-house day-care centers.

Beyond the church, other "parallel institutions" (Allen & Stukes, 1982) or those developed by blacks when denied entrance into those belonging to wider society, have also played a role in black healthy mental adjustment. Organizations such as fraternal societies, sororities, social clubs, and civic associations serve as providers of support (Jones, 1977; McPherson, 1971; Tomeh, 1973; Davis, 1980). Lewis and Looney (1983) found, in their study of working-class black families, that more competent families showed higher levels of social interaction.

Group Identification

The positive contribution to healthy mental functioning related to identifying oneself as a member of the black race has been discussed by a number of authors (McCarthy & Yancy, 1971; Nobles, 1974b; Gurin & Epps, 1975; Staples, 1976; Allen & Stukes, 1982). They describe such factors as blacks having a greater sense of purpose as a people united, often against a hostile dominant culture, in adding to feeling of security and an increased ability to accept and handle frustration.

Gary (1978) argues that "opinion leaders" or role models in the black community, such as politicians and entertainers, play important roles in promoting this group loyalty and racial identity. For example, it is reasonable to assume that most black people felt a special sense of pride when they watched Doug Williams lead his team to the Super Bowl championship and when they saw Rev. Jesse Jackson bring a hostage freedom from the Middle East when others had failed.

CONCLUSIONS

This brief discussion of literature concerning those internal, familial, and sociocultural factors related to the mental well-being of black people lends itself to drawing certain conclusions.

To begin with, although black families are varied and are affected by the often changing demands of the dominant culture, they continue to be the primary source of support in healthy mental functioning. However, the degree to which they are of benefit is dependent upon the way in which they respond to the needs for dignity, love, nurturing, and respect by the individual members. Families must be able to provide members with enough autonomy so as to feel empowered but, at the same time, provide the kind of structure and control that lead to feelings of stability and security.

As one expands out from the family to include friends, church, other social institutions, and group identification, it becomes apparent that the ability to relate in ever increasing circles of social interaction is another very important aspect in mental well-being. Here again, health is related to competence or the ability to adapt to one's environment in such a way as to provide for present needs. The broader one's worldview and openness to varied experience are, the more adept one is likely to be in meeting these needs for healthy functioning.

The area of internal factors that influence positive mental health among black Americans is very important and warrants further investigation. Evidence to date suggests that an open and flexible evaluation of perceptions and the ability to hypothesize and search effectively for alternative solutions give black Americans more options and alternatives. Blacks have been found to be more responsive to environmental feedback about performance. It is suggested that this external orientation leads to positive mental health because an awareness of the ambiguities and complexities of being a black American is present. The individual is therefore prepared to generate creative strategies for interacting with the larger society in an efficient and effective manner.

REFERENCES

Allen, W. R., & Stukes, S. (1982). Black family lifestyles and the mental health of black Americans. In F. U. Munoz & R. Endo (Eds.), *Perspectives on minority group mental health*. Washington, DC: University Press of America.

Anderson, L. P. (in press). Perceived stress and social support among single and married black mothers. In J. Stewart & L. Burton (Eds.), *The black family: contemporary issues*. University Park, PA: Penn State University Press.

Asher, S., & Allen, V. (1969). Racial preference and social comparison processes. *Journal of Social Psychology, 25,* 157–165.

Azibo, D. A. (1983, January). Some psychological concomitants and consequences of the black personality: Mental health implications. *Journal of Non-white Concerns, 1983,* 59–66.

Bachman, J. G., & O'Malley, P. M. (1984). Black-white differences in self-esteem: Are they affected by response styles? *American Journal of Sociology, 90*(3), 624–639.

Baldwin, J. A. (1984). African self-consciousness and the mental health of African Americans. *Journal of Black Studies, 15*(2), 177–194.

Baldwin, J. A. (1986). African (black) psychology: Issues and synthesis. *Journal of Black Studies, 16*(3), 235–249.

Battle, E. S., & Rotter, J. B. (1963). Children's feelings of personal control as related to social class and ethnic group. *Journal of Personality, 31,* 482–490.

Bewley, K. (1977). Self-esteem: The alternative to genetic inferiority. *Negro Education Review, 28,* 95–99.

Clark, M. L. (1985). Social stereotypes and self-concept in black and white college students. *The Journal of Social Psychology, 125*(6), 753–760.

Clark, K. B., & Clark, M. P. (1947). Racial identification and preference in Negro children. In T. M. Newcomb & E. L. Hartley (Eds.), *Readings in social psychology* (pp. 169–178). New York: Holt.

Davis, L. G. (1980). The politics of black self-help in the United States: A historical overview. In L. Yearwood (Ed.), *Black organizations: Issues on survival techniques*. Washington, DC: University Press of America.

Demo, D. H., & Parker, K. D. (1986). Academic achievement and self-esteem among black and white college students. *The Journal of Social Psychology, 127*(4), 345–355.

Dressler, W. W. (1985). Extended family relationships, social support and mental health in a southern black community. *Journal of Health and Social Behavior, 26*, 39–48.

Drury, D. W. (1980). Black self-esteem and desegregated schools. *Sociology of Education, 53*, 88–103.

Foster, M., & Perry, L. R. (1982, January). Self-valuation among blacks. *Social Work, 1982*, 60–66.

Franklin, J. H. (1974). *From slavery to freedom: A history of the Negro American*. New York: Alfred A. Knopf.

Frazier, E. F. (1939). *The Negro family in the United States*. Chicago: University of Chicago Press.

Frazier, E. F. (1964). *The Negro church in America*. New York: MacMillan Company.

Gary, L. E. (1978). *Support systems in black communities: Implications for mental health services for children and youth*. Occasional paper, vol. 3(4). Washington, DC: Institute for Urban Affairs and Research, Howard University.

Gary, L. E., Beatty, L. A., Berry, G. L., & Price, M. D. (1983). *Stable black families: Final report*. Washington, DC: Institute for Urban Affairs and Research, Howard University.

Gary, L. E., Brown, D. R., Milburn, N. G., Thomas, V. G., & Lockley, D. S. (1984). *Pathways: A study of black informal support network*. Washington, DC: Institute for Urban Affairs and Research, Howard University.

Goldberg, S. (1977). Social competence in infancy: A model of parent-infant interaction. *Merrill-Palmer Quarterly, 23*, 164–177.

Gurin, P., & Epps, E. (1975). *Black consciousness: Identity and achievement*. New York: Wiley.

Gurin, P., Veroff, J., & Feld, S. (1960). *Americans view their mental health*. New York: Basic Books.

Haan, N. (1977). *Coping and defending: Process of self-environment organization*. New York: Academic Press.

Harding, V. (1975). The black wedge in America: Struggle, crisis and hope. *Black Scholar, 7*(4), 28–46.

Harris, A., & Stokes, R. (1978). Race, self-evaluation and the Protestant ethic. *Social Problems, 26*, 71–85.

Hendrix, B. L. (1980). The effects of locus of control on the self-esteem of black and white youth. *The Journal of Social Psychology, 112*, 301–302.

Hill, R. (1972). *The strengths of black families*. New York: Emerson-Hall.

Hines, P., & Berg-Cross, L. (1981). Racial differences in global self-esteem. *The Journal of Social Psychology, 113*, 271–281.

Hoelter, J. W. (1982). Race differences in selective credulity and self-esteem. *The Sociological Quarterly, 23*, 527–537.

Horowitz, M. J. (1979). Psychological response to serious life events. In V. Hamilton & D. M. Warburton (Eds.), *Human stress and cognition: An information processing approach* (pp. 235–263). New York: Wiley.

Jackson, G. G. (1982). Black psychology: An avenue to the study of Afro Americans. *Journal of Black Studies, 12*(3), 241–260.

Janis, I. L. (1982). *Stress, attitudes, and decisions.* New York: Praeger.

Jenkins, A. H. (1982). *The psychological of the Afro American: A Humanistic Approach.* New York: Pergamon Press.

Jones, F. C. (1977). *The changing mood in America: Eroding commitment?* Washington, DC: Howard University Press.

Kardiner, A., & Ovesey, L. (1951). *The mark of oppression.* New York: Norton.

Lazarus, R. S., & DeLongis, A. (1983). Psychological stress and coping in aging. *American Psychologist, 38*, 245–254.

Lazarus, R. S., & Folkman, S. (1984). *Stress appraisal and coping.* New York: Springer.

Lewis, J. M., & Looney, J. G. (1983). *The long struggle: Well functioning working-class Black families.* New York: Brunner/Mazel.

Linblad-Goldberg, M., & Dukes, J. L. (1985). Social support in black, low-income, single-parent families: Normative and dysfunctional patterns. *American Journal of Orthopsychiatry, 55*(1), 43–58.

Martineau, W. (1977). Informal social ties among urban black Americans: Some new data and a review of one problem. *Journal of Black Studies, 8*, 83–105.

Mathis, A. (1978, November). Contrasting approaches to the study of black families. *Journal of Marriage and the Family, 1978*, 667–676.

McAdoo, H. (1978, November). Factors related to stability in upwardly mobile black families. *Journal of Marriage and the Family, 1978*, 761–776.

McAdoo, H. P. (1982). Levels of stress and family support in black families. In H. I. McCubbin, A. E. Cauble, & J. M. Patterson (Eds.), *Family stress and coping.* Springfield, IL: Thomas.

McCarthy, J., & Yancey, W. (1971). Uncle Tom and Mr. Charlie: Metaphysical pathos in the study of racism and personal disorganization. *American Journal of Sociology, 76*, 648–672.

McPherson, J. (1971). *Blacks in America: Bibliographical essays.* New York: Doubleday.

McQueen, A. J. (1977). The adaptations of urban black families: Trends, problems and issues. *Public Service Studies.* Oberlin, Ohio: Oberlin College.

Myers, H. (1982). Stress, ethnicity and social class. In E. E. Jones & S. J. Korchin (Eds.), *Minority mental health* (pp. 118–145). New York: Praeger.

Myers, H. F., & King, L. M. (1985). Mental health issues in the development of the black American child. In G. J. Powell (Ed.), *The psychosocial development of minority group children* (pp. 275–306). New York: Brunner/Mazel.

Milburn, N. G. (1986). *Social Support: A critical review of the literature as it applies to black Americans.* Occasional paper, No. 26, Washington, DC: Institute for Urban Affairs and Research, Howard University.

Milburn, N. G., Thomas, V. G., & Gary, L. E. (1984, March). *The nature of social network relationships among black Americans.* Paper presented at the 30th anniversary meeting of the Southeastern Psychological Association, New Orleans, LA.

Moynihan, D. P. (1965). *The Negro family: A case for national action.* U.S. Department of Labor, Office of Policy, Planning and Research. Washington, DC: U.S. Government Printing Office.

Nobles, W. (1974a). African root and American fruit: The black family. *Journal of Social and Behavioral Science, 20,* 52–64.

Nobles, W. W. (1974b). Africanity: Its role in black families. *The Black Scholar, 5,* 10–17.

Nobles, W. (1976). Extended self: Rethinking the so-called Negro self-concept. *Journal of Black Psychology, 4,* 21–27.

Norton, D. G. (1969). *Environment and cognitive development: A comparative study of socioeconomic status and race.* Unpublished doctoral dissertation, Graduate School of Social Work and Social Research, Bryn Mawr College, Bryn Mawr, PA.

Parham, T. A., & Helms, J. E. (1985). Attitudes of racial identity and self-esteem of black students: An exploratory investigation. *Journal of College Student Personnel, 1985,* 143–147.

Parsons, T., & Bales, R. (1955). *Family, socialization and interaction process.* Glencoe, IL: Free Press.

Pettigrew, T. (1971). *Racially separate or together?* New York: McGraw-Hill.

Piaget, J. (1955). *The language and thought of the child.* New York: A Meridian.

Powell, G. J. (1973). Self-concept in white and black children. In C. B. Willie, B. M. Kramer, and B. S. Brown (Eds.), *Racism and mental health.* Pittsburgh: University of Pittsburgh Press.

Rainwater, L. (1965). *Family design.* Chicago: Aldine.

Rice, P. L. (1987). *Stress and health: Principles and practice for coping and wellness.* Belmont, CA: Brooks/Cole.

Rosenberg, M. (1979). *Conceiving the self.* New York: Basic Books.

Rotter, J. B. (1966). Generalized expectancies for internal vs. external control of reinforcement. *Psychological Monograph, 80,* 1–28.

Rychlak, J. F. (1981). *Introduction to personality and psychotherapy: A theory-construction approach* (2d ed.). Boston: Houghton Mifflin.

Sameroff, A., & Chandler, M. J. (1975). Reproductive risk and the continuum of caretaking casualty. In F. D. Horowitz (Ed.), *Review of child development research* (Vol. IV, pp. 87–244). Chicago: University of Chicago Press.

Smith, W. D. (1980). The black self-concept: Some historical and theoretical reflections. *Journal of Black Studies, 10*(3), 355–366.

Sparks, C. T. (1980). Demographic and personal characteristics of professional black Americans: Toward a black mental health model. *Journal of Non-white Concerns, 1980,* 71–76.

Stack, C. (1974). *All our kin: Strategies for survival in a black community.* New York: Harper and Row.

Staples, Robert (Ed.). (1976). *Introduction to black sociology.* New York: McGraw-Hill.

Staples, R., & Mirande, A. (1980, November). Racial and cultural variations among American families: A decennial review of the literature on minority families. *Journal of Marriage and the Family, 1980,* 141–152.

Tomeh, A. (1973). Formal voluntary organization participation: Correlates and interrelationships. *Sociological Inquiry, 43*(3,4), 89–118.

Valecha, G., & Ostrum, T. (1974). An abbreviated measure of I-E locus of control. *Journal of Personality Assessment, 38*, 369–376.

Wahler, R. G. (1980). The insular mother: Her problems in parent-child treatment. *Journal of Applied Behavioral Analysis, 13*, 207–219.

Warren, D. (1975). *Black Neighborhoods: An assessment of community power.* Ann Arbor, MI: University of Michigan.

White, R. (1974). Strategies of adaptation: An attempt at systematic description. In G. V. Coelho, D. A. Hamburg, & J. E. Adams (Eds.), *Coping and adaptation* (pp. 47–67). New York: Basic Books.

Williams, D., & Anderson, L. P. (in press). The acculturated stress scale. In R. L. Jones (Ed.), *Handbook of tests and measurements for black populations.* Berkeley, CA: Price and Cobb.

Young, V. H. (1974). A black American socialization pattern. *American Ethnologist, 1*, 405–413.

15

COPING WITH COLOR: THE ANATOMY OF POSITIVE MENTAL HEALTH

Barbara J. Shade

In the issue of *Daedalus* which focused on color and race, Edward Shils wrote:

> In itself, color is meaningless. It is not like religion which is belief and entails either voluntary or hereditary membership. . . . It is not like kinship, which is a tangible structure in which the individual has lived, which has formed him, and to which he is attached. . . . It is not like intellectual culture which is belief and an attitude toward the world. It is not even like nationality which is a super-imposition of beliefs about a community of culture.
> Color is just color. It is a physical, a spectroscopic fact. . . . It is like height or weight— the mind is not involved. Yet it attracts the mind. (1967, p. 279)

For Afro-Americans, color is not "just color." When the term is ascribed to skin description, it becomes a mark of oppression, a pathological obsession, and an index of evaluation which invades every aspect of an individual's life. As one author explains it, "skin color, in and of itself, has no real meaning; yet somehow our society has given it meaning and attached to it the symbolic representation of exploitation, inferiority, injury, and insult" (Brown, 1969, p. 17). Because skin color has taken on such an orientation, it also has become a major psychological influence on Afro-American development and an important dimension to which an individual must adapt.

Adaptation, according to some theorists, is viewed as the behavior which results from an individual's ability to selectively meet the demands of an environment (Allerhand, Weber, & Haug, 1970). These scholars theorize that this response process may produce psychological stress for the adaptor if the environmental demands exceed or are incompatible with the coping strategies and resources available to the individual (Coyne & Lazarus, 1980).

Over the years, Afro-Americans anxiety levels have been strained to their limits to cope with an environment that uses skin color to keep individuals and the group, as a whole, from attaining their basic psychological needs, i.e., safety, security, belonging, and self-actualization (Shannon, 1973). Many scholars suggest that the stress of the situation has precipitated the development of an inferiorization pattern of adaptation which includes the display of such sociopsychological traits as subservience, ingratiating mockery, withdrawal, apathy, hostility, self-hate, and aggression (Adam, 1978). Studies such as A. Kardner and L. Ovesey's *The mark of oppression* (1951) and W. H. Grier and P. M. Cobb's *Black rage* (1968) cite evidence of these traits and interpret the behavior as demonstrations of mental illness.

Like other areas in the study of Afro-Americans, the study of adaptation techniques has concentrated on the negative and less productive modes of adjustment rather than on the more positive approaches. While there is little doubt that some individuals become psychologically crippled and use these styles, they are not the major coping techniques used by competent members of the community (Harrell, 1979; Huggins, 1977). Had it been so, the history of the group would have been nothing but stories of stagnation, failure, and possibly extinction. Instead, a careful look at Afro-Americans as a group depicts a portrait of growth and development (Smith & Welch, 1986). Unlike other threatened groups, Afro-American numbers have increased rather than decreased in size. This population has grown from around 750,000 in 1790 to over 28 million in 1987 without the addition of a large number of immigrants as occurred in the growth of the other population groups in America (Pinkney, 1975).

Although not as representative as should be expected, Afro-Americans have secured an increased proportion of the economic goods of this country. In 1986, the Afro-American community generated a gross national product of $206 billion and paid $84 billion in taxes. This economic indicator was produced by 83 percent of the families having an income holding only 9.8 percent of the jobs (Brimmer, 1987). Although this number is not as large as it should be, it does suggest that Afro-Americans participate in the economic life of this country with substantial results in spite of the color barrier and its attendant manifestations.

In the social mobility arena, more Afro-Americans than ever before have entered our colleges and universities. In 1985, over one million Afro-Americans were enrolled in higher education compared to 500,000 in 1950 (U.S. Bureau of the Census, 1987). Afro-Americans also are represented in all occupational levels throughout the social spectrum. This accomplishment has produced a growing middle class with incomes of between $25,000 and $50,000 (Landry, 1987). Based upon these and other statistics, one might conclude that, in spite of the color barrier and the inordinate emotional meaning attached to it, Afro-Americans have managed not only to survive, but also to progress.

Progress is not accomplished by individuals who are mentally ill, but by those who maintain a positive mental outlook in spite of environmental barriers. Examination of autobiographies and studies of individuals who are successful in adapting to color discrimination indicates that four basic tenets to positive mental health assist Afro-Americans to survive: (1) a strong sense of history and social knowledge about the Afro-American community (Stanfield, 1985); (2) a strong sense of self-identity which is generated by a strong inculcation of group culture (White, 1984); (3) the ability to be cognitively flexible and to assess situational and behavioral requirements (Harrell, 1979); and (4) a strong sense of control and the desire to control one's life (Dubey, 1971; Jenkins, 1984). The two latter factors are subsumed under the concept of personality. This chapter examines each of these areas and their relationship to successful adaptation.

FACTOR 1: A STRONG SOCIAL KNOWLEDGE BASE

The social history of a group represents the social memory base about its obstacles and accomplishments. From this history individuals obtain an understanding of how their community solved problems, developed resources, and managed their psychological stress. This knowledge serves as a reference point for individuals who belong to the group and helps them interpret the environment and their roles and expected responses (Stanfield, 1985). This is particularly important to individuals who wish to develop positive mental health because it helps them perceive their problems within a broader context.

To understand Afro-American social history and the adaptational strategies developed, a framework other than the traditional psychoanalytical theory must be used. When this perspective is used, the examination concentrates only on the effect of adaptational stress on the individual and ignores the effect the individual has on the environment (Sharpley, 1969; Comer, 1969). Instead, the social history of Afro-Americans should be examined using the ecological conceptualization. The assumptions of this perspective are that the environment, however it is defined, influences individual and group behavior (Barker, 1968) and that the development of the required cognitive and behavioral patterns by the individual influences the environment thus lessening the tension between individual needs and setting demands (Pettigrew, 1964; Ogbu, 1981).

When using the ecological perspective, one notes that the coping techniques developed within the history of Afro-America depended, in large measure, upon the geographical milieu and the time period in which they occurred. In each setting, color took on a different meaning and, thus, had a different impact on individuals and the community. The adaptation approaches Afro-Americans used to cope with color are, therefore, consistent with the demands of the historical period and the environment in which they functioned (Adam, 1978; Peeks, 1971).

Coping with the Decades of Immigration and Slavery

The settling of America occurred in several different regions. In addition to the South, with which most Afro-Americans and slavery are associated, the New England states, the Middle colonies, and the Upper Great Lakes territory were other sites to which people of African descent came. In all regions, Africans were both slaves and nonslaves, but their methods of coping within each area depended upon their numerical strength, the need for the labor supply, and the degree to which Africans were considered labor competitors by the other residents.

In the New England and Middle colonies, the coping techniques used varied as much as the background from which the African immigrants emerged. Citizens of these colonies were slaves, previous slaves, indentured servants, and freeborn persons (Quarles, 1964; Blassingame, 1979). They lived in common areas in cities and had the opportunity to exchange ideas, experiences, and information about the new society to which they had been brought, the color barriers that had been established, and the habits and mannerisms of Euro-American people. This exchange and neighborhood isolation served to solidify the group and its reactions.

One of the major responses to slavery and the caste system became the use of protest. For example, Richard Allen led a protest exit from the Methodist Church, and Frederick Douglass took every opportunity to write and speak on the injustice of slavery and color discrimination. While many individuals were not as famous as these gentlemen, throughout the historical records notes were made of many Americans of African descent who made use of newspaper editorials, race conventions, and church gatherings to protest conditions and encourage advancement (Quarles, 1964; Peeks, 1971). The engagement in these acts by individuals whom the legal and political system attempted to regulate was more significant than the results they obtained as it indicated that the massive acts of oppression had not killed their spirit or their desire for freedom. Many groups in similar circumstances become highly compliant (Frankl, 1966; Stampp, 1956).

P. Freire (1970) suggests that oppressed groups are more likely to engage in a struggle for freedom if they perceive that there is an exist from the oppressive situation. The Afro-American citizens of this early period apparently believed in the possibility of bringing a change in the slave system and chose to protest consistently the prescribed roles and expectations assigned to people of color. More important, these protests indicated a strong sense of community, self-respect, hope, and most of all a sense of control, which, as I. Katz (1969) indicates, is the most important attitude Afro-Americans can possess if they are to remain mentally healthy in an oppressive situation.

Another coping mechanism which assisted the Afro-American community and, ultimately, the Afro-American individual was the development of fraternal orders such as the Odd Fellows and the Prince Hall Masonic Order, as well as mutual aid and literary societies. On the surface, these organizations could be interpreted as evidence that Afro-Americans were merely attempting to replicate Euro-American society and to "identify with the oppressor." This was not the case. The organizations developed a distinct Afro-American character which evolved to differentiate these institutions from their Euro-American counterparts. Rather than serving only as social organizations and meeting places, the societies took on a function similar to the former tribal group. They became tools of socialization and social support networks, and they provided educational, political, and social information which helped the group understand the mores and mannerisms of Euro-Americans and the rules and laws of the country.

The cultural-loss advocates will, of course, point out that these organizations could have been organized around a pure African orientation instead of duplicating Euro-American structures. However, as historians have noted, the Afro-Americans deliberately made a commitment to remain in America and become a part of this society. Having made this commitment to citizenship, they assumed that, if the individuals and the group demonstrated similarities in actions, behaviors, and groups, acceptance as a full-fledged member of society would be forthcoming. So, although African in orientation and function, the organized groups were European in name and structure as a way of symbolizing the Afro-American's effort to belong to American society.

Africans in the South were not as fortunate as those in the North. In addition to the adjustment to the shock of capture, the inhumane mode of transportation, and the loss of freedom, these individuals had to adapt their psyche to being a commodity rather than a human being. As J. Blassingame (1979) and R. S. Bryce-LaPorte (1969) point out, this dehumanization process took place within the framework of a *total institution*. A total institution is a concept which epitomizes the idea that slavery and its accompanying codes and practices usurped the traditional socializing agencies such as the tribes and families, as well as the individual's right to think and make decisions. Through some standardized techniques, the Afro-American's sense of control over self and environment was erased, and individual personality traits of assertiveness and independence were replaced with subservience and compliance. The evolving coping pattern was labeled the "Sambo" personality (Elkins, 1959; Blassingame, 1979). However, the will to survive generated other reactions as well.

Based upon accounts of slave behaviors, whether serving in the domestics, crafts, or field-hand roles, traits such as vengefulness, aggressiveness, and assertiveness were just as common as conformance and dependence (Huggins, 1977; Peeks, 1971). There are indications that the more active and assertive personality may have been more common than usually portrayed since Afro-Americans also developed an adaptive technique known as "mask wearing." This behavior represents the individual's ability to veil a manipulative, hostile personality in a look of laziness, subservience, and loyalty.

Other coping devices centered around the concept of escape. If unable to escape physically, Afro-Americans had the ability to escape psychologically and did so through the use of folklore, songs, dance, and dreams of freedom. In D. C. McClelland's (1961) examination of an achieving society, it was suggested that the groups best able to tolerate difficult times and progress in the future are those that have a highly developed repertoire of fantasy because fantasy permits them to dream of the future and the removal of the obstacles hampering their success. Through stories such as *Brer Rabbit*, spirituals, and other artistic forms, Americans of African descent protected their psychological well-being and their sense of hope by visualizing the destruction of slavery (Levine, 1977). More important, the hope and dreams of freedom which Afro-Americans maintained seemed to inspire the escapes, revolts, self-purchases, and other freedom-producing acts undertaken by many individuals of color caught in the stranglehold of slavery.

Within the unchartered territories of the Northwest and West, Afro-Americans, both slave and free, from the North and the South developed Afro-American communities in various cities and towns bringing with them the coping devices found effective in their previous residences. In addition, a new technique was added—that of joining the community of other racial groups. There are numerous instances in which Afro-Americans sought and became integrated members of the Indian tribes who resided in their geographical area (Porter, 1970). This type of amalgamation was more likely to be engaged in by Afro-American males. Females chose amalgamation through marriage.

An example which illustrates this technique is the story of Mary Ann LeBuche DuChouquette Gagnier-Menard, a native of Prairie du Chien, Wisconsin. In his recollection of the early days of this settlement, James Lockwood, one of the more prominent frontier citizens wrote:

Among the other inhabitants of notoriety at that time was a Mrs. Menard, of mixed African and white blood. She came from one of the French villages below and then married to Charles Menard, a Canadian of French extraction. She had been married twice previously, first to a man by the name DuChouquette, by whom she had two sons, one of whom was in the employ of Mr. Astor in that unfortunate expedition of his trip in 1810 from the sea across the continent to the mouth of the Columbia River, now Oregon Territory. Her next husband was named Gagnier, by whom she had three sons and three daughters. After Gagnier's death, she married Charles Menard, by whom she had three sons and two daughters. (Lockwood, 1903, p. 100).

Mrs. LeBuche Menard's children also married Euro-Americans and later became a part of some other important incidents in Wisconsin history. While her obvious African features and heritage made her presence noteworthy, neither she nor her children seemed to suffer from the color barrier. Mrs. Menard, and others like her, continued to intermarry with Europeans, which resulted in complete color and cultural assimilation in succeeding generations; the badge of color was no longer an issue.

Coping in the Decades of Disappointment and Separation

When slavery was terminated, Afro-Americans throughout the country relished optimism and ambition. To pursue their hopes and aspirations, they sought landownership, work, and political, economic, and social participation. During this period, Afro-Americans also attempted to add to their repertoire of coping techniques through the acquisition of formal education. Throughout the community, individuals were told that participation in schooling would result in social acceptance in the larger society. The result was that school attendance became a primary focus during this period and people of African descent made every effort to become educationally literate, regardless of their age. Of this phenomenon, Booker T. Washington wrote:

This experience of a whole race beginning to go to school for the first time presents one of the most interesting studies that has ever occurred in connection with the development of any race. Few people who were not right in the midst of the scenes can form any exact idea of the intense desire which the people of my race showed for an education. It was a whole race trying to go to school. Few were too young, and none too old to make the attempt to learn. (Washington, 1959, pp. 20–21)

This attempt to obtain acceptance through education was met, however, with an even more devastating hardening in the color lines being drawn in every part of the country and in every facet of life. In the midst of the discrimination, segregation, and physical attacks, Afro-Americans found ways to maintain their ego integrity. One avenue that was used was the strengthening of their churches. In addition to its socialization role within the Afro-American community developed in an earlier area, the church became a community center to which Afro-Americans could retire for relaxation and recreation and receive help if they were sick or poor. It also enlarged its function as a training agent by providing opportunities to learn self-reliance, self-government, money management, and business management. The church's most important function, however, was to be a system of support, one in which individuals could gain personal recognition and status, things denied them in the larger society.

In areas of the country in which life proved unbearable due to exploitation, terrorism, and stringent controls, many citizens of African descent chose the avenue of flight to cope with color and migrated to the West or the North in search of a better life and acceptance. Sometimes this resulted in the establishment of their own towns and villages such as Boley, Oklahoma, and Nicodemus, Kansas, and it came very close to resulting in the establishment of an Afro-American state in Oklahoma (Peeks, 1971). Others went to the urban areas where they could become invisible among the already large number of Afro-American residents.

One of the most positive adaptation techniques of this period was the growth and enhancement of the Afro-American intellectual tradition through the creative outpouring of literature, art, and music by some of the greatest minds of the population. The sharing of these works provided not only an avenue of articulation of the discontent through an emotional release, but also the foundation of an esprit de corps through the development of a common body of literature (Levine, 1977).

Coping in the Decades of Necromachy

The period between the Harlem Renaissance and the Civil Rights era (1930s through the early 1950s) appear to have been the most difficult in the history of the Afro-American population. Not only was the color barrier further strengthened, but the assault on the black psyche grew in monumental proportions. It was during this period that the behavioral scientists imported and transformed the use of intelligence tests into widely accepted measures of intellectual and social inferiority. For Afro-Americans, individual differences on the test were equated with black skin color and a genetic base. W. E. Cross (1978) noted that it was during this period that "necromachy" set in. Necromachy is the seeking of approval and the need to be accepted as something other than what one is (Thomas, 1971). The driving force behind this need requires Afro-Americans to seek approval from whites in all activities and to use white expectations as a yardstick for determining what is good, desirable, and necessary, such as skin color, quality of hair, and mannerisms (Thomas & Thomas, 1971). Using the visual and communication media, the color *black* became synonymous with inferiority, shame, doubt, and evil.

Preoccupation with the color variation within the Afro-American community was evidenced in the scholarship published during this period as found in such series of psychological studies by Allison Davis (1943) and Kenneth and Mamie Clark (1939). This work set forth a thesis that color had a devastating impact on Afro-American self-esteem, self-image, motivation, and other stages of psychological development.

The constant bombarding of the community with the idea that "black" was unacceptable was apparently internalized finally by the Afro-American community itself. In their gaining understanding of color differentiation in the early stages of their development, it was found that children, in this time period, expressed the need to have light skin. Similar findings were evident in adult populations. For example, G. Bovell (1943) found that skin color variation made a difference in male-female relationships and in marriage selection; preference was given to women of light skin.

The coping strategy which evolved out of this focus on skin variation was that of "passing." The concept of passing represents the intentional transition into Euro-American society by Afro-American persons who have very light skin color. The individual deliberately leads others to believe that he or she is Euro-American rather than Afro-American (Conyers & Kennedy, 1963). Whether this is considered a positive or a negative strategy depends upon the underlying reasons Afro-Americans chose to engage in the practice. For some, it became merely a way to achieve various social, recreational, and economic advantages which were otherwise denied them because of color. In this instance, the technique might be perceived as merely an assertive technique for conquering an obstacle. On the other hand, some individuals chose to engage in this practice based upon denial of their heritage and the need to deny their backgrounds. This approach created stress and anxiety for the individual and demolished his or her self-esteem.

By the end of the era, apparently, there was a realization that no skin shade associated for African descent was immune to the difficulties associated with blackness so perceptions of what skin color was desirable changed within the Afro-American community. When C. Parrish (1946) examined how the young adults in the Afro-American community perceived the concept of color, he found that, although many of the accepted stereotypic traits generally attributed to the very light or very dark held true, both ends of the continuum received negative responses. Instead, a more moderate approach was taken, and individuals expressed preference for medium-brown skin. This change in attitude about the color complex precipitated the search for unity, self-concept, and equality. The turbulent decades of the Civil Rights movement was the result.

Coping in the Decades of Protest and Collectivism

While the Harlem Renaissance period provided the intellectual foundation, the Civil Rights period of the 1950s and 1960s provided the basis of solidification of an extremely diverse group into an identifiable force with a collective spirit. Examination of the individuals in that period found that, even if individuals did not participate in actual protest, there was a tremendous understanding of the issues and a support of the work in some way. From all indications, members of the community concluded that whether light or dark skinned, all individuals with African heritage were confronted with a myriad of social obstacles. This realization set the stage for unification and coalescing of Afro-Americans as a group through the identification of a common set of values, beliefs, and behaviors; and it became the basis for the second important factor.

FACTOR 2: SENSE OF SELF-IDENTITY

Although many members of the community during the protest years maintained the scars of the previous period and remained convinced of the need to conform to Euro-American standards, other members of the community engaged in activities directed toward the liberation of the black psyche and the establishment of a strong self-identity. Again, artists, poets, novelists, playwrights, lecturers, and scholars came to the forefront as they had in the 1920s to express the inner feelings of an entire group of people. For the first time, the community and its individual members recognized the uniqueness of their culture, their worldview, and their behavioral style. In the midst of the introspection and examination of Afro-American strengths, it became very clear that Afro-Americans had developed a distinct culture with norms and values which articulated the Afro-American perception of the world. More important, this culture provided the opportunity for Afro-American individuals to establish a bold self-identify which resulted in increased self-esteem.

Culture is a rather abstract term, but it is generally defined as the rules used by members of a particular group to govern the interaction with each other and with their environment. J. W. Berry (1976) defines culture as a way of life or a learned pattern of behavior which is unique to a group of people. E. Hall (1959) identifies it as the sum total of a group's behavior patterns, attitudes, and materialism which governs their way of life and represents that communication system.

Although the totality of the Afro-American cultural pattern has yet to be clearly identified, some aspects that have been elucidated are indications of the types of rules used by Afro-Americans in their interpreting of and reacting to the environment. Such things as rituals, color, dress, and music preferences become major devices for individuals who need to reaffirm their identity. Examples of these preferences include some common customs observed in their funerals, organizations, and churches within the Afro-American communities across the country. Outsiders would immediately notice differences in the type of funeral service procedures, the expectations of the behavior of the family, and, in particular, the importance of bringing food and having a large banquet after the funeral services. In church, the importance of having an old-fashioned songfest prior to the opening of the regular service and the ritual of walking around the church to place the offering rather than merely passing the plate by designated ushers are other examples. All of these become important identifiable rituals which are noted and accepted by Afro-Americans regardless of class or status. When encountering these preferences in various environments, Afro-Americans gain a sense of belonging and rootedness. It reaffirms their identity.

Artists who have examined aesthetic preferences note that there are apparently also unique cultural and symbolic representations evident in Afro-American art forms, dress, musical renditions, and literary efforts. These preferences include specific preferences for color intensity, style of dress, and environmental adornment (Logan, 1981; Schwartz, 1963; Myrdal, 1944). J. L. White (1984) and W. W. Nobles (1980) indicate that there is a group-specific perspective of time, work, rhythm, and spirituality which is a part of Afro-American culture. A. W. Boykin (1979) found that Afro-Americans differed from other groups in their preference for and toleration of a high noise level and the need for vividness and multiplicity of stimuli which they referred to as behavioral verve. This preference becomes most evident in the notable propensity for improvisation and spontaneity which seems evident in body movements and musical renditions within the community.

Over the years, Afro-Americans also have developed a cultural-specific view of values. R. Walker (1976) suggests that an important value in Afro-American culture is group unity, solidarity, and mutual aid. This value is particularly evident in the kinship system as noted by C. Stack (1974); in the need to focus and depend heavily on extended families and mutual support networks (Aschenbrenner, 1973); and in the participation of the group in the various social groups, community movements, and church culture.

Perhaps the most important psychological aspect of Afro-American culture to be noted is the existence of a high affective orientation and the preference for experiencing the environment from an emotional perspective (Pasteur & Toldson, 1982). Jacquelyn Brown (1976) calls this a cultural value system based upon person-to-person relationships. A. B. Pasteur and I. L. Toldson (1982) suggest that the degree to which individuals can become expressive and affective indicates the degree to which they have feelings relative to points of view. As T. S. Kochman points out,

Blacks' capacity to deal with intense emotional outputs is relatively greater than that of whites because blacks have greater experience of being confronted with them. Reciprocally, this capacity also gives blacks acting in response to their own feelings greater freedom to express them intensely, knowing that others have developed the capacity to receive them without becoming overwhelmed (Kochman, 1981, p. 117)

Y. Cohen (1974) suggests that this value system also provides group norms and guidelines for perceiving, explaining, and judging the world or weltanschauung. This worldview or weltanschauung of Afro-Americans seems to focus on adapting to the demands and challenges presented by people and social situations and serves as the basis for the following guidelines Afro-Americans use to decide on successful coping strategies:

1. Pay attention to the people and social interactions with which you are involved.
2. Pay attention to the entirety and gestalt of the situation and the idea rather than small details.
3. Cooperate, provide mutual aid, band together in a cohesive group rather than compete against each other.
4. Pay attention to the affective rather than the cognitive dimensions of the environment.
5. Nonverbal behavior tells more than verbal communication. Individuals from the community use these guidelines to determine the cues, ideas, information to which they will give their attention, how the information, ideas, events, or concepts should be interpreted, and what responses or decisions will be most appropriate for the situation.

These guidelines serve as mediating tools for the individual, and, as they become a highly socialized part of the individual repertoire for gathering, organizing, and interpreting information, they become a part of the individual personality.

FACTOR 3: THE ADAPTIVE PERSONALITY—SOCIAL INTELLIGENCE

Although it is ludicrous to suggest that 26 million people have the same approach and the same thoughts and choose the same response patterns, Hall (1966) has pointed out that culture does have an influence on the behavior and cognitive orientation of individuals. As one examines the Afro-American community, it appears that Berry (1980) is correct in his assumptions that cultures or communities with common guidelines and environments apparently develop a culturally specific personality which assists them in their adaptation and coping with various challenges faced in living. As Gordon Allport (1955) points out, personality represents a culturally induced configuration of the perceptual, cognitive, emotional, and motivational systems which determines an individual's responses to the environment.

The most healthy personality for Afro-Americans in a color-obsessed society appears to be one in which such characteristics as autonomy, independence, persistence, determination, and amicability are dominant (Clark, 1983). White (1984) also suggests that these are the individuals who are resourceful, inventive, imaginative, and enterprising. J. P. Harrell (1979) refers to this trait as having a cognitively flexible worldview. As such, the individual is able to assess accurately a situation, determine the need for change, and develop and use new, different, and creative strategies for overcoming obstacles.

One of the contributing factors to cognitive flexibility is the development of a socially attuned cognitive style. Cognitive style represents the executive system of the intellect which helps individuals monitor, evaluate, coordinate, and control their thoughts and actions as they move throughout the environment (Guilford, 1980). For Afro-Americans, the most successful style is one which focuses on the social domain and facilitates their understanding of social nuances, interpersonal interactions and relationships, and the people with whom they come in contact. H. Gardner (1984) in his identification of a myriad of intelligences refers to this skill in social cognition as interpersonal intelligence. This intellectual domain is best demonstrated in an individual's ability to perceive and recognize people and emotions, in his or her use and recognition of nonverbal communication patterns, and in his or her focus on the emotional, aesthetic, and affective attributes of people and situations.

Having a highly developed social intelligence is particularly helpful for Afro-Americans in their survival because they are able to determine insincerity, danger or threats, sensitivity, and acceptance, and, in general, they are then able to arrange for a more comfortable and less stress-producing environment. There is, of course, a possibility of misinterpretation and oversensitivity which could result in maladaptive rather than positive adaption.

An accompanying trait for mentally healthy Afro-Americans is the ability not to be easily immobilized by the oppressive and discriminatory experiences they encounter and to have a strong belief in their ability to control their own life chances (Dubey, 1971; Jenkins, 1984). Individuals with this temperament engage in active structuring of the world with the particular goal of effectivity and competence. Such individuals have a high degree of personal efficacy, seek to use every opportunity available to them to expand their knowledge and experience, and have a greater expectation to succeed. Rather than blame themselves for adversity and difficulty, they recognize the existence of a race barrier without letting it overwhelm them with despair and hopelessness. Using A. H. Maslow's (1962) terminology, these individuals would be self-actualized; A. H. Jenkins (1984) refers to them as assertive.

FACTOR 4: THE ADAPTIVE PERSONALITY—SOCIAL RESPONSIBILITY

An accompanying motivational system which seems important for Afro-American adaptation is one in which the individual sees the result of his or her actions as having an impact upon the race as a whole rather than just on his or her individual efforts. In the examination of individuals with this orientation, Jenkins (1984) noted that the studies concluded that individuals who perceived their achievements as having implications for Afro-American community development had a more positive approach to life and better mental balance than those who concentrated only on their own individualistic achievements.

The basic foundation of the Afro-American adaptational personality is self-confidence and the use of a high level of social intelligence to gain a clear understanding and a definition of the self, regardless of the definition given by the media or other significant others in the environment. Such a personality provides a bridge for the schizophrenic existence which W.E.B. DuBois described in his famous quotation as a

... peculiar sensation ... this double consciousness, this sense of always looking at one's self through the eyes of others ... two souls; two thoughts; two unreconciled strings ... being torn asunder. (1970, p. 3)

Only can the achieving personality provide the type of ego-integration individuals need to function in a color-conscious society.

SUMMARY

If you are an American with African heritage, one important message is consistently transmitted through numerous societal channels; i.e., "You are different"; "You are not wanted"; "You do not belong." The need to be accepted and become a part of the dominant group is a basic human developmental need which transverses sex, color, age, geographical region, or time. It is this desire to meet this basic need which is the core of all efforts in civil rights legislation, civil rights movements, and the general efforts of the Afro-American community. Unfortunately, the psychological message still is transmitted in subtle and not so subtle ways that having a black skin color creates a barrier to belonging that may never be overcome. How Afro-Americans cope with this state of affairs in a positive way, which facilitates their survival and mental health, seems to depend upon four major factors:

1. The possession of a historical sense of the Afro-American community and the adaptational strategies developed over time. Without such a background, individuals could develop a sense of despair, self-pity, and resentment as the messages of rejection become personally internalized.

2. A strong grounding in the cultural ethos and norms of the Afro-American community. This knowledge and perception provides the basis of self-identity and understanding; without his base, individuals will experience alienation, frustration, and isolation. They will have a perception of being an outcast without ties rather than having a sense of acceptance even on a limited basis.

3. The development and use of the culturally specific cognitive style which strengthens and emphasizes social cognition and social intelligence. This provides an important survival tool for it permits a rather keen observation and classification of people and situations within an environment which may or may not be an accepting one. The key for being able to cope and adapt is to be able to function well within any environment in which the individual finds himself or herself. This social intelligence provides the tool to help individuals maneuver the system by being cognitively flexible and highly creative.

4. The last, and most important, factor is the development of a strong, assertive, active concept of self which helps individuals achieve a sense of identity and a strong belief in their ability to control their lives. An accompanying behavioral trait is the ability to demonstrate purposefulness, self-motivation, and productivity. Studies of Afro-American personality throughout history also suggest that when both individual and group-oriented achievement become the focus of the effort of individuals with these traits, a more positive state of mind is achieved, and greater self-actualization is possible.

The epitome of good mental health for Afro-Americans is being competent and effective in a white man's world. This suggests that, if the Afro-American community is going to advance, it will do so through the development of a strong aggregation of individuals with this psychological background as epitomized by the identified characteristics. The major task facing educators, parents, the church, and other socializing agents is to initiate programs which facilitate the development of the successful personality throughout the community. Only with massive numbers of individuals who are self-assured, creative, committed, and socioculturally aware will Afro-Americans continue to progress in spite of the caste of color.

REFERENCES

Research which is the foundation of this chapter was supported in part by a postdoctoral grant from the National Endowment for the Humanities. An earlier version of this chapter was presented at the first annual seminar, Black Graduate Student and Professional Association, University of Kentucky, Lexington, Kentucky.

Adam, Barry D. (1978). Inferiorization and "Self Esteem." *Social Psychology, 41*, 47–53.

Allerhand, M. E., Weber, R. E., & Haug, M. (1970). *Adaptation and adaptability*. New York: Child Welfare League.

Allport, Gordon. (1955). *Becoming*. New Haven, CT: Yale University Press.

Aschenbrenner, J. (1973). Extended families among black Americans. *Journal of Comparative Family Studies, 3*, 257–278.

Barker, R. (1968). *Ecological psychology*. Stanford, CA: Stanford University Press.

Berry, J. W. (1976). *Human ecology and cognitive style: Comparative studies in culture and psychological adaptation*. New York: John Wiley & Sons.

Berry, J. W. (1980). Cultural ecology and individual behavior. In I. Altman, A. Rapoport, & J. F. Wohlwill (Eds.), *Human behavior and environment. Advances in theory and research*, Vol. 4. New York: Plenum Press.

Blassingame, J. (1979). *The slave community: Plantation life in the antibellum south*. New York: Oxford University Press.

Bovell, G. (1943). Psychological considerations of color conflicts among Negroes. *Psychoanalytic Review, 30*, 447–450.

Boykin, A. W. (1979). Psychological/behavioral verve: Some theoretical explorations and empirical manifestations. In A. W. Boykin, A. J. Franklin, & J. F. Yates (Eds.), *Research directions of black psychologists*. New York: Russell Sage Foundation.

Brimmer, Andrew F. (1987, April). Economic perspectives: Blacks fall short in taxes and income. *Black Enterprise, 17*, 35–36.

Brown, H. R. (1969). *Die, nigger, die*. New York: Dial Press.

Brown, Jacquelyn. (1976). Parallels between Alderian psychology and the Afro-American value system. *Individual Psychology, 13*, 29–33.

Bryce-LaPorte, R. S. (1969). The American slave plantation and our heritage of communal deprivation. *The American Behavioral Scientist, 12*(4) 2–9.

Clark, K. B., & Clark, M. K. (1939). The development of consciousness of self and the emergence of racial identification in Negro preschool children. *Journal of Social Psychology, 10*, 591–599.

Clark, R. M. (1983). *Family life and school achievement: Why poor black children succeed or fail*. Chicago: University of Chicago Press.

Cohen, Y. (1974). Culture as adaptation. In Y. A. Cohen (Ed.), *Man in adaptation: The cultural present* (2d ed.). Chicago: Aldine Publishing Co.

Comer, J. (1969). Racism: Its roots, form, and function. *American Journal of Psychiatry, 126*, 802–806.

Conyers, J. E., & Kennedy, T. H. (1963). Negro passing: To pass or not to pass. *Phylon, 24*, 215–223.

Coyne, J. C., & Lazarus, R. S. (1980). Cognitive style, stress perception and coping. *Handbook on stress and anxiety: Contemporary knowledge, theory and treatment*. San Francisco, CA: Jossey Bass, Inc.

Cross, W. E. (1978). Models of psychological nigrescence: A literature review. *Journal of Black Psychology, 5*, 13–31.

Davis, A. (1943). Racial status and personality development. *Scientific Monthly, 57*, 354–362.

Dubey, S. (1971). Powerlessness and the adaptive responses of disadvantaged blacks. *Human Organization, 30*, 149–157.

DuBois, W.E.B. (1970). *The souls of black folk*. New York: Washington Square Press.

Elkins, S. M. (1959). *Slavery*. Chicago: University of Chicago Press.

Frankl, V. (1966). *Man's search for meaning.* New York: Washington Square Press.

Freire, P. (1970). *Pedagogy of the oppressed.* New York: Continuum Press.

Gardner, H. (1984). *Frames of mind: Theory of multiple intelligences.* New York: Basic Books.

Grier, W. H., & Cobb, P. M. (1968). *Black rage.* New York: Basic Books.

Guilford, J. P. (1980). Cognitive styles: What are they? *Educational and Psychological Measurement, 40,* 715–735.

Hall, E. (1959). *The silent language.* New York: Doubleday Co.

Hall, E. (1966). *The hidden dimension.* New York: Doubleday Co.

Harrell, J. P. (1979). Analyzing black coping styles: A supplemental diagnostic system. *Journal of Black Psychology, 5,* 99–108.

Huggins, N. I. (1977). *Black odyssey: The Afro-American ordeal in slavery.* New York: Pantheon Books (Random House Publishing).

Jenkins, A. H. (1984). *The psychology of the Afro-American: A humanistic approach.* New York: Pergamon Press.

Kardiner, A., & Ovesey, L. (1951). *The mark of oppression.* New York: Meridian Books.

Katz, I. (1969). A critique of personality approaches to Negro performance, with research suggestions. *Journal of Social Issues, 25,* 13–27.

Kochman, T. S. (1981). *Black & white: Styles in conflict.* Chicago: University of Chicago Press.

Landry, B. O. (1987). *The new black middle class.* Berkeley, CA: The University of California Press.

Levine, L. (1977). *Black culture and black consciousness.* New York: Oxford University Press.

Lockwood, J. (1903). Early times and events in Wisconsin. *Wisconsin Historical Collections, 2,* 98–196.

Logan, O. (1981). *The black aesthetic.* Unpublished paper, University of Wisconsin, Madison.

Maslow, A. H. (1962). *Toward a psychology of being.* Princeton, NJ: D. Van Nostrand.

McClelland, D. C. (1961). *The achieving society.* Princeton, NJ: D. Van Nostrand.

Myrdal, G. (1944). *An American dilemma: The Negro problem and modern democracy.* New York: Harper and Son.

Nobles, W. W. (1980). African philosophy: Foundations for black psychology. In Reginald L. Jones (Ed.), *Black psychology* (pp. 23–35). New York: Harper & Row.

Ogbu, J. U. (1981). The origins of competence. A cross-cultural perspective. *Child Development, 128,* 241–257.

Parrish, C. (1946). Color names and color notions. *Journal of Negro Education, 15,* 13–20.

Pasteur, A. B., & Toldson, I. L. (1982). *Roots of soul: The psychology of black expressiveness.* Garden City, NY: Anchor Press/Doubleday.

Peeks, E. (1971). *The long struggle for black power.* New York: Charles Scribner's Sons.

Pettigrew, T. F. (1964). *Negro American personality: Why isn't more known? Journal of Social Issues, 20,* 4–23.

Pinkney, A. (1975). *Black Americans* (2d ed.). Englewood Cliffs, NJ: Prentice-Hall.

Porter, K. (1970). *The Negro on the American frontier.* New York: Arno Press.

Quarles, B. (1964). *The Negro in the making of America.* New York: Macmillan Publishing Co.

Schwartz, J. (1963). Men's clothing and the Negro. *Phylon, 24,* 51–58.

Shannon, B. E. (1973). The impact of racism on personality development. *Social Casework, 54*(9) 519–524.

Sharpley, R. H. (1969). A psychohistorial perspective of the Negro. *American Journal of Psychiatry, 125,* 91–96.

Shils, E. (1967). Color, the universal intellectual community and the Afro-Asian intellectual. *Daedleus: Color and Race, 96,* 270–286.

Smith, J. P., & Welch, F. R. (1986). *Closing the gap: Forty years of economic progress for blacks.* New York: Rand Corporation.

Stack, C. (1974). *All for kin.* New York: Harper and Row.

Stampp, K. (1956). *The peculiar institution.* New York: Alfred A. Knopf.

Stanfield, John H. (1985). The ethnocentric basis of social science knowledge production. In E. Gordon (Ed.), *Review of research in education* (Vol. 12, pp. 367–415). Washington, DC: American Education Research Association.

Thomas, Charles. (1971). *Boys no more.* Beverly Hills, CA: Glencoe Press.

Thomas, C., & Thomas, S. (1971). Something borrowed, something black. In C. Thomas (Ed.), *Boys no more.* Beverly Hills, CA: Glencoe Press.

U.S. Bureau of the Census. (1987). *Statistical abstracts of the United States.* Washington, DC: U.S. Government Printing Office.

Walker, R. (1976). *Society and soul.* Unpublished doctoral dissertation, Stanford University, Stanford, CA.

Washington, B. T. (1959). *Up from slavery.* New York: Bantam Books (1900).

White, J. L. (1984). *The psychology of blacks.* Englewood Cliffs, NJ: Prentice-Hall, Inc.

16

FACTORS CONTRIBUTING TO POSITIVE MENTAL HEALTH AMONG BLACK AMERICANS

Anderson J. Franklin and James S. Jackson

Passage through the life span is enriched with lessons of survival, adaptation, and adjustment (Levinson et al., 1978). Over time, these lessons form the basis of what we call the wisdom of age. For most people, traversing the life span is accomplished psychologically intact and with a matured perspective. This achievement in our opinion is the result of positive mental health. Positive mental health is a psychological orientation toward life experiences with attributes of inner strength, resiliency, optimism, and a capacity for mastery. Happiness, positive self-esteem, job success, good income, success in social roles, and good interpersonal relations have been found to be important factors in the psychological well-being of blacks (Franklin, 1988; Thomas & Hughes, 1986). However, these are only a few of the attributes of positive mental health (Jahoda, 1958). Knowledge about the dimensions of positive mental health is hampered by the mental health profession's preoccupation with domains of pathology (Williams, 1986). There is no better example of this than the sociohistorical characterizations of black people's behavior in the social and behavioral sciences literature (Billingsley, 1968; Ladner, 1973).

Despite the frequent representations of deviancy in black people's behavior, positive mental health is the foundation of black survival in a racist society (Wilcox, 1973). This chapter focuses on the psychological strengths among Americans of African descent which form this foundation of positive mental health. We offer descriptions, hypotheses, and speculations about the domains of positive mental health in blacks. Our objective is to further nurture a growing tradition among black scholars to examine the strengths within black people (Gary, 1978; Hill, 1971; Jenkins, 1982; Jones, 1972; McAdoo, 1987; Rodgers-

Rose, 1980; White, 1984). There is a deliberate intent to shift thinking away from the pervasive orientation of pathological explanations of behavior, where normality is considered to be the absence of abnormality.

Epidemiological Perspective

The sociohistorical representation of black behavior and mental health continues to portray sociopathy and affective and personality disorders as major community problems. Consistently, epidemiological studies have shown that urban inner-city neighborhoods, in comparison to other geographical locations, yield the largest numbers and more serious forms of psychopathology. Factors of race, locale, and social class, however, are often confounded in etiological interpretations (Faris & Dunham, 1939; Hollingshead & Redlich, 1958; Dohrenwend & Dohrenwend, 1969). The large representation of blacks in these neighborhoods implies a disproportionate prevalence (as well as incidence) of certain psychological disorders. The literature, however, is inconclusive about the extent to which environmental and social conditions contribute to stress and pathology in the black community (Ilfeld, 1978; Warheit, Holzer, & Arey, 1975; Myers, 1982; Neighbors, 1986). Moreover, the other statistic—the proportion of black people who do not exhibit these pathologies—is not discussed, nor are explanations tendered for how they survive oppressive conditions. Results from the Yale Epidemiological Catchment Area study confirm previous estimates that approximately five percent of the general adult population has a definable mental disorder (Weissman and Myers, 1978). The epidemiology of mental disorders among the black population is more problematic to ascertain, in spite of the progress made in methodology (see chapter 3).

In both the black and the general populations, the vast majority of people are not reported as having a definable mental disorder. Herein lies the difficulty in understanding the nature of normality across the life span (Offer & Sabshin, 1984). Normality is not simply the absence of abnormality, anymore than abnormality is the absence of normality. Complex theories and explanatory models have been presented to represent the etiology of abnormality (Taylor & Brown, 1988). It is no less important to provide such models in the quest to comprehend normality, in which positive mental health is an important component. Likewise it is important to explore the parameters of black behaviors that contribute to the successful passage through the life span psychologically intact (Levinson et al., 1978).

Positive Mental Health

Positive mental health is a relative concept, intrinsic to the definition of normality. There is an empirical and sociocultural definition of normality (Dressler, 1985). The empirical approach to a definition is in part based on the statistical inferences one can make from epidemiological studies representing the prevalence and incidence of mental disorders (Klerman, 1985). Epidemiology is the science used in determining the extent and distribution of mental disorders in a given population. Essential to this effort are reliable and valid diagnostic instruments. The National Institute of Mental Health recently undertook an extensive series of community studies to determine more accurately the distribution of mental disorders in the United States population (Eaton, Holzer, Von Korff, et al., 1984). The Diagnostic Interview Schedule (DIS), a standardized, structured lay administered instrument, was used to aid in the identification of symptoms and the classification of disorders. This study is a classic example of the empirical approach to defining mental health.

The Epidemiological Catchment Area (ECA) study was not designed to determine the distribution nor the parameters of normality in the population. There has been little effort to identify or classify the behaviors associated with positive mental health. To develop an empirical model of positive mental health one must in part rely on a strategy of inferring what is the opposite of the symptoms included in the formal classification systems of mental disorders (i.e., those used in the Diagnostic Statistical Manual (DSM) III-R or the DIS).

Another approach to conceptualizing positive mental health is to view it within a cultural context (Offer & Sabshin, 1984). Although groups may live in geographical proximity to each other, the United States is ethnically diverse and pluralistic (Wilson, 1979). Ethnic diversity requires us to view interpretations of mental health within the social conditions from which the rules of behavior evolved (Dressler, 1985). Comprehending positive mental health for blacks entails evaluating the normative experiences of black people, an experience which most include the role of prejudice and discrimination (Wilson, 1979; Akbar, 1979, 1985). Racism still plays a major role in the lives of black people (Williams, 1986). In the place of overt segregation in public accommodations, covert institutionalized racism in the form of discrimination in housing, employment, education, and health thrives. There are few black people who escape some form of racism, and, if queried, most black people can cite examples in which they have had to face and overcome prejudice and discrimination.

The social and behavioral science literature acknowledges the effects of racism on behavior and human development (Katz & Taylor, 1988). Many of the explanations of deviant and antisocial behaviors in blacks attribute their origin to the oppressive life conditions in black communities (Kardiner & Ovesey, 1951; Jackson, 1988; Jenkins, 1982; White, 1984). To conceptualize properly positive mental health for blacks it must therefore be relevant to the life conditions under which adjustment does or does not occur. This does not exclude the assumption of universal principles which govern human reactions to environmental stress (Myers, 1982), for example. Nor do we ignore that parallels may exist in how two individuals from different cultural contexts respond to comparable circumstances. We do, however, emphasize that, since distinctions exist in the quality of life for blacks in contrast to whites (Thomas & Hughes, 1986), a thesis of difference in a positive mental health model for blacks is a legitimate and viable presumption. Furthermore, the quest for understanding the dimensions of normality must incorporate the range, distribution, and variability of its attributes. Identifying the attributes related to normality requires disentangling implicit notions about normality, which only become apparent (i.e., through inference) when deviant behavior occurs.

We take normality for granted. To assume its presence when we observe no abnormality is as superficial a criterion as that good music exists when we hear no bad music. To go beyond this simplistic definition of normality requires examining those domains of behavior that are considered essential for growth and development, focused on how the processes and outcomes within these domains contribute to wholesome and healthy development (i.e., positive mental health).

Jahoda's Model of Positive Mental Health

In evolving a model of positive mental health for blacks, we begin by considering an earlier framework proposed by Marie Jahoda (1958) in the book *Current Conceptions of Positive Mental Health*. This book was part of a series of monographs, published by the Joint Commission on Mental Illness and Health, that was intended to contribute to the development of a national mental health program. Jahoda and her colleagues provided a scholarly delineation of what might constitute the dimensions of positive mental health. It is noteworthy that this effort seemingly went no further than the publication of the monograph, since few of the suggestions and recommendations were translated into public policy or extensive scholarship and research. Nevertheless some noteworthy concepts were presented which may have special significance for mental health among oppressed groups like blacks (Wilcox, 1973).

Jahoda offered two ways of defining mental health: "as a relatively constant and enduring function of personality, leading to predictable differences in behavior and feelings depending on the stresses and strains of the situations in which a person finds himself; or as a momentary function of personality and situation" (1958). In her review Jahoda identified the following six major dimensions that contribute to defining positive mental health and outlined research programs in each area:

1. Attitudes of the individual toward himself (or herself)
2. The degree to which a person realizes his or her potentialities through action
3. Unification of function in the individual's personality
4. The individual's degree of independence of social influences
5. How the individual sees the word around him (or her)
6. The ability to take life as it comes and master it.

Current literature related to the conceptions of positive mental health (Taylor & Brown, 1988) does not deviate markedly from the research areas outlined by

Jahoda in 1958. Our approach to developing a model of positive mental health for blacks draws heavily upon Jahoda's concepts. We examine domains related to self-concept and self-esteem; autonomy and control; environmental mastery; perceptions of reality; growth and development as they contribute to self-actualization and the accomplishment of life goals.

FACTORS IN POSITIVE MENTAL HEALTH OF BLACKS

Self-Concept and Self-Esteem

One of the more important constructs in the area of positive mental health is self-concept or self-esteem. Though some distinguish between them, they are often treated interchangeably (Gecas, 1982). Generally, self-concept has been considered to refer to the cognitive appraisals of self—the more objective personal assessments a person may make of self-dimensions. Self-esteem on the other hand has been referred to as the affective or emotional component of self-assessment, generally referring to the self-attitude and emotional evaluation dimensions of self. A recent study (Greenwald, Bellezza, & Banaji, 1988) indicates that self-evaluations (esteem) play a significant role in self-conceptions, even when these self-conceptions have little esteem-related manifest content.

Regardless of the distinctions that have been made between these constructs, their assessment in blacks has been consistent, and for the sake of clarity, we group such self-constructs under the rubric of self-evaluations. We view self-evaluations as forming the developmental key to positive mental health. It is the building block upon which other aspects of self, e.g., mastery, competence, social identity, and autonomy, are based (Spurlock, 1986).

An examination of the literature indicates significant shifts in views of black self-esteem and, by implication, individual pathology and lack of positive mental health (Spurlock, 1986). The first phase of research and writings ended in the 1930s and, contrary to popular opinion, viewed blacks as having little problems with self-esteem or self-concept. As R. M. Jennings (1975) documents, blacks were viewed as too uncomplicated to suffer from problems of esteem. The second phase of research, covering roughly the period from the 1940s through the 1960s, documented the lack of self-esteem among blacks (Jennings, 1975). In this period blacks were viewed as oppressed and subjugated to the whims of whites—their lack of self-esteem could be readily explained. Low self-esteem relevant to whites was viewed as consistent with low status and the denigrated group position of blacks in American society. This second phase of research on self constructs helped contribute to the notions of self-hatred, pathology, and the culture of poverty that were so prevalent during this period. It is notable that it was during this same period that many researchers began to report comparative findings of no essential differences among blacks and whites in self-esteem levels. Because the pathological model had become so firmly entrenched, this lack of differences was interpreted as "defensive" self-esteem—blacks responded positively to self-esteem items to hide and defend their inferior feelings about themselves (Spur-lock, 1986). Although they are still mentioned today, such explanations have become rare.

The third period of research began in the early 1970s and continues today. This research, which has become much more sophisticated, suggests a number of complicated reasons for the lack of differences in the average self-esteem levels on standardized measures between blacks and whites, and even in the superior performance of blacks over that of whites. J. G. Backman and P. M. O'Malley (1984) claimed that these observed differences are due to differences in response tendencies; blacks are more likely than whites to respond to extreme positions on the scales. This extreme responding accounts for the mean differences in black and white scores.

Others (Rosenberg, 1973, for example) have stressed the nature of the development of self and the nature of significant self-referents. Since interactions within the community and family form the context for self-esteem development, there is no reason to expect differences in self-evaluations between blacks and whites (Peters, 1987). Some researchers (e.g., Hare, 1985) suggest more complicated multi-dimensional models of self-evaluations. B. R. Hare (1985) has found that black and white adolescents base their global self-esteem on different subdimensions: Blacks tend to form their self-esteem on less intellectually based areas than whites, but global levels show no significant differences. Although Hare (1985) was concerned primarily with performance differences, the fact that different areas of life are used to form the basis of self-evaluations in black and white adolescents may have implications for later social and emotional adjustment.

In all of this research, however, few have directly tied self-evaluations to social pathology or mental illness (Spurlock, 1986; Taylor & Brown, 1988). Research findings indicate that black self-evaluations are as high or higher than those of whites. Methodological explanations (Bachman & O'Malley, 1984) and dimensionality (Hare, 1985) models do not detract from this fact. We believe that a healthy sense of self is a requisite for positive mental health. Some have argued that the maltreatment of blacks as a social group has formed a tighter social bonding, leading to an even more supportive socialization environment, contributing to even more positive self-evaluations among blacks than should be expected (Jackson, McCullough, & Gurin, 1987; Peters, 1987). In this view, the threat and negative evaluation of the social group contributes to more effective insulation and support of the developing black child (Peters, 1987).

Autonomy and Control

The concepts of autonomy and control have had a long history of research and scholarship. It is generally believed that perceptions of a sense of control (and actual control) form a key component of motivation and adjustment (Taylor & Brown, 1988). One of the major control constructs in the literature has been

J. B. Rotter's concept of internal-external control (1966). This concept gained popularity because of its relevance to the control of relevant reinforcements in the environment in the face of the powerlessness and alienation that faced oppressed groups like blacks (Gurin, Gurin, Lao, & Beattie, 1969; Jackson, Tucker, & Bowman, 1982). Gurin et al. (1969) made a major contribution to our understanding of the control concept among blacks (and in the general population) in the distinction that they drew between a sense of personal control and a sense of control on the part of the group. Similarly, they drew a distinction on the external side between luck and chance and perceptions of systematic environmental obstacles to group achievement (system blame) on the other. The multidimensionality of the I-E construct is now well established within the social science literature (Jones, 1980). In fact, the construct of control (and mastery) is becoming of increasing importance more broadly as a basic organizing framework in mental health research (Taylor & Brown, 1988; Wheaton, 1980).

In the mental illness literature, a sense of system blame and a belief in the existence of systematic external barriers are often referred to as fatalism (Wheaton, 1980). Fatalism has been linked with negative mental health outcomes, but system blame has been linked with positive outcomes of effective coping, particularly political responsiveness (Gurin et al., 1969). H. W. Neighbors (1987) notes that the mental health implications of these two competing notions has not been truly assessed. It could be that system blame is a necessary component of adjustment for an oppressed group, one that provides a sense of the limitations and defines the parameters in which an individual group member may aspire for achievement. While this may be an effective short-run strategy, it may prove in the long run (for example, over the individual life span) to be detrimental to one's motivation and perceptions of individual autonomy. These notions are speculative and have yet to be tested (Neighbors, 1987). What is clear, however, is that a sense of control and a realistic understanding of systemic barriers to achievement play an important role in perceptions of autonomy and adjustment and thus in any concept of positive mental health.

Environmental Mastery

Related to perceptions of control is the notion of environmental mastery (Taylor & Brown, 1988). Poor economic circumstances and social discrimination directly affect the etiology and nature of mental health status and the functioning of blacks. Conceptualizations of ethnic and racial minority group mental health status that do not take these external factors into consideration are inadequate. Mental health and mental illness of American blacks must be understood within the historical, political, social, and economic context of their lives (Akbar, 1979; Wilson, 1979). While mental health and mental illness are individual conditions, they are heavily influenced by individual and group interaction with the physical and social environment. Knowledge of the environment is crucial in understanding individual coping, informal and formal help seeking, and mental health status.

The environment provides a rich contextual background for understanding mental health and mental illness in black population groups (Jackson, 1988).

Theoretical perspectives and empirical information are nonexistent regarding the exact mechanisms and processes whereby environmental and social context factors affect the mental health status of blacks (Jackson, Neighbors, & Gurin, 1986). The growing poverty of black women and children, for example, provides a major source of environmental risks for the development of mental disorders. Not only does poverty have immediate effects on the nature of current functioning, it also curtails the types of life experiences needed for adequate growth and development of families and children. Thus, poverty, particularly among women and children, may play both important proximal and distal roles in the development of mental disorders among black Americans. A sense of control and actual mastery over one's immediate environment appears to be an essential aspect of positive mental health. Its absence among millions of black Americans may imply the widespread existence of important compensatory mechanisms or the lack of completely fulfilled positive mental health.

Perceptions of Reality

The perception of reality is a fundamental concept in mental health. It clearly helps to differentiate those who are seriously mentally disturbed and are out of touch with their environment, regardless of the basis of socially agreed upon standards. What is more difficult is to characterize one's perception of reality within a model of positive mental health. How does one's perception of events and circumstances in everyday life contribute to emotional stability and psychological health? Part of the dilemma in this task is similar to the overall definition of what is mental health. Behavior is judged by a normative standard established by social consensus. One's behavior is in part the outcome of how one perceives the world.

This fact is crucial in understanding how blacks achieve positive mental health. A classical controversy in this regard is the debate over the levels of paranoia in blacks. In our opinion any model of positive mental health for blacks must include certain features of paranoia as adaptive, although the individual may be classified as deviant by conventional criteria. Living in a racist society requires blacks to evaluate constantly the existence and nature of prejudice and discrimination that they face. It is essential for blacks to have a level of vigilance about racism. The inability to discern when one is a victim of prejudice and discrimination is to risk assuming that rejection is an accurate comment on personal worth, competence, and suitability. Repeated internalization of such assumptions leads to low self-esteem and psychological dysfunctioning. Black men, for example, who are the prime targets of white racism, frequently develop unconscious levels of rage and indignation from being treated as invisible entities (Franklin, 1989). Vigilance about racism, or what W. H. Grier and P. M. Cobbs (1968) call "cultural paranoia," normalizes the perception of reality for blacks, and permits constructive functioning.

Counteracting what A. J. Franklin (1989) calls the "invisibility syndrome" for black men requires not only vigilance but also validation of experiences. Validating one's perception of reality is fundamental to psychological stability. The mechanisms and processes used by blacks in the validation of experiences are central to a positive mental health model. It is an individualized process embedded within a group norm. In other words, the group norm acts as a frame of reference for the individualized experience of reality. Associating with other blacks and having a fundamental black group experience as a frame of reference are essential ingredients in a model of positive mental health for blacks. This assumption is based on the premise that blacks will be responded to racially, irrespective of nonracial societal ideals and values. In a racist society that response is often negative and degrading. Converting such a response into constructive behavior is in part determined by one's orientation to reality. That orientation must be governed by an "ethnic reality" (Wilson, 1979).

Growth, Development, and Self-Actualization

Passage through the life span connotes growth, development, and achievement of goals (Levinson, 1978; Schaie, 1981). An essential manifestation of positive mental health is whether life goals are achieved and individuals are satisfied with these accomplishments. Utilization of one's abilities is a key ingredient in the process. In any model of positive mental health, the identification and effective use of talents and skills are important to self-worth. For blacks, prejudice and discrimination are often obstacles to effective utilization of talents and skills. Compensation for these economic and social circumstances is a common practice, and a model of positive mental health for blacks must include the special compensatory processes which allow individual blacks to acquire competence plus gratification in the use of talents and skills.

Compensatory processes are utilized periodically by everyone, but the circumstances and content of experiences for blacks are uniquely influenced by racism. For example, blacks must be able to match their talents and skills with opportunities provided by a social structure that is limiting because of prejudice and discrimination. If there is a mismatch between talents and opportunity, one has to either rechannel skills toward allied areas or utilize secondary or tertiary skills that do match. Success in finding a match between talents and opportunity is crucial to self-worth (Spurlock, 1986), and this process highlights the dilemma in conventional mental health conceptualizations. The outcome of an individual's process of making the talent-opportunity match is judged by the prevailing norms of social expectations and acceptability. In other words, society structures, places values upon, and decides what are legitimate means and ends to the matching of talents with opportunities.

Athletic talents among blacks, for example, are encouraged by a relatively accessible opportunity structure in sports. There are available opportunities at the community level for nurturing such talents (e.g., playgrounds and schools). Unfortunately, the professional level is often viewed by black youngsters as the only end goal for athletic talents. The fantasies generated by this narrow path of limited opportunity can be counterproductive to how black youngsters construe success. On the other hand, finding accessible opportunity structures for talents in math and science is more problematic for blacks. Blacks very often have to be "super bright" to get attention and open up nontraditional opportunities; unlike the social and physical supports for athletic talents, there is not a comparable support structure to nurture scientific talents.

What should be focused upon in a positive mental health model is how survival in an oppressive society creates its own talent-opportunity structures. For example, drug dealing may be hated by many, but it is a role that allows the individual to express entrepreneurial skills. It offers quick rewards at great personal risk, but success elevates material status, self-esteem, and a sense of mastery. Expectations are formed within an existing context. This can also breed a "make do" attitude, complacency, and acceptance of injustices. The hallmark of colonialism was making subjugation a state of positive mental health (Fanon, 1967). Regardless of value judgments of the acceptable content for gaining a sense of positive mental health, it is crucial to understand that people will search for the opportunities that permit them to use their talents. The level of gratification attained in this quest is basic to mental health. Most black people find a level of gratification from this process that allows them to remain psychologically intact throughout the life span.

Empowering one's life within a racist society means overcoming despair and embracing hope. It means achievement and gratification in spite of barriers. It is a process of self-actualization that is personally defined. For example, a debate about immediate versus delayed gratification is a spurious argument if a meaningful future is thought to be problematic (Jones, 1980). In fact, under some circumstances, immediate gratification is more a sign of positive mental health than delayed gratification. Insisting that one stay in school when the gratification is low and future opportunities upon completion are blocked by discrimination is masochistic and difficult to rationalize in a positive mental health model. We return to one of our fundamental positions: social and cultural factors greatly influence the mechanisms and processes of individual mental health. Achieving a unified outlook on life and developing a personal philosophy provide the outlets for attaining inner peace.

The integration of one's life experiences into a personal philosophy of life that services positive mental health is therefore in part socially and culturally determined. For example, the black church has played a significant role in this process for blacks. Black people exhibiting talents of leadership could find an outlet in church clubs and offices. The spirituality and religion expressed in the church helped to reduce and facilitate the management of rage and indignation arising from racism. The black church insulated its members from the psychological ravages of prejudice and discrimination. It restored hope and combated despair through spiritual healing. Equally important, the black church provided a viable opportunity structure. As a social and economic institution controlled by its membership, a variety of opportunities are created to allow individual members to find freedom of expression in a supportive environment. This is underscored by the fact that most blacks consider their church both spiritually and institutionally an extremely personal experience; a place where one can seek one's own level of individual development protected somewhat from white racism. The principal psychological underpinning in this situation is "ownership." Therefore, in contemplating a model of positive mental health for blacks, understanding the ways in which black-controlled institutions, like the black church, contribute to individual development and emotional stability is essential.

IMPLICATIONS FOR RESEARCH AND CLINICAL APPLICATIONS

The mental health status of American blacks has been amply documented (e.g., Boxley & King, 1985). In fact, a wide variety of research has been conducted over an extensive period (Boxley & King, 1985; Jackson et al., 1986). This work has helped to delineate the nature and extent of the problems and directions for future research. On the other hand, little systematic research has been devoted to understanding the various dimensions of positive mental health and their interrelationships among blacks (Jahoda, 1958).

We are strongly convinced of the need to develop models of positive mental health that are sensitive to, and include estimates of, past and current social and environmental conditions. Over the years the amount of research on the mental health problems of blacks has increased (Miranda & Kitano, 1986), and a greater recognition of the role of social and economic disadvantage has emerged. Models and research knowledge, however, have not kept pace (Neighbors, 1984). In research on any population group, and in any particular scientific research problem, as the research accelerates so do the complexities and intricacies of the problems to be addressed.

We have reached the state of development that demands greater attention to the conceptual and model-building aspects of scientific mental health research on black populations. What is required is greater attention to the conceptual underpinnings and empirical research on the interaction and relationship of environmental conditions to psychological functioning, problem recognition and definition, the decision (or lack thereof) to seek help, the nature and efficacy of treatment, and the quality of treatment follow-up and the surveillance of continuing mental health conditions. This type of research requires greater conceptual clarity and multidisciplinary research approaches, focused on specific and concrete mental health strengths and problems of blacks (Jones, 1985; Bulhan, 1985).

Despite the fact that black Americans are disproportionately exposed to social conditions considered to be antecedents of psychiatric disorder, epidemiologic studies have not conclusively demonstrated that blacks exhibit higher rates of mental illness than whites (Neighbors, 1984; Williams, 1986). These findings make it obvious that to gain an increased understanding of the processes that influence racial factors in mental health status, a research approach which considers the stressors that blacks face and the various coping responses used by blacks, in addition to the rates of psychiatric morbidity, is needed (Myers, 1982; Neighbors, 1987).

Many studies have documented the fact that blacks (particularly the poor) have access to extensive informal social networks. Research shows that, when faced with serious personal problems, the vast majority of blacks make use of their informal helper network (Brown & Gary, 1985; Jackson et al., 1986). We also know that social support can reduce the impact of stress on psychological symptoms. Unfortunately, rarely are these bodies of literature linked empirically in studies primarily concerned with blacks. We do not know the extent to which black informal networks are actually supportive in the sense that they buffer the effects of stress on mental health outcomes. Because stress is rarely measured in studies concerned with race and mental health, there are no examples of how the ''stress-buffering'' effect of support might work for blacks. In addition to the study of the use of informal help and social support, people seeking professional help have been shown to have social and demographic characteristics that differ from those who tend not to consult professionals (Jackson, et al., 1986). Thus, it is not unreasonable to assume that there are other social, psychological, and cultural variables which might explain racial differences in access to and utilization of professional health and mental health resources. Because admission to treatment and the use of professional help are influenced by a number of social, psychological, and sociocultural factors, studies conceived within a narrow utilization approach have not been definitive (Neighbors, 1984; Williams, 1986).

Unfortunately, the nature of the various social and social-psychological processes that influence race differences in help-seeking behavior has been little researched. There are probably at least three important intervening variables (personal problem severity, personal problem definition, and informal social network characteristics) which should be built into analyses of black help seeking in order to help clarify sociodemographic differences in utilization. This approach has yielded valuable information in all three areas (Jackson, et al., 1986; Neighbors, 1984).

In addition to studying theoretical issues of help-seeking and illness behavior, more research is needed on the practical policy issues of access to, and utilization of, professional help sources (Neighbors, 1984). Because blacks tend to be physically less healthy than majority populations, physical health status may also play a major role in the nature of responses to risk factors, in the efficacy of individual coping capacities, and in the capability of utilizing informal and formal institutional resources. The role of physical health status, however, has gone largely unassessed in studies of blacks.

There is a need for different types of research approaches. Epidemiologic investigations are needed to examine distal and proximal risk factors. Survey research procedures can be fruitfully used to investigate individual coping capacities, help seeking, control, mastery, and mental health status. Clinical studies are needed to investigate the processes of diagnosis, the clinician/client interaction, treatment modes, and outcomes. Good theory and research on blacks, however, cannot progress without increased attention to the etiology and mechanisms of the social and economic factors related to positive mental health among black Americans.

Finally, mental health and mental illness are individual psychological conditions that have to be understood as consequences of individual perceptions and experiences in individuals' social and physical milieus. Each individual's physical experiences, perceptions, and ways of cognitively processing the environment is unique. The objective facts of deprivation, prejudice, and poverty create risk factors that curtail the types of positive life experiences necessary for adequate psychological growth of black children and families. Thus, there is an interaction among objective experiences, internal psychological resources, and personal problems (Harrison, Jackson, Munday, & Bleiden, 1989). Both the internal "subjective" psychological and the "objective" external contexts are needed to conceptualize adequately the complexities of mental health and mental illness (Jackson, 1988). Better understanding of their interrelationships is a necessary and fruitful area of research (Harrison et al., 1989). Traditionally designed mental health care delivery systems cannot keep pace with the problems that result from the poor life chances and life circumstances of black Americans (Jackson, 1988). In addition to research on increasing the efficacy of individual and family modes of service and treatment, public policies must be designed and implemented to address the proximal and distal environmental sources of mental disorders among racial and ethnic populations.

SUMMARY AND CONCLUSIONS

Continuing poor economic circumstances and social discrimination affect directly the etiology and nature of mental health status and the functioning of blacks. Conceptualizations of ethnic and racial minority group positive mental health statuses that do not take these external factors into consideration are inadequate. Mental health and mental illness of American blacks must be understood within the historical, political, social, and economic contexts of their lives. Mental health and mental illness are individual conditions that are influenced by individual and group interaction with the social environment. Knowledge of the environment and the individual's relationship to it is crucial in understanding mental status, individual coping, and informal and formal help seeking (Jackson, 1988).

Theoretical perspectives and empirical information are nearly nonexistent in regard to how environmental and social context factors may affect the mental health status of blacks (Jackson et al., 1986). Over the years, the amount of research on the mental health problems of blacks has increased (Williams, 1986), and a greater recognition of the role of social and economic disadvantage has emerged (Jackson, 1988). For example, the growing poverty of black women and children provides a major source of environmental risks for the development of mental disorders. Not only does poverty have immediate effects on the nature of current functioning, it also curtails the types of life experiences needed for adequate psychological, physical, and social growth and development of children and families. Thus, poverty, particularly among women and children, may play both an important proximal and distal role in the development of mental disorders among black Americans as well as serve as a major impediment to the receipt of adequate services.

Problems of persistent poverty, the growth of single-parent households, the lack of educational and employment opportunities, and barriers to adequate health care delivery can be addressed through the development of responsive public policies. Research has amply documented the human costs resulting from the lack of attention to these social and economic problems.

As we have stressed in this chapter, evolving models of positive mental health among blacks must be responsive to both internal and external sources of stress and satisfactions. These models must be sensitive to the interaction among these internal and external factors and must provide a description of and a theoretical accounting of their interrelationships.

REFERENCES

Akbar, N. (1979). Awareness: The key to black mental health. In W. D. Smith, K. H. Burlew, M. H. Mosley, & W. M. Whitney (Eds.), *Reflections on black psychology*. Washington, DC: University Press of America.

Akbar, N. (1985). Our destiny: Authors of a scientific revolution. In H. P. McAdoo & J. L. McAdoo (Eds.), *Black children: Social, educational, and parental environments*. Beverly Hills, CA: Sage Publications.

Bachman, J. G., & O'Malley, P. M. (1984). Black-White differences in self-esteem: Are they affected by response style? *American Journal of Sociology, 90*, 624–639.

Billingsley, A. (1968). *Black families in white America*. Englewood Cliffs, NJ: Prentice-Hall.

Boxley, R., & King, L. (1985). *Research in mental health: Assessment of the state of science on the mental health of black Americans: Issues, recommendations, and suggested implementation strategies*. Unpublished manuscript. Los Angeles: Fanon Mental Health Research Center.

Brown, D. R., & Gary, L. E. (1985). Social support network differentials among married and nonmarried black females. *Psychology of Women Quarterly, 9*, 229–241.

Bulhan, H. A. (1985). Black Americans and psychotherapy: An overview of research and theory. *Psychotherapy, 22(2 S)*, 370–388.

Dohrenwend, B. P., & Dohrenwend, B. S. (1969). *Social status and psychological disorder: A causal inquiry*. New York: Wiley-Interscience.

Dressler, W. W. (1985). Psychosomatic symptoms, stress, and modernization: A model. *Culture, Medicine and Psychiatry*, *9*, 257–294.

Eaton, W. W., Holzer, C. E., Von Korff, M., et al. (1984). The design of the epidemiologic catchment area surveys. *Archives of General Psychiatry*, *41*, 942–948.

Fanon, F. (1967). *Black skins, white masks*. New York: Grove Press.

Faris, R.E.L., & Dunham, H. W. (1939). *Mental disorders in urban areas: An ecological study of schizophrenia and other psychoses*. Chicago: Chicago University Press.

Franklin, A. J. (1988). Dimensions of psychological well-being among blacks. In R. L. Jones (Ed.), *Handbook of tests and measurements for black populations*. Richmond, CA: Cobb & Henry Publishers.

Franklin, A. J. (1989). *The invisibility syndrome among black men*. Unpublished manuscript. New York: City College of New York.

Gary, L. E. (1978). *Mental health: A challenge to the black community*. Philadelphia, PA: Dorrance and Company.

Gecas, V. (1982). The self-concept. *Annual Review of Sociology*, *8*, 1–33.

Greenwald, A. G., Bellezza, F. S., & Banaji, M. R. (1988). Is self-esteem a central ingredient of the self-concept? *Personality and Social Psychology Bulletin*, *14*, 34–45.

Grier, W. H., & Cobb, P. M. (1968). *Black rage*. New York: Basic Books.

Gurin, P., Gurin, J., Lao, R., & Beattie, M. (1969). Internal-external control in the motivational dynamics of Negro youth. *Journal of Social Issues*, *26*, 83–104.

Hare, B. R. (1985). Reexamining the achievement central tendency: Sex differences within race and race differences within sex. In H. P. McAdoo & J. L. McAdoo (Eds.), *Black children: Social, educational, and parental environments*. Beverly Hills, CA: Sage Publications.

Harrison, A., Jackson, J. S., Munday, C., and Bleiden, N. (1989). *Michigan research conference on mental health services for black Americans: A search for understanding*. Oakland, MI: Oakland University Press.

Hill, R. B. (1971). *The strengths of black families*. New York: National Urban League.

Hollingshead, A. B., & Redlich, F. C. (1958). *Social class and mental illness*. New York: Wiley & Sons.

Ilfeld, F. W. (1978). Psychological status of community residents along major demographic dimensions. *Archives of General Psychiatry*, *130*, 183–187.

Jackson, J. S. (1988). Mental health problems among black Americans: Research needs. *Division of Child, Youth, and Family Services Newsletter*, American Psychological Association, Division 37, *11*(2), 18–19.

Jackson, J. S., McCullough, W. R., & Gurin, G. (1987). Family, socialization environment, and identity development in black Americans. In H. P. McAdoo (Ed.), *Black families* (2d ed). Newbury Park, CA: Sage Publications.

Jackson, J. S., Neighbors, H. W., & Gurin, G. (1986). Findings from a national survey of black mental health: Implications for practice and training. In M. M. Miranda and H.H.L. Kitano (Eds.), *Mental health research & practice*. Washington, DC: U.S. Department of Human Services, National Institute of Mental Health.

Jackson, J. S., Tucker, M. B., & Bowman, P. J. (1982). Conceptual and methodological programs in survey research on black Americans. In W. T. Liu (Ed.), *Methodological problems in minority research*. Chicago: Pacific/Asian American Mental Health Research Center.

Jahoda, M. (1958). *Current conceptions of positive mental health.* New York: Basic Books.

Jenkins, A. H. (1982). *The psychology of the Afro-American: A humanistic approach.* New York: Pergamon Press.

Jennings, R. M. (1975). *The development of self-esteem in urban black high school students.* Unpublished doctoral dissertation, University of Michigan, Ann Arbor.

Jones, A. C. (1985). Psychological functioning in black Americans: A conceptual guide for use in psychotherapy. *Psychotherapy, 22(2 S),* 363–369.

Jones, J. M. (1980). Conceptual and strategic issues in the relationship of black psychology to American social science. In A. W. Boykin, A. J. Franklin, & J. F. Yates (Eds.), *Research directions of black psychologists.* New York: Russell Sage Foundation.

Jones, R. L. (Ed.). (1972). *Black psychology.* New York: Harper & Row.

Kardiner, A., & Ovesey, L. (1951). *The mark of oppression.* New York: Norton.

Katz, P. A., & Taylor, D. A. (Eds.). (1988). *Eliminating racism.* New York: Plenum Press.

Kessler, R., & Neighbors, H. W. (1986). *A new perspective on the relationships among race, social class and psychological distress. Journal of Health and Social Behavior, 27,* 107–115.

Klerman, G. L. (1985). Diagnosis of psychiatric disorders in epidemiologic field studies. *Archives of General Psychiatry, 42,* 723–724.

Ladner, J. (1973). *The death of white sociology.* New York: Vintage Books.

Lawson, W. B. (1986). Racial and ethnic factors in psychiatric research. *Hospital and Community Psychiatry, 37,* 50–54.

Levinson, D. J., Darrow, C. N., Klein, E. B., Levinson, M. H., & McKee, B. (1978). *The seasons of a man's life.* New York: Alfred A. Knopf.

McAdoo, H. P. (Ed.). (1987). *Black families* (2d ed). Newbury Park, CA: Sage Publications.

Miranda, M. M., & Kitano, H.H.L. (Eds.). (1986). *Mental health research & practice.* Washington, DC: U.S. Department of Human Services, National Institute of Mental Health.

Myers, H. F. (1982). Stress, ethnicity, and social class: A model for research with black populations. In E. E. Jones & S. J. Korchin (Eds.), *Minority mental health.* New York: Praeger.

Neighbors, H. W. (1984). The distribution of psychiatric morbidity in black Americans: Review and suggestions for research. *Community Mental Health Journal, 20,* 5–18.

Neighbors, H. W. (1986). Socioeconomic status and psychological distress in black Americans. *American Journal of Epidemiology, 124,* 779–793.

Neighbors, H. W. (1987). Improving the mental health of black Americans: Lessons from the community mental health movement. *The Milbank Quarterly, 65* (Pt. 2), 348–380.

Neighbors, H., Jackson, J. S., & Campbell, L., & Williams, D. (1989). The influence of racial factors on psychiatric diagnosis: A review and suggestions for research. (Under review).

Offer, D., & Sabshin, M. (1984). *Normality and the life-cycle.* New York: Basic Books.

Peters, M. F. (1987). Parenting in black families with young children: A historic perspective. In H. P. McAdoo (Ed.), *Black families*, (2d ed). Newbury Park, CA: Sage Publications.

Rodgers-Rose, L. F. (1980). *The black woman*. Beverly Hills, CA: Sage Publications.

Rosenberg, M. (1973). Which significant others? *American Behavioral Scientist, 16*, 829–860.

Rotter, J. B. (1966). Generalized expectancies for internal versus external control. *Psychological Monograms, 80*, 1–28.

Schaie, K. W. (1981). Psychological changes from midlife to early old age: Implications for the maintenance of mental health. *American Journal of Orthopsychiatry, 51*, 199–218.

Spurlock, J. (1986). Development of self-concept in Afro-American children. *Hospital and Community Psychology, 37*, 66–70.

Taylor, S. E., & Brown, J. D. (1988). Illusion and well-being: A social psychological perspective on mental health. *Psychological Bulletin, 103*, 193–210.

Thomas, M. E., & Hughes, M. (1986). The continuing significance of race: A study of race, class, and quality of life in America, 1972–1985. *American Sociological Review, 51*, 830–841.

Warheit, G. J., Holzer, C. E., & Arey, S. A. (1975). Race and mental illness: An epidemiological update. *Journal of Health and Social Behavior, 104*, 243–256.

Weissman, M. M., & Myers, J. K. (1978). Affective disorders in a United States urban community. *Archives of General Psychiatry, 35*, 183–187.

Wheaton, B. (1980). The sociogenesis of psychological disorder: An attributional theory. *Journal of Health and Social Behavior, 21*, 100–124.

White, J. L. (1984). *The psychology of blacks: An Afro-American perspective*. Englewood Cliffs, NJ: Prentice-Hall.

Wilcox, P. (1973). Positive mental health in the black community: The black liberation movement. In C. V. Willie, M. Kramer, & B. S. Brown (Eds.), *Racism and mental health*. Pittsburgh, PA: University of Pittsburgh Press.

Williams, D. H. (1986). The epidemiology of mental illness in Afro-Americans. *Hospital and Community Psychiatry, 37*, 42–49.

Wilson, R. (1979). The historical concept of pluralism and the psychology of black behavior. In W. D. Smith, K. H. Burlew, M. H. Mosley, & W. M. Whitney (Eds.), *Reflections on black psychology*. Washington, DC: University Press of America.

SELECTED BIBLIOGRAPHY

Adebimpe, V. R. (1981). Overview: White norms in psychiatric diagnostics of black patients. *American Journal of Psychiatry*, *138*(3), 279–285.

Akbar, N. (1979). Awareness: The key to black mental health. In W. D. Smith, K. H. Burlew, M. H. Mosley, & W. M. Whitney (Eds.), *Reflections on black psychology*. Washington, DC: University Press of America.

Allen, W. R., & Stukes, S. (1982). Black family lifestyles and the mental health of Black Americans. In F. U. Munoz & R. Endo (Eds.), *Perspectives on minority group mental health*. Washington, DC: University Press of America.

Amenson, C. S., & Lewinsohn, P. M. (1981). An investigation into the observed sex differences in prevalence of unipolar depression. *Journal of Abnormal Psychology*, *90*, 1–13.

Asher, S., & Allen, V. (1969). Racial preference and social comparison processes. *Journal of Social Psychology*, *25*, 157–165.

Azibo, D. A. (1983). Some psychological concomitants and consequences of the black personality: Mental health implications. *Journal of Non-White Concerns*, 59–66.

Bachman, J. G., & O'Malley, P. M. (1984). Black-White differences in self-esteem: Are they affected by response styles? *American Journal of Sociology*, *90*(3), 624–639.

Baldwin, J. A. (1986). African (Black) psychology: Issues and synthesis. *Journal of Black Studies*, *16*(3), 235–249.

Baldwin, J. A. (1984). African self-consciousness and the mental health of African Americans. *Journal of Black Studies*, *15*(2), 177–194.

Battle, E. S., & Rotter, J. B. (1963). Children's feelings of personal control as related to social class and ethnic group. *Journal of Personality*, *31*, 482–490.

Bell, C., & Mehta, H. (1980). The misdiagnosis of Black patients with manic depressive illness. *Journal of the National Medical Association*, *72*, 141–145.

Bell, C., & Mehta, H. (1981). Misdiagnosis of Black patients with manic depressive illness: Second in a series. *Journal of the National Medical Association*, *73*,

        101-107.
Bell, R., Leroy, J., Lin, E., & Schwab, J. (1981). Change and psychopathology: Epi-
    demiologic considerations. *Community Mental Health Journal, 17,* 203–213.
Bell, C. C. (1986). Coma and the etiology of violence. Pt. 1. *Journal of the National
    Medical Association, 12,* 1167–1176.
Bell, C. C. (1986). Impaired Black health professionals: Vulnerabilities and treatment
    approaches. *Journal of the National Medical Association. 78,* 1138–1141.
Bell, C. C. (1986). Preventing violence. *The New Physician, 35,* 7–8.
Bell, C. C. (1987). Preventive strategies for dealing with violence among Blacks. *Com-
    munity Mental Health Journal, 23,* 217–228.
Bell, C. C. (1980). Racism: A symptom of the narcissistic personality disorder. *Journal
    of the National Medical Association, 72,* 661–665.
Bell, C. C., & Kelly, R. P. (1987). Head injury with subsequent intermittent, non-
    schizophrenic, psychotic symptoms and violence. *Journal of the National Medical
    Association, 11,* 1139–1144.
Bell, C. C., Prothrow-Stith, D., & Smallwood-Murchison, C. (1986). Black-on-Black
    homicide: The National Medical Association's responsibilities. *Journal of the
    National Medical Association, 78,* 1139–1141.
Bell, C. C., Taylor-Crawford, K., Jenkins, E. J., et al. (1988). Need for victimization
    screening in a Black psychiatric population. *Journal of the National Medical
    Association, 80,* 41–48.
Bell, C. C., Thompson, B., Shorter-Gooden, K., et al. (1985). Prevalence of coma in
    Black subjects. *Journal of the National Medical Association, 77,* 391–395.
Boxley, R., & King, L. (1985). *Research in mental health: Assessment of the state of
    science on the mental health of black Americans: Issues, recommendations, and
    suggested implementation strategies.* Unpublished manuscript. Los Angeles: Fa-
    non Mental Health Research Center.
Brown, D., & Gary, L. (1987). Stressful life events, social support networks and the
    physical and mental health of urban Black adults. *Journal of Human Stress, 13,*
    165–174.
Brown, D. R., & Gary, L. E. (1985). Social support network differentials among married
    and nonmarried Black females. *Psychology of Women Quarterly, 9,* 229–241.
Cannon, M. S., & Locke, B. Z. (1977). Being black is detrimental to one's mental
    health: Myth or reality? *Phylon 38*(4): 408–428.
Christmas, J. J. (1978, Spring). Alcoholism services for minorities: Training issues and
    concerns. *Alcohol Health and Research World,* 20–27.
Clark, Kenneth B. (1965). *Dark ghetto: Dilemmas of social power.* New York: Harper
    and Row.
Collins, J. L., Rickman, L. E., & Mathura, C. B. (1980). Frequency of schizophrenia
    and depression in a Black inpatient population. *Journal of the National Medical
    Association, 72*(9), 851–856.
Congressional Budget Office (1982, February). *Improving youth employment prospects:
    Issues and options.* Washington, DC: U.S. Government Printing Office.
Curtis, L. A. (1975). *Violence, race and culture.* Lexington, MA: D. C. Heath and
    Company.
Davis, L. G. (1980). The politics of Black self-help in the United States: A historical
    overview. In L. Yearwood (Ed.), *Black organizations: Issues on survival tech-
    niques.* Washington, DC: University Press of America.

Demo, D. H., & Parker, K. D. (1986). Academic achievement and self-esteem among Black and White college students. *The Journal of Social Psychology, 127*(4), 345–355.

Dohrenwend, B. P., & Dohrenwend, B. S. (1969). *Social status and psychological disorder: A casual inquiry.* New York: Wiley-Interscience.

Dressler, W. W. (1985). Psychosomatic symptoms, stress, and modernization: A model. *Culture, Medicine and Psychiatry, 9,* 257–294.

Dressler, W. W. (1985). Extended family relationships, social support and mental health in a southern Black community. *Journal of Health and Social Behavior, 26,* 39–48.

Dressler, W. (1988). Social consistency and psychological distress. *Journal of Health and Social Behavior, 29,* 79–91.

Drury, D. W. (1980). Black self-esteem and desegregated schools. *Sociology of Education, 53,* 88–103.

Eaton, W. W., Holzer, C. E., Von Korff, M., et al. (1984). The design of the epidemiologic catchment area surveys. *Archives of General Psychiatry, 41,* 942–948.

Edelman, M. W. (1980). *Portrait of inequality: Black and White children in America.* Washington, DC: The Children's Defense Fund.

Fanon, F. (1967). *Black skins, white masks.* New York: Grove Press.

Faris, R.E.L., & Dunham, H. W. (1939). *Mental disorders in urban areas: An ecological study of schizophrenia and other psychoses.* Chicago: Chicago University Press.

Fischer, J. (1969). Negroes and Whites and rates of mental illness: Reconsideration of a myth. *Psychiatry, 32,* 428–446.

Foster, M., & Perry, L. R. (1982, January). Self-evaluation among blacks. *Social Work,* 60–66.

Franklin, A. J. (1988). Dimensions of psychological well-being among blacks. In R. L. Jones (Ed.), *Handbook of tests and measurements for black populations.* Richmond, CA: Cobb and Henry Publishers.

Franklin, A. J. (1989). *The invisibility syndrome among black men.* Unpublished manuscript. New York: City College of New York.

Franklin, J. H. (1974). *From slavery to freedom: A history of the Negro American.* New York: Alfred A. Knopf.

Frazier, E. F. (1939). *The Negro family in the United States.* Chicago: University of Chicago Press.

Frazier, E. F. (1964). *The Negro church in America.* New York: Macmillan Company.

Gary, L. E. (1978). *Mental Health: A challenge to the black community.* Philadelphia, PA: Dorrance and Company.

Gary, L. E. (1978). *Support systems in Black communities: Implications for mental health services for children and youth.* Occasional paper, Vol. 3(4). Washington, DC: Institute for Urban Affairs and Research, Howard University.

Gary, L. E., Beatty, L. A., Berry, G. L., & Price, M. D. (1983). *Stable Black Families: Final Report.* Washington, DC: Institute for Urban Affairs and Research, Howard University.

Gary, L. E., Brown, D. R., Milburn, N. G., Thomas, V. G., & Lockley, D. S. (1984). *Pathways: A study of Black informal support network.* Washington, DC: Institute for Urban Affairs and Research, Howard University.

Goldbert, S. (1977). Social competence in infancy: A model of parent-infant interaction. *Merrill-Palmer Quarterly, 23,* 164–177.

Good, B., & Good, M. (1986). The cultural context of diagnosis and therapy: A view from medical anthropology. In M. Miranda & H. Kitano (Eds.), *Mental health research and practice in minority communities: Development of culturally sensitive training programs*. DHHS Publication No. (ADM) 86–1466. Washington, DC: United States Government Printing Office.

Gorsuch, R., & Butler, M. (1976). Initial drug abuse: A review of predisposing social psychological factors. *Psychological Bulletin, 83*, 120–137.

Grier, W. H., & Cobbs, P. M. (1968). *Black rage*. New York: Basic Books.

Gurin, P., Gurin, G., & Morrison, B. (1978). Personal and ideological aspects of internal and external control. *Social Psychology, 41*, 275–296.

Gurin, P., & Epps, E. (1975). *Black consciousness: Identity and achievement*. New York: Wiley.

Gurin, P., Veroff, J., & Feld, S. (1960). *Americans view their mental health*. New York: Basic Books.

Haan, N. (1977). *Coping and defending: Process of self-environment organization*. New York: Academic Press.

Harper, F. (Ed.). (1976). *Alcohol abuse and Black America*. Alexandria, VA: Douglass.

Harper, F. (1981). Alcohol and its abuse. In L. Gary (Ed.), *Black men*. Beverly Hills, CA: Sage Publications.

Harris, A., & Stokes, R. (1978). Race, self-evaluation and the Protestant ethic. *Social Problems, 26*, 71–85.

Hendricks, L., Bayton, J., et al. (1983). The NIMH's diagnostic interview schedule: A test of its concurrent validity in a population of Black adults. *Journal of the National Medical Association, 7*, 667–671.

Hendrix, B. L. (1980). The effects of locus of control on the self-esteem of Black and White youth. *The Journal of Social Psychology, 112*, 301–302.

Hill, R. B. (1972). *The strengths of Black families*. New York: Emerson Hall Publishers.

Hilliard, T. (1981). Political and social action in the prevention of psychopathology of Blacks: A mental health strategy for oppressed people. In J. Joffee & G. Albee (Eds.), *Primary prevention of psychopathology: Prevention through political action and social change*. Hanover, NH: University Press of New England.

Hines, P., & Berg-Cross, L. (1981). Racial differences in global self-esteem. *The Journal of Social Psychology, 113*, 271–281.

Hoelter, J. W. (1982). Race differences in selective credulity and self-esteem. *The Sociological Quarterly, 23*, 527–537.

Horowitz, M. J. (1979). Psychological response to serious life events. In V. Hamilton & D. M. Warburton (Eds.), *Human stress and cognition: An information processing approach* (pp. 235–263). New York: Wiley.

House, J., & Harkins, E. (1975). Why and when is status inconsistency stressful? *American Journal of Sociology, 81*, 395–412.

Huba, G., Wingard, J., & Bentler, P. (1980). Longitudinal analysis of the role of peer support, adult models and peer subcultures in beginning adolescent substance use: An application of stepwise canonical methods. *Multivariate Behavior Research, 15*, 259–280.

Isaacs, M. (1984). *The determinants and consequences of intergenerational mobility among Black American males*. Unpublished dissertation, Brandeis University, The Heller School for Advanced Studies in Social Welfare.

Jones, B., & Gray, B. (1986). Problems in diagnosing schizophrenia and affective disorders among Blacks. *Hospital and Community Psychiatry*, *37*, 61–65.

Jackson, J. S. (1988). Mental health problems among Black Americans: Research needs. *Division of Child, Youth and Family Services Newsletter, American Psychological Association, Division 37*, *11*(2), 18–19.

Jackson, J. S., Tucker, M. B., & Bowman, P. J. (1982). Conceptual and methodological problems in survey research on Black Americans. In W. T. Liu (Ed.), *Methodological problems in minority research*. Chicago: Pacific/Asian American Mental Health Research Center.

Jackson, J. S., Neighbors, H. W., & Gurin, G. (1986). Findings from a national survey of black mental health: Implications for practice and training. In M. W. Miranda & H.H.L. Kitano (Eds.), *Mental health research and practice*. Washington, DC: U.S. Department of Human Services, National Institute of Mental Health.

Jackson, J. (1981). Urban black Americans. In A. Harwood (Ed.), *Ethnicity and medical care*. Cambridge, MA: Harvard University Press.

Jones, B. E., Gray, B. A., & Parson, E. B. (1981, May). Manic depressive illness among poor urban blacks. *American Journal of Psychiatry*. *138*(5): 654–657.

Jones, E. E., & Korchin, S. J. (Eds.). (1982). *Minority mental health*. New York: Praeger Publishers.

Kellam, S., Brown, H., Rubin, B., & Ensminger, M. (1983). Paths leading to teenage psychiatric symptoms and substance use: Developmental epidemiological studies in Woodlawn. In S. Guze, F. Earls, & J. Barrett (Eds.), *Childhood psychopathology and development* (pp. 17–51). New York: Raven Press.

Kessler, R., & Neighbors, H. (1986). A new perspective on the relationships among race, social class and psychological distress. *Journal of Health and Social Behavior*, *27*, 107–115.

Kleiner, R., & Parker, S. (1963). Goal striving, social status and mental disorder: A research review. *American Sociological Review*, *28*, 189–203.

Kramer, M., Rosen, B., & Willis, E. (1973). Definitions and distributions of mental disorders in a racist society. In C. Willie, M. Kramer, & B. Brown (Eds.), *Racism and mental health*. Pittsburgh: University of Pittsburgh Press.

Lazarus, R. S., & DeLongis, A. (1983). Psychological stress and coping in aging. *American Psychologist*, *38*, 245–254.

Lewis, J. M., & Looney, J. G. (1983). *The long struggle: Well-functioning working-class Black families*. New York: Brunner/Mazel.

Linblad-Goldberg, M., & Dukes, J. L. (1985). Social support in Black, low-income, single-parent families: Normative and dysfunctional patterns. *American Journal of Orthopsychiatry*, *55*(1), 43–58.

Linn, J. G., & Husaini, B. (1987). Community satisfaction, life stress, social support, and mental health in rural and urban southern Black communities. Unpublished manuscript. Center for Health Research, Tennessee State University, Nashville.

McAdoo, H. (1981). Patterns of upward mobility in Black families. In H. P. McAdoo, (Ed.), *Black families*. Beverly Hills, CA: Sage Publications.

McAdoo, H. (1978, November). Factors related to stability in upwardly mobile Black families. *Journal of Marriage and the Family*, 761–776.

McAdoo, H. P. (1982). Levels of stress and family support in Black families. In H. I. McCubbin, A. E. Cauble, & J. M. Patterson (Eds.), *Family stress and coping*. Springfield, IL: Thomas.

McCarthy, J., & Yancy, W. (1971). Uncle Tom and Mr. Charlie: Metaphysical pathos in the study of racism and personal disorganization. *American Journal of Sociology, 76,* 648–672.

McPherson, J. (1971). *Blacks in America: Bibliographical essays.* New York: Doubleday.

McQueen, A. J. (1977). The adaptations of urban black families: Trends, problems and issues. *Public Service Studies,* Oberlin, OH: Oberlin College.

Martineau, W. (1977). Informal social ties among urban Black Americans: Some new data and a review of one problem. *Journal of Black Studies, 8,* 83–105.

Mathis, A. (1978, November). Contrasting approaches to the study of Black families. *Journal of Marriage and the Family,* 667–676.

Milburn, N. G., Thomas, V. G., & Gary, L. E. (1984, March). *The nature of social network relationships among Black Americans.* Paper presented at the 30th anniversary meeting of the Southeastern Psychological Association, New Orleans, LA.

Milburn, N. G. (1986). *Social support: A critical review of the literature as it applies to Black Americans.* Occasional paper, No. 26. Washington, DC: Institute for Urban Affairs and Research, Howard University.

Myers, H. (1982). Research on the Afro-American family: A critical review. In B. Bass, G. Wyatt, & G. Powell (Eds.), *The Afro-American family: Assessment, treatment and research issues.* New York: Grune & Stratton.

Myers, H., Adams, L., Miles, R., & Williams, J. (1987). Role strains, social supports and depression in Black adults: The role of gender and social class. Unpublished manuscript. University of California, Los Angeles.

Myers, H., Alvy, K., Arrington, A., et al. (1987). Effective Black parenting: Preliminary results. Unpublished manuscript. Center for the Improvement of Child Caring, Fanon Research and Development Center, Charles Drew Medical School.

Myers, L. J. (1987). The deep structure of culture: Relevance of traditional culture in contemporary life. *Journal of Black Studies, 18*(1), 72–75.

Myers, L. J. (1986). Transcending oppression: A Black feminist perspective. *Women and Therapy, 5*(4), 39–49.

Myers, L. J. (1988). *Understanding an Afrocentric world view: Introduction to an optimal psychology.* Dubuque, IA: Kendall/Hunt.

Myers, H. F., & King, L. M. (1985). Mental health issues in the development of the Black American child. In G. J. Powell (Ed.), *The psychosocial development of minority group children* (pp. 275–306). New York: Brunner/Mazel.

National Center for Health Statistics (1980). *Data from advance report of final natality statistics.* Washington, DC: U.S. Government Printing Office.

National Research Council (1976). Advisory Committee on Child Development. *Toward a national policy for children and families.* Washington, DC: National Academy of Sciences.

Neighbors, H. (1984). The distribution of psychiatric morbidity: A review and suggestions for research. *Community Mental Health Journal, 20,* 5–18.

Neighbors, H. (1986). Socioeconomic status and psychological distress in Black Americans. *American Journal of Epidemiology, 124,* 779–793.

Neighbors, H. (1987). Improving the mental health of Black Americans: Lessons from the community mental health movement. *Milbank Memorial Fund Quarterly, 65*(2), 348–380.

Neighbors, H., & Jackson, J. (1984). The use of informal and formal help: Four patterns of illness behavior in the Black community. *American Journal of Community Psychology*, *12*, 629–644.

Neighbors, H., Jackson, J., Campbell, L., & Williams, D. (1988). The influence of racial factors on psychiatric diagnosis: A review and suggestions for research. Unpublished manuscript, Program for Research on Black Americans, Institute for Social Research, University of Michigan.

Newcomb, M., Huba, G., & Bentler, P. (1983). Mother's influence on the drug use of their children. *Developmental Psychology*, *19*, 714–726.

Nobles, W. (1974). African root and American fruit: The Black family. *Journal of Social and Behavioral Science*, *20*, 52–64.

Nobles, W. (1976). Extended self: Rethinking the so-called negro self-concept. *Journal of Black Psychology*, *4*, 21–27.

Nobles, W. W. (1974). Africanity: Its role in Black families. *The Black Scholar*, *5*, 10–17.

Norton, D. G. (1969). Environment and cognitive development: A comparative study of socioeconomic status and race. Bryn Mawr, PA: doctoral dissertation, Graduate School of Social Work and Social Research, Bryn Mawr College.

Parham, T. A., & Helms, J. E. (1985). Attitudes of racial identity and self-esteem of Black students: An exploratory investigation. *Journal of College Student Personnel*, 143–147.

Parsons, T., & Bales, R. (1955). *Family, socialization and interaction process*. Glencoe, IL: Free Press.

Pettigrew, C. A. (1971). *Racially separate or together?* New York: McGraw-Hill.

Pinderhughes, C. A. (1973). Racism and psychotherapy. In C. B. Willie, B. M. Kramer, & B. S. Brown (Eds.), *Racism and mental health*. Pittsburgh: University of Pittsburgh Press.

Powell, G. J. (1973). Self-concept in white and black children. In C. B. Willie, B. M. Kramer, & B. S. Brown (Eds.), *Racism and mental health*. Pittsburgh: University of Pittsburgh Press.

Reynolds, F. (1980, May). Homicide trends in the United States. *Demography*, *17*(2), 177–188.

Robins, L., Helzer, J., Crougham, J., & Ratcliff, K. (1981). National Institute of Mental Health Diagnostic Interview Schedule: Its history, characteristics and validity. *Archives of General Psychiatry*, *38*, 381–389.

Robins, L., Helzer, J., Weissman, M., et al. (1984). Lifetime prevalence of specific psychiatric disorders in three sites. *Archives of General Psychiatry*, *41*, 949–958.

Robins, L. (1985). Epidemiology: Reflections on testing the validity of psychiatric interviews. *Archives of General Psychiatry*, *42*, 918–924.

Ruiz, D. (1983). Epidemiology of schizophrenia: Some diagnostic and sociocultural considerations. *Phylon*, *43*, 315–326.

Russo, R. M. (1982, July). Poverty: A major deterrent to America's good health. *Urban Health*, 45–48.

Silverstein, B., & Krate, R. (1975). *Children of the dark ghetto: A developmental psychology*. New York: Praeger Publishers.

Smith, W. D. (1980). The Black self-concept: Some historical and theoretical reflections. *Journal of Black Studies*, *10*(3), 355–366.

Sparks, C. T. (1980). Demographic and personal characteristics of professional Black

Americans: Toward a Black mental health model. *Journal of Non-White Concerns*,
71–76.

Spurlock, J. (1975). Psychiatric states. In R. A. Williams (Ed.), *Textbook of Black-
related diseases*. New York: McGraw-Hill.

Stack, C. (1974). *All our kin: Strategies for survival in a Black community*. New York:
Harper and Row.

Staples, R., & Mirande, A. (1980, November). Racial and cultural variations among
American families: A decennial review of the literature on minority families.
Journal of Marriage and the Family, 141–152.

Staples, Robert. (Ed.). (1976). *Introduction to Black sociology*. New York: McGraw-
Hill.

Staples, R. (1981). *The world of Black singles*. Westport, CT: Greenwood Press.

Sussman, L., Robins, L., & Earls, F. (1987). Treatment-seeking for depression by Black
and White Americans. *Social Science and Medicine*, *24*, 187–196.

Taylor, S. E., & Brown, J. D. (1988). Illusion and well-being: A social psychological
perspective on mental health. *Psychological Bulletin*, *103*, 193–210.

Thomas, A., & Sillen, S. (1972). *Racism and psychiatry*. New York: Brunner/Mazel.

Thomas, C. S., & Comer, J. P. (1973). Racism and mental health services. In C. B.
Willie, B. M. Kramer, & B. S. Brown (Eds.), *Racism and mental health*. Pittsburgh: University of Pittsburgh Press.

Thomas, M. E., & Hughes, M. (1986). The continuing significance of race: A study of
race, class, and quality of life in America, 1972–1985. *American Sociological
Review*, *51*, 830–841.

U.S. Bureau of Census (1982). *Current population reports*. Marital status and living
arrangements: 1981. Series P–20, No. 372. Washington, DC: U.S. Government
Printing Office.

U.S. Bureau of Census (1982, July). *Current population reports*. Characteristics of the
population below the poverty level: 1980. Series P–60, No. 133. Washington,
DC: U.S. Government Printing Office.

U.S. Department of Health, Education and Welfare, National Institute of Drug Abuse.
(1977, December). *Drugs and minorities*. DHEW Publication No. (ADM) 78–
507. Washington, DC: U.S. Government Printing Office.

U.S. Department of Health, Education and Welfare, Public Health Service. *Health status
of minorities and low-income groups*. DHEW Publication No. (HRA) 79–627.
Washington, DC: U.S. Government Printing Office.

U.S. Department of Health and Human Services (1980, August). *The status of children,
youth and families: 1979*. DHHS Publication No. (ODHS) 80–30274. Washington,
DC: U.S. Government Printing Office.

U.S. Department of Health and Human Services (1981, September). National center on
child abuse and neglect. *Study findings: National study on the incidence and
severity of child abuse and neglect*. Washington, DC: U.S. Government Printing
Office.

U.S. Department of Health and Human Services (1981, December). *Health: United States,
1981*. DHHS Publication No. (PHS) 82–1232. Washington, DC: U.S. Government
Printing Office.

U.S. Department of Justice, Bureau of Justice Statistics (1982). *Sourcebook of criminal
justice statistics: 1981*. Washington, DC: U.S. Government Printing Office.

Vernon, S., & Roberts, R. (1982). Prevalence of treated and untreated psychiatric disorders in three ethnic groups. *Social Science and Medicine, 16,* 1575–1582.

Wagenfeld, M., & Jacobs, J. (1982). The community mental health movement: Its origins and growth. In M. Wagenfeld, P. Lemkau, & B. Justice (Eds.), *Public mental health.* Beverly Hills: Sage Publications.

Warheit, G., Holzer, C., & Schwab, J. (1975). Race and mental illness: An epidemiologic update. *Journal of Health and Social Behavior, 16,* 243–256.

Warheit, G., Vega, W., Shimizu, D., & Meinherdt, K. (1982). Interpersonal coping networks and mental health problems among four race-ethnic groups. *Journal of Community Psychology, 10,* 312–324.

Weissman, M., & Klerman, G. (1978). Epidemiology of mental disorder: Emerging trends in the United States. *Archives of General Psychiatry, 35,* 705–712.

Weissman, M. M., & Myers, J. K. (1978). Affective disorders in a United States urban community. *Archives of General Psychiatry, 35,* 183–187.

Wheaton, B. (1980). The sociogenesis of psychological disorder: An attributional theory. *Journal of Health and Social Behavior, 21,* 100–124.

White, J. L. (1984). *The psychology of blacks: An Afro-American perspective.* Englewood Cliffs, NJ: Prentice-Hall.

White, R. (1974). Strategies of adaptation: An attempt at systematic description. In G. V. Coelho, D. A. Hamburg, & J. E. Adams (Eds.), *Coping and adaptation* (pp. 47–67). New York: Basic Books.

Williams, D. H. (1986). The epidemiology of mental illness in Afro-Americans. *Hospital and Community Psychiatry, 37,* 42–49.

Young, V. H. (1974). A Black American socialization pattern. *American Ethnologist, 1,* 405–413.

INDEX

ABOUT THE CONTRIBUTORS

LOUIS P. ANDERSON, Department of Psychology, Georgia State University, Atlanta, Georgia.

MELANIE A. BAER, Psychologist, Philhaven, Mount Gretna, Pennsylvania.

CARL C. BELL, Clinical Psychiatry, University of Illinois; Community Mental Health Council, Inc., Chicago, Illinois.

JOSEPH BRENT, III, Department of History, University of the District of Columbia, Washington, DC.

DIANE ROBINSON BROWN, Institute of Urban Affairs and Research, Howard University, Washington, DC.

ALICE GRESHAM BULLOCK, Howard University Law School, Washington, DC.

JAMES L. COLLINS, Sr., Department of Psychiatry, Tripler Army Medical Center, Tripler AMC, Hawaii.

JAMES P. COMER, Yale University Child Study Center, New Haven, Connecticut.

PATRICIA J. DUNSTON, Commission on Mental Health Services, Chief, Planning Branch, St. Elizabeth Hospital, Washington, DC.

CHUCK L. EADDY, Department of Psychology, Georgia State University, Atlanta, Georgia.

ANDERSON J. FRANKLIN, Department of Psychology, the City University of New York, New York.

MARY S. HARPER, Long Term Care Programs, Mental Disorder of Aging Branch, National Institute of Mental Health, Rockville, Maryland.

JACQUELYNE J. JACKSON, Department of Psychiatry, Duke University, Durham, North Carolina.

JAMES S. JACKSON, Institute for Social Research, the University of Michigan, Ann Arbor, Michigan.

JOYCELYN LANDRUM-BROWN, Consultant, Accent on Success Consultants, Detroit, Michigan.

SUZAN LUMPKIN, School of Hygiene and Public Health, Johns Hopkins University, Baltimore, Maryland.

CLYDE B. MATHURA, Departments of Oncology and Psychology, Howard University, Washington, DC.

LINDA JAMES MYERS, Department of Black Studies, Ohio State University, Columbus, Ohio.

HAROLD W. NEIGHBORS, Department of Community Health, School of Public Health, University of Michigan, Ann Arbor, Michigan.

ALVIN F. POUSSAINT, Harvard University Medical School, Boston, Massachusetts.

DOROTHY S. RUIZ, Postdoctoral Fellow, School of Public Health, Department of Health Policy and Management, Johns Hopkins University, Baltimore, Maryland.

BARBARA J. SHADE, Division of Education, University of Wisconsin-Parkside, Kenosha, Wisconsin.

ELIOT SOREL, Transcultural Psychiatry Center, Washington, DC.

ERNESTINE A. WILLIAMS, Department of Psychology, Georgia State University, Atlanta, Georgia.